THE
GULF WAR
ASSESSED

THE
GULF WAR
ASSESSED

John Pimlott and Stephen Badsey
and members of the Department of War Studies
Royal Military Academy, Sandhurst

Foreword by
Brigadier Patrick A. J. Cordingley, DSO

ARMS AND
ARMOUR

Arms and Armour Press
A Cassell Imprint
Villiers House, 41–47 Strand, London WC2N 5JE.

Distributed in the USA by Sterling Publishing Co. Inc.,
387 Park Avenue South, New York, NY 10016-8810.

Distributed in Australia by Capricorn Link (Australia) Pty.
Ltd, P.O. Box 665, Lane Cove, New South Wales 2066.

British Library Cataloguing-in-Publication Data: a
catalogue record for this book is available from the British
Library

ISBN 1-85409-146-8

Cartography by Peter Burton.

Designed and edited by DAG Publications Ltd. Designed by
David Gibbons; edited by Philip Jarrett; typeset by Ronset
Typesetters, Darwen, Lancashire; camerawork by M&E
Reproductions, North Fambridge, Essex; printed and
bound in Great Britain by Hartnolls Ltd, Bodmin,
Cornwall.

Contents

List of Maps

Foreword

Brigadier A. J. Cordingley, DSO

Commander 7th Armoured Brigade during Operation 'Granby'

On 8 March 1991, the British 1st Armoured Division issued the order for troops to start returning from Kuwait to their bases in the United Kingdom and Germany. Morale, after six months in the desert, soared. Three weeks later the bulk of the 7th Armoured Brigade Group was back in Soltau and Fallingbostel.

This brought to a close my brigade's involvement in an international Coalition pitted against a moderately sized regional state. It now appears to have been a ridiculously unequal contest, with the Iraqi strength probably over-estimated. But we had studied their success in a different sort of war against Iran and focused on quantities of manpower, artillery and tanks rather than investigating human qualities. We had lived in harsh conditions through a long preparatory period and expected, when we went into the attack, to meet all sorts of horrors which did not materialise.

As we settled again in our peacetime routine, I hope we were forgiven for taking satisfaction in a job well done. Sometimes it had been difficult when deployed in the vastness of the Saudi Arabian desert to remember that we were only part of a huge Coalition force. Reality was brought home when we saw allied aircraft passing *en route* to bomb Iraq and when we heard of battles 200 miles away at Khafji. But we have been careful about the lessons we could learn from a war where we defeated a technologically inferior enemy on featureless terrain meeting very few reverses.

The fact that we all sustained ourselves throughout the long and often uncertain preparatory phase and the war itself owes much to our peacetime training and high standards of soldiering. For those Royal Military Academy Sandhurst graduates who served in the Gulf, the historical perspective and understanding of warfare, given to us by the members of the War Studies Department, also did much for our morale. The knowledge that our forbears had fought in the desert and elsewhere, and triumphed, gave us confidence for the task ahead. I am therefore grateful for this opportunity to pay tribute to the authors of this book and to the military historians of Sandhurst, both past and present, for providing an essential foundation for our understanding of the profession of arms.

And now, in this excellent book, the members of the War Studies Department have ably demonstrated the scale of the Coalition success in the Gulf while also assessing the relevance of the military campaign for the future of our armies. We should be in no doubt about the pivotal role that the United States played in this. If coalition operations are to be our most likely *modus operandi* in the future, a *lead* nation will always be necessary. In the Gulf this was provided by the Americans, and their commitment was enormous. Ours was also highly significant, and we were proud to be part of it.

List of Contributors

Duncan Anderson is a Senior Lecturer in the Department of War Studies at the Royal Military Academy Sandhurst. He has a doctorate from the University of Oxford and has contributed to a number of books on military history and contemporary affairs.

Stephen Badsey is a Senior Lecturer in the Department of War Studies at the Royal Military Academy Sandhurst. He holds a doctorate from the University of Cambridge, and has worked as a researcher for the Imperial War Museum and the BBC. He has written or contributed to numerous books and articles on modern warfare, his most recent work being on the Battle of Normandy 1944.

Andrew Lambert is a Lecturer in the Department of War Studies, King's College, University of London, and a former Senior Lecturer in the Department of War Studies at the Royal Military Academy Sandhurst. He holds a doctorate from the University of London. His most recent books are *The Crimean War* and *The Last Sailing Battlefleet*.

Sean McKnight is a Senior Lecturer in the Department of War Studies at the Royal Military Academy Sandhurst. He has published work on the Second World War and the Iran-Iraq War. He is currently researching into the 1914–18 Mesopotamian campaign, an interest that results from his having lived and worked in the Middle East.

John Pimlott is Deputy Head of the Department of War Studies at the Royal Military Academy Sandhurst. He holds a doctorate from the University of Leicester, and has written widely on modern military matters. His most recent book is *Vietnam: The Decisive Battles*.

Ray Sibbald is a Senior Lecturer in the Department of War Studies at the Royal Military Academy Sandhurst. He has recently completed a doctorate for the University of Liverpool, and has contributed to a number of works on both military history and Russian literature.

Francis Toase is a Senior Lecturer in the Department of War Studies at the Royal Military Academy Sandhurst. He holds a doctorate from the University College of Wales, Aberystwyth, and has contributed to a number of books on military history and contemporary affairs. His latest work is *Armoured Warfare*, to which he was co-editor and contributor.

Introduction

Whatever its origins, there is little dispute that the Gulf Crisis began with the Iraqi invasion and occupation of Kuwait on 2 August 1990, while the subsequent Gulf War began with the first Coalition airstrikes on Iraq and Kuwait on the night of 16/17 January 1991, and ended with the unilateral ceasefire by the Coalition forces on 28 February 1991. These dates have formed our main boundaries in distinguishing the course of the war from its background. The choice of 28 February 1992, the anniversary of the end of the war, as the date on which to end our assessment of its aftermath was dictated by a variety of competing factors, including our conviction that most of the short-term consequences of the war had become evident by that date.

All of the authors of this book are, or were at the time of the Gulf War, members of the Department of War Studies at the Royal Military Academy, Sandhurst, the British Army's officer training establishment. It is therefore particularly necessary for the editors to state that the opinions expressed in this book are those of the individual authors alone, and do not in any way represent the views of the Royal Military Academy, the Ministry of Defence, or of any other institution. The research and writing of this book was undertaken without institutional support, and formed no part of our official duties.

The two major antagonists in the Gulf War were the United States of America and Iraq, and our book reflects this fact. Inevitably, our own perspective on the war has been a British one, and we have also tried to provide an account of the British contribution to the war. Despite our affiliation, we have no particular case to make for any of the British armed services. We know that one of our authors, at least, would be distressed to be associated with the Army at the expense of the Royal Navy. We also hope that those whose own assessments of the war may differ from ours will not make the mistake of seeing our book as representing any particular national or political view.

The original suggestion for a book assessing the Gulf War came shortly after the war's end, from two of our authors, Ray Sibbald and Sean McKnight. Pressures of work and time led to our using a format and approach which had proved successful in the past on more general themes. The research and writing of chapters was left to individual contributors, reflecting their own areas of interest. At the same time, having all the authors within one academic department allowed us to share ideas and information freely, and to maintain a greater homogeneity of style and approach than is usual in casebooks of this kind. As a result, although the chapters of this book are self-contained, and may be read out of sequence if desired, they also provide a coherent narrative and analysis of the Gulf War without (we hope) excessive self-contradiction.

It is a pleasant duty for the editors to thank all the other authors, and everyone else who has helped make this book a reality. In particular, we would like to thank Mr Andrew Orgill, Librarian of the Central Library at the Royal Military Academy, Sandhurst, and all his staff, for their positive and enthusiastic assistance in the preparation of this book. We also wish to thank all our students, past and present. The interchange between research and teaching has been identified as one of the most satisfactory and productive elements in academic life. We hope that this book will go some way to repaying the debt that we owe to the officer cadets, student officers and officers who have passed through our hands. Our thanks also go to Roderick Dymott and his staff at Arms and Armour Press for their patience at times when it must have seemed that this book would never be completed.

It is traditional for editors to accept responsibility for any errors remaining in their book, and in this case, once again, it is particularly necessary. A very obvious feature of the Gulf Crisis or War was the absence of explanation and context for events as they unfolded. This book attempts a 'first history' to provide that context. More than one of our colleagues has warned us (from the best of motives) that such an assessment cannot be made within so short a time, and that much of what we now accept as fact may be soon overturned. Judgement on this must be left to history, the most unforgiving judge of all.

John Pimlott
Stephen Badsey

Department of War Studies
Royal Military Academy Sandhurst
Camberley, 20 March 1992

CHAPTER 1
Saddam Hussein and the Iraqi Army

Sean McKnight

> 'There is still — and I say this with a heart full of sorrow — no Iraqi people, but unimaginable masses of human beings, devoid of any patriotic ideal, imbued with religious traditions and absurdities, connected by no common tie, giving ear to evil, prone to anarchy, and perpetually ready to rise against any government whatever.'
>
> King Faisal I of Iraq, 1933

A new Arab hero

The 1990 crisis in the Middle East, induced by Iraq's invasion of Kuwait on 2 August, caught the outside world by surprise. In 1989 it had seemed that the region was settling down to a less turbulent period than it had endured in the recent past. The Iran-Iraq War of 1980–88 appeared to have exhausted Iran and to have forced Iraq to moderate its aspirations. Most outside observers believed that near-defeat in the war had compelled the Iraqi leader, Saddam Hussein, to replace his grandiose Pan-Arab ambitions with a newly born and sober Iraqi nationalism. The outside world rushed to do business with Baghdad, seeing Saddam as a pragmatist who would thenceforth play the game, mostly by its rules. This complacency was rudely shattered by Iraq's invasion of Kuwait. It seemed likely that, if he succeeded in retaining this conquest, Saddam would be in a position to redraw the map of the Middle East.

Iraq's initial military success in August 1990 sent shock waves across the Arab world, making Saddam a hero to Arabs as far away as Morocco. His apparent military might and audacity promised to right the wrongs which many Arabs felt the outside world had inflicted upon them. In contrast, the oil-rich monarchies of the Gulf saw Saddam's pre-eminence as a portent of their own political extinction, while chilling assessments of the possible costs of intervention dominated the media in the West.

Despite its geo-strategic and economic importance, the Middle East is a part of the world poorly understood by most Westerners, who tend to analyse the region from a Western perspective, expecting Arab nationalism to be similar to the European version. The state system of the Middle East is a relatively new one, with many of the familiar borders created only in the aftermath of the First World War. The collapse of the Ottoman (Turkish)

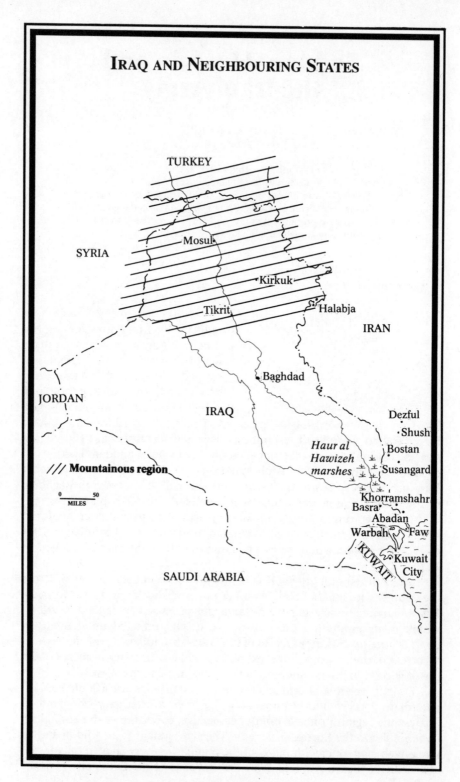

IRAQ AND NEIGHBOURING STATES

TURKEY

SYRIA

Mosul

Kirkuk

Tikrit

Halabja

IRAN

JORDAN

Baghdad

IRAQ

Dezful

Shush

Haur al
Hawizeh
marshes

Bostan

/// Mountainous region

Susangard

0 50
MILES

Khorramshahr

Basra

Abadan

Warbah

Faw

KUWAIT

Kuwait
City

SAUDI ARABIA

Empire in 1918 — the dominant power in the Arabian peninsula for more than 400 years — made Britain and, to a lesser extent, France, the effective arbiters of the region. The decisions taken by these two colonial powers in the subsequent two decades had far-reaching consequences. Britain in particular has been accused of imposing on the Middle East a political structure composed of artificial states, of ignoring the legitimate aspirations of the Arab people, and of leaving behind a legacy of political instability. The reality, in a region characterised by strong loyalties that divide just as much as they unite, is rather more complex.

Arabs are drawn together by historical, cultural, religious and, above all, linguistic ties. At its maximum extent the Arab world is enormous, but it is divided by local loyalties, focused on such things as the tribe or religious sect. Numerous attempts to unite separate Arab states have failed, and the Arab League, founded in 1945, is a large but relatively powerless organisation. The larger Pan-Arab loyalty is more than balanced by these stronger local loyalties, something which advocates of an Arab 'super-state' often prefer to ignore. Between the two extremes there is little to bind the citizen in loyalty to many of the existing states. This combination has produced states much less secure and cohesive than their Western counterparts, frequently destabilised by forces strong enough to upset the existing structure but insufficiently powerful to build a durable replacement.

The foundation of Iraq
In its own extreme way the Iraqi state serves as a microcosm of many of the problems of the wider Arab world. Created from Mesopotamia by the British in 1921, the area had for centuries been part of the Ottoman Empire. This gave it an administrative unity that did not reflect the diverse groupings within the region. Indeed, going back further, more than 2,000 years of recorded history provide very little evidence that this region was in any sense a nascent state.

In 1916 Britain and France secretly decided how they were going to divide their expected Middle Eastern conquests. This deal, known as the Sykes-Picot Agreement, placed what was to become Iraq in the British sphere of influence. After the First World War the League of Nations formalised British control by entrusting Iraq to Britain as a mandate. The theory was that Britain would guide Iraq to independence, a formula that gave a respectable façade to Britain acquiring control of an area already known to possess considerable reserves of oil.

The new Iraq included a Kurdish north, a Sunni-Arab centre and a Shi'a-Arab south,[1] with further important subdivisions within each. Smaller communities such as the Jews and the Assyrians were statistically significant; indeed, in Baghdad at the start of the century the single largest community was probably the Jews.

Despite British efforts to demonstrate the existence of popular enthusiasm for the establishment of an Iraqi state, there is little evidence of any such sentiment in 1921. In the north of the country popular aspirations seem to have leaned towards a continued union with Turkey, or towards regional independence. The American consul in the northern city of Mosul commented at the time: '... there is a large part of the population who would welcome with open arms the return of the Turks.'[2] The southern Shi'a people had been excluded almost totally from power in the Sunni-dominated Ottoman Empire, and remained separated by religion from their fellow Arabs even after its collapse. In 1920 they revolted openly, only to be suppressed by the British. Still organised in a traditional tribal structure, they remained a politically excluded and apathetic underclass in a new state which ignored their interests and wishes.

In creating Iraq the British, rather than divide their mandate into its three component communities or even create a Shi'a-dominated state, actually sought to placate Pan-Arab sentiment. Religious, communal and tribal loyalties seemed outmoded to the many British academics and officials who felt a genuine sympathy with the Arab cause. That Arab nationalism was neither as powerful nor as exclusive a focus of loyalty as nationalism was in Western Europe was ignored by these sympathisers. The result was an artificial state controlled by the Sunni-Arab minority as the only community in Iraq with any aspirations to be part of the larger Arab whole. This artificial country received an equally artificial monarchy with the investiture of King Faisal, who, together with most of his entourage, came from the Hijaz in Saudi Arabia. Iraq became formally independent in 1932, but remained bound to British interests by a treaty signed in 1930. Ironically, the charge levelled against Kuwait by Saddam Hussein in 1990 — that it was an artificial product of British imperialism — is a far more apt description of Iraq itself. Even so, the Pan-Arab nationalists should, in the circumstances, have been the last to complain, as they were substantial beneficiaries in this new creation.

The Hashemite monarchy of Iraq
In seeking to legitimise his monarchy, King Faisal had little choice but to appeal to the wider Arab nationalism, although his obvious dependence on Britain made his rhetoric unconvincing. In contrast, Iraq's army appeared to many as the true representative of Arab national aspirations, as an effective opponent to the British and as a force for modernisation. The army became a major power in Iraqi politics, partly because of the popular approval it won in suppressing an Assyrian 'revolt' in 1933. In 1936 a coup organised by General Bakr Sidqi overthrew the government.

Popularity of this sort enabled differing factions within the army to take power, but not to retain it, and by 1941 there had been no fewer than seven military coups in succession. Arab nationalist sentiment might bring the crowds temporarily on to the streets, but this mass enthusiasm was too ephemeral to sustain a government for any length of time. The alternative could have been to try to base a government on groups within Iraq, but any policy designed to win the support of one community would probably have alienated the others. Confrontation with internal and external enemies was the only way in which this weak state could create an appearance of unity. Indeed, in the absence of a genuine mandate, the politically dominant

Sunni-Arab minority actually had very little choice but to adopt Arab nationalism as its rallying cry.

Successive Iraqi governments were therefore driven into confrontation with Britain, an easy target against which to rouse the people. In 1941 the apparent imminence of British defeat by Germany tempted the government of Rashid 'Ali al-Kaylani, which had come to power that year, into direct military action. Although there were many demands on Britain's military power, it defeated Iraq's 46,000-man army with ease. The speed and economy of the British victory demonstrated the superficial nature of support for Rashid 'Ali's government. The British went on to suppress the political influence of the Iraqi Army, and several officers backing Rashid 'Ali were publicly executed by the new pro-British regime. Relatively modest external support enabled an unpopular monarchy to reoccupy a central position in the government of Iraq.

The fall of the Iraqi monarchy
The demand for change increased in the Middle East following the Second World War, particularly in Egypt, where the army overthrew the monarchy in 1952, opening the way to the emergence of Gamal Abdul Nasser as its leader two years later. Outside interference in the Arab world was resented, and when Nasser apparently humiliated Britain and France during the 1956 Suez Crisis, it gave a further boost to the radical forces challenging the old order in the Middle East. It was understandable that the Iraqi regime was particularly vulnerable to this revolutionary wave, as it was guilty in the eyes of many Iraqis of having too close an association with Britain.

On 14 July 1958 the Iraqi Army's 20th Brigade, led by Colonel 'Abd al-Salam 'Arif, overthrew the monarchy in a bloody coup. 'Arif did this on behalf of a loosely organised conspiratorial group of officers calling themselves 'The Free Officers' Movement', of which Brigadier 'Abd al-Karim Qassem was the most prominent figure. This was more than just another military coup. Although 'The Free Officers Movement' demanded fundamental change, it was more ambiguously motivated than subsequent history suggests, and Arab nationalism was just one of its many strands. The rejection of Western imperialism and of their own monarchy did not automatically make the Iraqi officers into Pan-Arabists, and Iraq remained divided into groups loyal to themselves rather than to the state or to the wider Arab nation. Almost as soon as the monarchy was overthrown, the erstwhile allies Qassem and 'Arif fell out; Qassem won this power struggle, and his regime stressed a programme of radical domestic reform rather than Arab unity.

The new Iraqi government enjoyed the backing of the communists, who in 1959 were the largest political party in Iraq, receiving most of their support from the Shi'a. For both Shi'a and Kurds, social reform and a share in political power were more important issues than Arab nationalism. However, Qassem alienated important sections of Iraqi society, and his reforms created lukewarm friends but determined enemies. His dictatorial approach drove political allies into opposition. In 1961 the government was further weakened by becoming embroiled in an unwinnable war against the

Kurds. Qassem's political enemies continued to plot his overthrow; one of the more determined and better organised of these was the Ba'ath Party.

The Ba'ath Party

The Ba'ath Party was founded in Syria, and its first congress was held in April 1947. It did not attract a large membership, but many Ba'athists were poorer members of the intelligentsia, giving the party disproportionate influence in Syria and the wider Arab world. The Ba'ath Party's founding theoretician, Michel 'Aflaq, wanted to improve the position of Arabs in the world and to transform their nature. The party acknowledged that most Arabs were not yet conscious of their historical mission, and concluded that it was justified in forcing backward brothers to realise their own appointed destiny. As with many totalitarian movements, the excesses of the moment were justified by the promise of a perfect future.

Organisationally, the Ba'ath Party was an ideal vehicle for gaining power in a state like Iraq. It was organised as a hierarchy, with a small number of elite full members and a leader supposedly possessing heroic virtues in command. Like the Bolsheviks, the Ba'ath was structured to win political power without enjoying majority support. 'Aflaq may have concluded that he himself lacked the virtues required to lead such a party, particularly after he recanted many of his beliefs following the strain of a spell in a Syrian jail. It is probable that he recognised the qualities he sought in the young Saddam Hussein, whose career in the party he furthered and whose regime he lived to praise publicly.

Three great issues enabled the Ba'ath Party to transform itself from one of many political factions to a ruling party with supporters throughout the Arab world. First was its advocacy of a single Arab nation, rejecting the division of the Arab world into separate states. Second was the Ba'ath version of socialism, which promised a measure of social justice in the unequal Arab world. Finally, the Ba'athists maintained a vision of an exclusively Arab road to modernisation, rejecting non-Arab imports and in particular the 'artificial progressivism'[3] of the West. This programme made a powerful appeal to Arabs, who felt humiliated by their position in the world, a position made even more galling by Israel's survival and expansion. The Ba'athists, with their advocacy of violence and air of ruthless efficiency, seemed to promise an effective answer to these grievances.

Iraq's first Ba'athist government

Ba'athist ideas spread from Syria to Iraq in the late 1940s, and in 1952 the 'National Command' recognised a Regional Command of the party in Iraq — the semantics making it clear that the party rejected the validity of the Iraqi state and claimed it as part of a larger Arab whole. The Ba'ath Party was only one of many advocates of Arab nationalism in Iraq, but it stood out by virtue of its organisation and deeds. In 1959 a Ba'athist attempt to kill Qassem failed, but the publicity from the resulting trial boosted their public profile. It was the Ba'ath Party, and a minority of dissident Arab nationalist officers, who took the risk of attempting to topple Qassem in February 1963. After two days of fierce street fighting, Qassem was dead and Iraq had its first Ba'athist government. It was a reflection of the lack of substance to the Iraqi state that a political party boasting only 830 full members[4] could force its way into power.

The first Ba'ath government of Iraq was able to attract some loyalty from most Iraqis beyond that which they felt to their immediate community. It was certainly neither a powerful nor consistent loyalty, but other than the communists no other political group in Iraq could command such popularity across the communal divisions of Iraqi society. Most of the army had stayed neutral during the February coup, although it possessed the real power in Iraq, and the survival of the Ba'athist government depended on military acquiescence. Aware of this, the Ba'athists had appointed 'Arif, the jailed 'hero' of the 1958 revolution, to what they hoped would be a purely honorary position as Iraq's President. As with several governments of the 1930s, a Pan-Arab aura legitimised the power of the army and, for a state in which the majority of the population was excluded from power, such legitimisation was important.

Saddam Hussein and the Ba'ath Party

The new regime was to be short-lived. The party settled old scores too blatantly and soon split into warring factions. In November 1963 the army pushed it aside, and President 'Arif became the dominant figure in the new military government. Support for the Ba'ath Party was sufficiently powerful for it to resist briefly, and its fall was accompanied by fierce street fighting in which the army crushed the party militia. The Ba'athists had secured more popular support than perhaps any other previous Iraqi regime, but in the peculiar creation that was Iraq such support was always likely to prove inadequate.

The Party's fall from grace was the opportunity for the 'centrist' faction of the party, headed by the respected General Ahmad Hasan al-Bakr, to secure control. After expelling the leftist faction of the Ba'ath in 1964, Bakr became Secretary General of the Party's Iraqi Regional Command. In a fashion typical of the politics of the region, his success boosted the position of his relatives, in particular the young Saddam Hussein.[5]

Saddam was born on 28 April 1937 near the town of Tikrit. His childhood was hard, because his father was unable to support his family, and much of Saddam's upbringing was entrusted to Khairallah Talfah, his maternal uncle. Khairallah was an army officer who had been jailed in 1941 for supporting Rashid 'Ali's government against the British, and his extreme views[6] strongly influenced his young nephew. In 1957 Saddam followed his uncle's example and became a committed supporter of the Ba'ath Party. His youthful activism earned him a spell in jail in 1958, while his growing reputation as a man of action led to his inclusion in a Ba'athist squad tasked to assassinate Qassem in 1959. The failure of the attempt drove Saddam into exile, where he favourably impressed 'Aflaq and became involved in Ba'athist politics in Egypt. His exile ensured that he played only a minor role in the 1963 Ba'ath government, but when its fall from power eliminated many senior party leaders, Saddam received his chance to emerge from obscurity.

Recognising that the Ba'ath Party needed to match the physical force of the army, Saddam reorganised the security apparatus of the Party. He set up the *al-Jihaz al-Khas*, literally meaning 'instrument of yearning', which became the core of the party's own armed forces and acted as an intelligence service as well. The *Jihaz* infiltrated other organisations, including the armed forces, and was to be invaluable in consolidating Ba'ath power when they next returned to government. It also assured Saddam's personal ascendancy. Saddam proved to be an excellent choice to organise the Party's clandestine struggle against the military government. Like Stalin, with whom he was often compared, he was good at the nuts and bolts of organisation. He also succeeded in building a reputation for daring, leading the underground Ba'ath resistance to the government, being arrested in 1964 and escaping spectacularly in 1966 — the career of a revolutionary hero.

Saddam's rise to power

The military government was weakened in April 1966 when President 'Arif was killed in a helicopter accident. Another military man was chosen as President, Abd al-Rahman 'Arif (the dead President's brother), but he was unable to keep different interest groups together. A dissident group of officers, headed by two colonels — Abd al-Razzaq al-Nayif and Ibrahim al Da'ud — offered their services to the Ba'athists in overthrowing the regime. Saddam persuaded his colleagues to take advantage of these ambitious military traitors as a way of returning to power, promising that he would find a way to deal with them afterwards.[7] This sealed the government's fate, as Nayif was Director of Military Intelligence and Da'ud commanded the Republican Guard which 'protected' the President.

It was a wiser Party that came to power in July 1968, determined neither to succumb to another military coup nor to see power fall into the hands of Ba'athist officers in the military, as had happened to its sister party in Syria in 1966.[8] It acted rapidly to remove its military 'allies' from office. By the end of August both Nayif and Da'ud had been stripped of power and sent into exile. Saddam played a prominent part in both removals, personally arresting Nayif as he lunched with the new President, Saddam's relative and patron Bakr. Within a matter of weeks the non-Ba'athist officers, who had hoped to control the government under a cloak of Ba'ath Party ideological respectability, were either removed or rendered politically impotent.

Saddam also moved against prominent Ba'athist officers by expanding the key decision-making body of the party, the Revolutionary Command Council (RCC). In 1968 all RCC members were officers, but in 1969 Saddam added nine members to the RCC, eight of them civilians (including himself). Shortly after this came a purge of the more important Ba'athist officers, including the formidable General Hardan al-Tikriti, one of a number of political exiles who were later assassinated. The political manoeuvres of this period confirm that Saddam was a masterly operator, promoting civilian rivals to deal with the immediate threat from the army while sowing discord among the military to prevent them making common cause against him.

The removal of the military threat enabled Saddam to turn his attention to potential civilian rivals. In the 1970s even close colleagues such as Abd al-Karim al-Shayhkli[9] were purged, and only a revolt in 1973 by Nadhim Kzar, Saddam's hand-picked security chief, briefly shook his position. Saddam personally headed the squad that tracked Kzar down, killing him and a prominent hostage he had taken.

In 1979 Saddam felt confident enough of his position to push aside President Bakr, formally assuming the powers which he had in reality exercised for several years. He crowned this achievement with a comprehensive purge of the Party leadership. A specially staged conference saw a tearful Saddam reveal details of yet another dastardly plot, and in a macabre touch the delegates personally executed the leading 'conspirators'. As they were bound to their new President by complicity in this bloody work, it would now be extremely hard for them to overthrow him safely. The parallels with Stalin are again striking. As Saddam himself declared: 'We are now in our Stalinist era. We shall strike with an iron fist against the slightest deviation, beginning with the Ba'athists themselves.'[10]

Iraq under the Ba'ath

The Ba'athist state was not simply a personal despotism. Rather, like many other totalitarian leaders, Saddam generated mass support for his rule. Iraq's annual oil revenue rose from $476 million to $26 billion between 1968 and 1980,[11] partly as a consequence of Saddam's bold decision to nationalise the Iraqi oil industry, a process completed in December 1973. This increased revenue was used to make dramatic improvements in social conditions. An expansion in state employment meant that by 1980 more than 835,000 Iraqis worked for the government[12] and had a vested interest in its survival. Millions of Iraqis became involved in aspects of state and party, an involvement that meant complicity without power. Underpinning the whole edifice, the rhetoric of Pan-Arab nationalism legitimised the government and turned opponents into traitors.

The other side of popular support for Saddam and the Ba'athist state was the existence of those instruments of control which permeated every aspect of Iraqi society, most notoriously the security services. The fragility of all previous regimes since the creation of Iraq had served to demonstrate that the temporary enthusiasms of the Iraqi people did not suffice to sustain governments. Ba'athists' confidence in their mission on behalf of a wider Arab cause made it easier for them to coerce the Iraqis into realising their destiny, something which could only be done as long as the Ba'athists themselves stayed in power. This vital task was performed by three separate institutions: the *Estikhbarat*, the principal role of which was to ensure the loyalty of the military; the *Amn* (or security service) and, most importantly, the party-based *Mukhabarat*, the *Jihaz* under a different name. Politics in Ba'athist Iraq soon became a series of plots and conspiracies. When real plots did not exist they were simply fabricated by a regime which needed enemies, and obscurity was no guarantee against attracting the attentions of the secret police. Mass support was created by this apparatus of coercion: the enraged mob ceased to be a spontaneous phenomenon, and the state stalked its victims backed by crowds celebrating their relief that this time it was not them.

Despite purging a considerable number of senior officers, the state continued to take precautions against a military bid for power. Legal execution, assassination and 'accidents' were repeatedly used to eliminate prominent officers, whose only crime may well have been their popularity. As soon as the Party returned to power, politically reliable junior officers were rushed into courses at the Military College for rapid promotion as part of a policy of 'Ba'athising' the officer corps. Officers were expected to be Ba'ath Party supporters, and non-Ba'athist political activity by active or retired members of the armed forces could be punished by death. In 1971, to keep an eye on the professionals, the regime introduced 'political guidance' officers throughout the army. Not content with this, the Ba'athists moved to ensure that the armed forces did not retain the monopoly on force, transforming politically reliable armed institutions that already existed into formidable forces capable of matching the army. The party militia or 'Popular Army', the Republican Guard and the Special Forces were only the most prominent of several such institutions, all outside the main body of the army, which insured the regime against its own armed forces.

The Iraqi Army up to 1980
Iraq in the 1970s was a peculiar mixture of ambition and weakness. By exaggerating its contributions to Arab causes, Iraq staked its claim to lead the Arab world; a pretension given some substance when Egypt signed the 1978 Camp David Accord with Israel, so isolating itself from the rest of the Arabs. Iraq joined in the general condemnation of Egypt while avoiding the extreme position taken up by states such as Libya, thereby securing a central position in inter-Arab politics. However, the Iraq which aspired to lead the Arab world was at the same time in danger of breaking up. The reality of the central government's weakness was exposed by its inability to suppress the endemic Kurdish rebellion in the north.[13] This in turn was only the most extreme manifestation of the failure of Iraqi governments during the previous 50 years to create any real loyalty to the state.

The hollowness of Iraqi aspirations is illustrated by the less-than-glorious history of its armed forces before 1980. Their one undoubted success was the suppression of the Assyrian 'revolt' of 1933, but since the founding of Iraq there had been a persistent conflict with the Kurds with which they were completely unable to deal. The situation became worse in the 1970s as Kurdish rebels received overt support from Iran and covert assistance from the United States. Numbers and heavy equipment enabled the Iraqi Army to gain control, but the revolt simmered on into the next decade.

Before Egypt's signing of the Camp David Accord, the one issue which had unambiguously united the Arab world was its hostility towards Israel. Iraqi forces had taken part in wars against Israel twice before the Ba'athists came to power — in 1948 and 1967 — but, despite the fact that in 1948 an Iraqi force of two infantry brigades and one armoured brigade had advanced to within 10km of the Mediterranean coast, neither of these conflicts had been a success for Iraqi arms. Repeated failures against the 'Zionist Entity' ironically boosted support for radical Arab movements such as the Ba'athists, and in 1968 the new Ba'ath regime in Iraq loudly proclaimed its solidarity with the Palestinian cause, even dispatching an expeditionary force to Jordan.[14] But Ba'athist policy was in practice more cautious than its rhetoric suggested, and the Iraqi forces wisely stood aside when, in September 1970, King Hussein of Jordan bloodily settled his differences with the Palestinians.

A much more substantial effort was made by Iraq in the October 1973 Arab-Israeli War, in which one of the surprises for Israel was the degree of co-operation achieved by the Arab world. Iraq committed two armoured divisions to the aid of Syria and fought three major engagements, which was far more than just a token effort. Iraqi troops did not lack determination in their engagements with the Israelis, although, despite a numerical advantage, they lacked the military skills necessary to win. Their first attack, on 13 October, was a disastrous divisional advance into a 'box' which the Israelis had prepared for them. The second attack, on 16 October, was poorly co-ordinated with their Jordanian allies and was eventually driven back by an Israeli counterattack from a flank. The largest action by the Iraqis, on 19 October, was comprehensively defeated when their Syrian allies retreated, uncovering their northern flank. The extent of the Iraqi commitment may be measured by the 217 tanks they left on the battlefield. The Israelis themselves assessed the Iraqis as tactically inept, unable to combine their different arms on the battlefield effectively.

What is often missed is that, in political terms, the Iraqi Army succeeded in many of these conflicts. Viewed from the outside, Iraq's military efforts were embarrassing failures, but just being involved in these conflicts was sufficient to generate a positive response from the public in Iraq itself. As with many of Iraq's military activities, the political symbolism of involvement in the 1973 War was far more important than the military performance.

Indeed, an inept army was actually in the interests of the Ba'ath regime, as greater competence would have posed a political threat because of the prestige which such competence would have generated. Ordinary Iraqis were so anxious to believe in the extraordinary qualities of their armed forces that a defeat had to be really rubbed in for it to register. Massacred Assyrians became part of Iraq's anti-imperialist struggle for modernisation (despite British support for Iraq's actions); humiliating defeat in 1941 could be represented as heroic defiance of the British; the debacle in 1973 could be transformed into a successful defence of Damascus. With the apparatus of a totalitarian state, it was easy to make people believe in a myth of military might, especially as it was what they wanted to believe.

The 1970s saw a considerable expansion in the size and equipment of the Iraqi armed forces, funded by increased oil revenues. Since 1958 Iraq had relied upon the Soviet Bloc for arms and training; this changed in the

1970s as Iraq sought to diversify its sources of military assistance. France in particular was keen to build up its military relationship with Iraq, agreeing in 1977 to export 40 Mirage F1 jet fighters.

Iraq still received large arms shipments from the USSR, and in the late 1970s was allowed to order some of the more advanced Soviet weapon systems, including 450 T-72 tanks.[15] As the following table shows, by 1980 Iraq had a formidable force at its disposal — on paper the country was in the front rank of Arab military powers. In reality, however, Iraq had an army that looked good rather than performed well, a direct consequence of the Ba'athist regime's determination to tolerate no potential challenger to its monopoly of power.

The Growth of the Iraqi Armed Forces in the 1970s

	1971	1975	1977	1978
Total Armed Forces	101,800	158,000	188,000	212,000
Main Battle Tanks	800	1,200	1,350	1,700
Other Armoured Fighting Vehicles	535	1,790	1,950	1,820[1]
Combat Planes	189	299	369	339[1]
Paramilitary Forces	18,000	54,800[2]	54,800[2]	79,800[2]

Notes: 1. These reduced figures are the result of phasing out some of Iraq's obsolete equipment and readjusting the 1977 estimate slightly downwards.
2. Most of which is the Ba'ath Party militia: the Popular Army.

Source: Estimates supplied from the International Institute for Strategic Studies' *Military Balances* for 1970/71, 1974/75, 1976/77 and 1977/78

Iraq's relationship with Iran

The fact that the army was expanded in this way reflected the regime's increasing confidence in the measures which it had taken to safeguard itself against internal military action. The army was also tangible proof that under the Ba'ath Party Iraq had become a modern state. However, the real impetus to expand the army was given by Iraq's easterly neighbour, Iran. Under the Shah, Iran had staked a claim to being the dominant state in the Gulf region. Iran's oil revenues were larger than those of Iraq, and its close relationship with the US meant that it could import such sophisticated weapons systems as the F-16 fighter, of which it ordered 160 at a cost of $3.4 billion in 1976.[16]

Iranian support for the Iraqi Kurds forced Iraq to sign the Algiers Agreement in 1975. In exchange for Iran cutting off aid to the Kurds, the Iraqis conceded Iranian demands for a revision of their mutual border, especially where it ran down the Shatt al-Arab waterway. This waterway was Iraq's principal access to the Gulf and, before 1975, Iraq claimed that its border with Iran ran down the eastern river bank; at Algiers Iraq recognised a new border running down the centre of the waterway. The man who reluctantly signed the Algiers Agreement on Iraq's behalf was Vice-President Saddam Hussein.

The war between Iraq and Iran which began in 1980 did not break out because of the historical antipathy between Arab and Persian, nor because of the territorial dispute over the Shatt al-Arab waterway, Iraq's only real access to the sea. These factors certainly made war more likely, but they were hardly sufficient reasons for conflict. The Algiers Agreement was not to Iraq's liking, but it was an acceptable compromise with its more powerful neighbour. Grudging co-operation was possible when both states recognised that it was in their interests. The specific cause of the war must be sought in the collapse of these shared interests, caused by Iran's apparent bellicosity but temporary military weakness.

After the 1979 revolution the Iranian armed forces were in chaos. The overthrow of the Shah had badly weakened Iran's impressive military establishment. Many members of the officer corps were closely associated with the Shah or, even worse, had been trained in the United States, and the revolutionary regime was busy purging these unreliable elements. The Imperial Iranian Air Force suffered most dramatically, losing half of its pilots by 1980.[17] The chaos accompanying the revolution led to many conscripts deserting from the ranks, while sophisticated high-technology weapons systems, dependent on the departed US maintenance experts, were rendered inoperable or irrepairable.

Nevertheless, Iraq's subsequent military adventurism makes it easy to forget the threat that revolutionary Iran, with its messianic fundamentalist message, appeared to pose to the status quo. Many commentators now explain Iraq's attack on Iran as a pre-emptive assault in the face of this Iranian menace. The dominant element of the Iranian revolution drew its power from Islamic militancy, which had a potentially powerful appeal to Iraq's downtrodden Shi'a majority. Revolutionary Iran spurned Iraq's tentative welcome, giving support to anti-Ba'athist forces within the Iraqi state, among them the Iraqi Shi'a group al-Da'wa, which almost succeeded in assassinating Iraq's Deputy Premier, Tariq Aziz, in April 1980. In response, in the months before the outbreak of war, thousands of suspect Iraqi Shi'a were labelled as illegal Persian immigrants by the Iraqi regime and expelled to Iran.[18] Given that it was only a matter of time before Iran recovered its military strength and added substance to its rhetoric, Saddam may well have concluded that a conflict was inevitable. If so, it would be logical to go to war sooner rather than later.

Such an explanation fits many of the facts but ignores some of the aspirations of Ba'athist Iraq. Saddam was laying claim to the status which President Nasser of Egypt had once enjoyed in Arab politics, and to win such a position he needed much more than just the temporary approval of the Arab League. Iraq had hitherto played an undistinguished part in fighting for Arab causes, but the defeat of the ancient Persian enemy would add substance to Saddam's pretensions. In addition, checking the menace of the Iranian revolution would earn Iraq the gratitude of the Gulf monarchies, who had plenty of reasons to fear Iran. From the perspective of 1980 it is easy to imagine the prestige that a short, victorious war would have brought Saddam, particularly as he was due to host the Non-Aligned Movement Conference in Baghdad in 1982. Expecting victory, Saddam made his demands on behalf of the entire Arab world.

These motives are plausible, and they are not mutually exclusive. Viewed in terms of Iranian-Iraqi tensions, the idea of a pre-emptive blow made sense, while modest gains won from Iran by waging a limited war were by no means incompatible with hopes of larger gains in the Arab world. In any event, it seems perverse not to regard Iraq's aims as a spectrum, ranging from the modest to the spectacular. With so many highly-placed Iranian exiles in Baghdad telling Saddam that the revolutionary regime would easily collapse, it is difficult to believe that Saddam did not hope to annex part of Iran. A particularly tempting prize would have been the oil-producing southern border province of Khuzistan, called Arabistan by those emphasising the Arab origins of many of those who lived there. It is sensible to assume that relief from the Iranian menace was the least he expected to gain from the war.

Iraq invades Iran

On 22 September 1980 Iraqi troops invaded Iran, and confidence was high enough for the RCC to leave some 50 per cent of the Iraqi Army inactive. In the north, two divisions advanced to protect the oilfields around Panjwin, and in the centre an armoured division with supporting units advanced to forestall any counterattack on Baghdad. The most ambitious attack was made in the south, into the southern Iranian province of Khuzistan. The two southern thrusts used two mechanised divisions and three armoured divisions, the lion's share of the more effective Iraqi troops. On the same day the Iraqi Air Force tried, but failed, to knock out the Iranian Air Force on the ground.

Iranian forces were initially capable of resisting the Iraqis only in urban centres, but even in the south the Iraqi advance was unspectacular. This reflected the poor performance of the Iraqi military, together with the limits which Saddam had deliberately placed on its advance. Halting his forces on 28 September, he optimistically offered to discuss terms for ending the war, only to have the offer rejected with scorn by the Iranians. The Iraqis' hope for a quick, cheap victory had evaporated, while the deliberate limits placed on their armed forces meant that they forfeited the opportunity to inflict greater damage on Iran.

A much slower advance was resumed in October. As Iranian resistance stiffened, it became clear that Saddam had overestimated the capacity of his army. Iraq's initial reluctance to storm large urban centres gave the Iranians time to strengthen their defences, and the sieges of Khorramshahr and Abadan proved to be particularly bloody. Khorramshahr finally fell on 24 October at a cost of over 8,000 Iraqi casualties, but Abadan was never completely taken. The limited enthusiasm of the Iraqi troops petered out in the winter rains; by November 1980 the Iraqi offensive had halted.

That the Ba'athist regime was facing a fight for its survival was not immediately apparent. Iran's initial attempt to drive out the Iraqi invader was a disaster, as political pressure forced the premature launching of an offensive in January 1981. Iran assembled the equivalent of a large armoured division with over 300 tanks, mostly Chieftains of British manufacture, and launched it into an attack near the town of Susangerd. What followed was a repeat of Israel's 'box' ambush in 1973, with the Iraqis on the other side and Iran on the receiving end. The battle took place in thick mud, with most of the firing at point-blank range. The Iranians left at least 140 tanks on the battlefield, and the jubilant Iraqis rushed the foreign press to the scene to record their triumph. But the sense of security induced by this victory was illusory; Iran's will to continue attacking was far from exhausted.

Changes in Iraq

Iraqi complacency was rudely shattered by a series of successful Iranian offensives later in the year. Iran's poorly equipped but enthusiastic troops exploited the marshes of the south, winning victories over their better-armed but reluctant opponents. The Iranians retook Abadan in September, attacking at night and catching the demoralised Iraqi defenders by surprise. Even worse followed in March 1982, when half the Iraqi IV Corps was surrounded defending Iraqi gains of the previous year in the Shush-Dezful area. Once again, Iranian human-wave tactics caught the Iraqis by surprise, causing many of the Popular Army militia to run away. In the fighting between March and May 1982 Iran inflicted over 50,000 Iraqi casualties, took 25,000 prisoners and captured 200 Iraqi tanks. The Iranian success was capped on 24 May by the recapture of Khorramshahr,[19] which was probably the closest they came to winning the war.

The progress of the war revealed much about the nature of the Iraqi state. On the advance Iraqi troops appeared cheerful, but morale rapidly collapsed in the face of Iran's successful counter-offensive. Any nationalist sentiment the Iraqis may have felt was inadequate to sustain them when things went badly. Tactics on the battlefield were dominated by a desire to avoid casualties, a sign that Saddam was aware how little popular support the regime possessed. The Iraqis made poor use of their material advantages, using weapons incompetently and being unable to combine their different arms effectively on the battlefield. The RCC attempted to manage the war centrally, and all serious decisions had to go up to this political level. Even though the Ba'athist regime had deliberately emasculated the officer corps, it was still unprepared to relax its political controls in this first stage of the war. At home, expenditure on public works rose rather than fell, and a major effort was made to prevent the demands of the war from reducing people's material well-being. Ba'athist Iraq employed all the rhetoric of a state sure of the loyal support of an Arab nationalist population, but recognised that the force of this nationalism was insufficient to sustain the state in any major military effort.

The Iranian victories in 1982 forced changes in Iraq. Many senior figures were purged, and at least one member of the RCC was executed — Minister of Health Riyadh Ibrahim Hussein. In the armed forces there were hundreds of executions of senior officers. Repression was accompanied by continued government efforts to minimise the impact of the war. It was no longer possible to improve the standard of living, but care was taken to look after families which had suffered a loss at the front, and a particular effort was made to direct funds into the neglected Shi'a south. The war accelerated the development of Saddam's personality cult, symbolised by the holding of elections to the National Assembly, the first since 1958.

Saddam made it clear that these elections 'must ensure that the thirteen and a half million [Iraqis] take the same road. He who chooses the twisted path, will meet the sword'.[20] Saddam had bypassed his own party, basing his power directly on the nominal consent of the governed.

While Saddam was safe against his domestic enemies, on the battlefield he faced an enemy intent on eradicating his regime. The absolute nature of Iran's war aims, and the possibility that they were realisable, alarmed the outside world. Arms, loans and gifts flooded into Baghdad, making it possible for Iraq to sustain an enormous expansion of its armed forces. Without this advantage it is doubtful if Iraq could have survived the onslaught of Iran.

Saddam's efforts to escape from the war

Saddam's miscalculation of Iraq's strength and Iran's weakness placed him in a dilemma. It was possible that Iraq could survive the war only if its army was permitted to become more competent, but allowing officers to make their own decisions required the regime to relax its controls. In particular, the criteria for promotion would need to relate to military competence rather than to political reliability. Changes such as these could well see the re-emergence of the army as a rival political force. Saddam's preference was to attempt to survive the war either by importing masses of equipment or by a strategic short cut that would obviate the need for basic reform of the military.

One possible 'short cut' for Saddam was to use Iraq's superior airpower. Crude attempts to coerce Iran by bombing urban centres were counter-productive, as each time a 'war of the cities' erupted it was Iraq which proved unwilling to sustain civilian casualties. A more sophisticated strategy became possible because Iraq was able to upgrade its air force, importing sophisticated equipment and sending trusted pilots abroad for training. The French supplied Iraq with variants of the Mirage F1, and the Soviets sold several of their more modern planes, such as the MiG-29.

Improvements in the Iraqi Air Force enabled Saddam to opt for a strategy of attacking Iran's economic infrastructure, in particular its oil-exporting facilities and tankers. In 1985 Iraqi planes successfully attacked the Iranian oil terminal at Kharg Island; their retrained pilots used French AS.30 laser-guided bombs and did sufficient damage to cut export production by 50 per cent. However, the Iranians found ways of countering these attacks, and Iraq never succeeded in doing more than temporarily halting Iran's oil exports from Kharg Island. The French loan of five Super Etendard fighters in 1983, and their replacement by Iraq's purchase of the Mirage F1EQ5 in 1985, gave Iraq an enhanced capacity to attack ships, as both aircraft could carry the Exocet anti-shipping missile. A 'tanker war' escalated in the Gulf and, as with the attacks on Kharg Island, Iraq succeeded in inflicting considerable damage but failed to cripple Iran's ability to wage war.[21]

Saddam hoped that events in the outside world could persuade Iran to end the war. It seems likely that Iraqi agents helped provide Israel with the pretext to invade Lebanon in 1982,[22] and Saddam used this to appeal to

Iran for a common front against Israel. Later in the war Saddam hoped that attacking targets in the Gulf would provoke Iran into an unwise response, and that in turn the West would intervene against Iran. The West did intervene, but proved unwilling to force Iran to end the war. Like Saddam's other 'short cuts' to victory, this one damaged Iran insufficiently to persuade it to stop fighting.

Iran invades Iraq

Contrary to Saddam's hopes, the war was to be decided by the course of the ground conflict. The 1,300 km-long front line seemed to give the Iranians a wide choice of directions from which to attack, but terrain, politics and a shortage of heavy military equipment narrowed their options. In the mountainous north the terrain favoured the defender and, despite the support of the Iraqi Kurds, a successful offensive could cause political complications with the Turks and Iran's own Kurdish minority. The centre of the front was relatively flat, dry and open — ideal for an offensive, but only if it could be conducted by armoured formations supported by airpower, neither of which Iran possessed in sufficient strength. At the southern end of the front numerous rivers made the area very marshy except during the hotter months; these marshes might nullify Iraq's advantages in armoured vehicles, but they were also formidable barriers that a defender could use to absorb attacks.

The pattern of the ground war from 1982 until 1987 was one of a series of Iranian offensives, mostly on the southern section of the front, blunted by Iraq's defences. Despite the enormous advantage in material enjoyed by Iraq, many of these attacks made initial progress. The Iranians became adept at surprising the Iraqis, and in particular in exploiting the extensive marshes on the southern section of the front. Two years in succession, Iranian forces infiltrated the Haur al-Hawizeh marshes, taking half of the Majnoon Islands oil complex in March 1984 and temporarily cutting the Baghdad–to–Basra highway in March 1985. An even more spectacular success was the seizure in 1986 of the Faw peninsula, which was held despite determined Iraqi counterattacks. To the outside world it seemed as if Iran might batter its way to victory.

Iraq continued to expand its armed forces and, as the following table shows, in material terms Iran was at a disadvantage.

A Comparison of Iraqi and Iranian Military Strength 1980 to 1988

	Iraq:			Iran:		
	1980	1985	1988	1980*	1985	1988**
Tanks	2,750	2,900	5,500	1,735	1,000	1,000
Other AFVs	2,500	3,000	5,100	2,250	1,060	600
Artillery	800	3,500	5,000+[1]	1,000	1,000	1,000
Combat aircraft	332	500	500+[1]	445	80	50
Helicopters	276	270	400+[1]	720	350	300+[1]

*Approximately half operational
**Very low % levels of operational equipment, especially planes and helicopters

A Comparison of Iraqi and Iranian Military Strength 1980 to 1988

Manpower					(figures in 1,000s)	
(regular)	200	475	475	150	250	305
Manpower						
(irregular)	75	650	650	75	250	250
Reserves	250	75	480	400	350	?

Notes: [1] There is a wide variation in the figures given in 1988, and these figures are estimates erring on the side of caution

Source: adapted from the International Institute for Strategic Studies' *Military Balance*

A policy of static defence enabled Saddam to keep a tight grip on his own forces, but, when Iranian attacks breached these defences, it became evident that a more professional and flexible army was required. Certain changes, such as improving the individual weapons skills of Iraqi soldiers, were initiated early in the war, but reforms that freed the armed forces from close political control were instituted reluctantly. After the defeats of 1982, the more incompetent officers were removed or transferred to duties in the rear. Political guidance officers remained with their units, although they had a reduced role in operational matters.[23] Senior officers were made members of the National Defence Council, which took over much of the day-to-day running of the war from the RCC. The army was taken into 'partnership' with the regime, although Saddam still had the last word on operational matters. In 1986, for example, it was Saddam's decision to launch an attack on Mehran rather than concentrate on recapturing the Faw peninsula.

Saddam turned to his 'elite' units to provide a force that could restore the situation in the event of the defences failing. The politically reliable Republican Guard were chosen to receive special training, and given more modern weapons. By 1987 over 30,000 Republican Guards had been retrained, enabling them to fight an all-arms battle and take important initiatives at brigade level. Hundreds of kilometres of new roads and a fleet of Soviet tank transporters enabled this force to be deployed as a last resort to counter an Iranian breakthrough. The Iraqis were fortunate to be receiving intelligence data regularly from the United States; this enabled them in most cases to have the Republican Guard on the move before Iran launched an offensive.

But Iraq could not have held its defensive line by having to call on the Republican Guard to stem every attack. It was equally important for Iraq to be able to take full advantage of its aerial and artillery assets. Iraqi artillery became much more accurate, being trained at co-operating with helicopters carrying artillery spotters. The pilots of helicopters and fixed-wing aircraft learned how to deliver accurate low-level attacks against tactical targets. These conven-tional approaches were supplemented by chemical weapons; after 1984, the Iraqis were using nerve gas in response to any Iranian penetration of their defences.

Iranian strategy in 1987 concentrated on attempts to take the southern Iraqi city of Basra. This made a tempting objective, full of Shi'a Arabs who could well be sympathetic to their Iranian co-religionists and less than

35 km from the front line. The Iranian problem was their inability to turn an initial tactical advantage into a strategic victory. Despite this, they failed to adopt a more cautious, attritional approach. Their modest gains were purchased at great cost in life; a sacrifice not matched by the defenders, who were able to substitute firepower for willpower. With virtually no exceptions, offensives cost Iran more lives than Iraq, even the offensives which the Iranians regarded as victories. Unfortunately for Iran, the Basra region was also the best defended section of the Iraqi front, multiplying the human cost of the offensives still further.

On 9 January 1987 the Iranians launched the 'Karbala 5' operation to capture Basra. Attacking by night, they achieved surprise, exploiting the marshes to nullify Iraq's advantage in armoured fighting vehicles. Initial Iranian progress forced the Iraqis to use their airpower recklessly, together with chemical weapons. The Iranians were unable to advance further, becoming very vulnerable to heavy artillery and aerial attacks, while Iraq gathered its resources, rather ponderously, for a counterattack. Major Republican Guard counterattacks were made on 31 January and 1 March, driving the Iranians back. The Iranians ended the offensive having gained a few kilometres at a cost of at least 20,000 lives. Iraq's loss of 6,000 lives was modest by comparison. Four lesser 'Karbala' offensives were launched by Iran between late December 1986 and April 1987; these were all indecisive and may have cost Iran 50,000 lives. Failure in these offensives eroded Iranian willingness to continue fighting the war.

Iraq resumes the offensive

Despite inflicting disproportionate losses on the Iranians, Saddam feared that Iran could continue accepting such casualties and would eventually wear Iraq down. However, after defeating the 'Karbala 5' offensive he was more confident of the fighting abilities of his troops. The result was a decision that in 1988 Iraq would once more take the offensive, which coincided with the wilting of Iranian fighting spirit.

To support the renewal of the offensive in 1988 the Republican Guard was enlarged to roughly 40,000 men. They were withdrawn from the line to rehearse the 'set-piece' offensives which Iraq hoped to execute. According to some Iraqi sources, they practised on life-sized models for the coming offensive. Advances were to be preceded by a heavy artillery bombardment and supported by tactical airpower. Unlike the Iraqi Army of 1980, these troops could expect accurate firepower to be delivered before and during their advance. This was a ponderous approach to waging an offensive, which would not have looked out of place in the First World War, but it did give Saddam, rather than front-line commanders, control of events.

Iraq opened its 1988 campaign in April with a well organised recapture of the Faw peninsula. It then moved on to an attack in the Basra area and on 25 May, in just ten hours of fighting, retook the territory that had been lost in 1987. The northern half of the Majnoon Islands, lost in 1984, was regained in June, and two more successful offensives followed. The only major check suffered by Iraq was the destruction of a force of anti-Khomeini Iranians fighting for Saddam, but that was at least partly due to indifferent Iraqi support for their advance.[24] At the same time Iraq's aerial attacks on targets deep inside Iran began to hurt the Iranian home front. A particular fear of Iranian civilians was that Iraq's new long-range Scud missiles might deliver chemical warheads against targets such as Tehran. Pressure also mounted against Iran in the Gulf, and by April US warships had sunk a considerable portion of the Iranian Navy. It seemed to Iran's clerical leadership that continuing the war might undermine the stability of the regime. Publicly, the Iranian leader, Ayatollah Khomeini announced that he would prefer to drink poison, but despite this he accepted a ceasefire on 20 July and on 8 August the fighting came to a formal end. At a conservative estimate it had cost the two states 367,000 lives to end up roughly where they had started. Many factors drove the Iranians to call for a ceasefire, but everything else pales in comparison to the way in which the ground war bled Iran's will to continue fighting.

Iraq's 'victory'

Although Iraq received massive help from the outside world, this does not by itself explain its surviving the war. It is not normal for a state lacking the wholehearted support of its citizens to endure such a conflict. It could be that the Iraqi Shi'a soldiers saw themselves as Arabs before they were Shi'a, an identification encouraged by Saddam's attention to their material needs. But although Iraqi propaganda stressed the theme of Arab against Persian, its appeal was clearly limited, and the Arab minority in southern Iran did not make common cause with Iraq. Another possibility is that a specifically Iraqi nationalism was forged by the trials of war. Certainly, during the war Saddam made an effort to include Kurds and Shi'a within the formal apparatus of the state, awarding them prestigious but powerless positions. But the major revolts by the Kurds and the southern Shi'a following the Gulf War in 1991 suggest that any newly created Iraqi nationalism was, at best, a limited motivating force. A less pleasant explanation comes from an examination of the sort of state the Ba'athists had built in Iraq. The regime drove people into a pseudo-mass involvement in which the security forces were ever present. Iraqis fought from fear of their own government, and because going through the motions was the safe thing to do. This was enough to make people fight, although without the conspicuous enthusiasm displayed by the Iranians. This explanation seems to account for much of the manner in which Iraq conducted the war.

Iraq's weakness as a state made it possible for a totalitarian regime to establish itself in power. A lack of a deep sense of loyalty to the state, and the ephemeral nature of Arab nationalist enthusiasms, made it likely that the Iraqi armed forces would be reluctant to fight a major war. This military weakness was compounded by the extreme measures the Ba'athist regime took to protect itself against its own armed forces. Saddam's misconceived invasion of Iran forced him to accept changes in the relationship between the regime and the armed forces, but throughout the conflict the survival of his regime remained more important than the effective conduct of the war. The help of the outside world, and the deficiencies of their Iranian opponents, enabled Saddam to survive the war without changing the political relationship between himself and the armed forces.

Surviving the war was a kind of victory for Iraq, and the regime's propaganda machine lost no time in trumpeting this triumph. Yet it is difficult to see exactly what the fruits of this victory were. Iraq had gained some small and totally valueless parts of Iranian territory. Diplomatically, Saddam had earned greater respect from his Arab brothers, but this was nothing noticeably more dramatic than he enjoyed before the war. The war had exhausted Iraq's previously healthy foreign exchange reserves and plunged the country into a $80 billion debt. The only tangible gain was that Saddam's armed forces had expanded dramatically and learned new skills. By 1989 Iraq certainly had the most formidable military establishment of any state in the Arab world. Unfortunately, the most obvious way to realise the advantage of such an asset was to use it.

Notes

1. The Sunni/Shi'a division is the most important in the Muslim religion. The Shi'a have traditionally made less distinction between the secular and the religious in government, whereas the Sunni have had a more secular approach to government. In many Muslim states the Shi'a are an underprivileged group, and only in Iran is Shi'a Islam the 'established' faith.

2. Elie Kedourie, *The Chatham House Version* (Weidenfeld and Nicolson, London, 1970), p 242.

3. Samir al-Kabir, *Republic of Fear* (Hutchinson Radius, London, 1989), p 193, quoting Michel 'Aflaq.

4. Ibid, p 228.

5. Ahmad Hasan al-Bakr was Khairallah Talfah's cousin and they were also close friends. Khairallah was Saddam Hussein's uncle and *de facto* foster-father.

6. Khairallah Talfah's extremist views are demonstrated clearly by the title of a book he published in 1981: *Three whom God should not have created: Persians, Jews and Flies* (Dar al-Hurriyya [Iraqi Government Press], Baghdad).

7. Efraim Karsh and Inari Rautsi, *Saddam Hussein* (Brassey's, London, 1991), quoting on p 30 Saddam's offer to deal with the Ba'ath's military allies once the 1968 coup succeeded.

8. Events in Syria split the Ba'ath Party. In 1966 Ba'athists in the Syrian armed forces overthrew a civilian Ba'athist government. This led to a dispute in the Ba'ath Party as a whole, partly because of the left-wing leanings of this new Syrian government. In Iraq, the faction led by Bakr and organised by Saddam defeated the pro-Syrian wing of the Iraqi Regional Command. In 1968 two Ba'ath Pan-Arab national commands existed, one based in Iraq and the other in Syria. Since 1968, except for a brief period, Syria and Iraq have had a very hostile relationship.

9. Abd al-Karim al-Shayhkli had been closely associated with Saddam since being involved in the 1959 attempt to assassinate Qassem. He temporarily saved Saddam from arrest in 1964, and in 1966 both men escaped from prison together.

10. Karsh and Rautsi, op cit, p 117.

11. Phebe Marr, *The Modern History of Iraq* (Westview Press, Boulder, Colorado, 1985), pp 242 and 336.

12. Samir al-Kabir, op cit, p 41.

13. Karsh and Rautsi, op cit, p 81, cite Saddam as admitting that the Kurdish conflict of the 1970s cost 60,000 Iraqi casualties, and that, at the close of the conflict, the Iraqi Army was almost at the end of its resources.

14. The idea of the expeditionary force was to protect Jordan and its Palestinian population from any further Israeli 'aggression' following the occupation of the West Bank in June 1967.

15. Efraim Karsh, 'The Iran-Iraq War: A Military Analysis', *International Institute for Strategic Studies Adelphi Paper No 220* (London, 1987), p 11.

16. Ibid, p 10.

17. Ibid, p 14.

18. Samir al-Kabir, op cit, p 19, puts the figure for 'Iranians' expelled from Iraq at 200,000.

19. Anthony H Cordesman and Abraham R Wagner, *The Lessons of Modern War*, Vol II, 'The Iran-Iraq War' (Westview Press, Boulder, Colorado, 1990), p 140.

20. Karsh and Rautsi, op cit, p 120.

21. Giacomo Luciani, in his essay 'Oil and Instability: The Political Economy of Petroleum and the Gulf War', in Hanns Maull and Otto Pick (ed), *The Gulf War* (Pinter Publishers, London, 1989), makes

a persuasive case that neither side did more than briefly halt the other's oil exports.

22. Dilip Hiro, *The Longest War. The Iran-Iraq Military Conflict* (Paladin, London, 1990), p 63, outlines Iraq's involvement in the 1982 attempted assassination of Israel's ambassador in London, which helped to trigger the Israeli invasion of southern Lebanon.

23. Shahram Chubin and Charles Tripp, *Iran and Iraq at War* (Tauris, London, 1988), p 117.

24. A fuller description of Iraq's 1988 offensives may be found in Cordesman and Wagner, op cit, pp 373–5, 381–4 and 387–90.

Further Reading

Anthony H Cordesman and Abraham R Wagner, *The Lessons of Modern War*, Vol II, 'The Iran-Iraq War' (Westview Press, Boulder, Colorado, 1990)

Dilip Hiro, *The Longest War. The Iran-Iraq Military Conflict* (Paladin, London, 1990)

Samir al-Kabir, *Republic of Fear* (Hutchinson Radius, London, 1989)

Efraim Karsh and Inari Rautsi, *Saddam Hussein* (Brassey's, London, 1991).

CHAPTER 2
The Gulf Crisis and World Politics

John Pimlott

'We are ready to use force to defend a new order emerging
among the nations of the world, a world of sovereign
nations living in peace.'

President George Bush, 1 January 1991

The invasion of Kuwait

At 2 am (local time) on 2 August
1990 Iraqi troops, spearheaded by
Soviet-designed T-72 tanks and
supported by fighter aircraft and
helicopter gunships, crossed the
border into Kuwait. Overwhelming
the inadequately prepared Kuwaiti
border guards, the main column moved south towards Kuwait City, while
heliborne special forces seized the strategically significant islands of
Warbah and Bubiyan. Despite some resistance around the Emir of Kuwait's
Dasman Palace (where the Emir's youngest brother, Sheikh Fahd, was
killed) and Royal Kuwaiti Air Force Headquarters, the Iraqis were in
effective control of the country by the end of the day. They may not have
achieved all their objectives — the Emir, Sheikh Salem al-Sabah, and most
of his family escaped to Saudi Arabia — but they had succeeded in taking
the world by surprise.

Background to the crisis

In retrospect this seems remarkable, for the crisis between Iraq and Kuwait
had been developing for some time. It had its origins in a mixture of
territorial, economic and political differences, exacerbated by more personal clashes between the Iraqi President, Saddam Hussein, and the leaders
of the Gulf states.[1] The latter represented the complacent, conservative, oil-
rich sheikhdoms, resented and envied by the poorer, more radical Arabs to
whom Saddam appealed in his quest for leadership of the 'Arab nation'.

Border disputes between Iraq and Kuwait were of long standing,
representing in Saddam's eyes all that was wrong with the territorial
arrangements in the Middle East. To him, the issue was clear. Kuwait
existed as a separate state only because of boundaries imposed by the
British in the aftermath of the First World War and the collapse of the
Ottoman Empire and, in reality, the area known as Kuwait was part of Iraq,
having originally existed as a *gaza* (lesser district) in the *vilayet* (province)
of Basra.[2] The invasion was therefore correcting an historical injustice, even
though, by exercising the 'right' of Iraq to expand territorially, Saddam was

undermining his own argument about the need for Arabs to overturn the state boundaries of a colonial past and come together as a single nation. Further reinforcement of Iraq's aggrandizement at the cost of a weaker neighbour came from the simultaneous seizure of Warbah and Bubiyan, vital islands on the route to and from Iraq's naval base at Umm Qasr.

But Iraq's claims to Kuwait were nothing new — they dated back at least to 1938, only six years after the British had withdrawn from what had been Mesopotamia — so other, more immediate reasons for the 1990 invasion had to apply. Chief among these was money, for by taking Kuwait Saddam stood to gain access to substantial oil wealth — a production of 1.8 million barrels a day, helping to create a Gross National Product (GNP) for the Emir of $22.1 billion a year in 1989 figures. Saddam certainly needed it, for although Iraq was itself producing 2.8 million barrels a day, helping to create a GNP of $67 billion a year, the country was effectively bankrupt. In August 1988, when Iraq celebrated self-proclaimed victory in the bitter eight-year war with neighbouring Iran, it was estimated that rebuilding the state to its pre-1980 condition would cost a staggering $230 billion, the equivalent of devoting every dollar of oil revenue for nearly 20 years to reconstruction. That this was impossible was shown by the fact that, in 1989, Saddam could not even balance the books. With oil revenues of $13 billion, his civilian and military imports alone totalled $17 billion, with debt repayments of $5 billion on top of that. The latter represented interest and minimal repayments on foreign debts, incurred during the war with Iran, said to total $80 billion.[3]

The knock-on effects of such an economic imbalance were substantial. Until some of the debts had been repaid, or at least rescheduled, foreign governments were understandably unwilling to lend more, and foreign companies were loath to invest in Iraq. Policies such as privatisation of key industries, introduced by Saddam in the late 1980s, did little to help, with few Iraqi entrepreneurs willing to risk their capital, and inflation was rising. By 1989–90 there were worrying rumbles of discontent among the Iraqi people, who faced hardships they had expected to avoid once the war with Iran was over. Like so many hard-pressed dictators before him, Saddam probably decided that a foreign adventure — especially one that seemed easy — would divert public attention from the very real problems at home.

If so, he gave ample warning. His solution to Iraq's economic problems was outlined as early as February 1990, at an Arab Co-operation Council (ACC) meeting in Amman, when he asked King Hussein of Jordan and President Hosni Mubarak of Egypt to put pressure on the Gulf states not only to declare a moratorium on all wartime debts to Iraq, but also to make an immediate additional grant of $30 billion. Saddam's justification was that Iraq had fought for eight years against Iranian fundamentalism on behalf of the Gulf states, so they owed him reparations. His threat if they did not agree — 'Let the Gulf states know that if they do not give this money to me, I would know how to get it' — was crystal clear.[4]

Saddam singled out Kuwait and the United Arab Emirates (UAE) for more substantial pressure, this time over oil production. The Organisation of Petroleum Exporting Countries (OPEC), responding to a glut in the world market, had laid down quotas for each of its members and set the price of oil at $18 a barrel. Saddam accused Kuwait and the UAE, with some justification, of deliberately exceeding their quotas, forcing the price down as they flooded the market. This inevitably affected the Iraqi economy. At an Arab summit in May 1990 Saddam pointed out: '. . . for every single dollar drop in the price of a barrel of oil, our loss mounts to $1 billion a year',[5] leading him to demand an end to quota violations, a permitted increase to Iraqi production and a price rise to at least $25 a barrel. Furthermore, he specifically accused Kuwait of 'stealing' Iraqi oil by slant drilling beneath the border in the Rumailla oilfield, and demanded compensation of $2.4 billion. The Kuwaitis angrily denied the accusation and refused to negotiate, maintaining oil-production levels and refusing to forgive any wartime loans to Iraq. To Saddam this was tantamount to a Kuwaiti declaration of 'economic war'; a neat excuse for imminent aggression.

While all this was going on, Iraqi relations with the West were deteriorating. In March 1990 the Iranian-born journalist Farzad Bazoft, caught investigating an explosion at a secret military base near Baghdad for the London newspaper *The Observer*, was accused of spying, put on trial and executed amid almost universal condemnation of Iraqi actions. At the same time Dr Gerald Bull, a Canadian ballistics expert reputedly developing a 'supergun' for Iraq, capable of launching non-conventional weapons many thousands of miles, was assassinated in Brussels. Soon after, British Customs confiscated eight long steel tubes, bound for Iraq, thought to be part of Bull's invention. On 28 March a joint Anglo-US Customs swoop added 40 electrical capacitators, usable as nuclear triggers, to the haul. Although interpreted by Saddam as part of a deliberate smear campaign against Iraq, evidence was growing that Saddam was a dangerous, unpredictable leader. On 2 April he took the process further by threatening to 'make fire eat half of Israel if it tries to do anything against Iraq', a reference to Iraq's growing chemical and biological weapons capability, already shown to be a reality in the Kurdish town of Halabja in March 1988.

At this stage both the USA and Israel seemed to take the threats posed by Saddam seriously. President George Bush publicly deplored Saddam's statement of 2 April, and Israel hinted that an Iraqi chemical attack would trigger a 'devastating' (presumably nuclear) riposte. If it did anything, however, this posturing diverted attention away from the growing crisis over Kuwait. This worsened on 16 July, when the Iraqi Foreign Minister, Tariq Aziz, reiterated the demands for an end to oil-quota violations and to Kuwaiti activities in the Rumailla oilfield. Twenty-four hours later Saddam openly accused Kuwait and the UAE of conspiring with 'world imperialism and Zionism' to destroy the economic livelihood of Iraq. He even went so far as to say that, if a peaceful solution was not forthcoming, he would 'have no choice but to resort to effective action to put things right'.[6]

The Kuwaitis played into his hands, underestimating the seriousness of the threats and refusing to negotiate beyond the minimum of concessions. On 20 July Kuwait and the UAE agreed to adhere to OPEC quotas, under intense pressure from Saudi Arabia, Iran and Iraq, but would go no further.

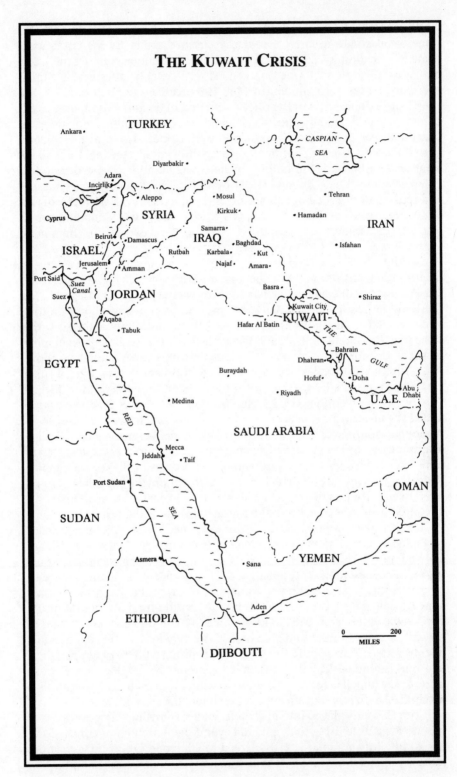

THE KUWAIT CRISIS

To Saddam this was merely reinforcement of their arrogance and intransigence; it may well have been at this point that he finalised his plans for invasion. Certainly, from 21 July Iraqi forces started massing close to the border with Kuwait.

But no Third World leader could afford to contemplate aggression, however justified in his own eyes, without reference to the international scene and, especially, to the likely reactions of the Superpowers. Here, Saddam made a major (although understandable) miscalculation, convincing himself that neither the USSR nor USA would respond to an attack on Kuwait with more than diplomatic or economic action. With reference to the USSR, preoccupied with events in eastern Europe and its own constituent republics, this was undoubtedly correct (anyway, a Treaty of Friendship between Iraq and the USSR, signed in 1972, was still in force),[7] but the USA was a different matter. From Saddam's point of view, President George Bush seemed irresolute, and available evidence certainly backed this up. At the time of Saddam's threat to Israel in early April, for example, an attempt by the US State Department to put together a sanctions package, refusing Iraq funds from the Export-Import Bank and cancelling the Community Credit Program (which allowed Saddam to purchase cheap US grain), had been undermined by the Commerce Department and by a visit to Baghdad by five US senators, all from farming states, reiterating a desire to do business with Iraq. Indeed, on 25 April Bush had even sent a message to Saddam, expressing a hope that 'the ties between the United States and Iraq would contribute to the peace and stability of the Middle East'. These were hardly the actions of an administration determined to contain Iraq, although they did fit the pattern of one obsessed with events elsewhere, notably in eastern Europe, and intent on 'damping down' potential crises which might affect the new relationship with the USSR.

All this coincided with growing reports from the Central Intelligence Agency (CIA), received via spy-satellites and the Israelis, that Iraqi troop movements suggested a serious threat to Kuwait, but the Americans still pursued a neutral policy. On 25 July, when Saddam granted an audience to the US Ambassador to Baghdad, April Glaspie, he received assurances that any disagreement between Iraq and Kuwait would be viewed as a local affair and that the USA had 'no opinion on inter-Arab disputes'. In saying this, Glaspie was undoubtedly reflecting the opinion of a State Department convinced that Saddam was doing no more than 'sabre-rattling' to force Kuwait to negotiate, but it effectively gave a green light to the Iraqi leader.[8] This was reinforced on 31 July, when the BBC World Service, monitored in Baghdad, carried reports of a meeting of a US House of Representatives Middle East subcommittee at which the Assistant Secretary of State with responsibility for the Middle East, John Kelly, admitted that the USA had no defence treaties with the Gulf states — a clear indication to Saddam that no military response was likely or, indeed, possible.

Thus, by late July, convinced that Kuwait was following a deliberate policy of economic sabotage against Iraq and spurred on by the prospect of seizing enormous oil wealth which would go some way towards solving Iraq's economic (and, by association, political) problems without triggering a Superpower reaction, Saddam had decided to act. A last-minute attempt by the Egyptian President, Hosni Mubarak, to mediate between Iraq and Kuwait on behalf of the Arab League, led Mubarak to declare: 'I've had it from the mouth of Saddam Hussein himself that he won't send troops and that he has no intention of attacking Kuwait.' But the effort ended in failure when a mini-summit between the two sides at Jeddah ended in acrimony early on 1 August. By then, Iraqi T-72s were preparing to move south.

US crisis management

Throughout 1 August, Eastern Standard Time, or EST (running about eight hours behind that in the Gulf), the US State Department held an inter-agency meeting to monitor events in Iraq. For much of the day the consensus remained that Saddam, if he attacked at all, would aim only to seize the disputed northern border with Kuwait as well as Warbah and Bubiyan — something that would not pose a threat sufficiently large to merit a full-scale US or Western reponse. By 11.30 pm EST (7.30 am, 2 August, Gulf time), however, it was apparent that Saddam was intent on taking over the whole of Kuwait, a move that would leave him in control of more than a fifth of the world's oil production, plus enormous Kuwaiti financial resources worldwide. Moreover, his forces might build up such a momentum that the advance would continue deep into Saudi Arabia or the Gulf states, leaving him all-powerful in the region. As far as the Americans were concerned, it was essential to react quickly to prevent such a scenario, but with President Bush already in bed for the night and Secretary of State James Baker on an official visit to the USSR as part of the preparations for the forthcoming Superpower summit in Helsinki, it had to be left to relatively junior members of the administration to initiate a process of 'crisis management', designed to restore an initiative lost by the preoccupation with events elsewhere in the world.

The key to such a process lay in the ability of the Americans to contain the crisis, minimising its impact on existing US policies and, if possible, enhancing opportunities for the realisation of policy goals. In terms of the Gulf, the existing policies were clear: to 'preserve and protect US and friendly access to Arabian peninsula oil resources, assist friendly states to provide for their own security against subversion and insurgency [and] prevent military coercion of friendly states'.[9] These had been formulated and refined in response to a perceived threat from the Soviet Union and, more particularly, from fundamentalist Iran in the aftermath of the Shah's overthrow in early 1979. At that time, President Jimmy Carter had reacted to the failure of US policies to protect the Shah by ordering the creation of a Rapid Deployment Joint Task Force (RDJTF), later expanded into Central Command (CENTCOM), and by initiating a variety of contingency plans for US political, economic and military commitment in the event of a future crisis. US resolution during the lead-up to the 1990 crisis over Kuwait may have been questionable, but once the Iraqi threat became obvious in terms of a full-scale invasion, the implementation of such plans was both swift and effective, reflecting well-practised processes. It was something that Saddam had not taken into account.

At 11.30 pm on 1 August a scrambled video link was set up in the Situation Room in the basement of the White House, enabling representatives of the White House, the Pentagon, the State Department, the CIA and Chiefs of Staff to hold initial discussions about the crisis and their reaction to it. The first priority was to co-ordinate an international mobilisation of support for US condemnation of Iraqi actions, isolating Saddam politically and seizing the 'moral high ground'. The US Ambassador at the United Nations (UN), already in close touch with his Kuwaiti opposite number, was directed to request an emergency session of the Security Council in New York. By 4 am on 2 August (EST), Resolution 660 had been adopted by 14 votes in favour to none against, with Yemen abstaining in the absence of clear instructions from its government. Based on the argument that Iraqi actions constituted a clear breach of international peace and security according to Articles 39 and 40 of Chapter VII of the UN Charter, the resolution condemned the invasion of Kuwait, demanded an unconditional withdrawal of Iraqi forces without delay, and called for immediate negotiations between Iraq and Kuwait to resolve their differences peacefully.[10]

But a UN resolution, however quickly adopted or universally backed, was only part of the American response. While diplomacy worked its course in New York, the crisis-management team in Washington was busy ensuring an economic isolation of Iraq and a denial of Kuwaiti wealth to Saddam. Justice Department lawyers were roused from their beds to draft the documents needed to freeze all Iraqi and Kuwaiti assets in the USA, while Deputy Treasury Secretary John Robson telephoned the governors of the central banks of all European and Asian capitals to ensure similar moves elsewhere. At 4.45 am on 2 August (EST), as Saddam's tanks closed in on Kuwait City, Bush was woken up, given a briefing on the response so far and presented with the asset-freezing documents to sign. He also agreed to an emergency meeting of the National Security Council (NSC) at 8 am, and to a proposal that Secretary of State Baker, then en route to Mongolia, should return to Moscow, meet with his Soviet opposite number, Eduard Shevardnadze, and ensure that a joint US-Soviet communique, condemning Iraq, was issued to prevent Saddam from playing one Superpower off against the other. By this time the British Foreign Secretary, Douglas Hurd, had also been informed of US actions and had been in touch with Prime Minister Margaret Thatcher, who was quite fortuitously in the USA for a conference with Bush at Aspen, Colorado, on 2 August. Her presence, and her experience of crisis management during the Falklands conflict of 1982, was to be invaluable.[11]

Thus, within the first few hours of the crisis, the basic components of the US response were apparent. Iraq had been politically isolated and condemned, Iraqi and Kuwaiti assets in the United States had been frozen (with other states, notably Britain, France and Italy, prepared to do the same), and key allies had been alerted. This gave the Americans a significant advantage at a very early stage but, if Saddam was to be forced out of Kuwait, the momentum had to be maintained. An essential element in this was to ensure support for US actions actually in the Middle East, for without allies among the Arab powers, any US response would seem to be little more than interference, alienating the people of the region and increasing Saddam's chances of 'getting away with aggression'. When Bush was awoken at 4.45 am on 2 August, he reportedly turned to General Brent Scowcroft, head of the NSC, and told him to 'make sure the State Department starts contacting the Arab nations to make sure they join in condemning the Iraqi invasion of Kuwait'. Scowcroft nodded, but must have been aware that this was going to be a difficult job. It was also one which, if carried out successfully, would put the Americans in a virtually unassailable position.

The Arab response
In fact, the Arab powers were already reacting to the invasion, though in ways that were to disappoint and frustrate the Americans. At 12.15 pm on 2 August (local time), an emergency meeting of the Arab League was convened in Cairo, but Kuwaiti calls for concerted action against Iraq failed to elicit a response, except from the UAE. The rest of the League, caught by surprise by Saddam's aggression, preferred to adopt a 'wait and see' approach, hoping that Iraqi forces would pull back as soon as concessions had been wrung out of the Emir. It was a poor response, reflecting the fact that the Arab League was neither designed for nor used to dealing with major crises between member states.[12]

There may have been more to it than that, for League members were probably aware — or may just have presumed — that peace initiatives were already being put forward by individual Arab states. The key player was Jordan, which found itself in a poor position (graphically described by an American commentator as 'caught between a rock and a hard place') once the crisis broke. Aware that if he supported Saddam he would alienate the West, and that if he supported the West he would alienate Saddam, King Hussein tried to take a neutral line, using his considerable influence as an 'elder statesman' of the Middle East to search for a peaceful solution. Moreover, with a collapsing economy and a population now more than 60 per cent Palestinian, the King could not afford a long-running crisis.[13] Saddam, aware of this, contacted him at 1 pm on 2 August (local time) to suggest a mini-summit in Cairo or Riyadh on 4 August, at which the problems between Iraq and Kuwait could be argued out. King Hussein, convinced that this was a genuine opportunity for peace, flew to Cairo and impressed on Mubarak the urgent need to prevent any anti-Iraqi statements from Arab League members, for fear of alienating Saddam. Although he was furious at having been lied to by Saddam about Iraqi intentions towards Kuwait, Mubarak agreed. Together, he and King Hussein contacted Bush, saying: 'We can settle the crisis, George. We can deal with it. We just need a little time.' They suggested 48 hours.

This seemed to suit Bush. At the NSC meeting early on 2 August it had been decided to review military options against Iraq at Camp David on 4 August, and with diplomatic, economic and allied aspects of crisis management already in place, the next 48 hours were hardly vital. But if this was the reasoning, it was not likely to increase any pressure on Saddam.

Indeed, it would provide him with a chance to consolidate his hold on Kuwait, and it may have been this that worried Thatcher when she met with Bush in Aspen later that day. Her reported admonition to the President that this was no time to go 'wobbly' may have reflected her fear that Saddam would use the lull to persuade fellow Arabs not to support any Western moves. If so, it seemed to work, for, in the immediate aftermath of the Aspen meeting, American resolve was renewed. Bush rang King Fahd of Saudi Arabia, offering US aid if Iraqi troops did not stop at the border, and C-141 transport aircraft were ordered to European airbases in case an airlift of forces to the Gulf was needed.

Nor did the Americans stop there. At 8.20 am on 3 August (EST) John Kelly, presumably acting under orders from the State Department and the NSC, sent a strong message to the Egyptian Foreign Minister in Cairo. It reminded the Egyptians, and other pro-Western Arab states, that they were dependent on the USA for arms supplies, adding that 'if they [the Arab powers] do not act, if they do not take a firm stance on the Kuwait affair, they can be sure that in future they will no longer be able to count on America'. The message was later denied by the State Department, but in the context of Bush's renewed determination it would seem logical. Without some indication of Arab support, the American reaction to the crisis was in danger of appearing irrelevant.[14]

If such a message was sent, it helps to explain the sudden shift in Arab opinion on 3 August, triggering a tougher and more overt anti-Saddam stance among selected states, much to the fury of King Hussein. Early on that day he flew to Baghdad and, after talks with Saddam, seemed to gain significant Iraqi concessions, including a promise to start withdrawing troops from Kuwait on 5 August. King Hussein then flew back to Amman, only to be greeted by the news that, regardless of previous agreements to keep quiet, Mubarak had issued a statement condemning Iraqi actions. Later the same day, at yet another emergency meeting of the Arab League, 14 of the 21 Arab states represented took their lead from Mubarak and voted in favour of a resolution condemning Iraq and calling for an immediate withdrawal of troops from Kuwait. The seven votes against — by Iraq, Jordan, Libya, Yemen, Sudan, Djibouti and the Palestine Liberation Organisation (PLO) — were predictable and, despite a rider to the Arab League resolution asking the Americans not to deploy forces, the Bush administration was pleased.[15] At the cost of a little manipulation (later conveniently denied), a deep split had emerged in the Arab camp, 14 Arab states had shown themselves willing to oppose Iraq, and King Hussein's peace plan (which, by offering concessions, seemed to reward Saddam's aggression) had been scuppered. By the end of 3 August, less than 48 hours after the crisis had begun, the Americans were in a position to make their response felt in the Middle East.

US military commitment

The opportunity was not wasted. At 8 am EST on 4 August Bush met with his advisers at Camp David to review military options presented by the Chairman of the Joint Chiefs of Staff, General Colin Powell. His view was that, if military force was to be deployed, it had to be capable of swift and decisive action, necessitating bases in Saudi Arabia, close to Kuwait. Coincidentally, earlier that morning the CIA had received a batch of spy-satellite photographs which seemed to show Iraqi troops already in the Neutral Zone between Kuwait and Saudi Arabia and massed along the border. Bush telephoned King Fahd, giving him the US assessment that his kingdom was in grave danger of attack and offering to send Secretary of Defense Richard ('Dick') Cheney to Riyadh for talks about protection. King Fahd agreed.

Bush now concentrated on preparing the way for military commitment — an unprecedented step, fraught with danger, not least of which was the alienation of potential Arab partners in an anti-Saddam Coalition if 'infidel' US troops seemed to be occupying sacred Moslem ground. By the evening of 5 August Bush had made 23 phone calls to 12 heads of state to elicit support, while initiating moves in the UN for another Security Council resolution, imposing mandatory economic sanctions against Iraq. On 6 August Baker rang Shevardnadze to ensure Soviet backing in the UN, using the opportunity to inform him of American intentions to deploy forces 'at the request of Saudi Arabia'. He even went so far as to suggest a joint US-Soviet 'peacekeeping force'. The latter was rejected by President Mikhail Gorbachev, under pressure from military hard-liners dismayed at the apparent abandonment of Iraq, a long-term ally, but he did not veto the idea of US troop commitment. Once again, the chance of Saddam playing one Superpower off against the other had been denied by some very careful pre-emptive diplomacy.

Meanwhile, also on 6 August, Cheney met King Fahd in Jeddah and persuaded him to accept US force commitment because of the apparent threat from Iraq. It was not a difficult process. Saudi Arabia, although in possession of some of the most sophisticated weapons in the Middle East, had only a small army, and the satellite photographs were convincing. This enabled Cheney to telephone Bush at 10 pm local time (2 pm in Washington) with the news. Two hours later Bush gave the go-ahead for Operation 'Desert Shield', although he would not make it public until the first US troops were actually on Saudi soil. It coincided with the adoption of UN Security Council Resolution 661 by a vote of 13 in favour to none against, with two abstentions (Yemen and Cuba). Under Chapter VII of the UN Charter, this imposed economic sanctions on Iraq, binding on all member states for as long as Saddam ignored Resolution 660 and remained in Kuwait.[16] One result was that, on 7 August, both Turkey and Saudi Arabia closed the pipelines carrying Iraqi oil across their territory, leaving Saddam with no major outlet for his main wealth-generating export.

The crisis was now five days old and the American position appeared to be strong. Building on the immediate response of international condemnation and financial 'punishment' of Iraq, the Bush administration, with help from its Western allies, had worked hard to sustain the pressure. Arab attempts to gain a compromise peace settlement that would have left Iraq in possession of key areas of Kuwait had failed to materialise, not least because of US manipulation; Saddam had been denied the opportunity to play one Superpower off against the other by a deliberate US policy of keeping the Soviets informed; and sanctions had been imposed. In addition, American resolve had been displayed, at least in the eyes of friendly Arab states, by the decision to commit forces to Saudi Arabia. As a bonus, when Bush appeared on television at 9 am EST on 8 August to announce that 'a line has been drawn in the sand' with 'Desert Shield', the latest Arab peace proposal, put forward by PLO leader Yasser Arafat, quickly fell apart. Instead of talking peace, Saddam further alienated world opinion in response to Bush's announcement by declaring the union of Iraq and Kuwait (altered to a formal Iraqi annexation of Kuwait on 28 August). Twenty-four hours later, on 9 August, he followed this up by closing all Iraqi borders and threatening to hold all foreign nationals in Iraq and Kuwait 'for security reasons'. Both sides were clearly digging in.

Bush must have been aware of the dangers inherent in 'Desert Shield', for although King Fahd had been persuaded to accept US forces, their presence in Saudi Arabia was potentially destabilising, working against the US political moves to create an anti-Saddam Arab Coalition. Not only was it anathema to many Moslems to depend on infidels for protection, but Saudi Arabia also contains two of the holiest Moslem shrines — at Mecca and Medina — which would be 'polluted' by foreign commitment to the region.[17] In this sense 'Desert Shield' was a propaganda coup for Saddam, who could now declare (as he did late on 10 August) that his aim was to rid the Middle East of infidel presence in a *jiyad*, or holy war, appealing to Moslems worldwide to support him, regardless of the problem of Kuwait. It was imperative for the Americans to counter this possibility by creating a solid bloc of Arab opinion against Saddam, stressing the danger of further Iraqi aggression along the lines of the invasion of 2 August. Bush therefore supported — some would say initiated — a call made by Mubarak on 9 August for an Arab summit, to be held the following day in Cairo.

The Arab split
By now the split in the Arab camp, first apparent at the Arab League meeting on 3 August, was deep. On the one hand, Egypt, Saudi Arabia and the Gulf states were firmly behind the American and international response, partly because of their vulnerability but also because of US pressure. On the other, Iraq could look to Jordan, the PLO and a variety of relatively peripheral Arab states for support, chiefly because they saw Saddam as a leader who was prepared to take action to correct apparent injustices and to defy the West. Indeed, one commentator described them as an 'alliance of the hungry and the angry'.[18] Some key players, notably the Syrians, were as yet uncommitted, and Bush had been careful not to be seen as too dependent on the Israelis, but it was obvious that much could be decided either way at the Cairo summit.

This was recognised by both sides in the 24 hours before the first plenary session on 10 August. Arafat, accompanied by his deputy, Abu Iyad, flew to Baghdad on 9 August to try to persuade Saddam to attend the summit, but he refused as long as the Emir of Kuwait was present. As an alternative, Arafat suggested, and Saddam accepted, that as soon as the first

session began the PLO would call for an adjournment to allow representatives of five 'key' Arab powers (Jordan, Yemen, Algeria, Egypt and
Palestine) to travel to Iraq for face-to-face talks with Saddam. This would
enable a compromise settlement to emerge, while effectively isolating Egypt
from the rest of the pro-American lobby. Probably aware of this danger,
Mubarak tried to forestall any such move by holding private meetings with
the Iraqi delegation, led by Deputy Prime Minister Saddoun Hammadi,
when it arrived in Cairo late on the same day. Nothing came of them.

The summit opened at 2.30 pm on 10 August (local time) with 14 heads
of state, five government representatives and PLO chief Arafat around the
table, but it soon became obvious that consensus was impossible. Mubarak
publicly called for an Iraqi withdrawal from Kuwait and the restoration of
the Emir, refusing to accept the PLO proposal for an adjournment. Instead,
he forced a vote on a seven-point resolution, the text of which was already
on the table when the session began. It rejected Iraq's annexation of
Kuwait, supported UN sanctions and called for the immediate formation of
an Arab 'expeditionary force' to aid Saudi Arabia. Twelve of the countries
represented — Saudi Arabia, Kuwait, Bahrain, Qatar, UAE, Oman, Egypt,
Syria, Lebanon, Morocco, Somalia and Djibouti — voted in favour, and
three — Iraq, Libya and the PLO — against. The rest, including Jordan,
abstained. According to some reports, King Hussein sat in stony-faced
silence throughout the proceedings, convinced that the resolution had been
suggested, if not actually written, by the Americans.[19] Whether that was true
or not, Bush could be pleased with the outcome of the summit. A bloc of
Arab support for US actions had clearly emerged, the PLO peace initiative
had been blocked and, although the resolution made no direct mention of
'Desert Shield', the principle of committing force to protect Saudi Arabia
had been accepted. The anti-Saddam Arab Coalition so crucial to American
plans was beginning to take shape.

Iraqi countermoves
Saddam, isolated and outmanoeuvred, hastily changed tack, aiming to split
the Coalition by appealing over the heads of Arab leaders directly to the
Arab people. On 12 August he put forward his own 'peace proposal',
linking any Iraqi withdrawl from Kuwait to similar withdrawls of Syrian
troops from Lebanon and, most emotive of all, of Israeli forces from the
Occupied Territories of the West Bank (including Jerusalem) and the Gaza
Strip. It was an astute move, for not only did it elicit an immediate rejection
from Bush, making him appear unwilling to discuss a peaceful settlement
(particularly one that might adversely affect Israel), but it also placed
Saddam in the forefront of Arab opposition to Israel, elevating the crisis
from a local level to one which affected the Middle East as a whole. Pro-
Saddam demonstrations swept the Moslem world, including many Arab
countries already committed to a pro-Western stance, and for a time it
looked as if the Iraqi leader had regained the initiative.[20] Furthermore, by
including a Syrian withdrawal from Lebanon in the projected 'package',
Saddam was deliberately putting pressure on his long-term Ba'athist rival
Hafez al-Assad, at a time when Assad, aware of Soviet weakness, was

veering towards the Coalition. According to the proposal, Syrian occupation of Lebanon was no different to Israeli occupation of the West Bank. Finally, Saddam succeeded in highlighting a double standard in the West. Whereas concerted action had been taken to oppose the occupation of Kuwait, no such action had been taken to force Israel out of the Occupied Territories, even though a UN Security Council resolution (242) had called for a withdrawal as long ago as 1967. The implication throughout that Iraq's occupation of Kuwait was similarly illegal was conveniently ignored.

There can be little doubt that Saddam's proposal embarrassed the Coalition, forcing it temporarily on to the political defensive. At first no specific response was forthcoming. Instead, Bush concentrated on consolidating the gains already made. On 15 August he rejected yet another peace proposal from King Hussein, confirming the isolation of Jordan[21] despite that country's adherence to UN Resolution 661, and continued to show his resolve by meeting Congressional leaders to discuss the call-up of 120,000 US reservists. This gave Saddam an opportunity to exploit his temporary advantage.

Saddam's next move was not only surprising, but also potentially damaging to the Coalition. He made peace with Iran. On 15 August, in a letter to Iranian President Ali Akbar Hashemi Rafsanjani, the Iraqi leader abandoned all claims to the disputed Shatt al-Arab waterway, one of the primary causes of the long and bitter war with Iran but now less important to Iraq, with its recently conquered Kuwaiti coastline and access to the northern Gulf. Saddam also promised an immediate exchange of prisoners of war, as well as a withdrawal of Iraqi troops from all remaining areas of Iran occupied during the war. This may have been an attempt to bring Iran into an anti-Western Moslem alliance, although even Saddam must have realised that this was unlikely so soon after such a costly war. A more likely explanation is that, by removing the threat from Iran, he was forestalling any Western pressure on Rafsanjani to join the Coalition and releasing substantial military units from border security before any conflict in or around Kuwait. But he did not stop there: on 16 August he publicly threatened to intern all US and British residents still in Kuwait, following this 24 hours later with an announcement that all Westerners in Iraq would be moved to 'strategic sites' to act as a 'human shield' to deter air attacks. Finally, Saddam sent Hammadi to Moscow to persuade the Soviets to adhere to the 1972 Treaty of Friendship with Iraq, so threatening Superpower consensus. It was a worrying time for the Coalition.

Fortunately for Bush and his allies, none of the Iraqi moves was particularly effective. If the aim of peace with Iran was to gain an ally, it failed. Rafsanjani merely accepted the offer and concluded a settlement, but went no further, preferring to maintain a neutral stance in the crisis over Kuwait. This was understandable. Iran was still recovering from the eight-year war with Iraq, and was unlikely to jeopardise gradually improving relations with the West for fear of losing the chance of economic aid. Also, of course, public and religious emotions in Shi'ite Iran continued to run high against Saddam as the Sunni leader responsible for the misery of the recent conflict.

Of more immediate concern to the Coalition were Saddam's threats against Western nationals in Iraq, but these backfired badly on him. He probably based his policy on memories of the impact of the Iranian hostage crisis (1979–81) on US public opinion, which had highlighted weaknesses of American resolve and led in part to the failure of President Carter to secure re-election to the White House in 1980. If so, Saddam seriously misread the mood of an American people determined to 'walk tall' in the world, exorcising the ghosts of Tehran and, by implication, Vietnam. The existence of Western hostages in Iraq was clearly a major worry to Bush and his allies, and it may have affected political decisions about the possible use of force to liberate Kuwait during this early phase of the crisis, but the US leadership remained firm in its commitment to oppose Saddam. A televised meeting with British 'guests' on 23 August did little to alter Western resolve, portraying Saddam as a personification of manipulative evil to many Coalition partners. Two days earlier Hammadi had arrived in Moscow, only to be told in no uncertain terms that the Soviets would do nothing to help Iraq as long as Iraqi troops remained in Kuwait.

Resolution 665

Such international solidarity allowed Bush to maintain the Coalition consensus and to increase the pressure on Saddam. As early as 17 August Baker made tentative proposals to Shevardnadze concerning yet another UN Security Council resolution, this time to authorise the use of force to impose the blockade against Iraq. Initially, the Soviets put forward no major objection, but Gorbachev was under mounting pressure from hard-liners not to associate himself too closely with the Americans. If he allowed Bush to dictate the scope and pace of the crisis, this would merely emphasise Soviet weakness in world affairs.[22] Thus, after the meeting with Hammadi on 21 August, Shevardnadze telephoned Baker to ask for a 48-hour (later extended to a five-day) delay in the introduction of the UN resolution, to give time for the Iraqis to respond to Soviet calls for a withdrawal from Kuwait. Although he was annoyed at this apparent moderation in Soviet policy, Baker agreed to compromise on a deadline of 24 August. On the 23rd Saddam rejected the Soviet demands, and almost immediately Shevardnadze indicated Moscow's willingness to support the resolution. At 4 am EST on 25 August UN Security Council Resolution 665, calling on those states 'co-operating with the Government of Kuwait, which are deploying maritime forces to the area' to use such measures as were needed to 'halt all inward and outward maritime shipping' to and from Iraq, was accepted. The voting pattern was familiar — 13 in favour and none against, with Yemen and Cuba abstaining.[23]

Resolution 665 was important for two main reasons. First, it showed that the true initiative still lay with the USA and its allies. Whatever Saddam had tried to do to widen the crisis or split the Coalition had failed, whereas the Coalition itself had stuck together and placed yet another brick in the wall of crisis management. Second, it significantly increased the pressure on Saddam, reinforcing Coalition resolve and, for the first time in the crisis, introducing the option of force to turn the screw. The crisis was still less than a month old, yet Iraq was politically, diplomatically and economically isolated, an anti-Saddam Coalition had been forged, military forces had begun to arrive in Saudi Arabia, and the principle of the use of such forces against Iraq, albeit in selected circumstances of preventing blockade-busting only, had been accepted by the international community. In terms of crisis management this was an impressive record, but the problems were by no means over.

Despite all the pressures, Saddam was showing no signs of actually pulling out of Kuwait. The nearest he had come to compromise was on 21 August, when Tariq Aziz declared a willingness to open negotiations with the USA, provided these were conducted without preconditions such as an immediate withdrawal of Iraqi troops, but this was rejected by both the United States and Britain straight away. Bush had to be aware, however, that the longer the crisis went on without resolution, the more the pressure would build inside the Coalition states either to force the issue by means of military action or to compromise with Iraq to avoid a costly war. In the USA, public opinion seemed to favour military action, but preparations were likely to take time, during which it was imperative to maintain Coalition consensus. By the same token, the spread of anti-Western demonstrations in certain Arab states (including some which were members of the Coalition), implied that splits could emerge to threaten the success of US policies, particularly if Saddam continued to stress a link between Iraqi withdrawal from Kuwait and Israeli withdrawal from the Occupied Territories.

Finally, as the plight of Western hostages in Iraq became apparent, redolent with the memories of Tehran, their families in the West began to exert pressure for a peaceful solution to the crisis to prevent bloodshed. This was by no means a major problem in late August, although Saddam, aware of the propaganda value, did his best to direct world attention towards the hostage question, releasing over 700 women and children on 1 September amid a blaze of publicity designed to stress his humanitarian concern. At the same time, however, he made no move to prevent the departure of non-Western nationals, presenting the UN with the problem of dealing with thousands of refugees (mostly Asian) who fled to squalid desert camps, principally on the Jordan-Iraq border.

With all these factors coming into play, Bush needed to work for time in which to consolidate the Coalition, build up military strength in Saudi Arabia and allow the economic sanctions to bite. Without it, he might be rushed into premature and costly action or unsatisfactory compromise, either of which could leave Saddam with permanent gains, in terms of propaganda or occupation of parts of Kuwait, from his original aggression. The onus was therefore laid very firmly on a continuation of crisis management, despite the apparent success achieved by 25 August. A key element in this was the maintenance of good relations with the Soviet Union. If Soviet resolve faltered, any hope of further action against Iraq through the UN Security Council would be dashed, and Saddam would be given an opportunity to exploit a Superpower split.

The Helsinki summit

On 4 September Baker declared that the American aim was to create 'a stable Middle East' once the crisis was over, and Shevardnadze supported the idea by suggesting an international conference, co-sponsored by the Superpowers, sometime in the more peaceful future. Five days later this consensus was reinforced when Bush and Gorbachev met in Helsinki for a summit organised before the Iraqi invasion of Kuwait. The official agenda was arms control and the future of eastern Europe, but it was too good an opportunity to miss in terms of the Middle East. What emerged was a *modus vivendi* between the Superpowers, designed to minimise any differences of opinion that might exist. Gorbachev had already made it clear, for example, that although he had no deep objection to the commitment of US troops to Saudi Arabia, he had no intention of contributing Soviet forces to the Coalition, and favoured a peaceful solution to the crisis. Bush accepted this, agreeing that Gorbachev should be free to exploit diplomatic links with Baghdad while the Americans, increasingly convinced that, in the end, Saddam would have to be forced out of Kuwait, continued with their military build-up.

This suited both leaders. Gorbachev, constrained by hard-liners in Moscow, realised that military involvement was politically impracticable, yet recognised that Soviet prestige would be significantly enhanced if a peaceful settlement could be negotiated. Moreover, such efforts might divert public attention away from domestic problems and would be sure to leave the Soviet Union in a leading position when any wider Middle East settlement was discussed. Meanwhile, Bush would be able to pursue the military option secure in the knowledge that, if it came to war, the dangers of escalation to Superpower confrontation were remote. Equally, Soviet peacemaking efforts would absorb world attention, allowing the military build-up to continue unhindered. The fact that Gorbachev's representative in the Middle East, Yevgeni Primakov, failed to persuade Saddam to negotiate was, to the Americans, unimportant: while he was trying to gain a settlement, time was available to the Coalition. It was a neat arrangement.[24]

The role of Israel

This was only part of the picture, for of equal importance to the continuation of crisis management was the maintenance of Coalition consensus in the Middle East. This was not easy, chiefly because the Americans, in creating the anti-Saddam Arab bloc, were forced to adopt a number of policies which seemed out of character, threatening their long-established links with the Middle East or pushing them towards states hitherto distrusted or openly opposed. Bush, for example, had to be extremely careful in his relations with the Israelis, for there was always the danger that pro-Western Arab powers would avoid any overt association with policies that seemed designed to strengthen the Jewish state. At the beginning of the crisis Bush deliberately marginalised the Israelis. He did not contact them during the first 48 hours for fear of creating unity in the Arab League which might lead to compromise with Saddam, and although there were clearly intelligence links between Washington and Tel Aviv, contact at a political level was kept to a minimum. This allowed the Coalition to emerge and the Israelis, recognising that US-led actions against Saddam might destroy or at least considerably weaken a dangerous enemy, seemed prepared to accept the situation. Unfortunately, it did not last, creating problems which, for a time, threatened American resolve.

On 8 October, 18 Palestinian demonstrators were killed by Israeli security forces on the Temple Mount in Jerusalem. The number of dead, and the fact that they appeared to have been shot after the demonstration had been dispersed, caused an international outcry and ensured that Israeli policies were brought before the UN Security Council for discussion and condemnation. There was nothing new in this. Since the beginning of the Palestinian *intifada* (uprising) in the Occupied Territories in December 1987, Israeli actions had been debated regularly, but in this particular case it presented the Americans with a problem. Normally they would be expected to exercise their veto in the Security Council, blocking any resolution critical of Israel, but in October 1990 this was impossible without threatening the anti-Saddam Coalition. If the veto was used, it would suggest that relations with Israel were more important to Washington than relations with the Arab powers, while highlighting once again the double standards of the West. After all, to many Arabs Saddam had done to Kuwait what Israel had already done to Palestine, yet the Israelis had not been subjected to Western-led pressures to withdraw.

After five days of debate, the Americans had no choice but to support Security Council Resolution 672, condemning Israel and setting up a UN delegation to investigate the shootings. The Israeli Prime Minister, Yitzhak Shamir, was reportedly furious. He refused to co-operate with the UN delegation and, despite previous promises to Bush, went ahead with the building of new Jewish settlements in East Jerusalem. Meanwhile, the Jewish lobby in the United States, always prepared to put pressure on the administration to adopt pro-Israeli policies, began to question the value of an American stance against Iraq that involved a shift of priority away from the Jewish state. At the same time, the Temple Mount shootings were a propaganda gift to Saddam, diverting world attention away from Kuwait and triggering anti-Israeli (and, by association, anti-American) demonstrations in many Arab states, some of which were integral members of the Coalition.[25] In the event Bush 'rode out' the crisis, although it was by no means easy to do so, especially when it coincided with visits to Baghdad by a variety of Western 'elder statesmen', such as Edward Heath and Willi Brandt, to negotiate with Saddam for the release of selected hostages. They did not come away empty-handed, but Saddam made the most of the attendant publicity, helping to raise arguments in the West that a more cautious policy towards Iraq would defuse the crisis.

US relations with Syria

In such circumstances the Americans needed to work hard to sustain and strengthen the Coalition, using whatever means were available, even if this meant a reversal of previous policies in the Middle East. A case in point was the renewal of relations with Syria, a country widely condemned before the

Kuwait crisis for having been allegedly involved in international terrorism, particularly the destruction of Pam Am Flight 103 over Lockerbie in December 1988, in which 270 people died. But Syria was important to the anti-Saddam Coalition, threatening Iraq — a long-term enemy — from the northwest, while adding considerable weight to the Arab side of Bush's support. Moreover, President Assad was more than willing to co-operate, as Baker discovered when he visited Damascus soon after the crisis began. Relations between Syria and Iraq were poor, Assad desperately needed to move away from dependence on a weakened Soviet Union, and the Syrian economy, drained by high military spending after nearly 15 years of involvement in Lebanon, was in dire straits. The advantages of joining the Coalition were obvious. A grateful West would lift the economic sanctions imposed in response to terrorist acts and would probably grant new loans to pay for Syrian commitment to 'Desert Shield'; other Arab powers, particularly those with petrodollars to spare, would be equally generous; Syria would regain an influential voice in Arab affairs and, with a bit of luck, the West (and, by implication, the Israelis) would do nothing to prevent Syrian advances in Lebanon to consolidate existing positions and impose a settlement by force.

This is essentially what happened. Baker's visit to Damascus led to a lifting of economic sanctions in exchange for Syrian troop deployment to Saudi Arabia and, on 13 October, Syrian forces wiped out the Maronite Christian militia in Beirut commanded by General Michel Aoun. This allowed the Syrians to strengthen their hold on Lebanon without causing an international outcry, and although no-one in the West seemed prepared to grant enormous loans to Damascus (the British, for example, refused even to renew diplomatic relations with Syria, broken off in the aftermath of the Hendawi affair in 1986, until after the resignation of Margaret Thatcher in November 1990), a number of Gulf states were not slow to show their gratitude, pouring an estimated $2 billion into Assad's hands before the end of the crisis.[26] Without American moves to rehabilitate Syria, none of this would have occurred. Without the need to maintain a coherent anti-Saddam Arab Coalition, Bush would have been extremely reluctant to approach Assad. Crisis management — an exercise in *realpolitik* — produces strange alliances.

The shift to crisis resolution
By November 1990 it was apparent that Bush had succeeded in sustaining the pressure on Iraq, allowing him to explore further measures by which to resolve the crisis. On 8 November he announced a doubling of US force commitment to the Gulf and began to clear the way diplomatically for a new UN Security Council resolution, authorising military action to liberate Kuwait if Saddam did not withdraw. On 18 November Bush and Baker flew to Paris to attend a previously scheduled meeting of the Conference on Security and Co-operation in Europe (CSCE), taking the opportunity to float the idea of further UN action to two other permanent members of the Security Council, France and the Soviet Union. A third, Britain, had already agreed to the plan.

It was at this point that Saddam, clearly aware of what was in the offing, and recognising that Bush was shifting significantly from crisis management to crisis resolution, seemed to lose his nerve. On the same day as the CSCE meeting, he suddenly announced that he would start releasing Western hostages from Iraq, beginning on Christmas Day. His intention was probably to pre-empt any deadline for a withdrawal from Kuwait by ensuring that the West would remain supine while hostages were being freed. Whatever his motive, it was a sign that he had been the first to blink in the face-to-face confrontation with the US-led Coalition.

Bush did not allow Saddam's offer to affect his resolve, realising that now was the chance to tighten the screw. On 29 November UN Security Council Resolution 678 came into force, authorising member states 'to use all necessary means' to implement Resolution 660 and subsequent relevant resolutions, unless Iraq complied by withdrawing from Kuwait by 15 January 1991. Twelve members of the Security Council voted in favour, two (Yemen and Cuba) voted against, and one (China) abstained.[27] But Bush did not leave it there. He recognised that, if he made war seem inevitable, less resolute allies might cease to support the Coalition. On 30 November he proposed a meeting between himself and Tariq Aziz in Washington, to coincide with a similar meeting between Baker and Saddam in Baghdad. It was an astute move, diluting any criticism that America was interested only in military action and placing the onus for peace firmly on Saddam: if he did not respond or the talks failed, he would be held to blame.

The ploy worked. King Hussein, Arafat and the Vice-President of Yemen, Ali Salam Al Beldh, all travelled to Baghdad on 4 December to try to persuade Saddam to comply with Resolution 678, or at least to offer some concessions in an effort to avoid war.[28] They appeared to succeed, for on 6 December the Iraqi leader, clearly worried, agreed to release all foreign hostages immediately and, 24 hours later, offered dates for the proposed negotiations — 17 December for the Bush-Aziz meeting and 12 January for that between Baker and Saddam. The Americans, convinced that they had him on the run, refused to accept the first meeting without a simultaneous date for the second, arguing that, if diplomatic contacts were still being made as late as 12 January, Saddam would drag them out beyond the UN deadline, rendering it meaningless. They could afford to be this precise for, once the hostages were safe, Saddam's only remaining trump card had been thrown away, leaving US planners free to choose bombing targets in Iraq without having to worry about killing their own people.

Saddam had been painted into a corner. He was politically isolated, diplomatically condemned, subject to economic blockade and under threat of imminent military action in Kuwait. He also had no cards left to play. To the Americans, this was exactly the situation they had striven to create and, although efforts continued to be made to organise diplomatic meetings, it was obvious that they stood little chance of success as long as Iraqi troops remained in Kuwait. Indeed, a whole series of peace moves materialised as the UN deadline approached, only to be dashed against the rocks of Iraqi intransigence and US resolution. On 12 December the Algerian President, Chadli Benjedid, tried to act as mediator between Saddam and Bush, exploiting the reputation his country had gained during negotiations for the release of US hostages in Tehran in 1980, but neither leader would agree even to meet him. Similarly, on 2 January 1991 the new President of the European Community (EC), Jacques Poos, declared his intention to travel to Baghdad after an EC Foreign Ministers' conference designed to hammer out a peace proposal, but he gained no support and stayed at home.[29]

The only chance of a last-minute peace came on 9 January when, at Bush's suggestion, Baker and Aziz met in Geneva. At first, as their talks went on for much longer than anticipated, optimism ran high, but by the end of the day the two sides were no closer to an agreement. By then time was rapidly running out, leaving the UN Secretary-General, Javier Pérez de Cuéllar, to make a final effort by travelling to Baghdad on 11 January. He was ignored by Saddam, who was now seemingly intent on war. Three days later the French announced their proposals for peace, but they were far too late. As the UN deadline passed with no sign of Iraqi compliance, the world held its breath. War was now inevitable.

An assessment of the crisis

In terms of American political, diplomatic, economic and military efforts — the basic components of crisis management — the period from 2 August 1990 to 15 January 1991 is impressive. After a poor start, allowing Saddam to achieve a position from which he felt safe to carry out aggression against Kuwait, Bush and his team of administrators and advisers worked remarkably quickly to condemn, isolate and put pressure on the Iraqi leader, orchestrating an international campaign against his blatant disregard for the sanctity of nations. The process was not easy, requiring the Americans to use all the tools of international politics at their disposal — their influence in the UN Security Council and among the powers of western Europe, their economic muscle among Middle Eastern states dependent on US aid, and their ability to deploy military force halfway around the world in response to aggression against a country they favoured — but it was carried out effectively. There is no doubt that such a response would have been impossible without Soviet weakness and splits among the members of the Arab League, but the recognition and exploitation of such opportunities is surely an integral part of crisis management. In this sense, the political run-up to the eventual war may be termed an American triumph, leaving Saddam so weakened before the fighting began that his chances of victory were negligible.

Nevertheless, it would be wrong to end on such a laudatory note, for it could be argued that the recourse to war in January 1991 was in fact a *failure* of crisis management. Bush's aim throughout the crisis was to put so much political, economic and diplomatic pressure on Saddam that the Iraqi leader would withdraw from Kuwait without the need for a potentially costly (and certainly unpredictable) military campaign. This he failed to achieve, being forced in November 1990 to shift away from crisis management towards crisis resolution, for a variety of reasons. Despite the success of US actions in creating a solid bloc of international support for condemnation of Iraq, Saddam refused to play by the rules of crisis management and remained firmly in possession of Kuwait. This, coupled to the slow-moving nature of economic sanctions, which seemed to be having little impact on Saddam's capability to maintain a large armed force, led inevitably to pressures for more effective action, particularly in the USA itself, where anti-Saddam propaganda and a widespread desire to exorcise the ghosts of Vietnam produced a mood of jingoistic patriotism. People came to expect a campaign designed to 'kick ass' and, with large Coalition forces in place in Saudi Arabia, raring to go, it would have taken an exceptionally strong (or foolish) political leader to deny the military option. At the same time, of course, to have refused to carry out the threat implicit in UN Resolution 678 would have been to appear weak and to have rewarded Saddam's aggression. When all this coincided with a lack of international restraint, occasioned by the weakness of the Soviet Union, Bush was presented with a unique opportunity to flex US muscle on the world stage. It was an opportunity he was unlikely to waste.

In the end, the politcal phase of the crisis over Kuwait may be viewed as an exercise in power rather than a sustained attempt to maintain peace. The Americans had been denied any chance of showing just how powerful they were by the 'balance of terror' inherent in the Cold War. Now that confrontation with the Soviet Union was a thing of the past, such power could be exercised with relative impunity, impressing on the world, and on the Middle East in particular, the fact that the USA was the most influential state around. Crisis management in its truest form, put into effect between August and November 1990, was undeniably impressive, but for once the Americans could go beyond merely containing aggression. As 'Desert Shield' became 'Desert Storm' on 16/17 January 1991, that aggression was also being punished. The outcome would determine the future of American influence.

Notes

1. For a full coverage of the background, see Efraim Karsh and Inari Rautsi, 'Why Saddam Hussein invaded Kuwait', *Survival*, January/February 1991, pp 18–30.
2. Dr Rosemary Hollis, 'At stake in the Iraqi invasion of Kuwait: Borders, Oil and Money', *The RUSI Journal*, Winter 1990, pp 17–24.
3. Karsh and Rautsi, op cit, p 19.
4. John K Cooley, 'Pre-War Gulf Diplomacy', *Survival*, No 2, March/April 1991, p 126.
5. Pierre Salinger with Eric Laurent, *Secret Dossier. The Hidden Agenda behind the Gulf War* (Penguin Books, London, 1991), p 31.
6. Ibid, p 41.
7. Graham E Fuller, 'Moscow and the Gulf War', *Foreign Affairs*, Summer 1991, pp 55–76.
8. A transcript of significant parts of the Saddam-Glaspie meeting appears in Salinger and Laurent, op cit, pp 48–56.
9. As outlined by General George B Crist, commander of CENTCOM, to the Senate Armed Services Committee on 27 January 1987, quoted in John Roberts, 'Oil, the Military and the Gulf War of 1991', *The RUSI Journal*, Spring 1991, p 12.
10. 'Kuwait: The Crisis', *UN Chronicle*, December 1990, pp 9–11. See also Hans Arnold, 'The Gulf Crisis and the United Nations', *Aussenpolitik*, 42/1, 1991, pp 68–77.
11. Salinger and Laurent, op cit, pp 90–5.
12. Yezid Sayidh, 'The Gulf Crisis: why the Arab regional order failed', *International Affairs*, 67/3 (1991), pp 487–507.
13. Ann Mosely Lesch, 'Contrasting Reactions to the Persian Gulf Crisis: Egypt, Syria, Jordan, and the Palestinians', *Middle East Journal*, Winter 1991, pp 30–50. See also Stanley Reed, 'Jordan and the Gulf Crisis', *Foreign Affairs*, Winter 1990/91, pp 21–32.
14. Salinger and Laurent, op cit, pp 112–3; Cooley, op cit, p 130.

15. 'Crisis in the Gulf: Transition to War?', *Royal United Serivces Institute for Defence Studies Aide Memoire III*, p 9.
16. 'Kuwait: The Crisis', pp 12–13.
17. Maha Azzam, 'The Gulf Crisis: perceptions in the Muslim world', *International Affairs*, 67/3 (1991), pp 473–85.
18. Professor Itamar Rabinovich, 'External Pressures, Internal Strains — The Middle East in 1990', *The RUSI Journal*, Winter 1990, p 46.
19. Cooley, op cit, pp 131–2; *RUSI Aide Memoire III*, p 9.
20. Azzam, op cit.
21. Reed, op cit.
22. Fuller, op cit.
23. 'Kuwait: The Crisis', pp 17–19.
24. Salinger and Laurent, op cit, pp 186–91.
25. Ibid, pp 192–5.
26. Lesch, op cit, pp 41–3.
27. The text of Resolution 678 appears in 'Desert Storm Almanac', *Military Technology*, Vol XV, Issue 6, 1991, p 139.
28. Salinger and Laurent, op cit, p 207.
29. Cooley, op cit, pp 135–8. See also Willem van Eekelen, 'WEU and the Gulf Crisis', *Survival*, November/ December 1990, pp 519–32, and Jonathan T Howe, 'NATO and the Gulf Crisis', *Survival*, May/ June 1991, pp 246–59 for European responses as the crisis developed.

Further Reading

John Bulloch and Harvey Morris, *Saddam's War* (Faber and Faber, London, 1991)
Adel Darwish and Gregory Alexander, *Unholy Babylon. The Secret History of Saddam's War* (Victor Gollancz Ltd, London, 1991)
Pierre Salinger with Eric Laurent, *Secret Dossier. The Hidden Agenda behind the Gulf War* (Penguin Books, London, 1991).

CHAPTER 3
The Doctrines of the Coalition Forces

Stephen Badsey

'In war, the general receives his command from the sovereign. Having collected an army and concentrated his forces, he must blend and harmonise the different elements thereof before pitching his camp. After that comes tactical manoeuvring, than which there is nothing more difficult.'

Sun Tzu, *The Art of War*

The meaning of doctrine

In the months following the Iraqi invasion of Kuwait in August 1990, President George Bush repeatedly affirmed that there were to be 'no more Vietnams'; that since the early 1970s something fundamental had changed in American political and military thinking on war and its conduct. Senior American military commanders were also keen to tell the public that this time their approach would be different, that 'the battle cry is *Fight Smart!*'. Even the US Marines, traditional exponents of the 'hey diddle, diddle, straight up the middle' style of tactics, boasted to the press that their thinking had been transformed by the philosophies of Sun Tzu, a Chinese general of the 6th century BC who stressed manoeuvre and subtlety in war. A new mood, a new attitude, was proclaimed throughout the American military.[1]

This new approach to war was encapsulated in the American doctrine of 'AirLand Battle', of which the Gulf War was the first serious test. In the course of the war, however, it became apparent that few outside the charmed circle of the Coalition military had any idea of what this expression meant, or even of what a military doctrine represents. 'How effective do you think that the AirLand Battle campaign has been?', General H Norman Schwarzkopf was asked at his press conference to announce the Iraqi defeat. The general's face, as he wrestled to provide a polite answer to this meaningless question, was a study.

As with many other terms used in the social and political sciences, there is no universally agreed definition of a military doctrine, but a broad consensus does exist. The Soviet *Military Strategy* gives a very precise definition:

A system of views adopted in a country, at a given time, on the nature, aims and character of a possible future war, on the preparation of the country and its armed forces for this, and on the methods of waging it.[2]

The North Atlantic Treaty Organisation (NATO) definition of doctrine is: 'fundamental principles by which the military forces guide their actions in support of objectives; it is authoritative but requires judgement in application.' The definition offered in 1979 by General Donn R Starry, then commander of the US Army's Training and Doctrine Command (TRADOC), which developed AirLand Battle, is: 'what is written, approved by an appropriate authority and published concerning the conduct of military affairs.'[3] Two further highly characteristic views of military doctrine are those of the Israeli Defence Force (IDF), whose doctrine includes a stipulation that there should be a continuous debate about doctrine, and the British Army, which two years before the Gulf War produced its first-ever written doctrine on military operations, despite fears that such a radical step was 'not the British way'. In practice, much of doctrine is not written down but is implicit in a common style or ethos, based on general and long-term aspects of a country's military culture, which cannot be easily or quickly changed. The US Army's *Field Manual* (FM) *100–5* 'Operations', the basic text on how the army fights, was completely revised and reissued three times between 1968 and 1982 without the chaos which would have ensued if doctrine were entirely a matter of going by the book.

Although military doctrine is often concerned with how things should be, rather than how they are, it would be a mistake to think of doctrine as theoretical, or remote from the conduct of war. Many of the crucial decisions in modern war are taken away from the battlefield, often before the war starts. The training of troops, the size and structure of armed forces, the design of tanks and aircraft, are all functions of doctrine. Further, without an understanding of how the Coalition forces expected to fight, no practical assessment of their actual performance is possible. Inevitably, as in other aspects of the Gulf War, questions about doctrine focused on the United States as the dominant member of the Coalition, and its influence on the doctrines of NATO, to which all the European members of the Coalition, together with Canada, belonged. But the Gulf War also saw, if only by proxy, the first test of a new NATO operational doctrine and its associated technology, of the complete restructuring and doctrinal changes to the French armed forces in the late 1970s, and of what its exponents called the 'revolution in doctrine' in the British armed forces during the 1980s. Soviet and Israeli doctrinal concepts were also tested at second hand by both sides during the war. It is particularly hard to understand the role of the Egyptian and Syrian forces in the ground war without reference to their own pre-war doctrines, based on Soviet concepts and on their own experience of past wars against Israel.

The term 'military doctrine' is usually applied only to land forces, or to land and air forces combined, and in the Gulf War it was these forces which created the greatest interest. The basis of US Navy action in the Gulf was the doctrine of the late Reagan era, often called simply 'Maritime Strategy', which was badly out of step with the ideas of the other American armed forces. The Navy saw its principal role as confronting major Soviet naval forces on the high seas with carrier and anti-submarine-warfare groups. It had no effective mine countermeasures vessels, and its ability to function in the narrow waters of the Gulf was called into question by the successful Iraqi Exocet missile attack on the frigate USS *Stark* in 1987 and the shooting down of an Iranian passenger jet in mistake for a hostile warplane by the cruiser USS *Vincennes* a year later. Fortunately, previous NATO acquaintance and shared doctrines made it possible for other forces, in particular the British Royal Navy, which since 1981 had moved closer towards a shallow-water role, to fill some of the gaps in the American naval deployment.

It was a feature of the Vietnam generation that it rejected the past in formulating doctrine for future wars. As Neil Sheehan put it in *A Bright Shining Lie*, 'Americans were different. History did not apply to them.'[4] As a reaction against this, the concepts of AirLand Battle and its NATO equivalents were based on historical study, the ideas of other armed forces (particularly the Soviet, Israeli and German), and what TRADOC called 'the tried and true principles of experience in war'. A list of these 'Principles of War', abandoned in the Vietnam era, was in fact reintroduced into US Army doctrine in 1978. Much of what appeared as new in the Gulf War, both in ideas and hardware, had been planned and discussed before many of those who took part in the war were born.

Limited War

A few months before the Iraqi invasion of Kuwait, President Bush gave his name to a short book, *The National Security Strategy of the United States 1990–1991*, replacing a similar work by Ronald Reagan. This took a broad view of strategy, integrating purely military tasks with more general political and economic goals, and setting out American policy at the highest level. One section outlined doctrine for possible American military involvement in the Third World:

> The growing technological sophistication of Third World conflicts will place serious demands on our forces. They must be able to respond quickly, and appropriately, as the application of even small amounts of force early in a crisis usually pays significant dividends. Some actions may require considerable staying power, but there are likely to be situations where American forces will have to succeed rapidly and with a minimum of casualties. Forces will have to accommodate to the austere environment, immature basing structure, and significant ranges encountered in the Third World. The logistics 'tail' of deployed forces will also have to be kept to a minimum, as an overly large American presence could be self-defeating.[5]

From this, it appeared that any American military response to the invasion of Kuwait would consist of small forces, striking at the earliest possible moment to bring about a quick victory. At the same time President Bush expressed fears of excessive casualties and uncertainty concerning America's technological supremacy. These political fears led to a very different kind of strategy, involving a massive military presence and supporting base which took almost half a year, from August 1990 to January 1991, to create. The very real possibility of a breakdown in Coalition solidarity while these forces were being assembled provided Iraq with its best hope for victory, or at least a compromise peace. This choice of strategy reflected a set of American uncertainties and difficulties which can only be understood in the context of Limited War doctrine and experience following the Second World War.

American defence planning in the first half of the 20th century was based on the reasonable assumption that the continental United States was virtually immune from attack. American armed forces could be held to extremely low levels in peacetime, and mass conscript armies and navies could be created almost from nothing after the outbreak of war by superior American industrial and administrative skills. American strategy would always be offensive, using overwhelming force to drive an enemy back and bludgeon him into defeat regardless of his superior defensive posture or battlefield skills. This use of business methods to achieve victory was the pattern for American involvement in both World Wars. On the battlefield it was manifest in a tradition going back at least to the American Civil War (1861–1865) of using technology as a substitute for tactical skill, in the belief that this compensated for the shortcomings of freshly-created and inexperienced troops, and reduced casualties. 'There is one thing that our government does that suits me to a dot', one enlisted man of that war said. 'That is, we fight mostly with artillery. The rebels fight mostly with infantry.'[6] Whatever its apparent novelty, the use of sophisticated bombardment weapons, mostly air-delivered, in the Gulf was a continuation of this tradition, which seeks to place a barrier of technology between the American soldier and the realities of the battlefield.

Following the Second World War, the development of thermonuclear weapons and their delivery by long-range bombers and missiles brought the continental United States itself under threat. Meanwhile, the growing American role as world policeman led in 1947 to the Truman Doctrine, a commitment of political, economic and military support to all nations under threat of communist aggression. By 1950 a Third World War of mass destruction against the Soviet Union, probably lasting several years, was seen as not only potentially catastrophic but less likely than a series of small wars or aggressions fought below the nuclear threshhold, of which the Korean War (1950–1953) appeared to establish the pattern. But if the USA was to fight this kind of war, the time to create large forces after the war had started would not be available. Indeed, the need in the early stages of Korea to deploy under-trained and poorly equipped troops on the battlefield while the USA rearmed itself led to an even greater reliance than in the Second World War on what became known as 'the meatgrinder' of artillery and aerial firepower. Equally, however, the social and economic cost of holding mass standing armies and navies in existence in peacetime was felt to be politically unacceptable. The solution adopted by the Eisenhower administration after Korea was the 'New Look', based on the belief that thermonuclear weapons had made open war with the Soviet Union extremely unlikely, and that the struggle between the Superpowers would be conducted over a long haul, largely in terms of economic strength. By building up nuclear weapons, conventional forces could be substantially reduced and domestic economic production expanded, enabling the USA to win the economic confrontation. From the perspective of 1991, with the collapse of the Warsaw Pact, this protracted economic strategy appeared to have succeeded. But in the form adopted by Eisenhower its main drawback was that it offered the USA little option in its use of force short of total nuclear war, caricatured as a 'Massive Retaliation' strategy. This military rigidity was amended in the subsequent Kennedy administration to a doctrine of Limited War.

The central problem confronting states in the era of nuclear weapons is how — if at all — to use force as an instrument of policy, when the potential destructiveness of the available force far outstrips any rational use. No war since 1945, including the Gulf War, has been conducted without reference to these weapons of mass destruction. The earliest American thinking on Limited War, advanced by writers such as Hermann Kahn in the decade after Korea, was on how to limit nuclear exchanges between the Super-powers. The essential idea was that victory in war had become a meaningless concept. Force should be used not to achieve victory in the conventional military sense, but as a precise political instrument first to deter the outbreak of war and then to keep its destructive violence to the lowest possible level consistent with American political objectives. A second important strand in Limited War doctrine was for medium-sized conventional American forces to be held at a high state of readiness in peacetime, enabling the USA to respond to aggression immediately, globally, and at an appropriate level below the nuclear threshold. By this method, confrontation with the Soviet Union would be held to a minimum, and wars could be conducted with little impact on American domestic society. The Korean War, in which the USA had deliberately limited its objectives, fighting after 1951 to maintain a military stalemate while reaching political accommodation, was seen as the archetype.[7] These concepts were taken up by Kennedy as the doctrine of Flexible or Graduated Response, adopted by the USA in 1962. As currently stated, the 'fundamental mission' of all American armed forces is to deter war rather than to wage it. With American prompting, Flexible Response was also adopted by NATO in 1967, and was the central military doctrine of all Coalition members in the Gulf which were also NATO members (except for France, which left the NATO integrated command structure in 1966). In theory, NATO doctrine applies only in the context of the NATO alliance and area; in practice none of those NATO members involved in the Gulf War could easily dispense with the doctrine within which they had planned and trained for decades, or wished to do so.

The problems of Limited War were revealed in its attempted appli-cation by the Americans to the Vietnam War (or Second Indochina War) between 1965 and 1973. Chiefly, although it sought to limit war in terms of political aim, geographical spread, use of weapons, and mobilisation of national resources, the doctrine contained no concept of limitation in *time*. This was exactly the criticism made by General Douglas MacArthur, whose refusal to implement a Limited War strategy in Korea led to his dismissal as US Commander-in-Chief Far East in April 1951. 'It seems to me,' MacArthur argued, 'to introduce a new concept into military operations — that of appeasement,' and that 'to me, that would mean that you would have a continued and indefinite extension of bloodshed'. Less formally, Mac-Arthur characterised the idea of fighting without military victory as a 'die for tie' strategy.[8]

A related problem was that the controlled use of force envisaged in Limited War ran contrary to the traditional popular American view of war as a moral crusade against an evil enemy to be obliterated without mercy. It was hard to justify limiting such a war to the American public, and so maintain political support for its prosecution. Both Truman in 1952 and Lyndon Johnson in 1968 stood down as President chiefly because of the unpopularity that their failure to resolve the Korean and Vietnam Wars respectively brought them. This political difficulty in prosecuting Limited War is part of a broader concern, first expressed just after the Second World War, that the checks and balances in the American Constitution (which never envisaged an active — far less an Imperial — Presidency), plus the conflicts between interest groups typical of a healthy democracy, have made the USA essentially ungovernable, placing it at a marked disadvantage in its dealings with more centralised and authoritarian states. In this view, it is not realistic to expect any American government to pursue a coherent foreign and defence policy, or to respond effectively to any military challenge short of a general war. The constitutional disaster of Watergate, resulting from President Nixon's attempts to centralise decision-making inside the White House between 1969 and 1974 in order to win the Vietnam War, seemed to prove the point.

A further drawback to Limited War was that, as a new concept of the use of force, it ran contrary to the fundamental military values which provided combat motivation for those who actually fought the war. As one senior US Navy commander in Vietnam told his pilots:

'Limited war' means to us that our target list has limits, our ordnance loadout has limits, our rules of engagement have limits, but that does *not* mean that there is anything 'limited' about our personal obligations as fighting men to carry out assigned missions with all we've got. If you think it is possible for a man, in the heat of battle, to apply something less than total *personal* commitment — equated perhaps to your idea of the proportion of *national* commitment being applied, you are wrong. It's contrary to human nature.[9]

The 'die for tie' approach produced morale problems and poor military performance from troops who could not understand why they were risking their lives without being allowed to win.

The concept of Limited War was applied by some theorists only to states with weapons of mass destruction, or even to a direct confrontation between the Superpowers. In practice, however, other nations have their own doctrines of Limited War, slightly different from those of the USA. Chiefly, as lesser powers, they are aware that their ability to use force is severely circumscribed by the threat of Superpower intervention. Both Israeli and British doctrines recognise time as one of the limitations placed upon them if they undertake conventional wars. The fundamental Israeli doctrine, as laid down by Prime Minister David Ben Gurion on the country's foundation in 1948, was that Israel must be prepared to fight any combination of its Arab neighbours simultaneously in a short war, but must never directly confront either of the Superpowers. Israeli restraint shown during the Gulf War derived ultimately from this doctrine. British Limited War doctrine, which has evolved piecemeal and pragmatically, also recognises the importance of Superpower involvement and the need for quick victory, which was a principal British concern during the Falklands conflict of 1982. Soviet doctrine rejected any concept of Limited War, arguing that the political objective is paramount in war, and that no arbitrary restrictions should be placed on the means to achieve it. France, together with Syria and Egypt, shares this doctrine, judging the amount of force required entirely in terms of the desired political result. The decision of all three countries to display a high profile in the Gulf War by deploying ground troops, while other Coalition members limited their involvement to air and naval forces, was therefore of great political significance.

The Vietnam legacy

The prosecution of Limited War in Vietnam was a mixture of traditional American methods and new ideas on how to employ the technology which became available in the course of the war. Ready to hand in the 1950s was a well developed airpower capability, including a US Air Force doctrine of independent or strategic bombing. Initially expounded just after the First World War, strategic bombing theory in its purest form argued that land warfare had been made obsolete by the ability of aircraft to strike directly at civilian population centres and economic targets, the destruction of which could by itself bring about victory. The practical results of strategic bombing in the Second World War were, at best, ambiguous, but by the end of that war airmen had begun to claim that, taking their strategic role together with their impact on the land battle, they had become the principal offensive arm in modern war, with land and naval forces as secondary. Airpower also fitted well into Limited War as being cheaper, lower in casualties and lower in political profile than deploying ground troops, and as a high-technology approach in keeping with American traditions. In both Korea and Vietnam the principal American offensive strategy was to attack enemy economic targets and infrastructure from the air, rather than invade with ground forces. Interdiction, the Second World War technique of strikes by aircraft and artillery at enemy forces away from the immediate battlefield, was also used with some success in both wars, while firepower on the battlefield came increasingly from 'flying artillery' in the form of air strikes. Airpower in all its forms, if not perhaps the absolute war-winner that the early theorists had promised, was clearly the developing weapon of the future.

The new idea most closely associated with the Vietnam War itself was airmobility, an extension of airpower. As early as 1954, former American airborne forces officers led by General Matthew Ridgway, who had commanded the XVIII Airborne Corps (82nd and 101st Airborne Divisions) in the Second World War, argued that the requirement of Limited War for troops to deploy globally at high speed, with the minimum adjustment to their equipment, organisation and tactics, could best be met by airmobile forces, consisting chiefly of lightly armed infantry deployed into battle from the air. By 1962 a new generation of helicopters had made this a practical proposition. Three years later, following the recommendations of the US Army's Howze Board, the 1st Cavalry Division (Airmobile), the world's first airmobile division, was deployed to Vietnam, followed by the 101st Airmobile Division. By the war's height, 'every infantry unit in Vietnam was, in fact if not in name, airmobile infantry, and its direct support artillery was airmobile artillery'.[10] Lieutenant-General William C. Westmoreland, head of Military Assistance Command Vietnam (MACV) for the critical years 1964–1968, was himself a former commander of the 101st Airborne Division.

A further crucial component in what was to become AirLand Battle to emerge from Vietnam was the electronic battlefield, brainchild of the American government's 'Jason Division' scientific think-tank, tasked in 1966 to solve the problem of an enemy hidden in jungle and skilled in infiltration tactics. The Jason Division's solution was a collection of electronic sensors, night-vision equipment, radars and data processing systems making it virtually impossible for enemy troops to escape detection regardless of terrain, night or weather conditions, in what has been called 'the transparency revolution'. This, coupled in 1962 with a satellite-based command and control system allowing instant communication worldwide, and the first use of precision guided weapons ('smart' bombs) in Vietnam by 1972, suggested a new kind of battlefield. In 1969 General Westmoreland as Army Chief of Staff predicted that increasing electronic capabilities, together with first-round kill probabilities approaching certainty from guided munitions, would reduce the need for large numbers of troops. Instead, highly mobile forces supported by equally mobile and sophisticated logistics would fight a high-technology war based principally on helicopters and electronics:

> Generals Howze and Wheeler and the late Lieutenant-General Bill Bunker conceived airmobility long before the machinery existed to fulfil the concept. Today we witness both the airmobile concept and the airmobile division proved in Vietnam.
>
> We are confident that from our early solutions to the problems of finding the enemy in Vietnam, the evidence is present to vizualise this battlefield of the future . . .
>
> In summary, I see an Army built into and around an integrated control system that exploits the advanced technology of communications, sensors, fire direction, and the required automatic data processing — a system that is sensitive to the dynamics of the ever-changing battlefield — a system that materially assists the tactical commander in making sound and timely decisions.[11]

In these three ideas — airpower, airmobility and the electronic battlefield — were the seeds of AirLand Battle doctrine as it existed by the time of the Gulf War.

That a new military means of prosecuting Limited War was required became apparent in Vietnam, as actual American conduct of the war revealed a fundamental mismatch between a political strategy of containment through minimum force and an attritional method of operations which still resembled the Second World War meatgrinder. The desire and capability for precise political control of the war led to a hopelessly confused and fragmented command chain, within which the Commander MACV had no control over significant portions of the war machine, while operational commanders were overridden or bypassed from Washington. As late as 1967, a major planning conference on the war found that a clear, concise, statement of American strategy in Vietnam could not be established. Meanwhile, operations consisted of the creation of 'a killing machine that subjected the enemy to the prodigious firepower that American technology provided'.[12] The resulting immense destruction, with no apparent purpose and no promise of victory, became itself a factor in growing American disillusion with the war. The unsuitability of the meatgrinder to Vietnam was encapsulated in the celebrated remark of a US Air Force officer in 1968, that: 'it became necessary to destroy the town [of Ben Tri] in order to save it'.[13]

In 1973, as part of the reaction to Vietnam, the USA replaced conscription with the All Volunteer Force (AVF), a smaller, professional body recruited on a competitive basis with the civilian workforce. The growing cost of troops and equipment, the likelihood of a declining recruitment pool, the challenge of new technology and the lessons of Vietnam all argued for a radical re-examination of American war-fighting methods. There was also pressure for the army to get away from wars in the Third World and concentrate on the Soviet Union as its main enemy. At the same time, officers demanded a more aggressive strategy, and in particular 'to be allowed to fight to win', to secure a definite military victory without excessive political interference. Traditionally, development of doctrine in the US Army had been geared to very general terms of reference and to a period of up to 25 years into the future. In July 1973 TRADOC was created, with General William E DePuy as its first commander, as a prestige organisation to produce doctrine for immediate use, related specifically to Soviet breakthrough operations in Europe. Considerable impetus was given to TRADOC's work by the October 1973 Arab-Israeli War (the Yom Kippur or Ramadan War). This was the largest clash of armoured forces since the Second World War, and for the first time gave practical demonstrations of new precision guided anti-tank and anti-aircraft missile systems, and produced levels of combat intensity (as measured by rates of ammunition consumption and casualties suffered) approximately double those of the worst Second World War fighting. In July 1976, following analysis of the Yom Kippur War, TRADOC produced its revision of *FM 100–5* under the name of 'Active Defense'.

Under the guidance of General DePuy, who had been Westmoreland's chief of operations and later commander of 1st Infantry Division in Vietnam, Active Defense was solidly in the old meatgrinder tradition. It saw new developments in airmobility and electronics chiefly as adjuncts to firepower, enabling American forces to defeat a Soviet attack in central Europe even if outnumbered. The lesson of Vietnam and Yom Kippur was that firepower would continue to grow more destructive, and so more important, as manpower declined. Whereas an attacking superiority of three to one was traditionally expected to ensure victory, a superiority of five or six to one was now required. Electronic battlefield technology, seeing into the enemy rear areas beyond the front line, would identify the path of the main Soviet thrust, and an active defence (hence the name) would ambush the penetration, using firepower to 'service' each target. Increased mobility would be used to concentrate units rapidly against the breakthrough point, abandoning the traditional concept of reserves held in depth, and leaving wide areas of the front very thinly defended by airmobile forces and light armour, both assigned a secondary role. Offensive operations were to be undertaken only in order to inflict heavier enemy casualties, or to secure a crucial objective. Geared to very specific terrain and battle conditions, Active Defense would permit American forces to win the first battle of the next war without the support of mobilised reserves.

The central objection raised to Active Defense was that it failed to deliver the promised chance of fighting to win. As with American strategy in Europe since the adoption of Flexible Response, the enemy was left with the initiative and American forces were condemned to progressive defeat and retreat up to the moment of nuclear release. Nor was it clear, in army exercises to test the new doctrine, that a main Soviet thrust could be identified, or that troops concentrating to meet the thrust would not themselves be ambushed or their flanks turned by other breakthroughs. By the time General Starry succeeded General DePuy as head of TRADOC in July 1977, further analysis had cast doubts on Active Defense's view of Soviet doctrine, its interpretation of the Yom Kippur War, and its basic assumption that increased firepower favoured the defence. The Egyptians and Syrians in 1973 had, after all, used their new precision guided weapons together with armour and aircraft to undertake an offensive war. Meanwhile, the Iranian revolution and the Soviet invasion of Afghanistan in 1979 forced the administration of President Jimmy Carter to think once more about possible military action outside Europe. The result of this general dissatisfaction with Active Defense was a further major revision of *FM 100-5* by the Department of Tactics at the Army Command and General Staff College, supervised by TRADOC. It appeared in August 1982, exactly a year after General Glenn K Otis has succeeded General Starry, as 'AirLand Battle'.

AirLand Battle

Unlike Active Defense, AirLand Battle was a global war-fighting doctrine, meant to be applicable anywhere, to any war, in any climate or terrain, and including the possible use of all available resources from nuclear weapons to psychological warfare in order to secure the military defeat of the enemy:

> Once political authorities commit military forces in pursuit of political aims, military forces must win something — else there will be no basis from which political authority can bargain to win politically. Therefore, the purpose of military operations cannot be simply to avert defeat — but rather it must be to win.[14]

This was in line with a broader political doctrine enunciated by the Reagan administration, that military operations in the Third World should use overwhelming force to achieve a quick victory, a major change from

Limited War as understood in the past. President Reagan himself was quoted as saying that MacArthur 'should have been allowed to lead us to victory' in Korea. The first practical demonstrations of this new approach were seen in Grenada in 1983 and in Panama in 1989.[15]

Also unlike its predecessor, AirLand Battle was intended to be forward looking, drawing on technology which already existed or would shortly come into service. As its name suggests, although developed by the army it relied heavily on the use of airmobility and airpower. As early as 1973 a joint Air-Land Forces Application Agency was established between TRA-DOC and the US Air Force Tactical Air Command (TAC) to co-ordinate doctrine, and a preliminary TAC-TRADOC agreement on doctrine was issued by the air force in 1981. A year earlier, the army and air force initiated a study for 'AirLand Battle 2000', intended to cover the period from 1995 into the next century. When Congress refused to fund this it was broken into two components, 'Army 21' and 'Air Force 21', which were still in development at the time of the Gulf War. Meanwhile, the US Air Force formally adopted AirLand Battle as part of its own doctrine in 1984.

AirLand Battle proposed that the new surveillance technology and computerised communications should be used not only to see deep past the front line (in military terminology the Forward Edge of the Battle Area or FEBA), but to strike deep, conducting offensive operations against the enemy rear. In 1979 the US Army Field Artillery School suggested to TRADOC that, whereas in the past interdiction fire had been largely random, increased ranges, accuracy and target detection had made an 'integrated battlefield' possible, with interdiction directly linked to fighting at the FEBA as part of the same battle. Meanwhile, the air force had developed a similar role for its ground-attack and interdiction aircraft, given the name Battlefield Air Interdiction (BAI) in 1976 and incorporated into the TAC-TRADOC agreement of 1981. The object was to produce what General Starry called an 'extended battlefield', stretching from the earth's surface to the stratosphere and beyond, and hundreds of kilometres from the FEBA into the enemy rear areas, in which all actions were part of a single orchestrated battle plan. As set out in *FM 100-5*, the four key concepts of AirLand Battle were 'Initiative, Depth, Agility and Synchronisation'. It marked a fundamental shift in American thinking from attrition warfare governed by superior firepower to manoeuvre warfare governed by superior skill.

AirLand Battle was also the first American doctrine directed specifically at the operational level of war, a term which itself needed careful explanation:

> The operational level of war uses available military resources to attain strategic goals within a theater of war. Most simply, it is the theory of larger unit operations . . . In AirLand Battle doctrine, this level includes the marshalling of forces and logistical support, providing direction of ground and air maneuvre, applying conventional and nuclear fires in depth, and employing unconventional and psychological warfare.[16]

This idea of operations (sometimes called 'grand tactics') as an intermediate level between strategy and tactics existed in American, French and British military thought in the 19th century but fell into disuse, continuing only in German and Russian (later Soviet) doctrine. AirLand Battle drew heavily on Soviet 'Operational Art', the science of organising and sustaining offensive operations by large forces over distances of hundreds of kilometres at high rates of advance, defeating tactically superior enemies by overwhelming them before they could mount a proper defence. It also adopted the related Soviet concept of 'Deep Battle', first propounded by Marshal Mikhail Tukhachevskii as early as 1928 and developed during the Second World War, of using mobile and airborne forces to strike at an enemy simultaneously throughout the depth of his deployment from the front line to the highest headquarters. AirLand Battle set out in some detail exactly how far ahead, in time and space, each level of command was to look and plan its actions. The role of Corps headquarters, assessed as the operational level of command, was to watch the enemy up to 300 km behind the FEBA, and to 'engage enemy forces which can *join or support the main battle within 72 hours*'[17] with artillery, airpower or airmobile forces.

When objections were raised to the inclusion of nuclear weapons and offensive action in AirLand Battle, its defenders argued that an operational commitment to the offensive did not imply a strategic attack, since 'the decision to cross an international border must reside with the strategic command authority', and that the same applied to the use of nuclear weapons.[18] Nevertheless, *FM 100-5* was reissued in 1986 with amendments clarifying this point, and NATO felt it necessary to state publicly that it would not conduct ground operations across the inner German border in the event of war.

Forward Command and Control Under AirLand Battle

Level of Command	Area of Interest	Area of Influence
Battalion	0–12 hours / 15 km	0–3 hours / 5 km
Brigade	0–24 hours / 70 km	0–12 hours / 15 km
Division	0–72 hours / 150 km	0–24 hours / 70 km
Corps	0–96 hours / 300 km	0–72 hours / 150 km
Echelons Above Corps	96+ hours / 1,000 km	72+ hours / 150+ km

Source: Field Manual (FM) *100-5* 'Operations' (Department of the Army, Washington DC, 1982 Edition)

One immediate and serious objection to AirLand Battle was that it was too sophisticated to work. It demanded a perfect level of communications (in military terms Command, Control and Communications, Information or C^3I) that could never be found in a real war. Even if C^3I were perfect, the cycle of orders and responses (known variously as a command loop, a decision loop, or particularly by the air force as a Boyd or OODA — Observation, Orientation, Decision, Action — loop) could not keep pace with such a fast-moving battle, nor could commanders engaged in actual combat plan so far ahead. Part of the American solution was to use 'flying command posts', advanced-technology aircraft to provide and process the information needed, in particular the Boeing E-3A/B Sentry Airborne Warning and Control System (AWACS), and the Boeing E-8A Joint Surveillance and Target Attack Radar System (J-STARS), a joint army-air force radar-equipped aircraft first used on operations in the Gulf War and reportedly capable of tracking enemy ground vehicles moving 185 km away.

The solution to the problem of C^3I breakdown on the battlefield itself was sought by adopting *auftragstaktik*, a style of issuing orders practised in the German Army since the late 19th century and given the name 'mission-oriented command' by the Americans. The basis of *auftragstaktik* is that, rather than being issued detailed orders, a subordinate should be given a broad understanding of the higher command mission and then left to carry out his part in it as he sees fit. By definition, even if C^3I failed completely, no-one would be left without orders, and the forces of AirLand Battle could get inside the enemy decision loop. 'Synchronization was more than the cliché of coordinated action. It meant a constant grasp by subordinate commanders of their commander's overall plan.'[19] Similarly, *FM 100-5* defined agility not simply as manoeuvre, but as units and leaders acting more quickly than their enemy could respond:

> They must know of critical events as they occur and act to avoid enemy strengths and attack enemy vulnerabilities. This must be done repeatedly, so that every time the enemy begins to counter one action, another immediately upsets his plans. This will lead to ineffective, uncoordinated and piecemeal enemy responses and eventually to his defeat.[20]

The object, on which General Starry laid considerable stress, was to bring about the physical and psychological 'collapse' of the enemy forces.

In 1978 TRADOC began its 'Division 86' study on the restructuring of forces needed to undertake AirLand Battle, planned to take place over the next eight years, and expanded after a year into 'Corps 86' and 'Army 86'. This led to the 'heavy division' as the basic tactical unit, including armour, mechanised infantry, long-range and rocket artillery and a regiment of air cavalry. The old designations of armoured and infantry (mechanised) divisions for the heavy divisions were continued only for historical reasons. While the 1st Cavalry Division became a heavy division as the 1st Armored Cavalry, the 101st Airmobile Division was upgraded to become the army's only air assault division. (In modern American terminology, air cavalry consist entirely of attack helicopters, while an air assault division includes also infantry and artillery with their own helicopter transport). Even the idea of an opposed paratroop drop, largely discredited since the 1950s by improved air defences, was revived by the 82nd Airborne Division for this new, agile form of war, and carried out in regimental strength during the invasion of Panama in 1989.

One prediction of the Vietnam era which proved accurate was that increased costs and a smaller recruiting pool led to Army 86 relying more on technology than on men. The decade 1981–1990 saw American military spending increase to an average of $292 billion a year, compared with $206 billion a year for the previous decade (constant 1989 dollars). Nevertheless, in 1990 the US Army had only two more divisions than in 1981 (both of them light divisions created without increasing the number of troops on active duty), and the US Air Force had one less tactical fighter wing.[21]

AirLand Battle and Army 86 provided a doctrine and a structure for many weapons systems first developed in the 1970s which achieved fame in the Gulf War, including the AH-64 Apache attack helicopter, the Multiple Launch Rocket System (MLRS) and the MIM-104 Patriot. However, one system which did not fit particularly well into this operational level concept was the M1 Abrams main battle tank, first ordered in 1976, the design of which owed too much to Active Defense, the concentration on Europe, and the tactical level of war. Powerful on the battlefield, the Abrams had a combat range of only 440 km (275 miles) and a fuel consumption which meant that a heavy division in the Gulf needed over 1,400 tons of fuel daily when attacking, compared with just over 100 tons for a Korean War armoured division.[22] Critics felt that Division 86, with the Abrams as its main weapons system, owed too much to the old attritional thinking, being too big and slow for manoeuvre warfare. This was important, since American doctrine placed a greater stress on armour than airmobility for desert war, and expressed concern about the practicality of manoeuvre in the desert:

> Armor and mechanized infantry forces are most suitable to desert combat; however, airmobile forces can also be advantageous. For the initial lodgment, airborne forces are valuable. Army and Air Force air may support airborne and airmobile forces in bearing the brunt of the fighting until heavy forces arrive ... Because of the sparse vegetation, concealment in the desert is more difficult than in many other environments. Concealment, however, is not only possible, *it is absolutely necessary* ... In general, easy observation and long fields of fire make undetected advances and withdrawals extremely difficult.[23]

It remained to be seen how much, in the reality of the Gulf, the USA would rely on airmobility and manoeuvre, and how much on the firepower of its tanks and attack aircraft.

One more ghost of the Vietnam era which AirLand Battle sought to exorcise was the problem in leadership and combat motivation. Since the Second World War the USA had consciously shifted from 'heroic' military leadership to a more managerial style made necessary by the increasing technological sophistication of war, producing a generation of man-managers and machine-managers as officers. As a result, a persistent criticism of American military performance for over a decade after Vietnam was that, at the lowest levels, officers lacked an understanding of the realities of war. The writers of AirLand Battle deliberately 'sought a doctrine firmly centered on how soldiers, not systems, fight',[24] and stressed effective, inspirational leadership as the crucial element in combat power. Reforms carried out in the 1980s were intended to boost traditional military attitudes and improve combat motivation. At the same time, other reforms sought to correct the *malaise* of the managerial style which had afflicted the highest American military commands. There was strong evidence that in Vietnam, and for a decade afterwards, bureaucratic conflict between the services had produced bad planning and inflexibility, even in the face of new intelligence which might render a plan unworkable. The future General Schwarzkopf experienced this at first hand in Grenada, afterwards cited as an outstanding example of American military incompetence.[25] Not until the Goldwater-Nichols Act of 1986 was the Chairman of the Joint Chiefs of Staff actually placed in the chain of command for the first time, changing his role from that of the head of four competing services to sole military adviser to the President, and service rivalry continued to present problems up to the very eve of the Gulf War.

Since inter-service co-operation and rapid response to new intelligence were the bases of AirLand Battle, critics could reasonably ask whether the American armed forces were deluding themselves in adopting this new form of war. Although the very bedrock of AirLand Battle was the co-ordination of air and ground forces, the US Air Force announced in 1989 that it would not replace its ageing A-10 Thunderbolt II close-support fighter, preferring a version of the F-16 Fighting Falcon, to be known as the A-16. As far as the army was concerned: 'Having an F-16 do close air support is like having a Maserati do double duty as a pickup truck. The air force would justify building more air superiority fighters by calling them close-support aircraft'.[26] It appeared that, when choosing between AirLand Battle and its older ideas of an independent role, the air force had let its unwritten doctrine dominate.

The chief difficulty with AirLand Battle was that it cut across the old, established organisational boundaries of the American war machine. What use were a separate army, navy and air force to a system requiring a fully integrated and orchestrated battlefield? It was warfare of the 21st century being attempted by the military institutions of the Second World War. Computers, electronics, precision guidance and airmobility demanded a completely different approach. Something very similar had happened on a small scale between 1915 and 1935, when the traditional 19th century arms (cavalry, infantry, artillery and engineers) had competed for control of the tank. But in that case there was an established interest group, the horsed cavalry, whose own arm was obviously in decline, and which in most armies took over the tank as its own, at some cost to early tank doctrine. Even if AirLand Battle were the future of war, the institutional problems it faced in gaining acceptance were far greater than those of the tank in the 1920s, and there was no obvious candidate for its champion. Only the US Marines, a force of under 200,000 men including virtually every form of land, sea and air component from fixed-wing aircraft to infantry, appeared to be properly structured for AirLand Battle. But, ironically, at the time of the Gulf War the Marines had not adopted AirLand Battle as their official doctrine.

Against these wider issues, the poor American fighting record over four decades since Korea, and the long-term pressures on American doctrine, there was some doubt if promises of taking the offensive by agility and fighting smart could be kept. 'Army doctrine can disparage attrition warfare as much as it likes,' wrote one critic, 'but the power of the US Congress will still ensure that American generals take more care to reduce casualties to their troops than the generals of most armies.'[27] These tensions between promise and past performance, between written and unwritten doctrine, produced the paradox in American strategy manifest in the Gulf War.

The other coalition forces

Among the various suggestions made by armchair generals before 'Desert Storm' began in January 1991 was one, from an eminent American military analyst, that the single divisions sent by France and Britain to the Gulf should be grouped together as a Coalition reserve corps. This idea, which caused some amusement on the European side of the Atlantic, reflected the weakness and small size of both divisions compared with Division 86, rather than a belief that French and British doctrines were compatible. Whatever its problems, the American approach to doctrine is highly systematic and businesslike, backed by the resources of the richest nation on earth. In contrast, although all Coalition members belonging to NATO were bound together by long familiarity, even the French and British experience difficulties in force structure, funding and competing strategic objectives, making it very difficult for them to establish doctrines in the American sense, particularly at the strategic and operational levels. For decades the transport and support systems of all European NATO armed forces have been vulnerable to political arguments on the need to concentrate on home defence, and on 'cutting the fat tail and leaving the teeth'. The result was that, instead of a long sharp spear, the best that both France and Britain could achieve in the Gulf was a short, blunt dagger.

Between 1977 and 1981 the French government under François Mitterrand carried through a major restructuring of its armed forces based on 'equipment rather than men',[28] the same technological solution that characterised the American approach. The most radical innovation was the *Force d'Action Rapide* (FAR), a toolkit of five small specialist divisions — one airborne, one airportable marine, one mountain, one airmobile and one light armoured — totalling 47,000 men, intended both to oppose Soviet attacks into Western Europe and to provide intervention forces for action outside the NATO area by taking units as necessary from each division. Although France retained conscription, all troops sent overseas were in practice volunteers, and FAR was the only such force in European NATO. The Gulf War was a major test not only of the new French doctrine but of the ability of middle-ranking European powers to provide such forces, which were being increasingly discussed in NATO at the time. The chief problem with FAR, recognised long before the Gulf War, was its lack of sea and air transport and protection, as well as deficiencies in communications, intelligence and support services. Although fighting as part of the Coalition with the Americans provided a partial solution to this problem, the sudden public revelation in 1990 of FAR's weakness produced violent arguments in France. The force actually sent to the Gulf, the *Division Daguet* (based on the 6th Light Armoured Division, with elements added from other divisions) was chiefly equipped with armoured cars and light tanks and trained for rapid operations in desert conditions, such as those carried out by French forces in Chad in 1978 and 1983. Its use as a flank guard for 'Desert Saber', the main Coalition land offensive, was consistent both with its specialist role and with France's aloofness from NATO common doctrines.

The British approach was very different to that of the French. Following the Second World War, Britain as a maritime power, a NATO alliance member, and heir to an old imperial role, had too many diverse commitments to predict with confidence any one opponent or function for its armed forces. Instead, the same forces prepared and trained for mechanised war in Europe and in support of NATO while carrying out a variety of police actions and low-intensity operations for which entirely different force structures and doctrines were required. Because of this, and for historical reasons, the institutional structure of the British armed forces, even at the time of the Gulf War, was extremely loose and decentralised. Almost unique in Europe in having all-volunteer forces, about a third the size of those of France or Germany, the British relied more than any other power on very high quality troops and leadership to solve their persistent problem — the likelihood of confronting at very short notice an enemy which they were not trained, equipped or structured to fight. The Falklands War, the largest British conventional war since Korea, was a classic example:

> Shifts in tactics or technology *might* have altered the outcome, but Britain's superior training, readiness and leadership *did* decide the outcome. This is a critical lesson to bear in mind in assessing low-intensity conflicts and the nature of any conflict fought under unique or improvised conditions. Regardless of force numbers and weapons, professionalism and innovation will often be the decisive 'force multiplier'.[29]

The institutional problem with this approach was that, particularly in the case of the British Army with its 'Regimental System' for armour and infantry, decentralisation often meant fragmentation, coupled with a resistance to change and new technology. As a Soviet general told his British opposite number a year before the Gulf War: 'You have the best troops in the world and the worst equipped, which is why we can afford to ignore you'. This was brought home by the Iraqi invasion of Kuwait. The sole British Army 'out-of-NATO-area' force, the 5th Airborne Brigade, was considered too weak and under-equipped to be sent to the Gulf.

Also in contrast to the French, who since 1966 have very much gone their own way, the British have a long political tradition as the most loyal American ally in NATO. In 1957 they adopted their own version of the Eisenhower 'New Look', and began a progressive concentration on their NATO role at the expense of 'out-of-area' commitments. This culminated in the 1981 Defence Review under Margaret Thatcher, which would have virtually eliminated any 'out-of-area' capability had it not been for the Falklands War in the following year. This concentration on NATO and Europe allowed the British, for the first time, to think about a single enemy, a single approach to war, and the development of a coherent doctrine. The same period also saw attempts at greater integration of the three armed services at higher levels. This culminated in the British Army producing its first-ever written doctrine, the short pamphlet *Design For Military Operations*, in 1989.

In 1983 NATO Supreme Headquarters issued *Allied Tactical Publication* (ATP) 35, a tactical doctrine for land warfare embodying many of the concepts of AirLand Battle, to which NATO members were requested to relate their own doctrines. Meanwhile, in 1979 the Supreme Allied Commander Europe (SACEUR), the American General Bernard Rodgers, began to promote his own concept for a unified NATO operational doctrine of Follow On Forces Attack (FOFA), which had many features in common with AirLand Battle, and which was approved as an official NATO long-term planning guideline in November 1984. FOFA was General Rodgers' response to the Soviet doctrine of mounting attacks in echelon, with repeated waves of armoured forces pressing down on a narrow enemy front, and fresh troops being pushed through the enemy lines at high speed to exploit and expand the initial breakthrough. This notion was already part of 'Deep Battle' before the Second World War, but reached its final form in the largest Soviet exercises for over 30 years, the *ZAPAD 81* (West 81) manoeuvres held in September 1981 on the Baltic coast of Lithuania and Poland at the height of the Solidarity crisis. These manoeuvres saw the Soviet use of an Operational Manoeuvre Group (OMG), usually the equivalent of a reinforced armoured division, held in reserve about 30km behind the FEBA and then unleashed once the break had been made to drive deep into enemy territory, converting a tactical victory into an operational-level advance. General Rodgers believed that in the event of war in West Germany his forces could hold the first Soviet wave at the FEBA, but that new technology should be used to strike both at OMGs in the immediate area and at Soviet rear echelon forces as they moved from western Russia and across Poland. Co-ordinating FOFA strikes with the battle at the FEBA would create opportunities for NATO forces to counterattack, take the initiative from the Soviets, and so win the war. Like AirLand Battle, with which it was obviously compatible, FOFA stressed electronics for intelligence gathering, good C^3I and deep strike.

By virtue of their own position within NATO and close association with the Americans, the British were highly receptive to both FOFA and AirLand Battle. The British Army ordered MLRS from the Americans to counter the OMG threat, and in September 1988 produced its first ever permanent airmobile formation, the 24th Airmobile Brigade. Similarly, the Royal Air Force (RAF) developed the Hunting JP233 low-level attack weapon as a way of striking at Soviet forces deep behind the FEBA. It also pressed for an air-launched Short Range Attack Missile (SRAM) to avoid the need to penetrate the last few kilometres of enemy airspace with manned aircraft, but this was not forthcoming by the time of the Gulf War. American doctrine also influenced the development in 1981 of new general concepts for I British Corps in West Germany under General Sir Nigel Bagnall. In 1983, on his promotion to command NATO's Northern Army Group (NORTHAG), General Bagnall attempted to extend the British ideas to the whole Army Group as a common doctrine. His work was continued by General Sir Martin Farndale as his successor at I British Corps and NORTHAG, although little clear progress had been made by the time of the Gulf War.

As with AirLand Battle, the British and NORTHAG concept tried to move away from the static use of firepower to mobility and manoeuvre warfare, gaining the initiative in offensive or counterstroke operations. In 1986 the British Defence Estimates spoke of this new method as 'giving the Alliance a much better chance of defeating the enemy rather than delaying him'.[30] The 1989 doctrine, written at the British Army's Staff College, re-introduced the operational level into British military thought, together with *auftragstaktik* under the name of 'mission analysis'. It was, however, a very quiet revolution. Although most of the British officers who fought in the Gulf knew about FOFA, few had heard of AirLand Battle.

Most reservations about the new British approach were couched in terms of cost and institutional pressures. With their small size, weak technology and resistance to reorganisation, it was not going too far to suggest that the British were attempting 21st century warfare with the institutions of the First World War. Indeed, critics had made exactly this point at the time of the Falklands War, arguing that: 'despite its achievements and reforms since 1906, the Army remains what it was then, *sans* doctrine and an unprofessional coalition of arms and services.'[31] A case in point was the 24th Airmobile Brigade, which was not an airmobile formation as the Americans used the term. It had no permanent control over its own transport helicopters, its infantry being carried by any helicopters that the RAF could spare temporarily from other duties. This, together with the small size and weakness of the British airmobile force, attributable to the concern of the armoured forces that money should be spent on tanks rather than on helicopters, meant that the 24th Airmobile Brigade, like the 5th Airborne Brigade, was not sent to the Gulf.

Nevertheless, the British shared a common language — in every sense — and something close to a common doctrine with the Americans, and had a long history of effective co-operation with them. Like all NATO forces, they had also based their planning for decades on the assumption that their enemy would be the Soviet Union rather than a much weaker power like Iraq. Of all the Coalition forces, the British might be expected to play the most prominent, effective and closely integrated supporting role in the American plan.

It is not reasonable to speak of doctrines for the smaller members of the Coalition, or even for Saudi Arabia, which has small forces for such a large and wealthy country. Of all the Middle East countries, only Israel, as the result of very specific circumstances and threats, has been able to develop doctrines in the usual sense of the term. However, the Saudis were familiar with the NATO forces of the Coalition through their purchase of American, French and British weapons, and with its other Arab forces by virtue of being near neighbours. As the Coalition's host country, Saudi Arabia could be expected to play a significant political role in maintaining smooth relations and co-operation, together with a small but prominent role in military operations. In purely military terms, the most significant Arab members of the Coalition were Egypt and Syria, both of which are often secretive about military matters, and whose armed forces tend to be seen by the outside world in the reflection of Israeli achievements. It should therefore be remembered that, at the time of the Gulf War, both nations had much more experience of modern mechanised war than any member of

NATO, and that between them they contributed more troops to the Coalition than the French and British. By close attention to their past doctrines and experience the two countries found a role within the Coalition which was entirely in keeping with their particular strengths.

Egypt and Syria share not only a common language but a common military doctrinal heritage in the form of massive Soviet military influence in the 1960s and 1970s, and had fought together as allies three times before the Gulf War. Indeed, the Iraqi defensive system which they faced was a crude but recognisable version of the 'Sword and Shield' defence which they themselves had used at the start of the 1967 Six-Day War, based on a Soviet concept going back to the Second World War. Similarly, the Iraqi air defence concept was based on the Soviet 'Layered Defence' doctrine used successfully by Egypt in the 1973 War and less successfully by Syria in 1982, when the Syrian forces in Lebanon had been subject to an Israeli air and ground attack which represented the closest that actual warfare had come to the ideals of the integrated battlefield before the Gulf War. Except for the Israelis themselves, no-one knew more about fighting Arab armies who had adopted Soviet doctrines, such as the Iraqis, than Egypt and Syria.

The experience of the Arab-Israeli conflicts had also had a major impact on AirLand Battle and its related doctrines. Indeed, the idea of 'collapsing' an enemy physically and psychologically, which formed the apex of AirLand Battle, was probably first suggested by Moshe Dayan, Chief of Staff of the Israeli Defence Force (IDF), in the Suez campaign of 1956. It reflected a fundamental Israeli doctrinal belief that armed forces should be viewed as social organisations, the product of their civilian societies, and that many Arab nations lacked the social cohesion characteristic of fully developed modern states. In the case of their enemies, the Israelis argued, political loyalty to the state was often more important than military competence at the higher levels of command, subordinate commanders would be discouraged from displaying initiative, and soldiers could not develop the mutual reliance and trust in their superiors typical of first-class fighting units. Effectively, therefore, such armies would be incapable of manoeuvre warfare. As Dayan expressed it during the Suez campaign:

> We must press forward and not stop to clean up isolated enemy positions. There is no need to fear that Egyptian units who will be bypassed will launch a counterattack or cut our supply lines. We should avoid analogies whereby Egyptian units would be expected to behave as European armies would in similar circumstances.[32]

Further, according to the Israeli 'collapse theory', if they were faced with a threat to which they were incapable of responding, such armies would experience a major failure in command and disintegrate into leaderless mobs. Although there is some dispute over the events of 1956, both the Egyptian and Syrian armies appeared to collapse in this manner during the Six-Day War of 1967. The British military theorist JFC Fuller believed that something similar had happened briefly to the British Army in March 1918, and the idea formed a central pillar of Sir Basil Liddell Hart's 'Indirect Approach' concept, also a major influence on AirLand Battle.

The 1973 Arab-Israeli War, in which Egypt and Syria took the offensive and inflicted a serious defeat upon Israel in the first few days of the war, appeared to disprove this theory. In fact, the Egyptians in particular had devised a battle plan that cleverly minimised their weaknesses. The crossing of the Suez Canal and piercing of the Bar-Lev Line defences, which caught the Israelis by surprise, was a set-piece attack which could be repeatedly rehearsed, and which required little sophisticated manoeuvre:

> Arab peasant armies can only be viable military forces in static warfare, where each man can fight on his own and the whole is no more than the sum of the parts. The most impressive feature of Egyptian planning in 1973 was the combination of the strategic offensive — the virtually unopposed crossing of the canal — with the tactical defensive, so that troops were only required to fight in a static manner to defeat Israeli counterattacks.[33]

When the Egyptians attempted to move out of their bridgehead in the second week of the war they exposed themselves to superior Israeli manoeuvrability and suffered rapid defeat. The war showed that the Egyptian Army was capable of conducting an effective but strictly limited attack through a difficult defensive position.

Following the 1973 War, Egypt made a conscious effort to move away from the Soviet orbit and confrontation with Israel. Instead, from 1975 onwards, the country sought to purchase American high-technology equipment and develop intervention forces for use outside its own borders. This was manifest in an increasing stress on professionalism in the Egyptian officer corps, as Egypt also moved towards the technological solution to declining manpower and rising costs. President Hosni Mubarak is himself a former head of the Egyptian Air Force. Syria, which remained loyal to Soviet concepts and equipment but experienced considerable difficulty affording them, might have been expected to play a lesser role. Although in 1986 the Syrian Army instituted training to improve its manoeuvre capability, an American assessment found that 'Syrian combined-arms and combined-operations capabilities remain poor by Israeli, Western and even Iraqi standards'.[34] With long and unsuccessful experience of fighting the Israelis in the air, neither Egypt nor Syria contributed air forces to the Gulf, preferring to rely on the air forces of Western members of the Coalition, which were expected to be, in technology and training, broadly comparable with those of the Israelis.

Conclusion

Of all the forms of warfare, coalition war is the hardest. And of all the ways to defeat an opponent, to outmanoeuvre him is the most difficult. After the disaster of Vietnam, the American planners for the Gulf War had to find a way to integrate the various elements of the Coalition into a unified structure, selecting a form of war and a strategy which would exploit the strengths of each member. At the operational level, they needed to reconcile a desire to fight sophisticated manoeuvre warfare with the limitations of the available forces and the tensions created by their various doctrines and past assumptions. In all this, the Iraqi enemy was almost a secondary consideration. Modern armed forces are so complex that by the time of the

Gulf War many military thinkers — particularly in the Soviet Union — had begun to argue that organised military force was becoming 'unusable'; that the machine must inevitably break down as it had done in Vietnam and Afghanistan. It was clear that in the Gulf, if they were to fight something as sophisticated as AirLand Battle, collapsing the enemy rather than annihilating him with firepower, the Americans in particular would spend most of their time in the institutional battle, in fighting themselves. It remained to be seen if this time they could really fight to win.

Notes

1. 'Spirit of Long-Dead General Hovering Over Two Armies', *The Guardian*, 19 February 1991; 'A New Breed of Brass', *Time International*, 11 March 1991.

2. V D Sokolovskii, *Voennaya Strategiya* (3rd Edition, Voenizdat, Moscow, 1968), p 54. See also the translation by Harriet Fast Scott, *Soviet Military Strategy* (Macdonald and Jane's, London, 1968), p 38; and Gregory Flynn, *Soviet Military Doctrine and Western Policy* (Routledge, New York, 1989); Harriet Fast Scott and William F Scott, *Soviet Military Doctrine* (Westview Press, Boulder, Colorado, 1988).

3. John L Romjue, *From Active Defense to AirLand Battle* (Historical Office TRADOC, Fort Monroe, Virginia, 1984), p 29; *US Department of Defense Dictionary of Military Terms* (Greenhill, New York, 1987), p 118.

4. Neil Sheehan, *A Bright Shining Lie. John Paul Vann and America in Vietnam* (Picador, London, 1989), p 43.

5. George Bush, *The National Security Strategy of the United States 1990–1991* (Brassey's, Washington DC, 1990), p 104.

6. Quoted in Paddy Griffith, *Rally Once Again* (Crowood, London, 1987), p 168.

7. Robin Brown, 'Limited War,' in Colin McInnes and G D Sheffield (ed), *Warfare in the Twentieth Century* (Unwin Hyman, London, 1988), pp 164–193. See also Robert Osgood, *Limited War* (Chicago UP, Chicago, 1957); David Rees, *Korea, The Limited War* (Macmillan, London, 1964); Lawrence Freedman, *The Evolution of Nuclear Strategy* (Macmillan, London, 1981).

8. Rees, op cit, pp 266–267.

9. Quoted in USG Sharpe, *Strategy For Defeat* (Presidio, London, 1978), pp 97–98.

10. D E Ott, *Field Artillery 1954–1973* (Vietnam Studies Series, Department of the Army, Washington DC, 1975), p 181. See also John J Tolson, *Airmobility 1961–1971* (Vietnam Studies Series, Department of the Army, Washington DC, 1973).

11. Quoted in Paul Dickson, *The Electronic Battlefield* (Morian Boyars, London, 1976), pp 221–222. See also Paddy Griffith, *Forward Into Battle* (2nd Edition, Crowood, Swindon, 1990); Frank Barnaby, *Future War* (Michael Joseph, London, 1984) and *The Automated Battlefield* (OUP, Oxford, 1987).

12. Sheehan, op cit, p 11. See also Martin van Creveld, *Command in War* (Harvard UP, Cambridge, Mass., 1985), pp 232–260; Peter M Dunn, 'The American Army: The Vietnam War 1965–1973', in Ian F W Beckett and John Pimlott (ed), *Armed Forces and Modern Counter-Insurgency* (Croom Helm, London, 1985), pp 77–111.

13. This famous quotation, repeated in various forms, was recorded by Peter Arnett. The officer himself was never identified. See John Simpson, *From the House of War* (Arrow, London, 1991), p 312.

14. Romjue, op cit, p 45.

15. Eugene J Carol Jr and Gene R La Roque, 'Victory in the Desert: Superior Technology or Brute Force?' in Victoria Brittain (ed), *The Gulf Between Us. The Gulf War and Beyond* (Virago Press, London, 1991), pp 43–60; John Halliday and Bruce Cummings, *Korea: The Unknown War* (Penguin, London, 1990), p 202.

16. *Field Manual* (FM) *100-5* 'Operations' (Department of the Army, Washington DC, 1982), p 2–3.

17. Ibid, p 7–15 (emphasis in the original).

18. Colin McInnes, *NATO's Changing Strategic Agenda* (Unwin Hyman, London, 1990), p 130.

19. Romjue, op cit, p 68. See also Martin van Creveld, *Fighting Power* (Arms and Armour, London, 1983), pp 35–41.

20. *FM 100-5*, p 2–2.

21. Lawrence J Korb and Stephen Daggett, 'The Defense Budget and Strategic Planning', in Joseph Kruzel (ed), *American Defense Annual 1988–1989* (Mershon Center, Ohio State University, 1988), pp 43–66.

22. Trevor N Dupuy, *How to Defeat Saddam Hussein* (Warrior, New York, 1991), p 103.

23. *FM 100-5*, pp 3–11 and 3–12.
24. Romjue, op cit, p 55.
25. Richard A Gabriel, *Military Incompetence* (Hill and Wang, New York, 1985), pp 149–186; Mark Adkin, *Urgent Fury* (Leo Cooper, London, 1989), pp 335–340. See also Hugh O'Shaughnessy, *Grenada: Revolution, Invasion and Aftermath* (Hamish Hamilton, London, 1984).
26. Joseph Kruzel, 'Perspectives,' in Kruzel, op cit, p 19.
27. David Robertson, *A Dictionary of Modern Defence and Strategy* (Europa, London, 1987), pp 104–105.
28. Douglas Porch, 'French Defense and the Gaullist Legacy,' in Lewis H Gann (ed), *The Defense of Western Europe* (Auburn House, Dover, 1987), pp 188–211; see also John Keegan (ed), *World Armies* (2nd Edition, Macmillan, London, 1983).
29. Anthony H Cordesman and Abraham R Wagner, *The Lessons of Modern War* (Westview Press, Boulder, Colorado, 1990), Vol III, 'The Afghan and Falklands Conflicts; p 351.
30. McInnes, op cit, pp 135–136.
31. Shelford Bidwell and Dominick Graham, *Fire-Power* (Allen and Unwin, London, 1982), p 295.
32. Moshe Dayan, *Diary of the Sinai Campaign 1956* (Sphere, London, 1967), p 42.
33. Edward Luttwak and Dan Horowitz, *The Israeli Army* (Allen Lane, London, 1975), p 286.
34. Cordesman and Wagner, op cit, Vol I, 'The Arab-Israeli Conflict' p 279. See also Keegan, op cit.

Further Reading

J P Harris and F H Toase (ed), *Armoured Warfare* (Batsford, London, 1990).
Edward Luttwak and Dan Horowitz, *The Israeli Army* (Allen Lane, London, 1975).
Colin McInnes, *NATO's Changing Strategic Agenda* (Unwin Hyman, London, 1990).
John L Romjue, *From Active Defense To AirLand Battle* (Historical Office TRADOC, Fort Monroe, Virginia, 1984).
Richard Simpkin, *Deep Battle* (Brassey's, London, 1987).

CHAPTER 4
The Build-Up

Duncan Anderson

'Amateurs talk about strategy; professionals talk about logistics.'

General of the Army Omar N Bradley

Central Command's plans

 Saddam Hussein was convinced that the United States was powerless to stop him invading Kuwait. Ironically, many top US military personnel shared his conviction. On 2 August 1990, the day of the Iraqi invasion, the USA had only a token military presence in the Middle East: a few warships in the Indian Ocean and the eight ships of No 2 Maritime Prepositioning Squadron anchored at Diego Garcia, an atoll 3,200km (2,000 miles) south of the Arabian peninsula. The nearest substantial US forces lay 3,520km (2,200 miles) to the north-west in Germany and 11,000km (6,800 miles) to the east in the Philippines. At best, the USA might be able to marshal some marines and aircraft, even some airborne forces. But a large-scale movement to match Iraqi forces would require the kind of resources the USA last had available when it had committed forces to Vietnam in 1965: an 18-division army and a correspondingly large fleet of troop transports. Twenty-five years later it possessed neither.

During the 1980s the USA had been developing contingency plans for moving forces into the Middle East. These were scarcely secret. Anyone following the hearings of the US Senate's Armed Forces and Foreign Relations Committees would have known of the formation in 1983 of the United States Central Command (CENTCOM). A group of prefabricated buildings on the edge of Florida's MacGill Air Force Base housed some 800 planning personnel, busy formulating schemes to move Marine Expeditionary Brigades (MEBs) and the US XVIII Airborne Corps to the Command's area of responsibility, a vast region extending from the Horn of Africa to the Indus Valley.[1]

CENTCOM's plans depended on the availability of forces in other 'real' commands. Nevertheless, it could boast some substantial achievements of its own. During the 1980s the CENTCOM-inspired 'Peace Hawk' programme had provided Saudi Arabia with airbases (including Dhahran) worth $5 billion. With its 560km (350-mile) perimeter fence, Dhahran was the largest airbase in the world. Bunkers at these bases were crammed with munitions, engine assemblies and avionic equipment — far more than the Royal Saudi Air Force could conceivably require (a policy which provoked sharp criticism from America's pro-Israeli lobby). At the same time, working in close collaboration with CENTCOM, the Bechtel Corporation (of which the then US Secretary of State George Shultz had been a vice-president) constructed a modern 16-berth port at Al Jubail and a 42-berth port at Dhahran, both equipped with giant cranes and vast roll-on/roll-off (Ro-Ro) capacity.[2] A subsidiary 'Earnest Will' programme in the late 1980s had concentrated on giving Saudi Arabia a modern command and control network, including the bunker complex in Riyadh which was to become HQ CENTCOM during the Gulf Crisis and War.[3] CENTCOM's planners had also secured the prepositioning at Diego Garcia, a British-controlled atoll in the Indian Ocean, of eight transport ships fully loaded with all the weapons and equipment which would be required by a 15,000-strong MEB.[4]

CENTCOM's plans had been developed to counter any potential threat to Saudi oilfields from the Soviet Union or Iran. In the event of a crisis, United States Air Force (USAF) fighter and attack wings would be flown into Saudi Arabia to secure control of the air, while the giant Lockheed C-5 Galaxy and C-141 Starlifter transports of Military Airlift Command (MAC) would establish an air bridge to fly in the personnel and some of the light equipment of the XVIII Airborne Corps, comprising the 82nd Airborne, 101st Airborne (Air Assault) and 24th Infantry Divisions. The bulk of XVIII Airborne Corps' equipment would come by sea in fast transports provided by Military Sealift Command (MSC). Simultaneously, the prepositioned transports would sail for Saudi ports, where the air bridge would deposit US Marine Corps (USMC) personnel who would then marry up with their equipment.[5]

During the 1980s the Ready Brigade of the 82nd Airborne Division ('All American') had deployed to Egypt on the biennial 'Bright Star' exercises. This was the only practical testing of any part of CENTCOM's plans, and the 82nd Airborne was the only division for which Time Phase Deployment Data (TPDD) had been prepared, vital sequential tables which would serve to minimise confusion. Otherwise plans remained wholly confined to blueprints and computer discs.[6] Much of the groundwork for planning deployments had been carried out in the 'Gallant Knight' exercises, which (despite their glamorous name) were a series of computer simulations. 'Gallant Knight' had no factual basis. Its smoothly synchronised operations lulled the senators on the Armed Services and Foreign Relations Committees into what proved to be a false sense of security.[7]

The crisis

On 4 August 1990 General H Norman Schwarzkopf, who had taken command of CENTCOM on 23 November 1988, had just finished running one of these simulation exercises ('Internal Look '90') when he was called to Washington to brief President George Bush on Operation Plan 90-1002. Forty-eight hours later, accompanied by Secretary for Defense Richard ('Dick') Cheney and Chairman of the Joint Chiefs of Staff (JCS) General Colin Powell, he gave essentially the same briefing to an audience in Riyadh. Here Schwarzkopf delivered what was to be the first of many vintage public performances during the Gulf Crisis. Briefed to convince the Saudis that the USA was not only willing but able to get forces to the Arabian peninsula quickly, he claimed that up to 250,000 troops and their equipment would shortly be on the way should the Saudis give the word. He must have been aware that the USA's ability to make good that promise was purely theoretical.[8]

In the hours preceding the briefing, Schwarzkopf's main anxiety stemmed from his conviction that Saddam Hussein was unlikely to sit idly by during a US build-up. If (as Schwarzkopf feared) he responded by sending his armoured divisions rolling 320 km (200 miles) south to overrun the ports of Al Jubail, Dhahran, Ad Damman and their airbases, a swift and major deployment of US forces would prove well-nigh impossible. So for CENTCOM's commander it was of paramount importance to get as many combat troops to Saudi Arabia as quickly as possible. Given this priority, the deployment would have to follow the reverse order of the move to Vietnam in March 1965, when logistic troops landed first and established bases for the combat forces. Now, fighter aircraft would fly in before their ground crews and maintenance equipment had arrived, and combat troops would fly in not only before requirements like food, water and accommodation had been arranged, but while the bulk of their ammunition and heavy equipment was still at sea. Not only were the military 'teeth' going before the 'tail', but the distance between teeth and tail was likely to be extended. Even more problematic was the fact that the tail — the once numerous logistic troops of the US Army — was no longer large enough to support all the teeth that Schwarzkopf was promising to send around the world.[9]

The reorganisation of the US Army 15 years earlier, after the debacle of Vietnam, was now to have far-reaching implications for the Gulf War. Eighty per cent of all combat-support forces had been placed in the reserve category. This decision had little impact on the USA's ability to sustain forces in well-developed theatres such as the Federal German Republic (FGR) or South Korea, but for so-called 'out-of-area' operations, such as the sending of troops to Saudi Arabia, the implications were serious. Mobilisation of combat support reserve forces required a political decision from the President. Even if the decision came quickly, mobilisation could take weeks, if not months. Meanwhile, the front-line forces would be largely on their own, possibly aided by such support from the Saudis as a handful of logistics officers in theatre had been able to secure.[10] Schwarzkopf knew he was taking an enormous risk. If Saddam Hussein decided to strike south at any time before the end of August, the Americans might suffer a resounding defeat on a par with the loss of the Philippines almost 50 years earlier.

On 7 August 1990, just five days after the invasion, CENTCOM began its deployment, when 48 McDonnell Douglas F-15C Eagles of the 71st Tactical Fighter Wing left Langley Air Force Base in Virginia on a 16-hour non-stop flight to Dhahran. They refuelled in flight six times, setting a new record for the longest overseas deployment ever made by US fighters. The record was soon matched by succeeding wings. But, even as the fighters

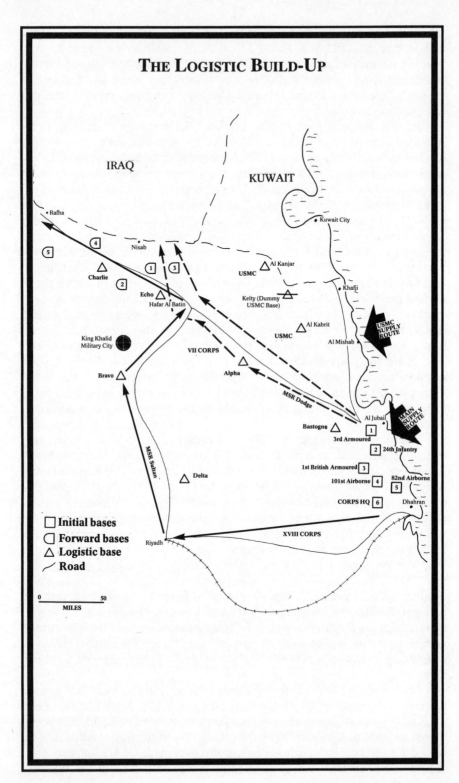

THE LOGISTIC BUILD-UP

IRAQ

KUWAIT

• Rafha

Kuwait City •

⑤

④

• Nisab

Charlie △

① ③

Al Kanjar △

② USMC

Echo △

Kelty (Dummy
USMC Base) △

• Khafji

Hafar Al Batin

King Khalid
Military City ●

Al Kabrit △

USMC

Al Mishab •

VII CORPS

USMC
SUPPLY
ROUTE

Bravo △

Alpha △

MSR Dodge

Al Jubail

MAIN
SUPPLY
ROUTE

Bastogne △

3rd Armoured

①

MSR Sultan

② 24th Infantry

△ Delta

1st British Armoured ③

101st Airborne ④

82nd Airborne ⑤

CORPS HQ ⑥

Dhahran •

□ Initial bases

◖ Forward bases

△ Logistic base

⌒ Road

Riyadh •

XVIII CORPS

0 ────── 50
MILES

were touching down at Dhahran, problems developed at Langley which soon spread to other bases. It proved difficult to arrange refuelling rendezvous between so many fighters. Ironically, the oil-rich kingdom of Saudi Arabia did not produce that one essential commodity, high-grade aviation fuel. Moreover, the Boeing KC-10 Extender tanker aircraft had to refuel at bases in Europe and the USA in order to build up fuel stockpiles in Saudi. The process took several days, during which the most modern US fighters sat on the Dhahran runway with scarcely enough fuel for the short publicity sorties they made for the benefit of television news crews. Meanwhile, chaos spread at US airbases. Every few hours giant C-5 transports of MAC arrived to pick up avionics, engines and munitions. Ground crews were simply unable to keep up the pace, and flying schedules were severely disrupted.[11]

At Pope Air Force Base, North Carolina, on 7 August the 2,300-strong Ready Brigade of the 82nd Airborne Division loaded their Humvees (High Mobility Multi-Purpose Wheeled Vehicles, the replacements for jeeps) and a handful of M-551 Sheridan light tanks into C-5s, then boarded C-141Bs for the flight to Dhahran. Fifteen hours later they disembarked into the burning heat of a Saudi summer, clad in full combat gear and helmets and carrying their personal weapons. They were met not by Iraqi tanks but by a fleet of dilapidated school buses. Logistics officers had been unable to hire any other form of transport to take the men to their accommodation in huge hangars near the airbase. Here they were issued with bottled water (with instructions to drink a bladder-straining 48 pints a day) and sat down to their first meal, a pre-packaged Meal Ready to Eat (MRE). Their second and third meals were also MREs, and a month later they were still eating MREs, now known throughout the rapidly growing US forces as 'Meals Rejected by Ethiopians'. The MRE was essentially a combat ration designed to sustain a soldier in the field for a maximum of roughly ten days. It had never been intended for the indefinite feeding of an army, but the US Army's former excellent Catering Corps had been one of the first casualties of the reorganisation of US forces during the mid-1970s. There was now no alternative but the MRE. Troops serving in the Gulf were worse fed than any other US Army in the 20th century.[12]

On the same day that the Ready Brigade of the 82nd Airborne Division touched down at Dhahran, Vice-Admiral Francis R Donovan, commander of MSC, ordered No 2 Maritime Prepositioning Squadron based at Diego Garcia to sail at full speed for the Gulf. As luck would have it, two of the ships were off station, one *en route* to the USA for routine maintenance and one already back at Wilmington, North Carolina, for an overhaul and repackaging of its supplies. Without waiting for orders, Donovan ordered the ship still at sea back to the Indian Ocean.[13] These seven ships carried enough armour, artillery and supplies to equip and sustain an MEB (about the size of a Second World War infantry division) for 30 days.

Two days later, on 12 August, leading elements of the 7th MEB boarded C-141s at Twentynine Palms in California for the first of 250 flights designed to transport the entire brigade to Al Jubail to meet up with the ships from Diego Garcia by 20 August. When the 7th MEB commander,

Major-General John L Hopkins, arrived at Al Jubail on 15 August (the day on which the ships from Diego Garcia docked), he encountered enormous problems. Although computer simulations had demonstrated the ease with which men could theoretically be married up with supplies, practice proved different from theory. Although Al Jubail was a modern container port with impressive facilities, the Marines, mindful of the Iraqi threat, worked the dockside equipment so fast and so hard that cranes jammed and container equipment handling broke down. Inevitably there were delays. The marines, still smarting from the disaster at Beirut seven years earlier, were reluctant to allow the regular port labourers — mainly Yemenis, Pakistanis and Filipinos — into their unloading areas. For ten days the marines worked as stevedores in the 140° Fahrenheit (60° Centigrade) heat with Hopkins working alongside them. On 25 August the 7th MEB, now 15,000 strong with 123 tanks, 425 artillery pieces and 124 aircraft, rolled 320 km (200 miles) north to the Saudi-Kuwaiti frontier.[14]

More marines were on the way. Already the advance elements of the Hawaii-based 1st MEB were landing at Al Jubail. The next day, 26 August, the Guam-based No 3 Maritime Prepositioning Squadron, ordered to sea at the same time as the Diego Garcia squadron, also docked at Al Jubail. Within hours the process of marrying up equipment and men was once more under way. Meanwhile, the advance guard of the 4th MEB, based in North and South Carolina, was also heading for the Gulf.[15] This was now the largest deployment of US Marines since the Second World War. The Marines were structured for a sudden assault rather than a long slog. They possessed both the experience and the ships to facilitate speedy travel to distant locations, but were less skilled at sustaining their forces in distant theatres over long periods.[16]

The 7th MEB was already suffering logistic problems. Although the USMC (unlike the US Army) had its own excellent on-board catering facilities and was expert at shifting large quantities of cooked food from ship to shore, it lacked the experience and the means to transport it the 320 km (200 miles) north from Al Jubail to the 7th MEB on the frontier with Kuwait. As it was considered unsafe to move the ships further up the Gulf, the cooked food was trucked north by Saudi contractors in unrefrigerated aluminium containers in 140° Fahrenheit heat on what often proved to be a five-hour trip. A subsidiary kitchen was set up at Al-Mishab, 45km south of the Kuwaiti border. But, even so, by the beginning of September about 20 per cent of the 7th MEB, some 3,000 men, had succumbed to a variety of intestinal disorders. The marines had proved their ability to get substantial forces to distant locations, but as yet they did not possess the logistic apparatus to feed them once they were there.[17]

Even with increasingly powerful air support, the marines and the lightly equipped airborne forces could not guarantee to stop an Iraqi drive south. They needed heavy equipment — the tanks, armoured personnel carriers (APCs), and heavy artillery of the 24th Infantry Division (Mechanised). The responsibility for transporting all this to the Gulf rested with Vice-Admiral Donovan's Strategic Sealift Force, part of MSC. Its key component was No 1 Fast Sealift Squadron (FSS), consisting of eight

55,000-ton Ro-Ro transports held in reserve at various ports in the south-eastern United States for just such a contingency. The Gallant Knight computer simulations had repeatedly demonstrated that from calculable factors — an average 24 hours to load the ships and a steady cruising speed of 30 knots — the FSS would take a total of 14 days to move the armour of the 24th Infantry Division from its embarkation port of Savannah, Georgia, to the Gulf. But no realistic exercises had been undertaken to provide a solid basis for these calculations since the ships had been acquired in the late 1970s. One naval officer commented:

> Imagine taking a 1978 car, draining the gasoline and all the fluids and putting it up on blocks for twelve years. Then you get a call saying the car has been taken off the blocks and has to be ready for a long trip in one week.[18]

His misgivings about preparing an FSS for sea after the same length of time seemed justified.

Against all the odds the first FSS, the USNS *Capella*, docked in Savannah only four days after the activation order. Then the real problems began. The Savannah Port Authority and the Coast Guard insisted on observing rigorous peacetime procedures which prohibited, among other things, the loading of ammunition in the inner harbour. Major-General Barry McCaffrey, the officer in charge of the 24th Infantry Division, was equally insistent that the tanks and APCs should be combat-loaded with fuel and ammunition. In the event of the pre-emptive Iraqi strike anticipated by Schwarzkopf, it was vital that they could fight from the very moment they disembarked in Saudi Arabia. A huge bureaucratic battle involving over 300 officials raged in Savannah.

Meanwhile, the vehicles of the 24th Infantry Division converged on the port from nine different bases in the south-eastern United States, movements which in themselves involved seemingly interminable negotiations with interstate highway authorities and the US railway system, Amtrack. It was little short of a miracle that the *Capella* sailed for Ad Damman on 14 August, loaded more or less in accordance with McCaffrey's wishes.[19] The second FSS ship activated, USNS *Antares*, sailed combat-loaded the following day, but after maintaining a punishing run of 27 knots for 48 hours, her engines burst into flames. *Antares* was towed ignominiously into the US base at Rota in southern Spain, where after several days her combat-loaded equipment was gingerly transferred to another FSS ship, the *Altair*, to complete the voyage to Ad Damman.[20]

Within a few hours of the activation order, MSC realised that the FSS needed assistance to transport the 24th Infantry Division's equipment to Saudi Arabia. On 10 August Donovan activated the so-called Ready Reserve Fleet (RRF), a fleet of 90 large Ro-Ro and container ships and freighters. The Ready Reserve was purportedly maintained at a level where it could put to sea within two to three weeks of an order being given. In fact the movement of 24th Infantry Division's equipment on two of the most modern ships fell ten days behind the planning schedule. Unfortunately one of them, the 45,000-ton *Admiral William F Callaghan*, hit a 'submerged object' on her return voyage through the Mediterranean and was towed to Greece for extensive repairs.[21]

Back in the USA crews were busy attempting to activate the RRF shipping necessary to sustain and reinforce US forces in the Gulf. The enterprise turned into a logistician's nightmare. It took an inordinate amount of time to make the 1970s-built large Cape-class Ro-Ros ready for sea: 45 days for the *Cape Johnson*, 61 for the *Cape Lambert* and a staggering 112 for the *Cape Diamond*. The *Cape Mohican* and the *Cape May*, pressed into service early, suffered engine breakdowns shortly after leaving port. Spectacular boiler explosions ended the equally short voyages of two older freighters, the *Gulf Bunker* and the *Washington*. By mid-September a storm of protest was brewing in the American press. Saddam Hussein had no submarines in the Atlantic; if the US merchant fleet continued to self-destruct with such apparently efficient regularity, taunted journalists, he would scarcely need them.[22]

American public opinion vented itself in frustrated outbursts, but the poor performance of the FSS and the RRF could have come as no surprise to anyone who had noted the steep decline in American merchant marine power since the 1960s. By 1990 skilled maritime manpower was thin on the ground. Few seamen understood how to operate the boiler technology of the 1960s and 1970s. Although Congress had voted $7 billion during the previous decade to maintain military sealift, the US Navy had diverted much of this sum to other purposes.[23] As *Time* magazine argued:

> The explanation of the logistic shortfall is simple enough: the armed services are not interested in spending money on programs that do not produce weapons. Promotions go to those officers who command warships and fly warplanes. Says a Navy captain: 'You don't make admiral driving freighters'.[24]

Within this context, it seems little short of miraculous that, by early November, MSC had activated and successfully sent to the Gulf some 70 ships.

From 8 August the man in charge of co-ordinating and orchestrating the arrival of US forces was Major-General William 'Gus' Pagonis. Pagonis had previously served as Deputy Chief of Staff in the Logistics Directorate of US Army Forces Command (FORSCAM) at Fort McPherson in Georgia. In the Gulf he faced a unique set of difficulties for which no training could have fully prepared him. Substantial logistic manpower support was unlikely to arrive for several weeks. It all depended on the mobilisation of reserves; and it was only on 22 August that President Bush signed an executive order authorising the call-up of 200,000 reservists. At first Pagonis, with a staff of five, literally operated from the back of a truck.[25] As his staff slowly expanded he occupied a headquarters at Dhahran (so as not to overlap with the virtually autonomous USMC HQ in Al Jubail). Pagonis had to find transport, accommodation, food, water, fuel and a thousand other essential commodities for the growing 'teeth'. His only option was to use what logisticians call Host Nation Support (HNS) — which in this case meant contracting from the Saudis. But existing Department of Defense regulations, not rescinded until 14 November, dictated an upper limit of $200,000 for any single contract. Consequently any large project had to be subdivided, with each component element negotiated under a separate contract. The task would have been hard enough in the USA. In Saudi

Arabia, where the US forces were dealing with Arab hosts who spoke a completely different cultural and legal language, frustration and misunderstanding severely impeded the process of negotiation.[26]

Several young captains experienced their first taste of real power in the organisation of HNS. They found themselves making $200,000 decisions daily and building rapidly growing empires. The buses which met the first elements of the 82nd Airborne Division on their arrival in Saudi Arabia had been hired by Captain James A Pabon, who controlled 35 buses and 10 flatbed trucks as the nucleus of his 9001st Medium Truck Company (Provisional). His drivers (largely Filipinos and Pakistanis) had some knowledge of English. Several also possessed excellent entrepreneurial skills. Pabon and his drivers together established the 9001st as one of the largest independent transport agencies in the Middle East. By December they were running nearly 500 buses and trucks. Captain Larry S Asbill, another of Pagonis's young officers, built up an impressive real-estate empire. He hired cold-storage facilities, hangars and land for tent cities. Through his real-estate contacts he managed to secure the exclusive use of Al Khobar Towers, a 4,000-unit apartment block in the town of Al Khobar. By the end of August he had filled each of its air-conditioned five-bedroom apartments with 15 to 25 troops: relative luxury compared with the squalid living conditions experienced by some units.

Captain John S Arellano's job, if less appealing, was even more vital to troop comfort. He ran the sewage and garbage disposal and laundry service with admirable effciency. Arellano's 'honey wagons', the sewage disposal trucks, became a familiar sight on the roads of eastern Saudi Arabia. Some of his drivers operated a lucrative sideline, transporting unaccredited 'non-pool' journalists to remote units. Transport by honey wagon offered advantages which outweighed the obvious drawbacks: speed (traffic gave them right of way) and immunity from Saudi and US military police searches. Arellano's laundry chain was a perfect model of free enterprise. US units often arrived in the Gulf wearing kit filthy from field exercises in the United States. Arellano, who had subcontracted virtually every launderette in the Gulf region, hired dozens of local van drivers to create a laundry delivery service which could almost rival the 24-hour claims of its US-inspired models. It was the biggest laundry service between the Nile and the Indus.[27]

Such ingenuity was worthy of the freewheeling logistic spirit displayed by Lieutenant Milo Mindebender and Sergeant Ernie Bilko, the fictional heroes of Joseph Heller's *Catch 22* and Phil Silvers' 1950s' television series. The enterprising logistics officer had become a familiar figure in American popular culture. But Pagonis faced problems more intractable than the establishment of an infrastructure. Since the early 1960s the US military had committed itself to the computerisation of logistic supply systems, since full-scale automation would enable it to cut down on expensive logistic manpower. By the early 1970s the Direct Support Unit Standard Supply System (DS4) had been issued to almost all units. When, for example, a tank commander required supplies for his troops and vehicles, he tapped the information on to his microcomputer keyboard. This would be transmitted in encoded form to the unit commander's system, then automatically consolidated and retransmitted to divisional, corps and army levels. Thousands of consolidated and sorted requests would then be transmitted via an electronic gateway to the appropriate depot in the USA. It was a more complex version of the technology used by most modern retail outlets to reorder stock from warehouses. At the depot the stores would be packed and sent out — by air if high priority, by sea if low priority. During the Second World War the ordering and despatching of supplies had taken weeks and millions of man-hours. In theory, the DS4 should have performed the same task in a matter of hours.

Computerisation generated its own standing jokes in the American Army. 'What happens if your finger slips when tapping in the code? You get a toothbrush instead of the transmission for a heavy tank.' In fact the computer system made built-in allowances for human error. The problems were far more serious, stemming, ironically, from the rapidity with which information technology had advanced since the 1970s. By May 1990 computer experts at the US Army Information Systems Software Development Center at Lee (DCL) in Washington were in the process of replacing the now obsolescent DS4 with a new system. The Standard Army Retail Supply System (SARSS), the latest in state-of-the-art technology, was infinitely faster and had almost unlimited capacity. By early August work was almost finished on updating the 82nd Airborne's computer system, but had yet to begin on those of the 24th Infantry Division or the 101st Air Assault Division. When the Gulf Crisis broke out, the 82nd Airborne possessed a computer system which, for all its sophistication, proved a white elephant. Not only was it incompatible with those used by the other two divisions of XVIII Airborne Corps, but it could not communicate with Corps or Army HQs, or for that matter with most depots in America.[28]

For a time the logisticians resorted to the methods tried and tested by their grandfathers — carbon invoices, file cards, despatch riders and telephone calls. Meanwhile, Pagonis flew-in computer experts from DCL and IBM to create interfaces between the different systems. The divisions had deployed with computers which spanned several generations of technology, from the late 1960s to the late 1980s. Linking-up systems proved extremely difficult, and breakdowns were frequent. The system was kept running only through the expertise and experience of a handful of computer troubleshooters.[29] As Pagonis later commented: 'Everything goes wrong every minute. What you do is fix it.'[30] The US Army computer system, in some cases held together by chewing gum and paper clips, soon began to resemble some vast Heath Robinson contraption: the ironic antithesis of minimalist microchip technology. It was now taking up to 12 days to process orders within Saudi Arabia before they could even be despatched from Riyadh. For all the billions of dollars invested, motorcycle despatch riders often proved faster.[31]

Pagonis and his staff followed the best logistic traditions. They begged, borrowed and improvised with impressive ingenuity. By the end of October they were sustaining the 97,000 troops of XVIII Airborne Corps. By then 42,000 US Marines had also arrived, close to one quarter of the USMC total active-duty strength. More than 31,000 were ashore with what was now known as the 1st Marine Expeditionary Force. The remainder, the 4th Marine Expeditionary Brigade and 13th Marine Expeditionary Unit, were kept afloat as the landing element of a strong amphibious task force. The fear that Saddam Hussein might exploit US weakness and attack was long since past.

The Coalition forces

Although the American build-up was by far the most spectacular, other nations had been committing forces to Saudi Arabia since early August. By 6 August a 2,000-strong Egyptian commando force had deployed to Hafar al-Batin. Meanwhile, 1,200 Moroccan troops deployed to Egypt, where they waited for the decision of the Arab League meeting on 10 August before flying on to join the Egyptians.[32] These were just the advance guard of what grew to be a numerically considerable Arab force. The Egyptians and Moroccans were soon joined by 10,000 troops of the Gulf Co-operation Council (GCC) Rapid Deployment Force. Shortly after, the Egyptians responded to the American cancellation of their $7 billion debt by reinforcing their contingent to 35,000 troops.

Syrian participation in the build-up created deep misgivings. By November President Assad had responded to Saudi promises of financial aid by sending a substantial contingent to the Gulf. The Syrian 9th Armoured Division, sailing to the Saudi Red Sea port of Yanbu in early November, joined up with advance forces. The Syrians deployed 19,000 troops, swelling the Arab Coalition commitment to a not inconsiderable 65,000 men. Arab governments were worried about too close a display of co-operation with the USA; they also feared that the similarity between their own and Iraqi enemy equipment would endanger their troops in a battle. Some Americans also harboured the unspoken suspicion that their Arab allies might display little enthusiasm in fighting fellow Arabs from opposing forces. It proved relatively easy to sustain the GCC forces, given that the drive from their own countries was only a matter of 400–480 km (250–300 miles). Sustaining Egyptian and Syrian forces proved more difficult and consequently more impressive. Both nations chose Yanbu as their main logistic base. They ran convoys from Yanbu across Saudi Arabia to where their troops were based at Hafar al-Batin, a distance of some 1,920 km (1,200 miles).[33]

The United States' relationship with France was just as ambiguous as its relationship with Syria. The French government was deeply divided about France's involvement in the Gulf conflict. After all, Jean-Pierre Chévènement, the French Defence Minister, had been a founder member of the Iraqi-French Friendship Society, and until 1990 France had supplied Iraq with military equipment worth some $25 billion.[34] But after Iraq seized the French ambassador's residence in Kuwait on 14 September, President François Mitterrand felt sufficiently confident to commit 4,000 ground troops along with armour and air support.[35] In early December these were reinforced to a full division of 14,000. At first, Mitterrand made it clear that these troops, commanded by Lieutenant-General Michel Roquejoffre, were to be integrated into the strategic group of Arab allies and were to have no direct link with the US forces.[36]

The French *Division Daguet* (the codename for their part of the deployment) was built around the regular core of the 6th Light Armoured Division. The conscripts who had formed more than half of the original 6th Light Armoured Division were not required to serve outside metropolitan France. For Gulf service, Chévènement was forced to replace them with regulars from other units. Although this led to several weeks of organisational confusion, the French deployment as a whole proceeded with admirable efficiency. Unlike the USA, France had over 30 years' experience of sending out light forces to intervene in trouble spots, chiefly in French-speaking Africa. French logisticians were skilled in deployment over long distances in relatively hostile environments; the Gulf deployment, albeit on a divisional rather than a brigade scale, posed no major difficulties. Some 50 SNCF (French railway system) trains moved the components of the division to Toulon and Marseilles, and they sailed to Yanbu on nine specially chartered French-owned Ro-Ro ships. Sustaining this force later involved another 40 ships. The French set up their logistic base — some 4,000 International Shipping Organisation (ISO) containers — between the Egyptians and the Syrians. Meanwhile, the bulk of the *Division Daguet* travelled overland to King Khaled Military City. Their AMX tanks, equipped with dual wheel/track capability, travelled on their tyres while their own heavy-lift equipment, 250 logistic transport trailer vehicles (VLTRs) and 55 tanker trucks, transported containerised supplies. US logisticians could only admire the clockwork precision of the French, although Schwarzkopf harboured a few doubts about their reliability as allies.[37]

Operation 'Granby'

The British Army was only minimally involved in the early stages of the Gulf commitment. The British deployment, codenamed Operation 'Granby', began as a British Royal Air Force (RAF)-dominated operation, controlled from a joint headquarters in a bunker complex at RAF High Wycombe. By the start of September 1990 the British Army had deployed only three companies of signallers and engineers in the Gulf, in sharp contrast to the large numbers of ground troops already sent by the Arabs and promised by the French. Instead, the British invested their efforts in air and sea reinforcements. Squadrons of Panavia Tornado F.3 air-defence fighters and SEPECAT Jaguar and Tornado GR.1 ground-attack fighters flew to bases in Saudi Arabia and Bahrain, and additional ships were despatched to the Armilla Patrol in the Gulf.

But the USA's commitment to sending in ground forces was steadily increasing; an indication that a major deployment would soon be coming from the British Army. August and early September 1990 witnessed frenetic activity in a number of army headquarters. Computer consoles hummed in the main Ministry of Defence (MoD) building in London, in the headquarters of United Kingdom Land Forces (HQ UKLF) in Wilton, Surrey, and at the headquarters of I British Corps (HQ 1 (BR) Corps) in the FGR, as officers arranged and rearranged orders of battle (orbats). No single brigade emerged as an obvious choice for despatch to the Gulf. Unlike the French, the British had no light division capable of operating in desert conditions. From HQ UKLF's viewpoint, a logical choice rested on the 24th Airmobile Brigade, accompanied by the 5th Airborne Brigade and the 3rd Commando Brigade. Pleas for a different type of deployment came from the cavalry and the Royal Tank Regiment. Like all units, they did not want to be left out. Moreover, on the horizon loomed defence cuts which gave the army little option but to reduce its numbers substantially. Armour-heavy units knew they would be severely affected, and it was scarcely surprising that German-based cavalry units pressed hard to be included in any expeditionary force to the Gulf.[38]

By early September four headquarters were involved in deciding orbats — HQ UKLF, HQ 1(BR) Corps, MoD and the Joint HQ at RAF High Wycombe. They were floating at least seven different deployment options. The USA helped the British to make up their minds. What they required above all was a large number of modern heavy tanks. This demand lay at the core of the appeal issued by James Baker, US Secretary of State, to the United States' NATO allies from Brussels on 10 September. Four days later a cheer went up from the officers of the British 7th Armoured Brigade assembled in the Jerboa Theatre in Fallingbostal in the FRG when they received confirmation that they were off to Al Jubail to be brigaded with the USMC.

The decision to deploy had been made, but lengthy disputes soon followed concerning the brigade's strength. Once again, economic and political factors coloured the debate. HQ 1(BR) Corps insisted that the brigade be at least 12,000 strong. The MoD, mindful of Treasury objections to excessive cost, argued for an upper limit of 6,000; too small a unit to function independently of American logistic support. For a time confusion reigned until the orbat was stabilised at 11,500.[39] HQ 1(BR) Corps decided that the 7th Armoured Brigade would deploy equipped with the very best tanks and vehicles that the British Army of the Rhine (BAOR) possessed, and with a sufficiently large set of stores and ammunition to sustain combat for at least 12 days. While the 7th Armoured Brigade's regiments trained, attached members of the Royal Electrical and Mechanical Engineers (REME) worked round the clock cannibalising tanks and vehicles which less fortunate units had been ordered to send to the 7th Armoured Brigade. Fallingbostal came to resemble a giant military scrapyard. The Royal Corps of Transport (RCT) and the Royal Army Ordnance Corps (RAOC) faced a new challenge. British logisticians in Germany (unlike those employed by USCENTCOM or France's *Force d'Action Rapide*) had never tackled the problem of moving *materiel* and personnel out of the FGR. One officer (with ironic British understatement) drily recorded the 'great interest' with which he and his fellow officers greeted the order that 'the deployment will be carried out by *reversing* the well-tried method of reinforcing BAOR'.[40]

Meanwhile, the Joint Forces HQ at High Wycombe worked hard to co-ordinate the land, air and sea movement of *materiel* and personnel. The first US deployment had been a mad dash against time. The British could afford to adopt a more logical and traditional sequence — the initial deployment of logistic troops followed by fighting troops. But problems still arose. One of the first units of the 7th Armoured Brigade to fly into Al Jubail was a small Local Resource Section (LRS) of the 9th Ordnance Battalion. It was tasked with contracting for transport, accommodation, food and labour from the local economy. But, owing to an MoD misunderstanding, no advance arrangements had been made to supply it with cash or letters of credit on its arrival. With a nerve that would do credit to many an impecunious subaltern, members of the LRS motored across the causeway to Bahrain, where they negotiated a £1 million credit with Kanoo Ltd, the shipping agents for the Royal Navy in the Gulf. They then got to work. By this time their American counterparts had been at work more than six weeks and had built up large transport fleets. The LRS operated in a seller's market and some of its officers were irritated by a policy that forced them to negotiate every contract on an *ad hoc* basis. Although such restraints were financially prudent, some officers involved in drawing up contracts felt that had they at times been granted more latitude they would have been more efficient. Operating in the wake of American logistic operations that had already contracted much of the local transport and accommodation, its achievement was impressive. Five months later it had organised more than 2,300 local purchase orders and some 40 major contracts at a cost of £29 million.[41]

Ordnance depots in Britain pulled out the stops to despatch supplies to the Gulf. Staff at the giant Donnington depot, working frenetically on 12-hour-on/12-hour-off shifts, managed to meet an incredible 28,000 logistic demands from the 7th Armoured Brigade. An unfortunate episode occurred when a visiting group of civil servants tasked with reducing army staff happened to chance on a group of men in the Donnington canteen slumped fast asleep after a gruelling 12-hour shift. One at least was sufficiently awake to overhear caustic remarks about overmanning which led to several equally frank ripostes. The Bicester Ordnance Depot stepped up an equivalent pace. Its normal load of 30 Red Star parcel priority issues per day surged to a staggering total of 2,643 per day.[42]

Meanwhile, RAF Strike Command worked to establish an air bridge to Saudi Arabia. BAOR, unlike the US XVIII Airborne Corps, had little experience of deploying by air, but soon learned to adapt to circumstances with a wartime flexibility that jettisoned official weights and tie-down schemes. When half-ton landrovers arrived at airfields such as Gutersloh weighing in at threequarters of a ton owing to modifications such as anti-mine armour welded to chassis undersides, official procedures became irrelevant. Loading staff simply emptied trucks of their contents and loaded them into aircraft on their sides, then crammed every available nook and cranny of the aircraft with loose stores. This *ad hoc* technique speeded operations but caused problems for RAF logistics officers at the receiving end at Al Jubail. Some airway bills bore so little relation to aircraft contents that one officer described them as mere 'sheets of fantasy'.[43]

Light equipment and most personnel travelled by air. Tanks, other vehicles and virtually all the ammunition went by ship. The Royal Navy's Royal Fleet Auxiliaries were the first to sail from Marchwood and Bremerhaven on 28 September, loaded mainly with ammunition. During the Falklands conflict of 1982 the army had relied on British 'ships taken up from trade' (STUFT). This time round the Defence Operations Movement Staff (DOMS) in the MoD decided to charter ships on London's Baltic Exchange, the world's largest system for matching cargoes to ships. So depressed was the world shipping market that several British shipping owners offered the use of their vessels, only to have them rejected in favour of foreign ships. Disappointed shipowners hinted darkly at all manner of corruption, but in most cases their vessels did not meet immediate requirements.

Contracting foreign ships certainly made financial sense, but it sometimes hampered the despatch of 7th Armoured Brigade. The vehicles, tanks and ammunition were assembled at Bremerhaven and Emden, where one REME officer recalled: 'the loading did not go as smoothly as planned, what with the ships' masters refusing to move loads they'd been hired to carry'. On some occasions the wrong vehicles were loaded. A driver who used a giant Foden recovery vehicle to tow a tank aboard the *Dana Cimbra* discovered that he did not have room to manoeuvre it off the ship again. The recovery vehicle sailed to Saudi Arabia with the tanks.[44]

Most regiments insisted that small parties accompany the ships. Those that did not sometimes found to their cost that, by the time their vehicles reached Al Jubail, they had usually been stripped clean of any personal kit. For the men themselves, the Mediterranean voyage was no cruise. Most ships left Bremerhaven and Emden in the early weeks of October, just in time to hit the full force of the gales produced by the autumnal equinox in the Bay of Biscay. Soldiers had ample opportunity to reflect on their good fortune in being chosen for Gulf service. Lieutenant Ian McDonnell of the RCT took 31 days rather than the 21 he had anticipated to get to Al Jubail.[45] A particularly unpleasant time was had by all who sailed on the *Oxfordshire*. One REME craftsman recalled:

> There was a lot of a swell on, the ship was going up and down, to and fro and apparently, although we know this cannot be true, round and round. From Bremerhaven to the Gulf we averaged three 'hughies' [bouts of vomiting] per day, per man. The chess board suffered a direct hit from Craftsman Dodger Green.[46]

The *Dana Cimbra*, the first ship carrying 7th Armoured Brigade vehicles, docked at Al Jubail on 18 October, just two months after the arrival of the USMC's prepositioned ships from Diego Garcia. A week earlier the RCT's 50th Movements Control Squadron had arrived to take over part of the port management from the USMC. It experienced some of the problems which had bedevilled the marines. When overworked cranes jammed the RCT were forced to resort to shipboard cranes to unload supplies. The antiquated side-mounted cranes on board some of the old merchantmen hired through the Baltic Exchange created serious worries. Swinging out over the quay, they caused the ship to rock violently during unloading —

very unnerving when the load was munitions. A REME non-commissioned officer recalled: 'one or two of the items got an unexpected wash when they were given an "ocean depth test" during unloading.' Even modern container ships presented problems. The British Army possessed only eight container unloading vehicles, five of which were soon at Al Jubail. The British were also far less familiar with handling ISO containers than were the US forces. Although skilled military personnel did their best to supervise the civilian workers who packed many of the containers, occasionally mistakes were made. Container manifests sometimes bore no relation to what was found inside the containers. In some cases more than eight weeks were to elapse before the contents of particular containers were identified and issued to units.[47]

Meanwhile, the 7th Armoured Brigade was arriving by air. The troops were quartered in two huge sheds on the docks at Al Jubail and in a rapidly growing tented encampment soon known as Baldrick Lines, after the hapless soldier in the popular 'Blackadder' BBC television series. Here they waited for their equipment to arrive on the slow boats from Marchwood, Emden and Bremerhaven. At first they depended on the marines for everything, particularly food. Many quickly rejected the MREs. By the time that it reached the British lines, the food supplied by the marines' galleys 15 km away had usually deteriorated beyond recognition. One soldier commented: 'After two or three meals, a Jerboa lightly tossed in sand and sautéed in camel fat became appetising.'[48]

By the end of October, when most of the brigade with its logistic support had arrived, the relationship between the marines and the British began to change. The marines were at the limit of their logistic system, still living on supplies taken directly off their ships. The British, with their newly-operational logistic system, now began to sustain the marines. Food became a bargaining counter. British soldiers with nicknames like 'Arfur Daley', 'Sharkey', 'Fingers', 'Fiddler' and 'Dodger' drove a hard deal. They traded British composite rations and Army Catering Corps cooked meals for a bewildering variety of US equipment — machine guns, Humvees, anti-tank missiles and the excellent US camp-bed, of which some 30,000 found their way into British lines.[49]

The reinforcements
Even before ships and aircraft had deposited the last elements of XVIII Airborne Corps and the French and British contingents at Dhahran, Al Jubail and Yanbu, Schwarzkopf at CENTCOM in Riyadh was urging Washington to authorise an offensive to clear the Iraqis from Kuwait. He was adamant that he needed more forces to guarantee a convincing victory. On 21 October Defense Secretary 'Dick' Cheney and General Colin Powell agreed to a massive increase in forces. President Bush gave his formal ratification on 30 October, but shrewdly delayed a press statement until 8 November, two days after the US Senate's mid-term elections. The new Gulf reinforcements were to be drawn from the US VII Corps stationed in Germany and the 1st Infantry Division (Mechanised) from Fort Riley in

Kansas. On 15 November the British responded by announcing that their own brigade would shortly be reinforced to division strength.

Germany had not witnessed such a large-scale movement of tanks, vehicles and troops since 1945. Long convoys rolled along the *autobahns* from southern and central Germany, heading for the North Sea ports. The US VII Corps alone mobilised some 50,000 vehicles, including more than 7,000 tracked armoured fighting vehicles (AFVs). Although on the British side only the 4th Armoured Brigade was involved, the process entailed moving British equipment more appropriate to a corps; some 10,000 vehicles, of which roughly 1,500 were tracked. United States and British ammunition depots embarked on a vast loading operation. When stocks ran low, the German *Bundeswehr* began an equally impressive movement from its own depots. Over 40,000 vehicles were required to shift the ammunition alone. If figures are included for the transportation of US and British servicemen to airheads, the entire operation used over 100,000 military vehicles.

It took the British some time to adjust to the new movement, known as Granby 1.5. During Granby 1, RCT officers had enjoyed a free run of the FGR's excellent transportation system. They now had to dovetail their plans into the much larger US movement which had begun a week earlier. The US forces had contracted virtually all of the FGR's rolling stock; only 150 covered railway wagons remained for British use. Consequently, nearly all the British movement, including 70 per cent of the ammunition, had to travel by road, but the expertise acquired by British logisticians during Granby 1 enabled them to overcome these minor irritations. The US troops, despite the advantage of a prior claim on German facilities, were often forced to employ British logisticians to sort out their log-jams and to expedite movements to ports. A good example was the vital role played by the RAOC's 154th Forward Advanced Depot (FAD) at Wulfen. The RAOC managed a substantial reduction in the trucking time for American ammunition convoys driving across southern Germany (a total of 2,200 trucks carrying 40,000 tons) by transferring their loads at Wulfen on to the German rail network. In all, 14 trains were crossloaded in this way and despatched northwards to Emden. The *Bundeswehr* stepped in with a company of the 192nd Panzer Grenadiers to provide vital base security against potential terrorist attack. Throughout Germany a similarly close and effective alliance of US, British and German troops prevailed.

MSC had been warned to expect a new deployment in mid-October. When Bush made his announcement on 8 November, 12 ships which had recently completed the movement of XVIII Airborne Corps lay docked in Germany's North Sea ports waiting for new cargoes. Unlike XVIII Airborne Corps, VII Corps was an armour-heavy formation with a correspondingly large number of heavy vehicles and substantial ammunition. This posed new large-scale logistic problems. MSC had to find shipping to move some 900,000 square metres (eight million square feet) of unit equipment from Europe and some 500,000 square metres (five million square feet) from the USA; more than the sum total stored by US forces in Britain for the liberation of France in June 1944. Donovan had already used 173 ships in the initial deployments. These would have to be supplemented by additional shipping contracted on the Baltic Exchange. By the time the operation had ended, over 25 per cent of additional US *materiel* had been carried on foreign-flagged ships. As with the German railways, the prior US claim to transport systems posed problems for the British. Although British DOMS had been contracting shipping well before 15 November, the US contractors got there first. The depressed shipping market enjoyed an unexpected fillip. Charter prices spiralled to giddy heights. According to experts at Lloyds of London, Britain paid far more than it should have for the operation. In all, it cost over £186 million.[50]

Much of the *matériel* required to sustain the new build-up was drawn from stocks held by US forces in six vast Prepositioned War Reserve Materiel Stores (PWRMS) located in Germany, Belgium, and the USA itself. The sheer size of the operation is indicated by the fact that, by February 1991, nearly 50 per cent of these war reserve stocks had been utilised. The demand on certain items, such as heavy-lift engines, was so great that new systems had to be devised to get them to Saudi Arabia as quickly as possible. The US Defense Logistics Agency, responsible for negotiating contracts with civilian manufacturers, ran a shuttle service from factories to MAC airbases for shipment on the newly established high-priority 'Desert Express' air service. A number of manufacturers, especially those engaged in heavy engineering, found the military demand so great that a 'guns and butter' system was no longer possible. Roger Penske, director of a leading motor engineering company, temporarily devoted his entire output to the Gulf cause. Other manufacturers, either more worried or less patriotic, tried to juggle military demands without forgoing civilian contracts. By the new year 1991 output was simply not meeting demand. On 9 January President Bush issued an Executive Order compelling civilian manufacturers to give first priority to military contracts. The strains of preparing for even a limited war had pushed the executive along the road towards a controlled economy.[51]

'Hail Mary'

On 10 November 1990, just two days after Bush officially announced the new build-up, Schwarzkopf presided over a meeting of senior staff in the officers' club at Dhahran. With a theatrical flourish he whisked the drape from a map board covered by broad blue arrows sweeping in a giant arc hundreds of kilometres from Saudi Arabia through south-eastern Iraq into northern Kuwait. Lieutenant-General Gary E Luck, commander of XVIII Airborne Corps, recalled that Schwarzkopf said: 'Okay, boys, this is what I wanna do, now you think about this and come back and tell me how I'm gonna do it.' Some of the audience gasped. One logistician reputedly gave a loud groan.[52] Schwarzkopf intended to outflank Iraqi defences along the Kuwaiti-Saudi border by sending the bulk of his forces well to the west and then trapping the Iraqi Army in Kuwait in a giant pincer. This entailed moving the XVIII Airborne Corps (then located in defensive positions between Dhahran and An Nuayriya) some 640 km north-west to the general area of Rafha, only 16 km from the Iraqi border, and 320 km (200 miles) to the west of the point at which the borders of Kuwait, Iraq and Saudi Arabia meet.

By this time the XVIII Airborne Corps had reached full strength — 118,000 personnel, 28,000 vehicles (of which 5,000 were tracked) and 1,000 helicopters. Moving such a large force to Rafha, let alone sustaining it once in position, would pose enormous difficulties. But Schwarzkopf's plans did not stop there. On their arrival in Saudi Arabia he proposed to move VII Corps (43,000 wheeled and 7,000 tracked vehicles and 150,000 men) more than 560 km (350 miles) inland to an area north-west of Hafar al-Batin. Had these moves been staggered over a period of several months they would have proved more than enough to test the ability of any logistic officer, but Schwarzkopf demanded the near impossible by insisting that they be carried out simultaneously. The time-window was further reduced by the need to wait until hostilities had broken out, when CENTCOM air attacks could destroy Iraq's ability to conduct aerial reconnaissance.

The need to move both formations quickly, secretly and simultaneously created additional problems. Only two roads existed along which forces could deploy. One of these, the Tapline Road, ran parallel to an oil pipeline which passed 1,600 km (1,000 miles) to the north-west from Dhahran to the Jordanian capital, Amman. At no point did it diverge more than a few kilometres from Iraq's southern border. The other route was a new highway which ran inland 480 km (300 miles) from Dhahran to Riyadh, before swinging 650 km (350 miles) to the north via the newly constructed King Khalid Military City to join the Tapline Road at Hafar al-Batin. Schwarzkopf proposed sending the bulk of XVIII Airborne Corps down the latter (codenamed Main Supply Route or MSR Sultan) to Hafar al-Batin, from where the corps would turn left for the 320-km (200-mile) drive west to its deployment area for the attack near Rafha. Meanwhile, VII Corps was to move directly north-west along the Tapline Road (codenamed MSR Dodge) to its pre-attack positions to the west of Hafar al-Batin. Logisticians predicted a large traffic jam at Hafar al-Batin when the convoys on Sultan and Dodge met up. Schwarzkopf proposed a means to avoid this: VII Corps would swing into the desert south of Hafar al-Batin and then move *across* MSR Sultan before swinging north again to cross MSR Dodge. This meant that VII Corps would cross over XVIII Airborne Corps' route of advance not once but twice. Schwarzkopf's transport officers were convinced that such an elaborate criss-cross exercise could not be accomplished without serious confusion.[53]

Only the French representatives greeted the plan with unqualified approval. Although still awaiting official sanction from Paris, *Division Daguet* had been placed on the extreme left flank of XVIII Airborne Corps. Schwarzkopf's plans would enable the French to play a major and spectacular role, advancing deep into Iraq. The British were less pleased. Their 1st Armoured Division remained deployed with the Marine Expeditionary Force on a coastal axis. This obviously subsidiary attack might also entail heavy casualties to no great effect. On 4 December Lieutenant-General Sir Peter de la Billiere, commander of the steadily growing British forces, gave his Headquarters Land Forces (HQLF) 72 hours to prepare a presentation for Lieutenant-General Calvin Waller, CENTCOM's deputy commander. HQLF's logistic officers proved that the British 1st Armoured Division had the logistic capability to deploy and advance with US VII Corps. It could be done — just. A few days later a presentation team from High Wycombe, using the same facts and figures, managed to convince Schwarzkopf of the operation's feasibility. The British 1st Armoured Division was now assigned to the right flank of VII Corps. Their place with the marines was assumed by the 1st Brigade of US 2nd Armored Division, the 'Tiger Brigade'.[54]

While the scale of Schwarzkopf's outflanking strategy was sinking in, the marines had been busy. The success of 'Hail Mary' depended on tricking the Iraqis into believing that an attack would come either directly from the south or from the sea. On 18 November the 4th MEB launched Exercise Imminent Thunder, a large-scale amphibious exercise given extensive media coverage. Two weeks later, marine logisticians began to construct a base at Kirbit, an old abandoned runway 40 km (25 miles) south of the Kuwait border and 80 km (50 miles) inland from the small port of Al Misha'ab. With the MEF 160 km (100 miles) to the south and only a screening force of GCC and Saudi troops between them and the border, the marines built what proved to be the largest logistic base in USMC history. On 6 February, nearly three weeks after the beginning of the air campaign, the marines went one better. At Gravel Plains, a location adjacent to the Kuwaiti border and within sight of Iraqi observation posts, they calmly set about constructing a 44-hectare (11,280-acre) depot. The ammunition supply point alone covered three hectares (780 acres), divided into 151 separate cells, each protected by berms which, if laid end-to-end, would have extended for 40 km (24 miles). It stored a cool 17.5 million litres (5 million gallons) of fuel. Al Khanjar, the Arabic word for dagger, was the name given the base by the marines' commander, Lieutenant-General Walter Boomer. Pointing directly north into Kuwait territory, it must have seemed just that to the Iraqis in their observation posts.[55]

Back in Dhahran and Riyadh, CENTCOM's logisticians were devising ways to implement the 'Hail Mary' ploy. The movement of such vast forces demanded considerable ingenuity, and Pagonis and his men rose to the occasion with their customary flexibility. They would use a railway running from Ad Damman to Riyadh to shift 5,000 ISO containers of XVIII Airborne Corps' supplies. This would reduce the pressure on the first leg of the journey along MSR Sultan. They also planned to make full use of available aircraft: C-130s were destined to carry virtually all of XVIII Airborne Corps' personnel to improvised airfields around Rafha. But logistic ingenuity was hard-stretched to solve the stubborn problem of how to shift so much heavy equipment within such a narrow time-window: more than 12,000 tanks and AFVs, close to one million tons of ammunition, and millions of gallons of fuel and water. The US Army simply did not have enough Heavy Equipment Transporters (HETs) in Saudi Arabia, or, for that matter, anywhere else.[56]

Christmas and New Year 1990–91 witnessed the 'great Arabian truck hunt'. The US forces contracted virtually every truck they could find in

Saudi Arabia and organised them into provisional truck battalions. The search became obsessive. When British logisticians somehow managed to find and contract 30 unclaimed trucks for their own use, the British Civil Secretary strongly advised that the contract be cancelled, ostensibly to avoid upsetting the Americans. Pagonis and his men looked further afield. They hired Egyptian tank transporters along with some Italian military trucks. The dissolution of the German Democratic Republic (GDR) proved an unexpected boon; former GDR tank transporters became available for hire. Czechoslovakia also provided the US forces with 100 heavy transporters. By early February Pagonis had secured 4,000 heavy vehicles of all types, including 1,300 HETs for transporting tanks. US Army transport companies were assigned to moving the XVIII Airborne Corps along MSR Sultan. The provisional truck battalions, manned largely by Filipino, Pakistani, Egyptian and South Korean drivers, were assigned to the movement of VII Corps along MSR Dodge.[57]

Pagonis knew that he had a massive task on his hands. He persuaded Schwarzkopf to allow some prepositioning of stocks before the air campaign began. This took place in three depots. Two were located along MSR Sultan, too far from the Iraqi border to arouse the enemy's suspicions. The third, codenamed Log Base Alpha, was located along MSR Dodge, so close to the Kuwait border that the Iraqis would probably think it was designed to support an offensive directly into Kuwait. The prepositioning of supplies at these bases formed Phase Alpha of the logistic plan Pagonis outlined to his staff on 4 December. The second part of the plan, Phase Bravo, the deployment of the troops and fighting vehicles of XVIII Airborne and VII Corps, would begin as soon as the air campaign had effectively blinded the Iraqis.[58]

US Army transport plied along MSR Sultan in relative safety, but those who travelled along MSR Dodge literally took their lives in their hands. The horrifically graphic accounts later given by those who made the journey show just how deeply the experience had seared itself on their memories. Many of the US provisional transport battalions' trucks were close to falling apart. Sergeant Sheila Jansen, one of four Women's Royal Army Corps (WRAC) non-commissioned officers (NCOs) in the Gulf to hold a heavy goods vehicle licence, was drafted in to drive one of the few 'Choggie' wagons, a Mercedes HGVI articulated fuel tanker, which the British had been allowed to hire. She remarked:

> The vehicles would not have passed an MOT [Ministry of Transport road-worthiness test] back home. They were very basic to say the least. A cushion and a plank of wood made a very neat driver's seat. Who needed a stereo when the gear box made such good vibes?[59]

The road was appalling. Dodge began as a six-lane dual carriageway but soon degenerated into what one RCT officer described as 'a narrow two-lane death trap'. Another RCT officer recalled:

> The road was not wide enough for large vehicles, road markings were non-existent, many vehicles did not have lights that worked, vehicles travelled too quickly, drivers were tired and the local drivers drove like men possessed.[60]

On MSR Dodge an RCT NCO warned one new arrival 'to expect the unexpected, especially if overtaken by a civilian driver in a 50,000-litre tanker on the outside of a blind bend going uphill'. Warrant Officer D G McLaughlin of REME gave a vivid account of his trip to Log Base Alpha:

> Crashed pickups, overturned trucks and tankers littered both sides of the road amidst multiple lanes of speeding American trucks tearing along each side of the road regardless of direction. Even this chaos had to grind to a halt when an American ammunition truck caught fire and exploded a couple of hundred yards ahead of our convoy.[61]

More Coalition servicemen and civilians contracted to the Coalition were killed on MSR Dodge than in the actual ground war. The fact that the US and British forces were able to build up substantial stocks says much for their skill and fortitude.

Once the air war began, the speedy movement of vehicles along the MSRs would prove vital. Supervision of the task was assigned to the 318th Transportation Agency (Movement Control), a New York-based US reserve unit. Its members keyed vital information into their computers: vehicle numbers, distances to be covered, time available. Military police posts and hundreds of signposts lined the routes. The corps' movements, broken down into individual convoys, were ready and waiting for the air assault to start. The British decided to begin their move early. On 14 January the 7th Tank Transporter Regiment RCT began moving the British 1st Armoured Division's 3,000 armoured and heavy vehicles westwards. It was just as well, because someone in the 318th had forgotten to key in the existence of the British, with nearly 15,000 vehicles. The 318th managed to find space along the route for the 1st British Armoured Division, but it was a close-run thing.[62]

On the night of 16/17 January Coalition aircraft screamed down on Iraq and Kuwait. An endless ribbon of headlights suddenly pierced the darkness as the corps began their movement. Some 21 days later the Coalition forces were in position — 12,000 AFVs, 250,000 men and one million tons of ammunition. It was now that the waiting began.

Notes

1. For background to CENTCOM, see Raphael Iungerich, 'US Rapid Deployment Forces — US CENTCOM — what is it? Can it do the job?', *Armed Forces Journal International*, October 1984, pp 84–106.
2. Amitav Acharya, *US Military Strategy in the Gulf* (Routledge, London, 1989), pp 45 and 113.
3. Roger Cohen and Claudio Gatti, *In the Eye of the Storm: The Life of General H Norman Schwarzkopf* (Bloomsbury, London, 1991), p 194.
4. R J C Dicker, 'RDF Sealift Programs — the long-term maritime prepositioning force takes shape', *International Defense Review*, July 1983, pp 956–8.
5. Anthony H Cordesman, *The Gulf and the Search for Strategic Stability* (Wentworth Press, Boulder, Colorado, 1984), pp 810 and 857.
6. Murray Hammick, 'Lost in the Pipeline', *International Defense Review*, September 1991, p 998.
7. Acharya, op cit, p 78.
8. Cohen and Gatti, op cit, p 185.
9. John Boatman, 'Success behind the "storm" front', *Jane's Defence Weekly*, 11 May 1991, p 783; C W Kolburger Jr, 'The Gulf War: A More Distant Look', *Navy International*, November 1991, p 392.
10. John Reed, 'Deployment Out of Area: Did "Desert Storm" Change the Rules?', *Defence*, April 1991, pp 17–19.
11. Robert F Dorr, *Desert Shield* (Motor-

books International, Osceola, Wisconsin, 1991), p 41.

12. Lieutenant-Colonel David Evans USMC (Rtd), 'Desert Shield', *United States Naval Institute Proceedings (USNIP)*, January 1991, p 77.
13. L Edgar Prina, 'Two If By Sea: Are We Ready?', *Army*, December 1990, p 20.
14. Brigadier-General Edwin H Simmon USMC (Rtd), 'Getting Marines to the Gulf', *USNIP*, November 1991, p 52.
15. Ibid.
16. Brigadier-General James A Brabham USMC, 'Training, Education were the Keys', *USNIP*, November 1991, p 52.
17. Ibid.
18. Gordon Jacobs, 'Desert Shield Sealift', *Navy International*, November 1990, p 389.
19. Cohen and Gatti, op cit, p 199.
20. Jacobs, op cit, p 388; James Blackwell, 'An Initial Impression of the Logistics of Operation Desert Shield', *Military Technology*, December 1990, p 58.
21. Evans, op cit, p 84.
22. Prina, op cit, p 6; Jacobs, op cit, p 389; Captain Douglas M Norton USN, 'Sealift, Keystone of Support', *USNIP*, January 1991, p 43.
23. Major Bradley E Smith, 'Maritime Challenges to Sustaining the Force', *Military Review*, September 1989, p 28.
24. *Time International*, 10 September 1990.
25. *The Daily Telegraph* (London), Tuesday, 12 February 1991.
26. Hammick, op cit, p 998.
27. James C Hyde, 'Logisticians pave way for Desert Storm Troops', *Armed Forces Journal International*, March 1991, pp 28–9.
28. Rheta S Phillips, 'Logistics Automation Support for Desert Storm', *Military Review*, April 1991, pp 9–13.
29. Ibid, pp 12–13.
30. Cohen and Gatti, op cit, p 200.
31. Lieutenant-General Jimmy D Ross, 'Victory: The Logistics Story', *Army*, October 1991, p 134.
32. *The Sunday Times* (London), 26 August 1990.
33. *The Independent* (London), Wednesday, 19 September 1990; *International Herald Tribune*, Thursday, 10 January 1991.
34. *The Sunday Times*, 26 August 1990; *The Independent*, Thursday, 23 August 1990.
35. *The Independent*, Friday, 21 September 1990.
36. General Carbonneaux, 'Daguet: Logistics in Broad Daylight', *Military Technology*, August 1991, pp 33–5.
37. Ibid, p 35.
38. Colonel J C Lucas OBE, 'Down the Hole with the Bunker Rats of Granby 1', *Royal Corps of Transport Review*, July 1991, p 5.
39. Ibid, p 8.
40. Ibid, p 7.
41. *Royal Army Ordnance Corps Gazette*, April 1991, p 499.
42. Ibid.
43. Lieutenant-Colonel M Dowdle, 'Operation Granby — 25 Transport and Movements Regiment', *Royal Corps of Transport Review*, July 1991, p 13.
44. *The Craftsman* (Journal of the Royal Electrical and Mechanical Engineers), August 1991, p 266.
45. *The Waggoner* (Journal of the Royal Corps of Transport), March 1991, p 22.
46. *The Craftsman*, February 1991, p 38.
47. Ibid, April 1991, p 123.
48. Lieutenant-Colonel C R Chambers, 'Joint Headquarters — an RCT Perspective', *Royal Corps of Transport Review*, July 1991, p 6.
49. *Royal Army Ordnance Corps Gazette*, January 1991, p 385; *The Waggoner*, June 1991, p 116.
50. Michael Ranken, 'The Gulf War — Logistic Support and Merchant Shipping', *The Naval Review*, July 1991, pp 198–206; Lieutenant-Commander K Napier, 'With the British in the Gulf', *USNIP*, June 1991, pp 65–6.
51. Ross, op cit, p 129; Lieutenant-Colonel Richard D Hill, 'Depot Operations Supporting Desert Shield', *Military Review*, April 1991, pp 25–6.
52. Cohen and Gatti, op cit, p 240.
53. Lieutenant-General William G Pagonis and Major Harold E Raugh, 'Good Logistics is Combat Power', *Military Review*, September 1991, pp 34–7.
54. Chambers, op cit, p 7.
55. Brigadier-General Charles C Krulak, 'A War of Logistics', *USNIP*, November 1991, p 56.
56. Colonel Peter C Langenus, 'Moving an Army. Movement Control for Desert Shield', *Military Review*, September 1991, pp 41–2.
57. Ibid.
58. Lieutenant-Colonel G B L Fox, 'The Base Rat's Eye View of Transport Operations in the Gulf', *Royal Corps of Transport Review*, July 1991, p 24.
59. Sergeant Sheila Jansen, 'Class I Sandbaggers', ibid, p 23.
60. Anon, '27 Regiment RCT', ibid, p 36.
61. *The Craftsman*, September 1991, p 317.
62. Major D J A Bergin, 'The Gulf War — A Personal Account', *Journal of The Royal Military Police*, September 1991, p 10.

Further Reading

Roger Cohen and Claudio Gatti, *In the Eye of the Storm: The Life of General H*

Norman Schwarzkopf (Bloomsbury, London, 1991).

Norman Friedman, *Desert Victory: The War for Kuwait* (Naval Institute Press, Annapolis, 1991).

Dilip Hiro, *Desert Shield to Desert Storm. The Second Gulf War* (Paladin, London, 1992).

CHAPTER 5
The Air War

Ray Sibbald

'Airpower is the most difficult of all forms of military force
to measure, or even to express in precise terms.'

Winston Churchill, 1948

The potential of airpower

During the first days of the Gulf War, in January 1991, BBC correspondent John Simpson described the effects of Coalition air attacks on Baghdad:

> As I looked out from the fifth-floor window at the skyline it felt like being in the middle of a very big chessboard: every now and then, at apparently random intervals, a gigantic hand would reach down out of the sky and take away one of the major pieces on the board, without touching any of the others. One day the piece might be Baghdad's electricity supply. The next it would be its communications or its stocks of fuel. With great deliberation, Iraq was being bombed back into the age of the Abbasids.[1]

Reports such as this seemed to confirm to many observers that airpower had finally attained the scientific status that its proponents had long claimed. Even before the advent of powered flight in 1903, people had speculated about the vast potential of flying machines, especially in the field of warfare. At an exposition in Chicago in 1893, for example, Major J D Fullerton of Britain's Royal Engineers spoke of 'a revolution in the art of warfare ... that would require changes in the design of naval ships, dispersion of armies on the battlefield and new standards for the construction of fortresses'.[2] He went on to conclude that, in future, wars would end as a result of an air fleet arriving over the capital city of one of the combatants and bombing it into surrender.

Subsequent theory followed similar lines. In 1917, after a series of raids on London by German Gotha bombers, the South African politician Jan Christian Smuts wrote a report, commissioned by a worried British government, on the feasibility of creating an effective defence against air attack. In it, he speculated:

> The day may not be far off when aerial operations, with their devastation of enemy lands and destruction of industrial and populace centres on a vast scale, may become the principal operations of war, to which the older forms of military and naval operations may become secondary and subordinate.[3]

Four years later, the Italian Giulio Douhet, in his book *The Command of the Air* (Rome, 1921), reinforced Smuts' pessimism when he argued that it was impossible to mount an effective defence against the bombers. This view has been expressed before every major conflict since the First World War, with the refinement that, although the early theorists concentrated on the role of strategic bombing, later advocates stressed the wider use of airpower and therefore its potential in all aspects of warfare. The Gulf War was no different, with some American commentators openly stating that airpower alone could win the conflict. On the face of it, the events of 16/17 January-28 February 1991 would seem to lend credence to their views, although, as always, the true picture is significantly less clear.

The Coalition build-up

One of the main advantages of air capability is that it can be deployed quickly, and the crisis in the Gulf in 1990–91 showed this well. By 7 August 1990, only five days after Iraq's invasion of Kuwait, 301 Coalition fixed-wing aircraft were already in the theatre. After 35 days this number had risen to 1,220, and on the night that the air offensive against Iraq began (16/17 January 1991), Coalition strength stood at 2,430. Nor did it end there, for by the start of the land campaign to liberate Kuwait (23/24 February 1991), the Coalition had increased the number of aircraft either in-theatre or capable of projecting force into the area of operations to 2,790. An example of the rapid movement involved is presented by the British Royal Air Force (RAF). On 8 August 1990 the British government took the decision to commit forces to the Gulf to protect Saudi Arabia. Within 48 hours a squadron of Panavia Tornado GR.1s had arrived in the kingdom. Two hours later it was ready for action.

Such a rapid build-up was made possible only by the provision of base facilities in Saudi Arabia. Over a period of some ten years the Saudis, with the United States' help, had constructed a network of airbases. During peacetime many of these were used to house 'guest-workers', but were prestocked and prepared for an emergency. Others lacked almost any facilities except runways — as one US airman commented in August 1990: 'The tallest thing on the base when we got here was the two-inch-high taxiway lights'[4] — and the United States Air Force (USAF) had to call in its integral civil-engineering component. This group, comprising both civilian and military personnel, worked wonders. Perhaps their finest achievement was the building of an entire base from scratch in about 40 days.[5]

Coalition air deployment may well have been a decisive factor in deterring Saddam Hussein from launching an attack on Saudi Arabia in the early days of the crisis. Throughout the first month, Coalition Intelligence was aware that large numbers of Iraqi troops and armoured vehicles were massed in apparently offensive formations along the Kuwait-Saudi border. This was taken to be a clear indication that Saddam planned to continue his programme of regional aggression before Coalition ground forces could arrive in sufficient numbers to provide a credible defence. The build-up of air strength by the Coalition seemed to remove this threat, forcing Iraqi troops to shift to a defensive posture. Without such a bloodless victory, Coalition ground deployment would have been severely disrupted and the outcome of any war with Iraq left hanging in the balance.

Coalition air defence

Iraq's ground forces were not the only threat, for although Saddam's air force was later to be discredited by its lack of effectiveness in the Gulf War, its reputation and size posed a danger that could not be ignored during the early weeks of the crisis. Air attacks on targets in Saudi Arabia, including the Coalition bases, had to be seen as a possibility and guarded against by means of an integrated air-defence system. Its creation became a top priority.

To give warning of any Iraqi airstrike, the Coalition maintained continuous Airborne Warning and Control System (AWACS) patrols, using Boeing E-3A/B Sentry aircraft. They were backed by Boeing RC-135 signals intelligence aircraft (codenamed Rivet Joint) and by Boeing/Grumman USAF/US Army E-8A Joint Surveillance and Target Attack Radar System (J-STARS) assets. If an airstrike should materialise, the first line of defence was provided by combat air patrols (CAPs), comprising at least 20 Coalition interceptors in the air at all times. Should this outer shield be penetrated, an area-defence system employing MIM-104 Patriot and MIM-23B Hawk surface-to-air missiles (SAMs) provided a second line of protection. Finally, a short-range anti-aircraft screen was deployed around key installations such as airfields, troop concentrations and cities. Uppermost in the minds of Coalition planners and commanders was the possibility of an Iraqi attack using chemical or biological weapons. Fortunately it later transpired that Iraqi capabilities in this field had been greatly exaggerated.

The air balance

A similar judgement may be made about most aspects of the Iraqi Air Force. Despite remarkably widespread views in both the West and the Arab world that Saddam had access to an experienced and well equipped air element, it was in truth a 'bargain basement' formation. Its reputation rested on contributions to the Iran-Iraq War (1980–88) that were, on investigation, less than impressive,[6] and although it fielded some modern aircraft, such as the Soviet-supplied Mikoyan/Gurevich MiG-29 and Sukhoi Su-24, and the French-built Mirage F1, the bulk of its front-line strength of 602 aircraft was, by Coalition standards, obsolete. By comparison, the final Coalition strength of 2,790 fixed-wing aircraft represented an air armada of overwhelming numerical superiority.

Nor was this all, for the Coalition also enjoyed a marked advantage in terms of technology. Many of the aircraft it deployed were at least one and in some cases two generations more advanced than the best that the Iraqis could field. The United States, France and the United Kingdom, for example, all deployed the most advanced aircraft in their inventories, helping to create an air weapon of devastating potential. In the end, Saddam stood little chance of winning the air war, regardless of the tactics employed.

A prime example of Coalition technological superiority was the Lockheed F-117A 'stealth fighter', the first aircraft in the world to be designed specifically to avoid radar detection. With a top speed of 880 km/h

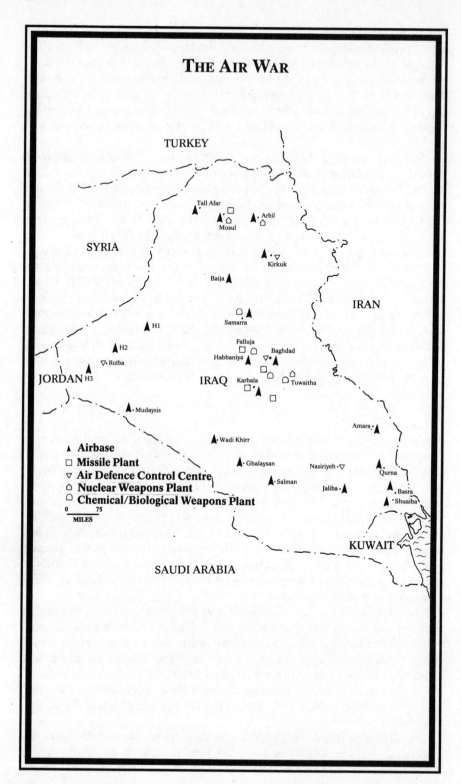

THE AIR WAR

TURKEY

SYRIA

Tall Afar

▲· □

▲· ⌂ ▲ Arbil
Mosul   ⌂

▲ ▽·
Kirkuk

Baija ▲

IRAN

▲ H1

□ ▲
Samarra

▲ H2

▽· Rutba

Falluja
□ ⌂ Baghdad
Habbaniya ▲ ▽·⌂
⌂ ⌂
Karbala ⌂ ▲
□· ▲
□

JORDAN H3

IRAQ

Tuwaitha

▲· Mudaysis

Amara · ▲

▲· Wadi Khirr

▲· Ghalaysan

Nasiriyeh ·▽

▲ Qurna

▲ Airbase
□ Missile Plant
▽ Air Defence Control Centre
⌂ Nuclear Weapons Plant
⌂ Chemical/Biological Weapons Plant

0 _____ 75
MILES

▲· Salman

Jaliba ·▲

▲· Basra
▲ Shuaiba

KUWAIT

SAUDI ARABIA

(500 mph), it was equipped with a computer-assisted flight-control system and an advanced avionics package, details of which remain classified. Bombs and other weapons were carried in internal bays to reduce the surface area and radar sensitivity of the aircraft, and although the details of the weapons deployed remained clouded in official secrecy, it was believed to have a bomb capacity of about 1,800 kg (4,000 lb), delivered by means of a laser-guidance system. The F-117's range of 1,770 km (1,100 miles) could be extended using mid-air refuelling, even in darkness. It was something to which the Iraqis had no effective counter.

Other Coalition aircraft were no less impressive. The Boeing E-8A J-STARS, for example, was rushed to the Gulf from the USA, where its Norden synthetic-aperture side-looking airborne radar was undergoing trials. This radar unit was capable of detecting the movement of a single vehicle at a range of 185 km (115 miles), and was an integral part of the 'see deep' capability of AirLand Battle. Along the same lines, examples of the Lockheed TR-1 high-altitude monitoring aircraft, developed as part of the Precision Location Strike System, also central to AirLand Battle, were made available, although they may only have been used, along with Lockheed U-2Rs, for reconnaissance.

The Coalition arsenal of air-delivered weapons was no less advanced, with the whole spectrum of television (TV), infra-red, radar and laser-guided munitions on offer. A typical example of the 'smart' munitions used in the Gulf War was the GBU-15, a 900 kg (2,000 lb) Mk-84 warhead linked to either a TV or infra-red targeting system that relayed an image of the target back to the launch aircraft. The weapons operator could either guide the bomb on to the target or switch it to 'homing mode' and leave it to do the job itself. In addition, the Coalition possessed a wide variety of conventional and specialist 'dumb' (unguided) bombs that included the seven-ton BLU-28 'Daisy Cutter'. Originally designed to clear helicopter landing zones in the jungles of Vietnam, the Daisy Cutter was capable of flattening every standing object within a one-kilometre (0.6-mile) circle of its impact point.

Finally, the Coalition was able to field a variety of aircraft that acted as 'force multipliers', enhancing the performance of front-line combat aircraft without actually carrying or delivering weapons themselves. Air-to-air refuelling tankers such as the Boeing KC-135R, for example, increased the range of Coalition aircraft as well as the time that they could spend in the air, enhancing the air cover available without having to increase the number of aircraft in theatre. All in all, the Coalition air forces represented a gathering of the best of Western technology, in overwhelming numbers across the whole spectrum of aircraft types and capabilities. As one commentator noted: 'The "mix and match' possibilities of such a varied force [were] a tactical planner's dream and a defender's nightmare.'[7]

Planning the air war
Planning for an air campaign against Iraq began within days of Saddam's invasion of Kuwait. A special 'Checkmate' committee was set up in the Pentagon in Washington to draw up a list of specific objectives, out of

which an overall air plan emerged. The American planners, looking back to the experience of bombing North Vietnam (Operation 'Rolling Thunder', 1965–68, and Operation 'Linebacker', 1972), identified a number of key factors that they believed would be essential if airpower was to contribute to the eviction of Iraqi troops from Kuwait. At the top of the list was the need for unity of command (a failing in Vietnam, where five separate air campaigns were conducted simultaneously, each under different commanders), and this led to the establishment in August 1990 of a Joint Forces Air Component Commander (JFACC). Second was the importance of striking at Iraqi governmental centres and command, control and communications systems, in an effort to blind and confuse the enemy, opening the way to his military defeat. Clearly this would not be possible without gaining air supremacy by ensuring the suppression and destruction of Iraqi air defences, so that, too, was given priority, as was the use of electronic warfare to increase the survival rate of aircraft and their chances of hitting the targets assigned to them. In short, the aim was to take out the 'brain' of the enemy by means of a closely controlled and technologically superior use of airpower, leaving the front-line Iraqi 'muscles' to wither and die.[8]

None of this was feasible without accurate information about Iraq and the targets to be hit. American planners drew on a wide range of intelligence sources. They examined the records of Western construction firms to find details of Iraqi military and industrial installations, while deploying spy satellites to create accurate maps of Iraq, essential if the necessary information was to be fed into the Terrain Contour Matching Guidance System (TERCOM) of the BGM-109 Tomahawk cruise missiles. At the same time, the Checkmate planners identified five major objectives of the air campaign: the suppression and destruction of Iraq's air defences; the elimination of Iraq's nuclear, biological and chemical capability; the disruption and destruction of military and civilian communication networks within Iraq and Kuwait; the destruction of key industrial and economic sites, such as power stations and oil facilities; and the degradation of the Iraqi Army's physical and psychological resources to render it incapable of opposing the proposed Coalition ground offensive to liberate Kuwait. The first version of this plan, codenamed Instant Thunder, was delivered to Central Command Air Force (CENTAF) in Riyadh as early as 20 August 1990.

Refinements were added, but by early September CENTAF had finalised a plan that was, in essentials, the one that was executed during the war itself. It was made up of four phases. Phase One would encompass the suppression and eventual destruction of the Iraqi air-defence network, something that was originally scheduled to take seven days, although in the event this exaggerated the level of resistance offered by the enemy. Phase Two was to cover a variety of objectives, such as strategic economic targets, military and civilian communication networks, including roads and bridges, as well as some military-industrial complexes. Phase Three envisaged the destruction of the Iraqi Army's physical capacity to fight and its psychological will to resist. Phase Four called for Coalition air forces to provide close support to ground units as they advanced into Kuwait and southern Iraq.

It was envisaged that the first three phases would take 30 days to complete. Because of poor weather conditions (heavy rain, sandstorms and low visibility) and the need to divert resources to search for mobile Scud-missile launchers once the air campaign began, Phase Three was not completed until Day 38, but this did not detract from the overall effectiveness of the plan, within which the various phases tended to merge and overlap. The air campaign became a seamless learning process, in which each successive phase acted as a bridge to the next, rather than a separate event. A slight hiccough occurred in September 1990, when the Chief of Staff of the USAF, General Michael J Dugan, was dismissed from his post. He had given a press interview in which he made it clear that the air plan was based on strategic bombing of targets in Iraq, including if possible the command bunkers containing Saddam Hussein and his close associates. This was deemed politically embarrassing to an American administration still engaged in diplomatic negotiation and apparently dedicated to a peaceful solution to the crisis. An air plan existed, but for the moment it needed to be kept a closely guarded secret.

Air tasking

Once the basic air plan had been finalised, there remained the complex business of determining target priority and assigning resources to attack each target. It was rendered even more complex by the fact that this was a Coalition operation, requiring the integration of not only the various air assets of the USA, drawn from the Air Force, Army, Navy and Marine Corps, but also those of several other national air elements, including the United Kingdom, Canada, France, Italy, Saudi Arabia and the Gulf states. This, coupled to the fact that large numbers of aircraft would have to be airborne at any one time (during the campaign the Coalition air forces flew between 2,500 and 3,000 sorties a day), reinforced the need for a single central command. As the USA was providing the bulk of the air capability, the post of JFACC had to go to an American officer and control of the air war had to be placed firmly in American hands. The only exception to this was a French insistence that they should retain a right of veto over any targets assigned to their aircraft, but the JFACC who was appointed, Lieutenant-General Charles A ('Chuck') Horner, found that this did not significantly undermine the fundamental principle of centralised command.

Horner's initial priority was to provide Air Tasking Orders (ATOs) for the aircraft in the Gulf theatre, designed to cover all aspects of operational activity. The preparation of ATOs was delegated to the Director of Operations, United States Central Command Air Force (USCENTAF), but they were of necessity largely inflexible, having to be worked out on computers which imposed their own rigidity and restrictions. Although the computers were extremely powerful, such was the complexity of the problems involved in designing an ATO that, on average, each one took 48 hours to produce. The process began with a JFACC decision as to where the emphasis of air operations would be placed, after which targets were selected by a group drawn from the US services possessing air assets, plus a representative from the RAF. This group was joined in October 1990 by an officer from the Royal Saudi Air Force. The ATO thus formulated often ran to a document of several hundred pages.

When the air war began on 16/17 January 1991, JFACC had produced ATOs for the first three days of the offensive. An obvious advantage of the system was that it allowed a single command centre to control a vast array of aircraft as they went about their various tasks. A constant worry among Coalition air chiefs was that aircraft might be lost to 'friendly fire', and it is to the credit of the planners and operational forces that no such incident occurred during the campaign. However, this sort of highly structured plan could work only if the enemy operated from static defensive positions. The problems experienced by the Coalition in trying to eliminate the Scud launchers were indicative of the difficulties that the system had in coping with a more mobile foe.

The Coalition air forces tried to temper the rigidity of their planning in two ways. During Phase Three of the campaign (the assault on the Iraqi Army), areas to be attacked under the ATOs were divided into 'kill zones', with aircraft scheduled to appear at specific times to attack any enemy formations found there within a given period. As the same aircraft were seldom used to assault a particular kill zone on successive occasions, it was obviously difficult to monitor the progress of the attacks, and it soon became clear that the Iraqis were exploiting this by mounting a successful deception campaign, building mock tanks or using previously damaged vehicles as decoys. Coalition spotter aircraft were deployed in an effort to counter the problem, but traditional piston-engined spotters such as the Grumman OV-10 Bronco proved susceptible to Iraqi ground fire. Because of this, the Coalition resorted to a spotting and control system called Fast Forward Air Control ('Fast FAC'), in which a General Dynamics F-16 Fighting Falcon multi-role fighter, minus its ordnance, flew low and fast over the target area before the strikes went in, checking for Iraqi deception ploys. It was a system that had been tried in Vietnam, using the McDonnell Douglas F-4 Phantom, but heavy ground foliage had rendered it inoperable; it worked in the Gulf only because of the vast field of vision afforded by desert conditions.

The second option open to the Coalition planners was to abandon the ATO system for certain tasks. This was viable if it was confined to the periphery of the theatre of operations, as any suspension of ATOs elsewhere would have caused chaos. In fact, it was possible to use this alternative only because both the US Navy and Marine Corps were reluctant to accept USAF control over their air assets — something that puts a slightly different perspective on American claims that full air co-ordination was achieved. The aircraft of the two 'aquatic' services were often available for assignments outside the areas covered by the ATOs, providing that the targets were away from the main area of air activity.

An integral part of any planning process was access to accurate and usable intelligence, and in this the Coalition was fortunate. A good example was the material provided by J-STARS, which enabled the Coalition to build up a very detailed picture of Iraqi transport movement preparatory to the destruction of the enemy's logistic chain. The information provided by J-STARS was so accurate that Coalition planners could predict where Iraqi vehicles would be at almost any given time and arrange for aircraft to meet them as they arrived at their destinations.

The situation was less advantageous in terms of bomb damage assessment (BDA), upon which ongoing planning needed to be based. There was a lack of specialist reconnaissance aircraft such as the Lockheed SR-71 'Blackbird', while TV cameras on some combat planes proved unsatisfactory. However, local improvisations solved many of the problems. Tomahawk cruise-missile missions, for example, were often timed to reach their targets an hour before spy-satellite runs so that the surveillance pictures could be used for BDA. In addition, two Defence Support Program (DSP) early-warning satellites, equipped with heat-sensitive infra-red telescopes, had their orbits altered to provide warning of Scud launches, while two (possibly three) photo-reconnaissance satellites, each capable of identifying objects as small as 76 mm (3 inches) square, were deployed to cover the Gulf area. Poor weather did not hamper the use of such sophisticated assets, but, even if it had, the Coalition also had access to the Lacrosse radar-imaging satellite, which used radar beams to build up a picture of the terrain below it, regardless of conditions on the ground. All in all, the Coalition intelligence-gathering system proved to be more than capable of meeting the demands made on it during the crisis and subsequent war.

Phase One: gaining air supremacy

By 15 January 1991, when the United Nations' deadline for Iraq's withdrawal from Kuwait passed without any move from Saddam, the Coalition had assembled its aircraft and completed its plans for what was to become an overwhelming display of aerial might. The air campaign began at midnight (GMT) on 16/17 January. US Army AH-64 Apache strike helicopters fired the first shots of the air war when, as a prelude to the main attack, they destroyed Iraqi radar sites to create a number of 'safe lanes' for Coalition aircraft.

The initial objective of the Coalition air forces was the suppression and destruction of the enemy's air-defence systems. With this in mind, the first raids, carried out by a combination of F-117A 'stealth' aircraft and sea-launched Tomahawk cruise missiles, were aimed at the core of Iraq's air-defence command, control and communications capabilities. Such was the precision and success of these attacks that, within minutes, the Iraqi air-defences were effectively 'blind', a situation that was to continue through-out the war, enabling the Coalition to carry out its other air tasks with a significant degree of impunity. The F-117A's attacked in pairs, one aircraft using precision laser-guided weapons to destroy targets illuminated for it by its partner, which also carried out almost instantaneous BDA. Each of the F-117's 900 kg (2,000 lb) GBU-27 laser-guided bombs could penetrate up to five metres (16 ft) of reinforced concrete, making it ideal for destroying heavily fortified command centres. On the first day F-117As attacked 31 per cent of the Coalition's primary targets.

Tomahawk missiles were launched from naval vessels in the Red Sea, Persian (Arabian) Gulf and eastern Mediterranean, either independently or in conjunction with F-117A raids. They proved to be highly effective. One of the most remarkable images of the air war was provided by BBC correspondent John Simpson, when he described witnessing a cruise missile as it flew below roof height along a street in Baghdad towards its target: 'The Al-Rashid hotel was a turning point for cruise missiles . . . One flew across the front of the hotel, turned at the corner and flew across the back of it before striking its target just opposite'.[9] In all, 284 cruise missiles were fired during the conflict. Of these, 196 were launched in the first two days.

The Coalition air offensive therefore got off to an impressive start, although some problems did occur. On the second day of the campaign, for example, eight Tornado attack aircraft of the Italian *Aeronautica Militare* took off to attack Iraqi positions. Because of air-refuelling problems, only one of the aircraft managed to reach the target, and that fell victim to Iraqi ground fire.

Once the enemy air-defence system had been suppressed, the way was clear for the Coalition to destroy the Iraqi Air Force and the actual weapons of the air defences — the surface-to-air missiles (SAMs) and anti-aircraft artillery (AAA or 'Triple A'). This task was undertaken mainly by McDonnell Douglas F-15E Strike Eagles, General Dynamics F-111s and Tornados of the Coalition air forces, flying round-the-clock raids on Iraqi airfields and air-defence installations. The RAF Tornados' initial role was to attack enemy airfields in low-level missions using the JP-233 runway-cratering bomb, something that was vividly described by a British pilot at the time: 'It was the most scary thing I have ever done in my life. We went in low over the target, as low as we dared, dropped the bombs and ran like hell.'[10] Low-flying hazards were significantly increased because these raids took place at night, and the degree of danger involved is clearly indicated by the fact that the RAF lost five Tornados in the first week of the air war, even though only one of them was officially listed as having gone down while carrying out a low-level attack. When it became clear that the Iraqi Air Force had no intention of committing mass suicide by attempting to challenge the Coalition control of the air, the Tornados were withdrawn from low-level raids and reassigned to tasks in the next phase of the offensive.

Initially, the Iraqis did try to defend themselves, and Coalition pilots reported heavy concentrations of AAA and a mass use of SAMs over some targets. But it should be stressed that, impressive as these 'firework displays' were on television, they were almost totally ineffective in reality, lacking radar guidance. The few Iraqi interceptors that actually got into the air were more of a danger to themselves than to Coalition aircraft. On the first day of the war, two Iraqi MiG-29s were involved in a remarkable incident which typified Iraq's response to the Coalition aerial onslaught. Flying in close formation, one MiG managed to shoot down its wingman before colliding with the debris and being destroyed itself. Apparently unaccustomed to the sophisticated air-to-air radar of the MiG, the Iraqi pilot had simply taped the radar button down so that it locked on to the first target it acquired. Of course, being of a nervous disposition, the pilot also kept his fire button permanently depressed, with devastating results as the system locked on to his wingman. One of the very few examples of aerial combat took place on 24 January 1991. Captain Ayhed Salah Al-Shamrani of the Royal Saudi Air Force, flying an F-15C interceptor, engaged two Iraqi Mirage F1s, destroying both with AIM-9 Sidewinder missiles.

As the Iraqi Air Force showed no inclination to engage the Coalition in the air, attacks were made on Iraqi aircraft on the ground. The success of this approach may be seen from two events. First, in response to Coalition strikes on their reinforced aircraft shelters, the Iraqis moved some of their remaining aeroplanes away from military airfields and placed them in urban centres or even close to important archaeological sites such as the ziggurat at Ur.[11] Second, some Iraqi pilots began to seek refuge in Iran, where they and their aircraft were promptly interned for the duration of the war. A number of theories have been advanced to try to explain why Iraqi pilots 'deserted' in this way, but what is certain is that their actions largely removed any lingering threat that the Iraqi Air Force posed to the Coalition, particularly as all of Iraq's potentially effective Su-24s were in the forefront of the flight across the border. When events such as these are taken into account, there can be little doubt that the Coalition had achieved air superiority within hours of the start of the campaign. Indeed, the only thing that prevented a claim of complete air supremacy was an American insistence that all Iraqi air defences, including AAA, had first to be destroyed. Coalition commanders announced air supremacy on 22 January 1991.

This achievement was made possible to a large extent by the widespread Coalition use of electronic warfare (EW) measures, taking as an example Israeli experiences during the invasion of southern Lebanon in June 1982 (Operation 'Peace for Galilee'). Attacks against Iraqi SAM batteries in particular benefited from the deployment of EW aircraft. General Dynamics EF-111A Ravens, accompanying strike aircraft, penetrated the defence network and disrupted the few early-warning and surveillance radars that had survived the first hours of the air war. The only course of action open to the Iraqis once they had been blinded in this way was to try to fire their SA-2, SA-3 and SA-6 missiles using the manual-optical override mode. Even when this proved possible, EF-111As and Grumman EA-6B Prowlers were able to divert the missiles by using their jammers against the SAM command links.

By comparison, the US Navy used EW tactics copied directly from the Israelis, employing large numbers of Tactical Air Launched Decoy (TALD) drones. These were deliberately flown over Iraqi SAM batteries to trigger the radars, the frequencies of which were monitored by EA-6Bs or Vought A-7 Corsair IIs. Once the signals had been identified, the aircraft fired either AGM-45 Shrike or AGM-88 HARM anti-radiation missiles which locked on to the beams and destroyed the missile radars. The USAF did not possess

TALDs, depending instead on Wild Weasel F-4G Phantoms to trigger the Iraqi radars and to fire HARMs down the beams. Iraqi missile operators, faced with the option of firing blind (and ineffectually) or switching on their radars and being destroyed, in most cases decided that discretion was the wiser course and loosed off their weapons indiscriminately. The Chairman of the US Joint Chiefs of Staff, General Colin Powell, summed up the Coalition achievement on 23 January 1991: 'We were able to attack the [Iraqi] air-defense envelope with great success by first taking out the early-warning capability, blinding them, and then going after the operating centers, the various sector operating centers that they used to wire this all together.'[12] It was a crucial Coalition victory, for without it the other air objectives would have been difficult, if not impossible, to attain.

Phase Two: hitting strategic targets
Once Iraqi air defences had been suppressed, Coalition air forces could begin to shift to the next phase of the air plan: the destruction of strategic military and economic targets inside Iraq and Kuwait. It is important to be aware that, because of the quick successes in the initial phase, attacks on key military and economic sites began while Phase One was still going on. For instance, Tomahawk and F-117A strikes were launched against nuclear power plants and chemical and biological installations during the first two days of the air war. As a result, the Osiriq nuclear reactor and the chemical and biological plants at Salman Pak, Samara and Abu Gharib were either destroyed or severely damaged.

Typical of this phase of the offensive was an attack launched by the French *Armée de l'Air* on 18 January 1991 against a large Iraqi ammunition depot at Ras-al-Quilayah, south of Kuwait City. Twelve SEPECAT Jaguar ground-attack aircraft carried out the raid, returning the next day to complete the task of destroying this important installation. In similar vein, on 27 January the RAF attacked and blew up a massive arms dump near Basra. In the same area on the following day, while the explosions from the arms dump were still lighting up the sky, another RAF raid destroyed an Iraqi oil refinery. The Coalition was in the ideal situation of being able to pick out its targets and bomb them without having to worry about effective air defences.

Phase Three: interdiction and battlefield preparation
The third phase of the air plan was designed to prepare the way for the ground offensive. At no time during either the planning or the execution of the air war was it assumed that the Iraqis would surrender because of air action alone. Interdiction was vital to the removal of the Iraqi Army from Kuwait, in that its overall objective was the 'shaping' of the battlefield to help Coalition ground forces to achieve their aims. The first step in this shaping process was to isolate Iraqi forces in southern Iraq and Kuwait from their sources of supply and reinforcement further north. Iraqi troops thus isolated could then be subjected to a relentless aerial bombardment that would destroy both their will and their capability to resist. In the words

of General Powell: 'First we are going to cut it [the Iraqi Army] off, then we are going to kill it.'[13]

Isolating the Iraqi Army began in the first days of the air campaign, when key command, control and communication centres in Baghdad and elsewhere were taken out. It continued with Coalition attacks designed to sever the physical communication links that the Iraqi military relied on for its logistic support: roads, railways and, above all in Iraq itself, bridges across the Tigris and Euphrates rivers, many of which carried the cables for important parts of Saddam's communication system. The Iraqi Army employed a logistic chain derived, like many of its other organisational structures, from a Soviet model. To cite just one example, that of ammunition supply to armoured formations, very little ammunition was actually held by individual units — a policy geared more to the prevention of rebellion than to successful campaigning. Resupply was via a distribution system that required time-consuming and labour-intensive loading/unloading of trucks at various depots, rather than direct delivery to the front line. Such a system increased the number of potential targets available to the Coalition air forces and enhanced the chances of catching large amounts of supplies at the depots, before they had been distributed to combat troops.

The aircraft used by the Coalition in the interdiction phase were principally Tornados (used by the RAF in conjunction with Hawker Siddeley Buccaneer S.2s as laser-designation aircraft until the Tornados could be fitted with their own thermal imaging airborne laser designators), F-111s, Jaguars, Grumman A-6 Intruders and Fairchild A-10 Thunderbolt IIs. Such aircraft operated 24 hours a day, attacking road and rail links, bridges and supply depots. The blitz on the Iraqi bridge network began on the night of 5/6 February 1991, when British and American aircraft destroyed the Bridge of the Republic in the centre of Baghdad. On 10 and 11 February the bulk of the British Tornado and Buccaneer assets were devoted to the campaign. By 15 February 27 of the 36 principal bridges on Iraq's major transport routes had been downed, and Coalition aircraft went on to destroy a further eight before the war's end, leaving the Iraqis with only one major bridge intact. A vivid example of the 'bridge-busting' effort was provided on 20 January, when General Norman Schwarzkopf displayed a video of an American plane destroying an Iraqi bridge with a single missile.[14] This was undoubtedly impressive, although it should be compared with the RAF estimate that, on average, it required 24 aircraft sorties to destroy a bridge.

At the same time, using the information provided by J-STARS, the Coalition was able to ensure a clean sweep of Iraq's transport network. The ability of J-STARS to monitor ground movement 24 hours a day meant that Iraqi convoys were denied even the sanctuary of night movement. So effective were the Coalition road-convoy raids that the Iraqis were rapidly reduced to sending out individual trucks in an effort to avoid the air onslaught, although this, too, proved unsuccessful in the face of the electronic wizardry of J-STARS. Again, television pictures provided a dramatic illustration of the effectiveness of such attacks, Western audiences being shown images of Iraqi trucks in convoy or singly being destroyed from the air.

The Coalition anti-logistic campaign quickly reduced the amount of supplies getting through to Iraqi front-line troops. Within two weeks of the start of the air war, Coalition commanders were claiming to have cut the total of Iraqi supplies reaching the front in Kuwait by more than 50 per cent. By the beginning of the ground offensive, on 23/24 February 1991, the Iraqi supply system had ceased to function in any meaningful fashion.

Cut off from resupply, short of even the bare necessities of existence such as food and water, and shorn of its command, control and communication network, the Iraqi Army in Kuwait was, by about mid-February 1991, little more than a collection of slowly starving units. This ragged and dispirited horde was then subjected to a constant aerial bombardment that was both intense and extended. Coalition air forces used just about every munition in their arsenals to destroy both the morale and *matériel* of the enemy. Boeing B-52Gs, for example, flew 1,624 'carpet-bombing' sorties, dropping 25,700 tons of munitions principally on targets in the Kuwait Theater of Operations (KTO), aiming specifically for Iraqi troop and armour concentrations. A cell of three B-52Gs could lay waste an area about 1,000 m (3,300 ft) wide and 3,000 m (10,000 ft) long, arriving over the target at high altitude to drop bombs on radar co-ordinates fed into on-board computers. The results were often devastating, as were similar raids using fuel-air explosives, drenching an area with an aerosol cloud of propylene oxide vapour which ignited as it mixed with air to produce a fireball of searing destruction.[15]

Nor was this all, for the Coalition also dropped several very large single bombs on enemy locations, the most effective of which was the BLU-28 Daisy Cutter, launched from the tail ramp of a Lockheed C-130 transport aircraft. To heighten the psychological impact of this fearsome bomb, leaflets were dropped over the intended target zone three days before the intended attack, explaining what it was and what its effects were likely to be. Each succeeding day until the event, more leaflets were dropped, counting down the days. Once the first Daisy Cutter had been used and its effects observed by Iraqi troops, the issue of the three-day leaflets was enough to induce severe anxiety on the part of Iraqi soldiers receiving the unwelcome news. Interestingly, the first Daisy Cutter raid, producing a loud explosion and a distinctive fireball, could be heard and seen as far south as Al Jubail in Saudi Arabia, where Coalition troops thought for a moment that the war had somehow gone nuclear.

Nevertheless, according to some Intelligence reports, it was precision-guided munitions that had the greatest impact on Iraqi morale, greater even than the use of the most monstrous 'dumb' bomb. Iraqi soldiers watching the destruction of vehicles picked out by Coalition aircraft, frequently hitting a target with each missile fired, rapidly concluded that their safest course of action was to separate themselves from their tanks and armoured personnel carriers (APCs). The effect that this had on the cohesion of the Iraqi Army in Kuwait and southern Iraq was, by all accounts, considerable.

As this example implies, the Coalition waged a devastating campaign against the Iraqi Army's physical ability to wage war by destroying its most effective weapons — its tanks and APCs. By 17 February 1991 US Central Command in Riyadh was able to announce that Coalition aircraft had destroyed 1,300 of the estimated 4,000 Iraqi tanks in Kuwait. By the start of the ground offensive, six days later, further announcements specified the elimination of 1,508 artillery pieces and 1,210 APCs. It is difficult to believe such exact claims, however, when the BDA problems experienced by the Coalition at the time are taken into account. During the air war, disputes over the number of targets destroyed were common, with some commentators in Washington displaying a healthy scepticism about damage estimates prepared in Riyadh. Whatever the correct figures, it is beyond doubt that Coalition aircraft destroyed considerable numbers of Iraqi armoured vehicles, easing the way for the ground offensive to liberate Kuwait.

Faced with the destruction of entire armoured units, Iraqi commanders frequently attempted to disperse large formations so as to present smaller targets. As Coalition aircraft had the ability to hit single vehicles with accuracy, the only discernible effect of this ploy was further to degrade the cohesion of the Iraqi defenders. By the start of the ground war the Iraqi Army in Kuwait had been subjected to weeks of intense round-the-clock aerial bombardment. It had been isolated from its sources of supply, and to a large extent it was leaderless, because its central command network no longer functioned. Indeed, the Iraqis had no clear idea of the overall situation in Kuwait, nor any real appreciation of what the Coalition ground forces intended to do. In addition, a large proportion of the Iraqi Army's armoured fighting vehicles had been destroyed or incapacitated. Those that remained were short of both fuel and ammunition.

Perhaps even more significant in terms of the course of the ground offensive, the aerial onslaught destroyed the morale of many Iraqi soldiers. Before Coalition troops crossed the border into Kuwait and southern Iraq they were encountering mass desertions and surrenders of enemy forces. On at least two occasions large numbers of Iraqi troops actually surrendered to American attack helicopters and were escorted into captivity by their aerial captors. Prisoners such as these provided Coalition Intelligence with graphic descriptions of poor Iraqi morale, although it should be remembered that the Iraqi Army was for the most part made up of poor-quality troops, lacking in discipline or any sort of *esprit de corps*. It was therefore highly unlikely that the mass of Iraqi conscripts would be able to resist the intense psychological pressures generated by a concentrated and extended aerial bombardment. Whatever the details, the prolonged air attacks rendered the Iraqis virtually helpless when Coalition ground forces went on to the offensive.

'The Great Scud Hunt'
The Coalition air plan took longer to complete than originally envisaged, partly because of unexpected bad weather, but also because of the time that had to be devoted to what the media called 'the Great Scud Hunt'. From the

moment that Coalition personnel began to arrive in Saudi Arabia in August 1990, the threat from Scud-missile attack was perceived as perhaps the greatest danger to Coalition lives, particularly if the Scuds were armed with chemical or biological warheads. The elaborate precautions taken to counter this possibility may be regarded as an admirable attempt to cover any eventuality, although it is worth bearing in mind that the Soviets, who had supplied the Scuds to Saddam, assured the Coalition that Iraqi missiles were not capable of carrying unconventional warheads.

Once the war began, it soon became clear that the Soviets were right. Not only were the 86 Scuds fired by the Iraqis incapable of carrying anything more than high-explosive warheads, but they were also grossly inaccurate. This implies that Saddam's objective was political rather than military, for when he authorised the missile attacks on Israel and Saudi Arabia he must have known that they could only be indiscriminate. In the case of the attacks on Israel, the intention was clearly to provoke an Israeli reaction that would split the Arab Coalition states from the Western powers, something that did not require the precise destruction of targets in the Jewish homeland. Indeed, one of the missiles that landed on Israeli soil was armed with nothing more lethal than a concrete warhead,[16] apparently an empty container for chemical or biological material. Similar motives can be ascribed to the attacks on Saudi Arabia. They were a futile attempt to show that Iraq could strike back against the overwhelming aerial might of the Coalition.

The Scud campaign failed to achieve its aims for two reasons: the uncharacteristic restraint shown by Israel and the effectiveness of the American Patriot anti-missile system, which destroyed the vast majority of Scuds launched against Israel and Saudi Arabia. Inevitably, a proportion did get through. On 26 February 1991, for example, a Scud (or part of the missile) hit a warehouse in Dhahran, killing 28 US service personnel, while the Patriot battery assigned to cover the area was undergoing modifications to improve its effectiveness — but the fact is that incoming Scuds were not the main problem.

What was far more important, both in terms of reassuring the Israelis and Saudis and protecting the Coalition forces, was the prevention of Scud launches in the first place. It was this that led to an extension of the air campaign over Iraq, for it has been estimated that the resultant 'Scud hunt' prolonged the air war by about seven days. The Iraqis used mobile launchers that proved extremely difficult to locate. Even the very effective J-STARS could only identify vehicles, not their purpose. To complicate matters further, the Iraqis constructed large numbers of dummy launchers in an effort to divert Coalition air efforts. Because of these factors, the Scud attacks could not be stopped completely, despite a Coalition search involving 150-200 aircraft sorties a day. Bearing in mind the air superiority enjoyed by the Coalition, this was not a major success.

Integral to the 'Scud hunt' were Coalition special forces, operating deep behind enemy lines throughout the war. At the start of the air campaign Schwarzkopf was quoted as saying that there were 'a lot of special forces out there . . . It was a special forces' theme park'.[17] Men from the British 22nd Special Air Service Regiment (22SAS) and American Special Forces carried out activities across the spectrum of covert warfare, including actions in direct support of the air offensive. Special forces' teams located several Scud launchers in Iraq, destroying them or calling in Coalition aircraft to do the job. Equally, the pin-point accuracy of some Coalition air attacks, particularly in urban areas, owed a great deal to special forces' activity. Infiltrating target areas, the teams would illuminate selected buildings and facilities using portable laser-designators, creating 'beams' along which incoming attack aircraft would fire their weapons. A full picture of special forces' involvement in the Gulf War will probably take years to emerge, but what is certain at this stage is that they made a significant contribution to the success of the air campaign.

Phase Four: close air support
The final phase of the air war was support of the ground offensive to liberate Kuwait, something that Coalition air forces performed with great skill and effect. As ground forces advanced into Kuwait and southern Iraq, they had available to them an unprecedented level of close air support. At any time, and in any location on the battlefield, ground troops could call in massive air assets. Indeed, it could be argued that the amount of support was out of proportion to the threat posed by a demoralised and badly mauled Iraqi Army. An example of this came at the end of the war, when American aircraft engaged Iraqi troops caught on the Mutla Ridge, on the road north to Basra, as they tried to flee Kuwait. Hundreds of Iraqis were killed by aircraft operating in close support of the American ground units that had blocked the highway, yet during the five hours of the action only one American casualty was suffered. In these circumstances, the decision to continue prosecuting a sustained close air support campaign could be criticised as overkill, and the one-sided slaughter involved was reportedly one of the reasons for President George Bush's unilateral ceasefire on 28 February.

As in many 20th-century conflicts, however, close air support in the Gulf did prove to be a double-edged weapon, occasionally doing as much damage to Coalition forces as to the enemy. On 29 January 1991, during the Iraqi attack on Al-Wafra that preceded the battle at Khafji, several US Marines were killed when a Coalition aircraft fired in error on their APC, and incidents of so-called 'friendly fire' continued throughout the war. Even the introduction of various preventive measures, such as the use of brightly coloured panels and inverted 'Vs' to distinguish Coalition vehicles from the air, did little to alleviate the problem. On 17 February 1991 two American M2 Bradley Infantry Fighting Vehicles were destroyed by 'friendly' air attack, leaving two soldiers dead and a further six injured. Even worse, on 26 February an American A-10 strafed two British Warrior Mechanised Combat Vehicles belonging to the 3rd Battalion, The Royal Regiment of Fusiliers, killing nine soldiers. Details of this incident are unclear, but it appears from eyewitness reports that the attack took place in conditions of good visibility, while the Warriors were stationary and with their identity markings clearly displayed. After the war was over, JFACC

General Horner observed that 'rapid battlefield movement requires improved capabilities for the identification of friendly forces. It is critical that we acquire systems that will allow pilots attacking forces on the ground to quickly distinguish friend from foe'.[18] Until these 'distinguishing systems' have been developed, the only way to avoid tragedy is to keep a very tight control over aircraft involved in close air support.

Conclusions
A few facts and figures will illustrate the extent of the Coalition air effort in the Gulf. During the conflict, Coalition air forces flew an average of 2,500-3,000 aircraft sorties a day; 88,500 tons of munitions, of which 6,250 tons were delivered by 'smart' weapons, were dropped on Kuwait and Iraq.[19] The results were devastating. American spokesmen were reported as saying that Iraq had been bombed back into a pre-industrial period, an assessment confirmed by independent observers such as UN relief workers, who visited Iraq after the ceasefire. In the battle against the Iraqi Air Force, the Coalition was equally successful: for a loss of 43 of its own aircraft, all to ground fire or accident, the Coalition destroyed 277 Iraqi aeroplanes. When the 116 aircraft that fled to Iran are added, it may be seen that the Coalition achieved a truly crushing aerial victory.[20]

Nevertheless, there were a number of claims made about various aspects of the air war that did not bear close examination. Possibly the most prominent feature of the Gulf War was its hi-tech nature, with the air campaign often being likened to some sort of video game. 'Smart' munitions, for example, were credited with unerring accuracy. Figures of one missile fired, one tank destroyed, were broadcast around the world, together with countless video tapes of direct hits on Iraqi targets, and were accepted as the norm. A former US Navy Secretary tried to put the claims in perspective by stating that laser-guided munitions had a 60 per cent hit capability,[21] but even this figure was for missiles fired under test conditions. It ignored the 40 per cent that missed their test-range targets, often by as much as five kilometres (three miles). To expect such munitions to improve their performance suddenly under the arduous conditions of war was unrealistic in the extreme. 'Smart' munitions were undoubtedly far more accurate than conventional bombs, but they were not infallible. No-one was shown the videos of missiles missing their targets.

The exaggeration surrounding the 'smart' munitions can be understood only when two factors are taken into account. First, the Gulf War took place against a background of intense inter-service rivalry within the American armed forces. Each service tried to emphasise its own achievements in order to influence the post-conflict allocation of funds devoted to defence in the aftermath of the Cold War. An example of this was the praise heaped on the F-117A 'stealth fighter' by the USAF, even though several other aircraft performed just as well. Reports of the F-117A's 'invisibility' appear to have been overstated, particularly as all Coalition aircraft were effectively 'stealthy' once Iraqi air defences had been blinded in the first few hours of the air war. In addition, it soon became clear that F-117As did not operate independently of radar-suppression assets, enjoying the benefit of some clever radar-jamming devices. It was therefore misleading to claim that the performance of the F-117A proved the case for developing a future generation of USAF 'stealth' aircraft. Secondly, throughout the war in the Gulf, the American military did all it could to reassure domestic opinion, and one of the most effective ways of doing this was to present the conflict as a 'clean' war, free from the collateral damage associated with Vietnam — in other words, war as an arcade video game.

Such inter-service rivalry inevitably spilt over into discussions about which service had actually 'won' the war. Again, it was the USAF that was most vociferous in its claims, epitomised by General Merrill McPeak, the USAF Chief of Staff, when he stated: 'This is the first time in history that a field army has been defeated by air power.'[22] He clearly had his own definition of the word 'defeat'. In a war against Iraq, defeat meant the removal of occupying troops from Kuwait, something that required ground forces to engage the enemy and liberate the territory belonging to the Emir. After all, people live on the ground, not in the airspace above it. At no time during the air war was it suggested that the Iraqi Army was going to vacate Kuwait or surrender *en masse* just because of the intensity of aerial bombardment. A more accurate summation of the role of airpower in this and other conflicts may be found in the words of a USAF colonel who actually fought in the Gulf: 'airpower can only do so much; the Army must go in on the ground to defeat the enemy's ground forces finally to win the battle.'[23]

Great claims were also made about how effective the Coalition aerial onslaught had been on the Iraqi Army. It was true that Iraqi military morale in Kuwait had been largely destroyed by the exposure to Coalition bombing, but this may be attributed in part to the poor quality of Iraqi troops. Recent history is full of examples of good-quality soldiers withstanding devastating bombardments and then fighting back against ground attack, so to claim that the Iraqi Army's poor performance in 1991 was attributable to airpower alone is to ignore reality.

Finally, there can be little doubt that the Iraqi Air Force was no match for the forces deployed against it. Perhaps the best assessment of its equipment came from Soviet Major-General Nikolai Kutsenko, who stated in *Izvestiya*: 'Iraq's armament, including that which is Soviet-made, was primarily developed in the 1960s-1970s and lags at least one-to-two generations behind the armament of the multinational forces.'[24] Well trained, well motivated personnel using such antiquated systems might have been able to offer some resistance to Coalition airpower, but it is inconceivable that the poorly trained, dispirited Iraqi Air Force could have done more than it did in 1991. Its failure against Western-equipped air forces enjoying overwhelming numerical and technological superiority was hardly surprising, but was crucial. Once the Coalition had achieved air superiority, the outcome of the war was virtually guaranteed.

Notes
1. Brian MacArthur (ed), *Despatches from the Gulf War* (Bloomsbury, London, 1991), p 104.
2. Quoted in Peter Paret (ed), *Makers of Modern Strategy* (Oxford University Press, 1986), p 627.
3. Ibid, pp 628-9.
4. US Department of the Air Force, 'US Air Force Performance in Desert Storm', *Military Technology*, Vol 15, No 6, 1991, pp 146-56.
5. Ibid, p 156.
6. Anthony H Cordesman and Abraham R Wagner, *The Lessons of Modern War*, Vol II, 'The Iran-Iraq War' (Westview Press, Boulder, Colorado, 1990), pp 456-529.
7. Mike Gaines, 'Paper Tigers', *Flight International*, 9-15 January 1991, pp 21-2.
8. Lieutenant-General Charles A Horner, 'The Air Campaign', *Military Review*, September 1991, pp 17-27.
9. MacArthur, op cit, p 104.
10. Ibid, p 61.
11. I D Oppenheim, *Gulf: Diary of the Micro Chip War* (Country Press, Sussex, 1991), p 53.
12. Tamir Eshel. 'The Most Successful Air Campaign Ever?', *Military Technology*, Vol 15, No 4, 1991, pp 36-44.
13. Ibid, p 41.
14. BBC News Report, Sunday 20 January 1991.
15. Frank Barnaby, *The Automated Battlefield* (Sidgwick and Jackson, London, 1986), p 84.
16. Andrew Hull, 'The Role of Ballistic Missiles in Third World Defence Strategies', *Jane's Intelligence Review*, October 1991, pp 464-70.
17. MacArthur, op cit, p 251.
18. Horner, op cit, p 26.
19. Eshel, op cit, p 44.
20. Ibid.
21. *The Washington Post*, Sunday, 3 February 1991.
22. Ibid, Saturday, 16 March 1991.
23. Quoted in Lieutenant-General Edward M Flanagan Jr, 'The 100 Hour War', *Army*, April 1991, p 4.
24. *Izvestiya*, Sunday 24 February 1991.

Further Reading
Norman Friedman, *Desert Victory: The War for Kuwait* (US Naval Institute Press, Annapolis, 1991).
Dilip Hiro, *Desert Shield to Desert Storm. The Second Gulf War* (Paladin, London, 1992).
Stan Morse (ed), *Gulf Air War Debrief* (Aerospace, London, 1992).
Bruce Watson (ed), *Military Lessons of the Gulf War* (Greenhill Books, London, 1991).

CHAPTER 6
The Naval War

Andrew Lambert

'The Navy did not play the press. We tend to avoid the
press; the US Air Force embraced the press. The results
were viewed almost around the clock during the course of
the war by people all over the world.'
   Rear Admiral Riley D Mixson, USN, 9 May 1991.

Navies and the Gulf

Naval forces played a vital, if under-
publicized, role in the Gulf Crisis in
1990-91, both in the immediate
aftermath of the invasion of Kuwait
and in the operations of 'Desert
Storm'. Those operations need to be
placed in context, and lessons
drawn from them for the future of seapower.

The fact that the Gulf War coincided with the end of the Cold War,
combined with the large scale of the military effort and the comprehensive
success of the American-led Coalition, will have a major impact on
subsequent defence decision-making. Nowhere will this be more important
than in the world's naval forces. The value of seapower has been given a
powerful restatement, but few navies are capable of exploiting the
opportunities. In addition, long lead-times for new equipment meant that
few ships deployed in 1990-91 had been designed with the benefit of Royal
Navy (RN) experience in the Falklands campaign of 1982. Force levels and
packaging will have to be modified in the light of the Gulf War. Therefore it
is vital to establish how seapower contributed to Coalition success.

The Persian Gulf: a strategic assessment

The Persian Gulf (hereafter the Gulf), by its geography and climate, limits
the role of naval forces in any regional conflict. The Gulf is no open ocean,
it is nowhere more than 350 km (217 miles) from west to east, only 1,046
km (550 miles) divide Kuwait from Dubai, while the maximum depth of
water is only 200 m (650 ft). Further complications are caused by large
inshore areas of shallow water, which cannot be used by ocean-going
warships. This accounts for the offshore oil-pumping platforms in the area,
and the wealth of deep-water harbours that have been built and improved
since 1945.

In maritime strategic terms, the Gulf is a poor theatre for sea-based
operations. A long, narrow arm of the Indian Ocean, the only entrance is
through the narrow choke-point of the Straits of Hormuz, where the sea
room for large warships is restricted both by shallow waters, ideal for

mining, and by the ease with which land-based missiles can command the passage. The Gulf has always been considered unsuited to the operation of large warships. Although the sea is deep enough, there is inadequate sea room within which to disperse a carrier battle group or to manoeuvre at high speed in the event of sustained air attack. In addition, every part of the Gulf can be covered by land-based, high-performance fighter/strike aircraft. These two factors explain the marked reluctance of the United States Navy (USN) to move any carriers into the Gulf. However, any naval forces operating in the Gulf require sustained air cover. If this is to be provided by carriers operating in the Indian Ocean, the aircraft must be brought up close to the Straits, relying on in-flight refuelling and overflying part of the Arabian peninsula. The former is time-consuming; the latter has serious diplomatic repercussions.

Maritime power in the Gulf can be exercised by frigate/destroyer-sized units, where they can operate under air cover. In this role carrier aviation has the advantage, having more experience of naval tasks and over-sea navigation and better data links. Operations without air superiority are too dangerous to be contemplated. Nations that cannot guarantee air superiority are forced to rely on high-speed units; for this reason the Fast Patrol Boat (FPB) and the Hovercraft have been taken up extensively within the Gulf.

The Naval balance

The regional Gulf powers have largely relied on aircraft and coast-defence forces for seapower. Iran, under the Shah, built up a modest deep-water sea-control navy and placed orders for an impressive range of warships, including four very capable air-defence destroyers based on the American 'Spruance' class. This ambitious programme was terminated by the 1979 Revolution, the four destroyers being taken over by the USN. The more recent Saudi *Sawari* programme created a balanced sea-control force, albeit with a very limited air-defence capacity. Both Iran and Saudi Arabia wanted to extend their strategic reach out into the Indian Ocean, but such forces were too vulnerable to operate effectively in the Gulf. Both nations therefore operate light forces inside the Straits.

The nature of the Gulf prompted many naval analysts to question why Iraq, at the north-western extremity, furthest from the Straits of Hormuz, should have spent so much money on four frigates, six large corvettes and a replenishment vessel. The answer is simple enough. The Italian 'Lupo' and 'Esmerelda'-class units were designed for high-speed operations (35-37 knot), under air cover, to launch heavy anti-shipping missiles. The intended targets — Iranian tankers — would require the larger OTOMAT warhead, rather than the warship-orientated Exocet, while the virtues of a large warship for local policing and interdiction cannot be overstressed.

Iraq never took delivery of these impressive vessels. Had she done so, they would have been very effective for attacking Iranian ships during the Iran-Iraq War (1980-88). After that war ended, the Iranian threat to treat any Iraqi warship passing the Straits of Hormuz as hostile did nothing to encourage Iraq to complete the payments, leaving the ships in the

Mediterranean, out of harm's way. As a result, in August 1990 the largest unit of the Iraqi Navy was a small training frigate, the *Ibn Khaldum* (renamed *Ibn Marjid*), laid up owing to a shortage of spares for her Rolls-Royce engines. In addition there were two Soviet 'Osa I' and five 'Osa II'-class FPBs, three 1,100-ton 'Polnocny'-class landing ships (each with a capacity of 100 troops) and a number of patrol boats and minesweepers. The seizure of the Kuwaiti Navy made a major addition to Iraqi strength. Six of the eight German-built Type 45 and 57 FPBs, armed with Exocet missiles, provided a considerable capacity to attack maritime targets under favourable circumstances. In addition, the Iraqi Air Force had some experience of air-dropping Exocet, additional stocks of which had been held by Kuwait for helicopter launch. It has been estimated that Iraq had 400 Exocets available at the beginning of the crisis, along with 80 to 100 Soviet Styx surface-to-surface missiles for the Osa-class, and an unknown quantity of Chinese Silkworm, a copy of the Styx. In total, Iraq possessed a modest sea-denial force with the capacity to land small forces from the sea. There could be no question of any attempt to assert sea control. However, the Iraqis did possess two weapons that might redress the balance: land-launched Exocet and Silkworm missiles and large stocks of sea mines, ranging from crude contact versions to sophisticated plastic-cased bottom mines using pressure and magnetic influence detonators. As with all their hardware, the mines had come from a variety of suppliers, from the Soviet Union and North Korea to Italy.

The strategic situation was complicated by the stance of Iran. While Iran remained neutral throughout the 1990-91 crisis, its position along the northern shore, and in particular at the Straits, gave it the potential to block off the Gulf, albeit temporarily, using land-based missiles, mines and a small air force, whenever it chose. The ability of the Iranians to threaten surface shipping was their strongest card. If they had elected to join Iraq, Iranian forces would have complicated the situation, forcing the Coalition to rely on forces already within the Gulf until control of the Straits of Hormuz could be regained. This, more than any threat of Iraqi action, kept the American Carrier Battle Groups (CVBGs) outside the Gulf until the war began.

The Coalition possessed an overwhelming naval superiority in the weight and sophistication of its equipment. Furthermore, this was not even counterbalanced by Iraq's local advantages, for the USN and RN had been operating at a high level in the Gulf during the latter stages of the Iran-Iraq War. The USN alone, with 14 aircraft carriers, a Marine Amphibious Force (MAF) of one division with integral air support and another brigade-sized force, had the ability to crush the Iraqi Air Force and launch a sea-based invasion. The major weakness of the USN lay in its limited mine countermeasures (MCM) force. With two new classes under construction, the USN had to rely on ships from the early 1950s and their solitary new Mine Countermeasures Vessel (MCMV), the USS *Avenger*. The strength and experience of RN and European MCM forces gave them a clear role, and made their presence a matter of urgency if the USN was to operate safely in waters which had already seen one mine campaign. Moreover, following experience in the Falklands, and more recently in the Gulf itself, the Western navies had upgraded their anti-air and anti-missile defences and improved damage control.

The US maritime strategy and Coalition doctrine

Although the Coalition had an overwhelming naval superiority in 1990-91, this would be of little use unless it were prepared to operate in the Gulf. In the 1980s the USN had developed a 'Maritime Strategy' based on the offensive use of conventional seapower assets to degrade the ability of the Soviet Navy to threaten Western communications, and to penetrate Soviet ballistic-missile submarine bastion areas. To carry out this mission, the Reagan administration tried to build a 600-ship navy and equip it to take on and defeat Soviet land-based air forces, as well as the numerous submarines of the Northern Fleet. Although this policy can be seen as merely a more coherent and public way of expressing age-old concepts of taking the fight to the enemy, which has a continuous history in war at sea dating back to Drake's raid on Cadiz in 1587, if not before, it did have the singular merit of forcing the USN to prepare for the most difficult conceivable task. This has been compared to the use of naval forces to draw out and destroy the Imperial Japanese Navy in the Battles of the Philippine Sea and Leyte Gulf in 1944. In both cases the real edge for the Americans was technological.

After Vietnam the USN had been seen as increasingly irrelevant to a 'hot' war in Europe, but the maturing of naval weapons technology in the late 1970s allowed the USN to contemplate offensive operations. Central to its new war-fighting capacity were two systems that featured in the Gulf. These were the AEGIS long-range air-defence missile and phased array radar combination, capable of tracking 100 targets and engaging up to 20 at the same time, installed aboard 'Ticonderoga'-class cruisers; and the Tomahawk sea-launched cruise missile (SLCM), intended to neutralise specific hard targets in the Soviet air defence system, facilitating the use of conventional carrier air forces.

Improved anti-submarine warfare (ASW) capability, partly provided by RN support groups, would not be tested in 1991. In any war with the Soviets the USN anticipated a four-carrier battlegroup moving into the Northern Ocean, drawing out Soviet air and submarine assets, degrading them and then pushing the battle closer to the Soviet bases on the Kola peninsula. If they had the capacity to do this, which American analysts believed they did, then the defeat of Iraq should be a simple matter. Further advantages were drawn from the carrier strikes against Libya in 1986, when three carriers destroyed a number of Libyan aircraft, in the air and on the ground, along with air-defence missile batteries and warships. These operations revealed teething troubles in the AEGIS system, but overall the lesson was that Soviet-supplied air-defence systems could do nothing against the sophisticated American electronic warfare (EW) and electronic countermeasures (ECM) packages, while the range and flexibility of American weapons would quickly destroy the selected target. Hostile warships were particularly vulnerable.

By contrast, the Maritime Strategy downplayed the threat of mines, both from the nature of the ocean areas in which it anticipated operating, and from the sheer impossibility of MCM forces keeping up with a CVBG. The use of less-capable helicopter minesweeping was forced on the USN by the speed of fleet operations.[1]

The lessons of Allied naval operations in the Iran-Iraq War

Western and Soviet naval forces were deployed in the Gulf during the Iran-Iraq War, initially to demonstrate concern and later to safeguard economic interests and attempt to influence the course of the conflict. The Soviet presence was limited to escorting three Soviet tankers that had been chartered to Kuwait. By contrast, the USN took an increasingly active role. The graduated American response to Iranian actions has led some to conclude that it merely encouraged further Iranian pressure. The obvious point that should have been drawn from this episode — that a graduated deterrence posture will not impress regimes that have a different concept of international relations — appears not to have been picked up in the Pentagon. In 1987 Iran was perceived as anti-Western and anti-Soviet, yet American policy-makers behaved as though they were still thinking in a manner more appropriate to deterring World War Three. With the Soviets employing a minimal force and working to keep oil supplies open, there was no need to tread so gently. However, if American diplomacy was half-hearted and riddled with confusion, naval operations were carried out successfully and kept within limits that precluded escalation. In addition, they reassured the Arab world that, in the wake of the Iran-Contra scandal, the USA was not going to cave-in to Khomeini.

Iran threatened the sea lanes through the Straits, but this merely hastened the deployment of Western forces to protect Kuwaiti oil shipments, and then to chastise Iran. Yet by a curious fatality, the first serious incident had nothing to do with Iran. On 15 May 1987 the frigate USS *Stark* was hit by two Exocets fired by an Iraqi Mirage F1EQ. One warhead exploded and the fuel tanks of both rockets burned, resulting in the death of 37 men. This made the Gulf a major political issue, and may have encouraged the Iranians to try to pressurize the US over the reflagged tankers, believing there was a real division between the Western powers.

The subsequent mining of the tanker lanes to Kuwait exposed American weakness in MCM. The 414,266-ton USS *Bridgeton* struck a mine on 24 July 1987, only 30 km (19 miles) from the Iranian naval guards' base on Farsi Island. For the remainder of the Iran-Iraq War the USN, with its European allies, built up naval forces in the Gulf to sweep for mines and to escort tankers. On 13 April 1988 the frigate USS *Samuel B Roberts* struck a mine. Although ten men were injured and the ship was very badly damaged, the calm water and well drilled crew kept her afloat. In response, the Americans attacked Iranian oil platforms that had been used as naval bases. In the resulting battle two Iranian frigates were sunk and a third disabled; several small craft were also destroyed. The air cover was provided by USS *Enterprise*, operating inside the Gulf. This allowed the USA to offer protection to all ships within the Gulf from 21 April. On 3 July the AEGIS cruiser USS *Vincennes* moved to protect a Danish tanker, threatened by Iranian boats. Under pressure her inexperienced crew misread their sensors, shooting down an Iranian Airbus with 290 civilians on board, which they took for a hostile F-14. This incident provided a catalyst for Iran to end the war.

The 1987–88 naval war made the USA wary of limited involvement and anxious to have the full support of her allies, particularly Britain, which could provide vital MCMV. Although the USN could demolish any surface or air threat with ease, it was less happy with regard to mines. The damage inflicted on the *Roberts* was a lesson that the world's most powerful navy would not forget.[2]

Naval forces and the crisis: August 1990 to January 1991
In the immediate aftermath of the Iraqi invasion of Kuwait on 2 August 1990, American options were limited. Iraq was too large for any conceivable air strike or strikes by the forces in the area to be decisive. Indeed, they would have been counter-productive before the diplomatic processes had been exhausted and the Coalition built up. An attack might give Saddam a justification for invading Saudi Arabia. In addition, it was clear that ground forces would be required to defeat the Iraqi Army and recover Kuwait, however badly Iraqi nuclear, biological and chemical facilities were hit from the air. Nevertheless, if Saddam had invaded Saudi Arabia, local naval air assets (the *Independence* was available for strike operations from 5 August, the *Eisenhower* only three days later) would have been used to slow the Iraqi advance while a reinforceable defensive position was established, analogous to the Pusan perimeter during the Korean War.

The analogy with the air raids on Libya in 1986 should not be carried too far, however, as those carrier strikes were used to demonstrate weakness, not to fight a war. In the short term, naval forces were the best symbols of American commitment, being highly visible and in-theatre. Deploying troops would take time and require a major logistics build-up, the latter almost entirely by sea.

It is not without significance that, on 5 August, one day before King Fahd requested American aid, President Bush ordered 50 USN warships to deploy to the Gulf. Forces available locally comprised the US Joint Force Middle East (JTFME) — one cruiser, one destroyer and five frigates, with the flagship USS *La Salle*. The Royal Navy had the destroyer HMS *York*, the frigates HMS *Battleaxe* and *Jupiter* and the storeship RFA *Orangeleaf*. France had two small corvettes, and the Soviet Union a large destroyer. Additional US forces in the wider theatre included the CVBG led by USS *Independence*, which was temporarily in the Indian Ocean, and the *Eisenhower* group in the Mediterranean. The *Saratoga* CVBG was despatched to relieve *Eisenhower*, accompanied by the battleship USS *Wisconsin* and an amphibious component. When the *Eisenhower* moved into the Red Sea, two carriers were available to strike at Iraq three days before any air force assets reached Saudi Arabia. The forces on the spot were assigned to enforce the blockade and operate against Iraq if any further aggression was committed.

Economic sanctions

While the diplomacy of alliance building was conducted, the United Nations agreed to wage economic war. Under Resolution 661, passed on 6 August, the UN approved a range of economic sanctions, including an embargo on the purchase of Iraqi oil and an end to sales to Iraq. One immediate effect of these measures was to ensure that most of the Iraqi Air Force's MiG-21s would remain in Yugoslavia, where they were being serviced. More significantly, it also included food, in which Iraq was not self-sufficient. Unable to raise money abroad by selling oil, Iraq would find it increasingly difficult to purchase food and munitions. The rapid institution of food rationing, on 1 September, and tighter regulations imposed on the 14th, indicated the weakness of Iraq against this old form of coercion. Although the embargo was imperfect, the use of Jordan and air links could not replace the massive sea-based import trade in such staples as rice and flour. In addition, Iraq had not kept adequate stocks of spare parts for military and civil equipment. The cumulative impact of the blockade over five months seriously degraded the Iraqi response to the air war. However, there is no example of sanctions forcing an aggressor to relinquish his prize, so it was almost inevitable from the start that military action would have to be prepared for, and taken. In the interval, the blockade would keep up pressure.

The blockade was conducted by a relatively small Multinational Interception Force (MNIF), relying on the computer and tracking facilities of the Tomahawk SLCM system, with a specially modified P-3C Orion aircraft to identify ships. This sophisticated equipment was critical when several thousand ships had to be monitored at any one time. The Americans employed small Coast Guard detachments familiar with the legal issues at stake, after experience with drug enforcement patrols. Resolution 665 gave the Coalition forces latitude to employ lethal force if the circumstances required. The USS *John I Hall* intercepted the first Iraqi ship, the tanker *Al Fao*, on 17 August in the Red Sea. On the same day two more were stopped in the Gulf. By the time of the ceasefire almost 7,000 ships had been intercepted — between 30 and 40 a day. As the deadline for Iraq to evacuate Kuwait came closer, this task was increasingly left to the less-capable ships of the Coalition forces. Some 1,000 ships had to be boarded, often by helicopter. With the Gulf easily closed, most cargoes were routed through the Jordanian Red Sea port of Aqaba, so some 93 per cent of all ships intercepted were in the Red Sea. Iraqi efforts to run the blockade, ignore warning shots, resist the boarding parties or to stage an incident to discredit it were unsuccessful. This operation continued after the war, as the object under UN Resolution 661 was to enforce the withdrawal of Iraq from Kuwait and ensure the payment of reparations.[3] The immediate effects were to reduce Iraq's GNP by half. However, it was clear that the embargo could not bring sufficient pressure on the Iraqi regime, in the medium term, to secure UN objectives. In future, naval coercive action must be viewed from the outset as a combination of economic and military pressure.

Strategic options

When Operation 'Desert Storm' began, in January 1991, there were approximately 120 US and 50 Coalition warships available in the theatre of operations. These provided General Norman H. Schwarzkopf with a range of options, and posed a serious threat to Iraq; one that, it must be concluded, was underestimated by Saddam. There is now a danger that post-war analyses will make the same mistake.

Naval command

The naval component of CENTCOM (NAVCENT), under Schwarzkopf as CENTCOM Commander, was initially commanded by Vice Admiral Henry Mauz of the JTFME. He was superseded in October by Vice Admiral Stanley Arthur, Commander of the US Seventh Fleet aboard the USS *Blue Ridge*, a specialist command flagship normally based at Yokosuka. Among the Coalition naval forces the American, Australian and NATO forces adopted standard NATO operating procedures and secure signalling systems, but the remaining units were hampered by having to rely on normal ship-to-ship radio. This determined the operating patterns of the various Coalition ships. The command, control and communications (C^3) aspect of the naval war proved to be very successful. By contrast, there were serious weaknesses in human and terrestrial intelligence gathering, which can be attributed to the Carter era run-down of these assets in favour of satellite reconnaissance. The most obvious result of this weakness was the overestimation of Iraqi strength, based on published figures of equipment and divisions rather than a close-up appreciation of manning levels and operability.

The USN controlled all naval forces in the northern half of the Gulf and in the Red Sea. The southern Gulf was placed under the command of the Western European Union, at the time under French presidency. SLCMs were also fired from the Mediterranean, where a multinational allied effort served to escort the supplies and guard against the vague threat of Libyan or terrorist intervention. Following the Goldwater-Nichols Act of 1986, new American command and control arrangements tended to assert air force/army concepts over those of the navy. As a result, USN air assets were placed under control of the air force. The unified air component for 'Desert Storm' was placed under the Joint Forces Air Component Commander (JFACC), Lieutenant General Charles A. ('Chuck') Horner. This co-ordinated the air war against fixed targets in Iraq, but proved less successful in responding to the fluid air-sea battle along the coast. The structure did not satisfy the USN, which was under-represented, and may have played a part in the low level of publicity accorded to naval forces. Despite the best intentions of General Horner, and the efforts of naval officers assigned to JFACC, the USN is conscious of having lost a major battle: the battle for post-war public support in funding struggles. The lack of ranking naval representation at Riyadh did weaken the naval case with the media.[4]

The naval build-up

As 'Desert Shield' was put in place, the naval forces in the area were reinforced. American assets included the movement of the CVBG led by USS *Midway* from Japan in September 1990, and the despatch of the battleship USS *Missouri* to the Gulf. While the carriers spent their time outside the Gulf, the battleships were available to support the land forces. The battleships, the only two in commission, were a major asset, combining the awesome firepower of 16-inch guns with a large battery of SLCMs. The guns were considered vital for any amphibious landing, while the SLCMs were a key part of the air war. The two carriers in the Arabian Sea remained largely outside the Gulf — *Independence* moved in between 2 and 6 October as a demonstration — but they were far safer outside the Straits, and remained there until the air war began. They could operate against Iraq only at extreme range from outside the Gulf.

In mid-August the *Eisenhower* CVBG was relieved in the Red Sea by the *John F Kennedy*. The USS *America* arrived in the Red Sea in November, while the *Ranger* relieved the *Independence* in January 1991, and carrier strength was finally brought up to six CVBGs when the *Theodore Roosevelt* entered the Gulf on 21 January. Further carriers were available — the *Nimitz*, *Abraham Lincoln*, *Forrestal* and *Independence* were all considered for urgent dispatch. The arrival of substantial Marine forces allowed the navy to pose an amphibious threat to the seaward flank of the Iraqi position, tying down troops and equipment.

In addition to the forces deployed within range of Iraq, the Coalition relied on the RN light CVBG based around HMS *Ark Royal* to replace the American presence off Libya, with support from the Spanish *Principe De Asturias* group and the Italian *Guiseppe Garibaldi*. The NATO exercises Operation 'MedNet I' (2–6 February) and 'MedNet II' (14–27 February 1991), tracked shipping of special interest throughout the Mediterranean. In addition, the NATO fleet, without an American carrier, exercised its air-defence capabilities. With reinforced MCM assets, including a French force in the Suez Canal, these forces were a powerful reminder to all concerned that NATO had a strategic role, forces to spare, and a very effective C^3 system. Finally, on 21 January the USS *Forrestal* was ordered to the eastern Mediterranean, from Florida, to provide reinforcements, while a German MCM force covered the northern entrance to the Suez Canal. Both covered the logistic tail of 'Desert Shield'. As an indication of his limited strategic vision, Saddam appears to have made no effort to interdict Coalition supplies, or the port and airbase facilities in Saudi Arabia. However, the danger was real, and had to be guarded against. The possibility of even one success against the Coalition logistic supply line, with so few national-flag ships, was one of the most serious challenges to the entire operation. Once again the requirement for a significant deep-sea, nationally owned merchant marine was restated. Unfortunately the very success of the covering operation, and Saddam's weakness, have ensured that nothing will be done. The threat of terrorist action, however, did have an impact on civil air traffic.

Within the Gulf, in addition to the American forces, the Royal Navy provided three air-defence destroyers, three modern frigates, one aviation training ship, five MCMVs, and part of the replenishment fleet. The British ships were the only ones to join the Americans in the firing line. Australia and the Netherlands each provided a pair of modern frigates with a replenishment ship, and these reinforced the *Midway* CVBG when it entered the Gulf. Italy and Spain reinforced patrols in the eastern Mediterranean, while Argentina, Belgium, Canada, Denmark, France and Greece contributed to the blockade. The French effort was the only one to achieve a high profile, through the sorry cruise of the light aircraft carrier *Clemenceau*, which was unable to operate her obsolete air group and then suffered a serious engineering failure in the Red Sea. It is noteworthy that none of the European navies sent MCMVs to join the British at the head of the Gulf until after hostilities had ended. Precluded from operating outside the NATO area, German forces were deployed to the Mediterranean to replace ships sent to the war zone and to reinforce NATO forces in the absence of the American carriers.[5]

The Defence of Kuwait

Saddam believed that he could avoid war by raising the possible cost of a Coalition attack. To this end, the numerous high-technology weapons paraded at the 1989 Baghdad Air Show, specifically the sea mines, were publicised. Considerable effort was put into reinforcing the seaward defences north and south of Kuwait City against an amphibious landing, as demonstrated on an Iraqi sand-table captured in Kuwait City. Six divisions were dug in along the coast. While these preparations were in process, Saddam used the Western hostages to buy time.

Naval operations

Naval forces, which had imposed the blockade and thus degraded Iraqi defences since August, remained a major asset. They did not receive their due weight of publicity at the time, and have not done so since. The slow strangulation of a blockade makes poor news copy.

The naval contribution to the air war

The strike assets of the USN — six CVBGs, two battleships, many more Tomahawk-armed ships, and an unknown, and as yet still classified, deployment of submarines armed with SLCMs — were a major asset. Being mobile, the CVBGs were safe from the threat of a Scud attack, something that could not be said for any fixed base after the hit on Dhahran. In addition, they gave the Coalition the ability to strike Iraqi air defences from hitherto unexpected quarters. Flying from the Red Sea, the air groups of USS *Saratoga* and *John F Kennedy* could outflank Iraqi air defences, although the aircraft did require air-refuelling on both legs of the mission. These two ships were primarily flying strike missions, but those in the Gulf were orientated towards providing fighter cover and support for ground and sea forces. The four carriers in the Gulf (USS *America* was switched from the Red Sea in time to support the land operations), were closer to Iraq than any shore-based aircraft, at times only 240 km (150 miles) from the target zone, and so could achieve very high sortie rates. USS *Theodore Roosevelt* was particularly active attacking the Republican Guard concentration areas. This was the first time that four large carriers had operated together, posing a series of new command and control problems, all of which were overcome with ease. In addition, the horror felt by the deep-water USN at the prospect of operations in the confined waters of the Gulf proved to be unfounded. The four ships had adequate sea room because there was no air threat.

During 'Desert Storm', about 30 per cent of all air missions were flown by USN assets. Indeed, American carrier aviation played a critical role in the air war. In August 1990 the USN had just completed a detailed examination of Iraqi air defences. This information, along with the five-month respite provided by 'Desert Shield', gave the US Air Force time enough to plan its attack. Electronic reconnaissance was largely conducted by land-based EA-3B, EP-3E and P-3 Orions operating from Crete and Jeddah. These were supplemented by RAF Nimrods. The Coalition edge in signals intelligence (SIGINT), electronic intelligence (ELINT) and communications intelligence (COMINT), while as yet unclear, must have been at least as marked as that in other areas of electronic warfare. Although the Iraqi system was integrated, the individual elements were not particularly impressive. If the command structure could be removed, the whole would be far less than the sum of its parts. USN experience in dismantling a similar, if smaller, Soviet-based system in Libya in 1986, provided a guide. Navy EA-6B Prowlers could jam radars, launch AGM-88 high-speed anti-radiation missiles (HARM), and employ tactical air-launched decoys (TALD). These aircraft would be accompanied by fighter-bombers with the firepower to destroy the blinded and confused radar sites. The USN employed a different tactical approach to the air force, emphasising the flexibility of its assets. The navy also successfully deployed the new AGM-84E stand-off land attack missile (SLAM), based on the Harpoon. The naval contribution was particularly important, the Prowler being the only Coalition aircraft equipped to jam non Soviet-bloc radars, of which Iraq had several. The majority of the first night-strikes against air-defence missiles were carried out by USN and Marine Corps aircraft. Naval units also fired Tomahawks to knock out fixed radar positions. These were timed to precede air-strikes, confusing enemy radar.

The launch of an overwhelming strike on 16/17 January 1991 allowed the Iraqis no time to become acclimatised to air attack, or to repair their air-defence system. It was far more effective than the same weight of munitions dropped over a longer period, as a comparison with the gradual build-up of the air war against Vietnam should emphasize. The rapid turn-round of carrier-based aircraft in the Gulf added weight to the opening move. Once air superiority had been seized, the USAF Checkmate plan — a detailed and inflexible target list — came into operation, attacking targets built up from satellite intelligence. While this provided the detailed mapping required for Tomahawk, and pinpointed fixed targets, it lacked the flexibility to take on the Scuds and other mobile targets. This showed up clear divisions of emphasis between the USAF and USN. The air force wanted to win a strategic air war, while the navy thought more in terms of supporting the ground war. However, the sheer number of attacking aircraft over Iraq and Kuwait required detailed central targeting control, the success of which can be seen in the absence of 'blue-on-blue' (friendly fire) air engagements.

The inherent flexibility of carrier air groups (demonstrated by the movement of the *America*), with the close proximity of the CVBGs in the Gulf, ensured that the USN carried out at least 60 per cent of the operations to suppress Iraqi air defences. With the Coalition air forces short of strike reconnaissance assets for bomb-damage assessment, this role was taken on by 17 USN F-14s with the tactical air-photo reconnaissance pods (TARPS). They proved to be the best source for such intelligence, underlining the folly of relying solely on satellites for intelligence gathering.

The carriers in the Red Sea, commanded by Rear Admiral Riley D Mixson, concentrated on targets in western Iraq and around Baghdad, while those in the Gulf worked over the Basra area and the naval base at Umm Qasr. The availability of laser-guided and other precision munitions gave a particular advantage to carrier air groups. In the past, carrier aviation has suffered from limited bomb stowage, but this was far less important when almost every weapon could be expected to hit. However, there were serious shortages of the most important high-tech weapons. Admiral Mixson reported from the Red Sea that he was down to his last 37 laser-bomb guidance kits at the ceasefire. In addition, the carriers lacked the capability to deliver really heavy weapons, while the F/A-18s and F-7s lacked laser designators and thus had to operate with A-6s. All suffered from limited organic refuelling capacity. This last placed them entirely in the hands of JFACC for missions beyond 320 km (200 miles). Six USN aircraft were lost in action: five strike aeroplanes and one F-14.

In addition to aircraft, the USN deployed an estimated 350 Tomahawk SLCMs, of which 284 were fired, about 80 per cent hitting their targets. USS *Louisville* became the first submarine to launch one of these weapons in anger. By firing Tomahawk from all round the borders of Iraq it was possible to complicate the already disastrous air-defence scenario. Because the SLCM does not depend on visual information, it provides the navy with the capacity to strike even in conditions that preclude manned air operations.

The overall contribution of the USN to the air war, taking into account the six carriers, the Marine Corps' assets and Tomahawks, cannot be rated below 30 per cent. This figure is impressive enough, without adding in the potential of the carriers held in reserve. The specialist anti-air-defence skills of the carrier squadrons were a vital asset, the SLCMs added a new element, while the Marine Corps was able to conduct the great bulk of its own air support. These aspects of the air war have to be restated, because they are in danger of being subsumed into an air force and army war.

Deterrence
In addition to the prosecution of the air war, the USN also carried the Coalition's deterrent against Iraqi chemical, biological and possibly nuclear

weapons. The cruiser USS *San Jacinto* was designated a 'special weapons ship', which has been taken as meaning that she carried nuclear-armed SLCMs, ready to respond to any Iraqi use of weapons of mass destruction. Her vertical launch battery was entirely armed with 122 conventional SLCMs, and although she was the first warship to fire the new missile in combat, she did not fire anything like her entire load. Two more cruisers, the *Antietam* and *Philippine Sea*, were also armed with an increased ratio of SLCMs. This threat had been made clear in a series of statements by President Bush.

The naval war
To support and protect carrier operations, Coalition naval forces pushed up the Gulf, taking the opportunity to attack Iraqi naval and sea defence assets, clear mines, and eventually retake Kuwaiti islands. With so little danger, the carriers could replenish (which they had to do every three to four days) without leaving the battle zone.

Among the first targets for carrier air attack was the Iraqi naval base at Umm Qasr. The base was bombed and its approaches mined, forcing the Iraqis to abandon their naval assets, or to move them out into the Gulf where they could be destroyed. This was part of a concerted plan for operations in the northern Gulf, intended to open the way for amphibious operations. It began with the removal of Iraqi observers from the offshore islands and oil platforms, which were being used as observation posts to replace the lost air-defence radar coverage. On 18 January 1991 USS *Nicholas*, under the cover of P-3 Orion radar surveillance, deployed army special force units and helicopters, with a Kuwaiti FPB, to clear 11 oil platforms in the Durrah field. Following this demonstration, the Iraqis evacuated as many of the remaining platforms as they could, and further attacks met with little or no resistance from demoralised and hungry Iraqis. On 22 January two Iraqi minesweepers were destroyed; one was disabled by Sea Skua missiles and then sunk by an A-6 from USS *Ranger*, and the other sank after running into a minefield. Two days later Qaruh Island was retaken, providing a wealth of information on Iraqi minefields. Pushing the enemy back on to the mainland deprived him of the ability to see what lay over the horizon, giving emphasis to the latent threat of the amphibious power of the US Marine Corps.

The battle for Khafji
Saddam's plan for the attack on Khafji, which began on 29 January, involved cutting off a Marine Corps' unit by land and sea. Seaborne forces would be landed in the rear of the town, to complete the circle. A convoy of 17 small boats carrying Iraqi commandos was picked up on the radar of a British frigate, attacked by RN Lynx helicopters firing Sea Skua, and then by further Coalition helicopters and USN A-6s. The entire convoy was destroyed; 14 boats were sunk and three driven ashore. At the same time the battleships provided fire support to the Saudi forces. Further up the coast, US Marines reoccupied the deserted Kuwaiti island of Umm al Maradir, which had been used for early warning of air attacks.

On the 30th a more substantial convoy, including three ex-Kuwaiti TNC 45s, three Polnocny landing craft and a Type 43 minesweeper, was detected by USN P-3 Orions and then engaged by Coalition air assets off Bubiyan Island. While it has been suggested that these vessels carried a reinforced Iraqi combat team, and were intended to link up with the Khafji operation, it is now clear that they, like the air force, were running for Iran. Sea Skua missiles knocked out all seven ships. The majority were then sunk — the Polnocnys by RAF Jaguars and the TNCs by A-6s. One Osa reached Iranian waters, badly damaged and still burning. The Type 43 survived to regain harbour. There was no attempt to provide air cover for either convoy.

The destruction of defenceless and slow-moving light ships in such a hostile environment was not surprising, although the Iraqi decision to put them in harm's way can only be explained by Saddam's ignorance of the realities of naval war. The attempted flight of the more powerful units made sense only if they could reach Iran. They would not survive if they remained in Iraq or Kuwait, and had little chance of damaging Coalition naval units. With the benefit of hindsight, it is clear that this operation wasted the best naval units available to Iraq. All Iraqi missile-firing warships had been accounted for by 3 February, the day the *Missouri* crept through the minefields to bombard the coast of Kuwait. The *Wisconsin* supported a Marine Corps' probe into southern Kuwait on 8–9 February with 112 16-inch rounds, paving the way for land operations along the coast.

The amphibious threat
When the battleships moved into firing positions, the amphibious threat became real. The Marine Corps prepared plans for an operation to land inside the Shatt al-Arab and cut off the Iraqi forces in Kuwait. These were not adopted, but the final decision of General Schwarzkopf appears to have been delayed until mid-February. The old concept of opposed amphibious landings, in the style of D-Day, required some revision. The US Marine Corps combines a wealth of assets, from 50-knot air cushion landing craft to heavy helicopters, that make a modern landing into a wide and deep assault that can outflank or leap-frog defences. The non-employment of this option was conditioned by factors other than its viability. It was obvious that, as the Iraqis had been allowed five months in which to prepare their seaward defences, any assault landing would be expensive. However, very few people were informed of the decision against the amphibious operation, sustaining the deception plan.

The sea defences of Iraq — naval forces, shore missile batteries and naval air strength, largely based around Exocet — were rapidly demolished. They had never posed a serious threat to the Coalition. Even the modern TNC 45-class Kuwaiti boats were defenceless against Sea Skua, their limited fire control radar being easily confused by the movement of the helicopter, particularly if the FPB accelerated to anything like top speed, when vibration reduced radar performance. Developed to counter the Soviet deployment of heavy missile corvettes, such as the 'Nanchuka' class, the small Sea Skua was not lethal against an FPB, though it was powerful enough to disable the boat, leaving it to be finished off by aircraft dropping unguided bombs. Fifteen hits were observed, including those on five ex-Kuwaiti FPBs, two T43 minesweepers, two Polnocny landing ships, two 'Zhuk'-type patrol boats and two smaller assault boats. These engagements were carried out well inside the 15 km (9 mile) range of the missile.[6]

It is indicative of the level of threat that, by the end of the war, the Lynx were leaving off their 'Yellow Veil' (ALQ-167‹V›) jammer pods to make room for two additional Sea Skua. The American frigate helicopter, the SH-60, was not armed with an anti-FPB missile, and as a result it often worked in combination with the RN. The USN had purchased the Norwegian Penguin missile for this task, but had yet to deploy the system.[7]

While it has been argued that the next generation of FPBs will be able to carry duplicate C^3 and better point defence, this will probably also ensure that they are both too big and too expensive for their role. The FPB myth was one of the larger illusions to be exploded by the Gulf conflict. In fact, the whole concept of coast defence by light warships has, once again, been shown up as little more than a waste of effort. Superior naval forces can always deal with FPBs, SSMs and mines if they have air superiority. With air superiority, the defenders will not require FPBs or SSMs, merely air-dropped weapons of adequate performance. Modern surface-to-surface missiles have the range to strike targets well out to sea, removing the requirement to send a ship out to hit them. The only surface-to-surface missiles actually fired at Coalition naval forces, a pair of Silkworms aimed at USS *Missouri* on 24 February, were, significantly, shore-launched. The only attempt to air-drop Exocet — by a solitary Mirage F1EQS with another Mirage as an escort on 24 January — was dealt with by a Saudi F-15C vectored in by Hawkeyes.

While both the USN and RN have refused to comment on the deployment of submarines, two British 'Oberon'-class diesel-electric sub-marines were employed in the Gulf. Both HMS *Otus* and *Opposum* returned home painted in an unusual camouflage, the former displaying a pennant which indicated that she had been involved in clandestine operations. This would appear to have involved the insertion of special forces, a task for which the older submarines are well configured. The Americans employed 18 nuclear-powered boats as part of the escort force for the CVBGs, for reconnaissance, and for missile launching.[8]

Mine warfare
The most significant threat to the freedom of Coalition naval forces to operate in the northern Gulf, and thus to an amphibious operation, was posed by mines. The Iraqis used only five basic types, despite claims that they had obtained the design of the latest British 'Stonefish' type through Cardoen Industries. The types deployed were the plastic-cased Italian Manta acoustic ground mine, with an additional magnetic sensor; the Lugum 145, a locally made version of the old Soviet moored contact mine; the Soviet KMD 500 multi-influence ground mine; the hitherto unidentified UDM 500 bottom-mine; and another Soviet designed ground mine, built in Iraq but employing Soviet electronics. The Iraqi plan called for 60 mines per nautical mile in water between 3 and 12 m (10 and 40 ft) deep, between 800

and 1,600 per nautical mile between the 3 m (10 ft) line and the beach, and 3,200 to 6,400 simple landmines per 1.6 km (1 mile) on the beach. No mines were encountered on the beach, but the 3 to 12 m depths were mined according to plan. More than 1,200 sea mines appear to have been laid. Those furthest from the Iraqi bases were often out of position, and in many cases were still fitted with their safety devices. This range of types increased the problems facing the American and British clearance units. When the Coalition forces moved into the northern Gulf, the Iraqis released about 150 floating mines from Ra's-al-Qulay'ah, most of which washed-up ashore. These weapons, being very difficult to pick up on sonar or radar, forced the Coalition warships to employ visual bow lookouts.

The American effort comprised six MH-53E Sea Stallion helicopter sweepers aboard the helicopter carrier USS *Tripoli*; the Royal Navy contributed up to five of the outstanding 'Hunt'-class MCMVs, and controlled the surface clearance operation. Australian and Saudi clearance divers were also employed. Britain and America had had some experience of sweeping during the latter stages of the Iran-Iraq War, but the task was more complex in 1991. The Iranians had relied almost entirely on contact mines, so this time the seabed would have to be cleared by detailed investigation — a slow and laborious task that made heavy demands on air cover and surface escorts for the helicopters and vessels involved. Preliminary sweeping by the Sea Stallions for acoustic and magnetic mines was of some benefit, reducing the risk to the surface sweepers, but there can be no substitute for surface operations if the sea is to be used by other surface ships. The five-month build-up to the conflict allowed the Coalition to generate a good picture of where the mines had been laid, and the ships that had been laying them. The latter should have been a major target for naval air attacks, and were often tracked by satellite, but the rigid air targeting orders employed at JFAAC hampered efforts to destroy the large salvage tug *Aka*, which laid several fields during the war. The waste of assets at Khafji reduced the already limited capability of the Iraqis to reinforce their fields.

The main task of the sweeping effort was to clear two lanes into the Kuwaiti coast, together with safe areas close to the shore for the battleships. Mines did slow the pace of Coalition naval operations, and by doing so made it harder to pose the threat of an amphibious landing that was to become part of Coalition strategy. Some American ships were fitted with a high-definition mine-avoidance sonar, a direct result of the 1987–88 naval war in the Gulf. USS *Nicholas* used this system on 3 February to pilot the *Missouri* into a firing position off Kuwait.

Mine damage to USS *Tripoli* and USS *Princeton*, both of which were hit on 18 February, demonstrated the limits of mine clearance. *Tripoli* ran into a field of contact mines, striking one at 4.30 am. This blew a hole some 4 by 6 m (16 by 20 ft), 3 m (10 ft) below the waterline on the starboard side. Three compartments were flooded and the ship was temporarily left dead in the water. Although she suffered only local damage (in the paint store, to be precise), she had to be dry-docked at Bahrain, and her helicopter mine-sweepers were transferred to her sister ship, USS *New Orleans*.

The AEGIS cruiser *Princeton*, which was co-ordinating local anti-air and anti-missile cover for the mine-clearing forces, triggered a ground mine at 7.16 am, while travelling a very low speed. She had taken up a position between the minehunters and the possible site of Silkworm batteries. Sources inside the Pentagon have suggested that the *Princeton* made a simple error in navigation, leaving the swept channel, although this has not been confirmed. The main effect of the mine was to lift the stern of the ship bodily out of the water by up to 3 m (10 ft), causing a severe whiplash effect and a cycle of vertical and then lateral shock waves. The lateral motion was caused by a second mine, apparently a sympathetic detonation, 275 m (300 yards) off the starboard bow. Because the majority of the crew were at breakfast, or in their quarters, and therefore well away from the bow and stern, only three crewmen were medevaced, and none was in any danger. The *Princeton* was badly damaged. Half of her powerplant was knocked out, the port rudder and propeller shaft were disabled, and the hull suffered severe distortion. The quarterdeck was badly buckled and the keel strained. As a result, her aft gun and missile systems were also out of service. However, she had been designed to 'fight hurt', and remained on station until relieved. *Princeton* was dry-docked at Dubai for repairs before proceeding home. Reaction and damage control on both ships was well conducted.

The Coalition effort succeeded in clearing a path through the minefields, making the amphibious threat a real one. More worrying for the USN was the degree of dependence on British expertise. There is little point having the world's only oceanic power-projection navy if you cannot then cross the last few kilometres to the beach. In addition to a general lack of American experience in surface MCM, the USS *Avenger* suffered mechanical problems with her engines.[9]

By contrast, the efforts of the five RN Hunt-class MCMVs — *Atherstone, Cattistock, Dulverton, Hurworth* and *Ledbury* — were a great success. Over 270 mines were destroyed, largely by RN ships with additional USN divers. They opened up the sea approaches exploited by the two battleships, and formed the vanguard of the Coalition naval effort. When the Coalition forces returned to Kuwait, Rear Admiral Taylor, USN, signalled HMS *Cattistock* to take the lead as 'the fleet was used to following a "Hunt".' The need to use a survey ship and the Tank Landing Ship *Sir Galahad* (which had arrived on station carrying part of the British 1st Armoured Division) as a base, pointed out the limitations of these craft for sustained operations in distant waters. They required a full support package, which had to be both local and mobile. In 1987 the purpose-built MCMV support ship HMS *Abdiel* had been deployed, but by 1991 she had been sold without being replaced.

The naval war continues

Despite the two mine hits, the amphibious warfare ships remained on station, while the *Missouri* shelled Faylakah Island on 23 February, sustaining the threat. On the 24th the British MCMVs led the amphibious assets towards the coast, at which point two Silkworms were fired. One never reached the danger zone; the other was shot down by two Sea Dart missiles from HMS *Gloucester*. During the conflict a Type 42 destroyer was permanently assigned to 'ride shotgun' on the battleships. The missile battery was then destroyed by aircraft, the four carriers having moved up to the central Gulf in support of the land, and sea, attack. The Marine forces were always ready to land, but the progress of the land war made this expensive operation unnecessary. On the 26th the battleships fired their final salvoes.

Fire support

Because of the wide coastal area of shallow water in the Gulf, the only Coalition ships with artillery capable of hitting the land were the two American battleships. The 16-inch, 50-calibre gun might have been the oldest weapon in service, but it was a major asset, offering sustainable bombardments at low cost and without recourse to aircraft. The 2,500 lb shells were capable of penetrating any concrete bunkers on the coast of Kuwait. The presence of these guns was seen as a major precondition for a successful amphibious operation by the Marine Corps. Spotting for the guns was conducted by small Pioneer remotely piloted vehicles (RPVs), operated by the battleships themselves. This harked back to the pre-1939 era, when all battleships carried floatplanes for the same task. The range of heavy guns made visual spotting from the ship impossible. Later in the war the Iraqis realised the significance of the RPVs. When one flew over a target the Iraqi troops surrendered, rather than face what was to follow. Over 1,100 16-inch shells were fired, adding weight to the threat of an amphibious landing and helping the progress of Marine Corps units along the coast.

Marine Corps plans for a seaborne operation were serious; Schwarzkopf's very public wielding of the Marine Corps' assets was always a part of his overall war plan to deceive the Iraqi command as to the exact point of attack. In this respect the public (and rather unsuccessful) Exercise 'Imminent Thunder' 160 km (100 miles) south of the Kuwaiti border on 15 November 1990, Exercise 'Sea Soldier IV' on 24 January 1991 (the largest amphibious landing since Inchon in 1950), and the widely reported arrival of amphibious units from the American West Coast, had a dual role. First, they reminded Saddam of the danger to his flank; second, they drew the media off the scent of the great leftward deployment of the army. During the ground war CENTCOM made further use of the amphibious feint, reporting that the offshore islands of Faylakah and Bubiyan were under attack, and later that they had been taken. Marine Corps Harriers and the battleships did attack the islands, but no troops were landed. The men of the 5th Marine Expeditionary Brigade (MEB) were eventually flown ashore, shortly before the land war began, to form the operational reserve for the 1st Marine Division. However, the 4th MEB, which had the greater helicopter assets, was kept afloat throughout the campaign, to meet any unexpected eventuality.

The naval lessons for the future

The lessons, both strategic and tactical, to be drawn from the naval and amphibious aspects of 'Desert Storm' fall into two categories: new experience, and salutary reminders.

Strategic implications

The United States Navy, assisted by Coalition forces, provided the first deterrent to further Iraqi aggression, blocking any easy advance beyond Kuwait; enforced an effective trade embargo; prepared the way for the ground and air forces; shipped in 95 per cent of all stores used to fight the war; provided 30 per cent of the air assets, the majority of which were strategically mobile, including some that could not have been duplicated; posed a real, and strategically significant, threat to the seaward flank of the Iraqi position; and offered Schwarzkopf the option to employ this capacity if the situation required. The speed of response and flexibility of American seapower has no rival. It is hardly possible that another war will arise in which the allies have five months to get ready, a well prepared air and land base with excellent port facilities on hand, and an all-but-comatose enemy willing to have his air-defence system probed and analysed. If the land and air components of 'Desert Storm' have stolen the thunder, they have done so by building on the foundations laid by the naval forces, and in circumstances that are unlikely to recur.

Although Iraq was not the Soviet Union, and Kuwait was hardly equivalent to the Kola peninsula, the range of electronic warfare assets, missile technology and airpower available to the USN make it uniquely capable. No other navy has the airpower to take on a regional power like Iraq. Had Saddam pushed on in August 1990, carrier airpower would have crippled his operations and earned the Coalition time to react, even if that required two CVBGs to take on the entire Iraqi Air Force. The strategic mobility of carrier aviation, which requires no friendly overflight rights, no local bases and embodies years of experience of operating at the end of a long logistic line, should ensure its future.

Similarly, there can be no doubt that only the biggest carriers make sense. The *Midway* did well with her light air group, but F-14s are essential to cover long-range offensive operations. As the veteran carrier will soon be paid off, the USN will operate only the large post-1945 carriers. For the navies with a limited air capability the point is less palatable. The best that can be expected from the planned French *Charles de Gaulle* and the Russian *Tblisi/Kuznetsov* is a measure of local air defence. Their air groups will be too small to mount a long-range strike. Naval power-projection forces require air superiority, and only big carriers can guarantee this. Seapower remains a many-layered cake, but only the Americans have access to the icing.

Under the cover of carrier aviation, the US Marine Corps can still mount a serious landing at divisional level. The Corps lacks for nothing in terms of close air support, under its own control, and has a powerful ground-combat capacity. This combination of sea and amphibious power will be vital to the defence of Western/American interests. The Marines and

USN together can be moved unilaterally, are highly visible, and carry the most formidable punch. With the Soviet threat no longer present, the 'New Naval Policy' will ensure that the USN is configured for power projection in a more fluid world situation.

From the Iraqi perspective, the basic lesson is simple. Naval forces that cannot operate in a hostile air environment are of no use against an American-led Coalition. Mines and submarines are the only option. However, Third World navies are not built solely to take on the USN; consequently the mix of forces will never be ideal.

Smaller Western navies are left with a less fundamental, if equally significant, choice. With the reduction of East-West tension, there will be less requirement for specialist ASW assets designed to take on the latest Soviet nuclear submarines. Surface warships will become more general-purpose, with attention given to range, habitability, anti-aircraft point defence, helicopter(s), a medium gun for blockade and other tasks. Fleets will require more replenishment assets, along with the ability to extemporise bases in less-well-equipped, and less-friendly, regions than the Gulf. While it might appear, from a technical and financial perspective, that this would be best organised in collaboration, the political problems inherent in such arrangements would cripple the employment of the resulting force. The fact that the Western navies worked together in 1991 should not obscure the fact that the USN and RN were the only forces committed to battle, and that nations with a greater stake in the outcome of the war, particularly Japan, preferred to pay rather than enter the war zone, even for purely ecological tasks where the Self Defence Force has a large and capable flotilla of oil-slick dispersal vessels.

Other strategic 'lessons' are easily stated, but no less important. Blockades are effective, but they do not force aggressors to submit within a timescale that the world is prepared to accept. 'Desert Shield' was built on a logistic chain that used the sea for 95 per cent of all stores and equipment. If that supply line had not been secure, a task taken on by the Coalition navies, there would have been no 'Desert Storm'. Surface navies — the only forces that can exercise a measure of control over the sea lanes — have a major role in the future of Western security, particularly as the old bipolar world order is ending. To protect vital overseas resource areas, it is first necessary to get overseas, and then to stay there.

Tactical implications
The lesson that mine warfare is still the best option for local sea-denial navies will come as no surprise after 1987. The concomitant that the USN must improve the size and availability of its own MCMV forces is also an old lesson. It has been recognised, and is being addressed; more MCMVs are on order, while the helicopter sweeping package is to be upgraded and simplified.

The FPB myth, dating back to the sinking of the Israeli gunboat *Eilat* in 1967, was finally laid to rest by the ease with which RN Lynx helicopters were able to knock out any Iraqi assets that put to sea. Again, there was nothing new in that. The success of the USN off Libya in 1986 encompassed the destruction of far more capable naval units than Osa and TNC-45s. However, in 1986 the ships were hit by Harpoon, a large and expensive weapon. In 1991 it was possible to deal with this threat at the most basic level. Any helicopter-capable surface ship now has the answer to FPBs, in a friendly air environment.

Few naval weapons were given a serious trial, but the American and British systems that were used worked well. Technology pays dividends, in the right hands. The Tomahawk was an undoubted success, providing a new precision element in air warfare, in concert with the F-117A 'stealth' fighter. For the British, it was particularly pleasing to see the Sea Dart-armed Type 42 destroyers escorting American battleships and engaging in anti-missile warfare. Upgrades to the warhead, radar and software since 1982 have made a marked difference in the capability of this system.

If the amphibious threat is to be taken seriously, the venerable 16-inch guns of the battleships will be required. These ships and their guns were quite outstanding, both in combat and psyops terms. The USN will have to replace them eventually, but it would be difficult to suggest how this could be done.

Navies, deterrence and signalling

The two conflicts in the Gulf (1987–88 and 1990–91) should raise serious doubts concerning the value of naval forces in the role of limited threat of force, as defined in Sir James Cable's *Gunboat Diplomacy*.[10] The graduated level of deterrence and carefully constructed political signalling that this requires are utterly wasted if the intended target of such efforts does not understand, and, like both Iran and Iraq, treats forbearance as weakness. In addition, some nations used limited naval forces to signal their adherence to the Coalition, but then so bound up those forces, either by sending units of limited value, or by restrictive rules of engagement, that the real signal derived from their effort was one of half-hearted acquiescence. Belgium in particular came in for considerable criticism for her initial deployment, in addition to her attitude in regard to supplying other Coalition nations with ammunition. The incongruous voyage of the *Clemenceau* might have had as much to do with the pro-Iraqi stance of French Defence Minister Jean Pierre Chévènement as any operational requirement. The only conclusion to be drawn from this experience is that deeds speak louder than gestures. If naval powers want to be heard they must be prepared, and equipped, to act, not merely to show the flag and hope that their forbearance will be understood.

Navies and the media

The USN is particularly conscious of having 'lost' the media war to the US Air Force. This will have serious repercussions when the victory comes to be translated into new funding. A combination of factors, some institutional, some technical, left the USN with few assets in the battle for headlines. Awe-inspiring footage of the *Missouri* and *Wisconsin* conducting 16-inch night shoots, and launching Tomahawks, could not be faulted. However, the great bulk of the navy's work was subsumed into the

Coalition air effort, both by being placed under the Air Force Strike Cell, and more immediately because the USN A-6s lacked the high-resolution video cameras used by the USAF. Some 98 per cent of video footage shown to the world was produced by the USAF. In consequence, the world was treated to the results of USAF action, but only to library-issue film of the launch of USN strikes. Even the destruction of Iraqi shipping on 29 and 30 January provided little material for television. Mine damage to two major US warships added a negative image to the limited number of positives. This was unfortunate, as it emphasised the popular perception that the Gulf War was an air force and army conflict only. In reality, the naval involvement was crucial.

Notes

1. Norman Friedman, *The Maritime Strategy* (US Naval Institute Press, Annapolis, 1988), especially pp 1–15 and 194–234. See also Eric Grove, *The Future of Seapower* (London, 1990), pp 205–12.
2. H W Maull and O Pick, *The Gulf War: Regional and International Dimensions* (London, 1989), pp 121–38 and 184–5. See also Efraim Karsh (ed), *The Iran-Iraq War: Impact and Implications* (London, 1987); H Cordesman, *The Gulf and the West* (London, 1988), pp 361–455; and Norman Friedman, *Desert Victory: The War for Kuwait* (US Naval Institute Press, Annapolis, 1991).
3. Rear Admiral E W Carter III, 'Blockade', *United States Naval Institute Proceedings (USNIP)*, November 1990, pp 42–7; Commander T Delery, 'Away the Boarding Party', *USNIP*, May 1991, pp 66–71.
4. Rear Admiral R D Mixson, 'Where we must do better', *USNIP*, August 1991, pp 38–9.
5. P Gilchrist, *Seapower: the Coalition and Iraqi Navies* (London, 1991) for a basic listing of ships; J T Howe, 'NATO and the Gulf Crisis', *Survival*, May/June 1991, pp 246–59.
6. D Foxwell, 'Contending with Iraq's Patrol Boats', *International Defence Review*, May 1991, p 486.
7. Anthony Preston, 'Naval Aspects of the Gulf Conflict', *Military Technology*, April 1991, pp 58–61.
8. D Miller, 'UK Forces in the Gulf War', *Military Technology*, July 1991, p 39; also B L Cyr, Bruce Watson, R Luraghi, Bruce George, T Lister and J Piriou, 'Naval Operations', in Bruce Watson (ed), *Military Lessons of the Gulf War* (Greenhill Books, London 1991), p 123.
9. Rear Admiral C F Horne III, 'Mine Warfare is with us and will be with us', *USNIP*, July 1991, p 63. See also B K Brown and David Foxwell, 'MCM and the threat beneath the surface', and S Truer, 'Lessons from the Princeton incident', in *International Defence Review*, July 1991, pp 735–8 and 740–1.
10. See the discussion in Grove, op cit, pp 192–6 for the best modern analysis of this subject.

Further Reading

Vice Admiral S Arthur and M Pokrant, 'Desert Storm at Sea', *USNIP*, May 1991, pp 82–7: an early report by the C-in-C of the naval effort.

Captain L G Bien, 'From the Strike Cell', *USNIP*, June 1991, pp 58–60; Bien was senior naval officer at JFACC.

Commander R Brooks et al, 'If it was there, P-3s found it', *USNIP*, August 1991, pp 41–3.

B L Cyr, Bruce Watson, R Luraghi, Bruce George, T Lister and J Piriou, 'Naval Operations', in Bruce Watson (ed), *Military Lessons of the Gulf War* (Greenhill Books, London, 1991): a brief survey, with few 'lessons'.

Vice-Admiral Dunn, 'After the Storm', *USNIP*, June 1991, pp 60–1.

Norman Friedman, *Desert Victory: The War for Kuwait* (US Naval Institute Press, Annapolis, 1991): the first informed account of the Gulf War, with a strong naval influence.

'A Chronology of Events', *Military Technology*, June 1991, pp 118–40.

M Palmer, 'The Navy did its job', *USNIP*, May 1991, pp 88–93.

Anthony Preston, 'Ships and Naval Weapons', in *Weapons of the Gulf War* (Bison Books, London, 1991): a well informed picture book.

Survival, Vol XXXIII, No 3, The Gulf War issue: an important collection of essays on the war, but containing virtually nothing on the naval-air aspect.

CHAPTER 7
The Land War

Francis Toase

'Thus it is that in war the victorious strategist only seeks battle after the victory has been won, whereas he who is destined to defeat first fights and afterwards looks for victory.'

Sun Tzu, *The Art of War*

The Coalition plans

On Saturday 23 February, 1991, at 8 pm Eastern Standard Time (EST), President George Bush made a televised announcement from Washington that was to herald the final stage of Operation 'Desert Storm'. On the previous day, Bush had given President Saddam Hussein of Iraq an ultimatum to begin withdrawing his forces from Kuwait by noon on 23 February (EST). Bush's ultimatum was disregarded by Saddam, and eight hours after its expiry the American President announced that on behalf of all the Coalition governments he had directed General Norman Schwarzkopf, commanding the Coalition forces in the Gulf, 'to use all forces available, including ground forces, to eject the Iraqi Army from Kuwait'.[1] As Bush spoke, Coalition forces in Saudi Arabia began to push forward at selected points along a 480-km (300-mile) front. The Coalition land offensive, soon to be known as 'the Ground War' or 'the 100 Hours War', had begun.

Coalition force commanders had begun laying plans for this ground offensive as early as October 1990, albeit on a contingency basis only. At first, Schwarzkopf's primary mission was to defend Saudi Arabia, a mission which was reflected in his concentration of Coalition forces in defensive positions to the south of the Saudi-Kuwaiti border. But, on his arrival in Saudi Arabia in August, Schwarzkopf had also been tasked by Washington to 'conduct other operations as directed'.[2] The meaning of this became clearer when he was ordered in mid-October by General Colin Powell, Chairman of the American Joint Chiefs of Staff (JCS), to prepare contingency plans for an offensive, thus providing a military option in case diplomatic and economic sanctions failed to induce Saddam to withdraw his forces from Kuwait. Schwarzkopf duly prepared his plans, but also protested that he needed more troops in order to launch a successful offensive. This proviso was accompanied by a further protest from Schwarzkopf to Washington that he needed an immediate decision on the dispatch of such reinforcements, so as to have them 'in theater' before March 1991, after which the Arabian summer heat would effectively foreclose the option of offensive action until the following September.

Although the exact dates and sequence of events remain obscure, the CENTCOM commander's protests appear to have had the desired effect. President Bush decided on 30 October to double United States' troop levels in the Gulf to some 400,000 men. Bush delayed the announcement of this decision until 8 November, after the American Congressional elections, proclaiming that the Coalition should have an 'adequate offensive military option, should that become necessary to achieve our common goals'.[3] This decision, together with Bush's diplomatic drive to press the United Nations (UN) Security Council to authorise the use of force against Iraq, meant that from the end of October 1990 Schwarzkopf was in a position to formulate realistic plans for the reconquest of Kuwait.

As they proceeded to draw up these plans, Schwarzkopf and his CENTCOM staff acted on the assumption that the Iraqi Army was a formidable adversary, both quantitatively and qualitatively. It was understandable that CENTCOM planning was based on preparing for the worst. Most obviously, the attitude of the US commanders and staffs was coloured by their country's experience in Vietnam between 1961 and 1973, in which American leaders had made the mistake of underestimating the determination and capability of their foes. In addition to this, Coalition thinking was undoubtedly influenced by intelligence assessments suggesting that the Iraqi Army was every bit as redoubtable as Saddam Hussein claimed. It was by all accounts an extremely large force, with over a million men under arms, and was widely reported to possess a cornucopia of modern weaponry. Typical assessments gave Saddam between 5,500 and 6,000 main battle tanks (including numerous Soviet-made T-72s), 4,000 armoured personnel carriers (APCs), 3,200 artillery pieces, including some which could outrange comparable Coalition artillery, and between 800 and 1,000 modern combat aircraft, together with a proven capability for chemical warfare and a potential capability for biological and nuclear warfare.

Moreover, the Iraqi Army was reputed to be battle-hardened and confident after eight years of war with Iran (1980–88). In a paper published in April 1990, as respected a body as the US Army War College's Strategic Studies Institute had made reference to the Iraqi Army's reputation for being superb on the defence and adept at building intricate defensive systems. Ominously, the Institute had alluded to the Iraqis' inclination to 'lure their enemy into pre-arranged killing zones' where they could use their artillery to break the momentum of the enemy's attack and their armoured forces to launch a counterattack.[4]

As the Coalition monitored the Iraqi build-up in and near Kuwait (referred to in CENTCOM plans as the 'Kuwait Theater of Operations' or KTO), they found this scenario especially worrying, and with good reason. By October the Iraqis had already begun to array their forces in the type of elaborate defensive system identified by the Army War College. They had fortified the Kuwaiti-Saudi border with a continuous belt of obstacles, including sand berms, minefields, barbed wire and oil-filled trenches which could be turned into a wall of fire, backed by entrenched infantry and covered by artillery. This entire defensive line was supported by mobile and armoured formations, better trained and equipped than the somewhat mediocre troops in front of them, tasked to reinforce any sector of the front threatened by enemy attack. Beyond the outer defensive line and the pockets of mobile reinforcements, straddling the border between northern Kuwait and southern Iraq, was the theatre reserve, a concentration of Iraq's best trained and equipped armoured and mechanised formations, mostly belonging to the 'elite' Republican Guard.

The Iraqi layout thus conformed broadly to a Soviet-style 'sword and shield' defence, the outer layer and supporting forces being the shield, which was supposed to halt — or at least degrade the impact of — any attack, and the theatre reserve being the sword, tasked to provide the *coup de grâce* if any enemy formations penetrated beyond the shield. Whether the Iraqis also intended the sword formations to launch a *counteroffensive* deep into the enemy rear, as in the Soviet model, or simply a *counterattack* to restore their own line (as in their previous war with Iran) remains open to question. The general Iraqi intention, however, seemed clear enough: they would attempt to turn any Coalition offensive into the sort of grinding, head-on confrontation which had finally worn down the Iranians, presumably in the belief that their enemies would not be able to sustain a bloody and lengthy conflict. Coalition commanders were certainly agitated by the prospect of such a *slugfest* (the graphic American coinage for an attrition battle). As Schwarzkopf himself was later to say, the 'nightmare scenario' was to storm Iraq's so-called Saddam Line of defences covering the Kuwaiti border, only to 'get hung up in this breach', and 'then have the enemy artillery rain chemical weapons down' on the trapped Coalition forces.[5]

Moreover, Coalition commanders were agitated by the sheer size of the Iraqi Army. Even after Bush's decision to double American troop numbers in the KTO, the force ratios were hardly reassuring for the Coalition. Pentagon Intelligence assessments suggested that the Iraqis were building up to a deployment level that would reach 545,000 troops, 4,300 tanks, 2,700 APCs and 3,000 artillery pieces in the KTO by January 1991, organised into 12 armoured and 30 infantry or mechanised divisions.[6] Schwarzkopf himself later claimed that, at the start of 'Desert Storm', he was at an overall disadvantage of 2:3 in troop numbers and 1:2 in combat soldiers, as well as being significantly outnumbered in tanks and artillery. He did assume that his forces would have the edge in training and equipment, despite the doubts expressed by some observers as to whether some of the latest weapons systems, such as the M1A1 Abrams tank, the M2 Bradley IFV (Infantry Fighting Vehicle) and the AH-64 Apache attack helicopter, would actually work in desert conditions. But Schwarzkopf also professed to be uncomfortable at not having the classic 3:1 ratio of advantage which military tradition says an attacker should have in order to guarantee victory, not to mention the 5:1 ratio of advantage supposedly needed against a defender in well-entrenched positions. The Coalition, Schwarzkopf claimed, needed 'to come up with some way to make up the difference' by skill and ingenuity.[7]

Schwarzkopf and his staff concluded that their principal means of compensating for the Coalition's presumed quantitative inferiority on the

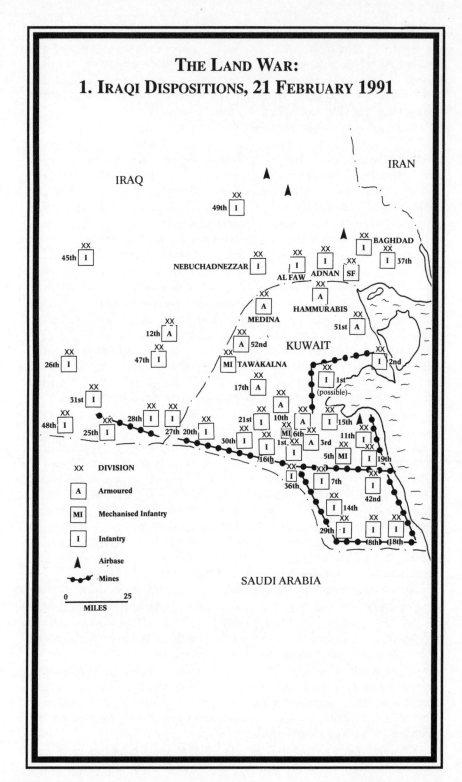

THE LAND WAR:
1. IRAQI DISPOSITIONS, 21 FEBRUARY 1991

IRAN

IRAQ

49th I

45th I

NEBUCHADNEZZAR I

BAGHDAD

I

I 37th

AL FAW ADNAN SF

A

MEDINA HAMMURABIS

A

12th A

51st A

47th I

26th I

A 52nd

KUWAIT

MI TAWAKALNA

17th A

I 2nd

31st I

I 1st
(possible)

A

48th I

28th I I

21st I 10th

I 15th

25th I

27th 20th A MI 6th

11th

30th I 1st A 3rd I

I 5th MI I 19th

16th

I 7th

I

36th

I 42nd

I 14th

29th I I I

8th 18th

DIVISION

XX	DIVISION
A	Armoured
MI	Mechanised Infantry
I	Infantry
▲	Airbase
••••	Mines

0   25
MILES

SAUDI ARABIA

ground should be to exploit its vast air armada, which was eventually to number nearly 2,800 aircraft. The CENTCOM commander had become aware soon after arriving in Saudi Arabia that the Coalition had a distinct edge over Iraq in terms of airpower, both quantitatively and qualitatively. This advantage could be of enormous benefit in the desert terrain of the KTO, especially as Saddam had gained little experience of dealing with substantial air attacks during his war with Iran. Accordingly, Schwarzkopf pressed his air commander, Lieutenant-General Charles A ('Chuck') Horner, USAF, to devise a plan whereby Coalition airpower could be used to reduce Saddam's warmaking capability in general, and the effectiveness of his forces in the KTO in particular.

The Coalition also had the advantage of almost total superiority at sea. Its naval and amphibious assets included a force of some 17,000 US Marines which might be used to mount an amphibious landing on the Kuwaiti coastline, so outflanking the Saddam Line. Schwarzkopf duly set in motion a series of naval-amphibious exercises,[8] culminating in mid-November 1990 in Exercise 'Imminent Thunder', a dress rehearsal for a coastal landing, and persisted in keeping this option open even after the Iraqis extended the Saddam Line up the coast to Kuwait City in response.

At the same time, Schwarzkopf was secretly preparing a plan to outflank the main Iraqi defences not from the east by sea, but from the west or landward side. Here, beyond the point at which the Iraqi, Saudi and Kuwaiti borders meet, Saddam and his generals had failed to extend their fortifications to cover their exposed western flank. The reasons for this Iraqi failure remain obscure. It may have stemmed from a conviction that the Coalition would decline to violate Iraq's territorial integrity. It may have arisen out of confidence that the Coalition would be unable to move forces so far out into the desert without being discovered and thwarted. It may simply have been from a lack of further military resources. Whatever the reason, the Iraqis had left an open flank, and Schwarzkopf, having examined the terrain personally at an early stage to check its suitability for armour, had become increasingly convinced that his point of main effort (in military terminology the *schwerpunkt*) should be in that area.

Schwarzkopf's proposal

These two themes, of seeking to degrade the military capabilities of the Iraqi Army by exploiting Coalition air assets, and to confound Iraqi defensive organisation by shifting the *schwerpunkt* away from the heavily fortified southern border of the KTO to its unguarded western flank, came together as an outline plan which Schwarzkopf presented to his army, navy, air force and marine component commanders at Dhahran airbase on 10 November.[9] At this meeting, Schwarzkopf proposed that, if a Coalition offensive became necessary, it should take the form of a massive combined air and land assault, supported also by naval assets, which would paralyse and overwhelm the Iraqi forces quickly and decisively. His plan for the projected ground offensive featured a wheeling movement from the far west of the KTO, together with direct attacks from the south and a feint amphibious attack from the east (retaining the option of making this a reality). The overall aim was to hold the Iraqi forces in the KTO in place and crush them, thus not only liberating Kuwait but also destroying Saddam's offensive capabilities into the bargain. This ground offensive, Schwarzkopf asserted, should be preceded by a sustained air offensive both within the KTO and deep into Iraq itself, tasked to smash Saddam's strategic capabilities in general, isolate the Iraqi forces in the KTO, and prepare the battlefield.

This outline proposal incorporated many of the elements of the US Army-Air Force doctrine of AirLand Battle,[10] including the use of relentless attacks to keep the enemy off balance, deep thrusts and strikes to isolate the battlefield, and co-ordinated air-land operations. This was reflected even in Schwarzkopf's choice of codename for the plan, 'Desert Storm', conjuring up visions of a ubiquitous, unrelenting and irresistible offensive.

One aspect of Schwarzkopf's plan which caused particular apprehension was his insistence that the two US Army corps tasked to carry out the left flanking movement, the US XVIII Airborne Corps to block and seal off the KTO and the US VII Corps to attack at the *schwerpunkt* of the offensive, should not move to their pre-attack positions until after the day on which the air offensive began, the latter being designated by CENTCOM, using standard military terminology, as D-Day. Schwarzkopf's motive in holding back the move until after his air component had defeated Saddam's air force, and so taken out Iraq's 'eyes', was to maintain secrecy. Not starting until after D-Day, XVIII Airborne Corps and VII Corps were expected to complete their move west within 14 days, so that the start of the ground war — G-Day — might come as early as D+14. But at the time of Schwarzkopf's proposal XVIII Airborne Corps was concentrated near Dhahran, with VII Corps to its west, south of the Wadi al-Batin. Schwarzkopf was in effect asking these two huge formations to swap over while moving westwards along the same line of communication, in the notoriously difficult military manoeuvre known as the 'passage of lines', with VII Corps moving 400 km (250 miles) and XVIII Airborne Corps moving 800 km (500 miles) through it, to take up positions on its left.

The choices of roles were themselves not in dispute: XVIII Airborne Corps was configured for a fast flanking drive over open desert, while VII Corps, with its four heavy divisions, was highly suitable for the *schwerpunkt*. The speed and scope of the proposed redeployment did, however, raise questions of logistic plausibility. Schwarzkopf's insistence that the 17,000 US Marines waiting offshore should mount an amphibious feint rather than a genuine attack also drew fire, as did his refusal to countenance a parachute drop by the US 82nd Airborne Division ('All American') into the River Euphrates valley. After what has been described as a 'drawn-out and sometimes bitterly argued process'[11] between Schwarzkopf and his commanders, lasting two months, he succeeded in retaining the essentials of his original proposals within the final plan.

What emerged as CENTCOM's plan in mid-January 1991 was a preliminary air offensive to be conducted along the lines adumbrated at the meeting of 10 November, followed in due course by a ground offensive accompanied by continuing air and naval operations. The Coalition ground forces were to use the time provided by the air campaign to move into their pre-attack positions and make preparations for the forthcoming offensive. Special Forces, which were already doing much to provide the Coalition with HUMINT (Human Intelligence, as opposed to ELINT and SIGINT or Electronic and Signals Intelligence), were to mount reconnaissance operations deep into Iraq's open desert flank, to make sure it had not been left open as a trap and to monitor Iraqi movements, if any.

For the purposes of the offensive, Coalition ground forces were to be organised into four groupings along a 430-km (270-mile) front. In the west, on the far left of the deployment, would be XVIII Airborne Corps, with VII Corps to its right as proposed, between them comprising ARCENT (Army Central Command). At the start of the ground offensive, ARCENT reverted in public to its more familiar title of US Third Army, although it also included a French division in XVIII Airborne Corps and a British division in VII Corps. To the right of VII Corps, east of the Wadi al-Batin, would be Arab forces from Egypt, Syria, Saudi Arabia and Kuwait, collectively known as Joint Forces Command North (JFCN). To their right, along the 'elbow' of the Saudi-Kuwaiti frontier, would be two divisions of US Marines in MARCENT (Marine Central Command), and, completing the deployment up to the coast, forces from Saudi Arabia, Kuwait, Oman and the United Arab Emirates (UAE) would comprise Joint Forces Command East (JFCE). Two US Marine Expeditionary Brigades (MEBs), also under MARCENT, were to remain offshore.

Order of Battle of the Coalition Ground Forces

As a courtesy to the host country, all Coalition forces and commanders were officially subordinated to the Saudi Defence Minister, General Prince Khalid bin Sultan.

In practice, operational command was vested in US Central Command (CENTCOM) under its commander-in-chief, General H Norman Schwarzkopf. The only non-American given a place on Schwarzkopf's central planning staff was the commander of the British Forces Middle East (BFME), Lieutenant-General Sir Peter de la Billiere.

General Schwarzkopf's deputy commander-in-chief was Lieutenant-General Calvin A Waller (US Army). His component commanders were Vice-Admiral Stanley H Arthur (US Navy), Lieutenant-General Walter E Boomer (USMC), Lieutenant-General Charles A Horner (USAF) and Lieutenant-General John Y Yeosock (US Army).

Lieutenant-General Yeosock commanded ARCENT or the US Third Army, with XVIII Airborne Corps being commanded by Lieutenant-General Gary E Luck and VII Corps commanded by Lieutenant-General Frederick M Franks Jr. JFC forces were under Saudi command.

Arcent (US Third Army):
US XVIII Airborne Corps:
   French 6th Light Armoured Division (*Daguet*)
   US 82nd Airborne Division
   US 101st Airborne Division (Air Assault)
   US 24th Infantry Division (Mechanised)
   US 3rd Armored Cavalry Regiment
US VII Corps:
   US 1st Armored Division
   US 3rd Armored Division

US 1st Infantry Division (Mechanised)
US 1st Armored Cavalry Division (theatre reserve under ARCENT until G+2)
British 1st Armoured Division
US 2nd Armored Cavalry Regiment

Joint Forces Command (JFC):
JFCN:
Syrian 9th Armoured Division
Egyptian 3rd Mechanised Division
Egyptian 4th Armoured Division
Saudi 4th Armoured Brigade
Saudi 20th Mechanised Brigade
Kuwaiti 35th Mechanised Brigade
Kuwaiti 15th Mechanised Brigade
JFCE:
Saudi 8th Mechanised Brigade
Saudi 10th Mechanised Brigade
Saudi National Guard 2nd Mechanised Brigade
Kuwaiti Mechanised Brigade
Omani Mechanised Brigade
Qatari/UAE Mechanised Brigade

Marcent:
US 1st Marine Division
US 2nd Marine Division
1st ('Tiger') Brigade of US 2nd Armored Division
US 4th Marine Expeditionary Brigade (afloat)
US 5th Marine Expeditionary Brigade (afloat until G+3)

Order of Battle of the Iraqi Ground Forces

The actual Order of Battle of the Iraqi Army in the Kuwait Theater of Operations is a matter of considerable dispute. This table represents the Iraqi Order of Battle as the Coalition believed it to be at the start of the ground war, and on which the Coalition planning was based.

Although the Iraqi Army established a theatre headquarters in Kuwait City, for practical purposes command was exercised directly from Baghdad by Saddam Hussein.

Kuwait Theatre
Republican Guard Forces Command (RGFC):
'Hammurabi' Armoured Division
'Medina' Armoured Division
'Tawakalna' Mechanised Division
'Adnan' Infantry Division
'Al Faw' Infantry Division
'Baghdad' Infantry Division
'Nebuchadnezzar' Infantry Division
II Corps:
51st Armoured Division
1st Infantry Division (identification uncertain)
2nd Infantry Division
37th Infantry Division
III Corps:
3rd Armoured Division
5th Mechanised Division
7th Infantry Division

8th Infantry Division
11th Infantry Division
14th Infantry Division
15th Infantry Division
18th Infantry Division
19th Infantry Division
29th Infantry Division
42nd Infantry Division
IV Corps:
6th Armoured Division
10th Armoured Division
17th Armoured Division (attached to RGFC?)
52nd Armoured Division (attached to RGFC?)
1st Mechanised Division
16th Infantry Division
20th Infantry Division
21st Infantry Division
30th Infantry Division
36th Infantry Division
VII Corps:
12th Armoured Division
25th Infantry Division
26th Infantry Division
27th Infantry Division
28th Infantry Division
31st Infantry Division
45th Infantry Division
47th Infantry Division
48th Infantry Division
49th Infantry Division

The Coalition plan envisaged a three-phase ground offensive designed to trap and eliminate Iraqi forces inside the KTO. During the first phase, ARCENT's XVIII Airborne Corps was to move into the Euphrates valley to cut off the Iraqi Army from escape and to protect the Coalition's western flank. At the same time, MARCENT and JFCE forces were to attack northwards towards Kuwait City to confirm Iraqi expectations of a direct attack. In the second phase, ARCENT's VII Corps would move north and then north-east and east to take the Iraqi theatre reserve in the flank, while the JFCN troops moved northwards into Kuwait. Finally, in the third phase, the JFCE and JFCN troops, together with MARCENT, would complete their advance to Kuwait City, while ARCENT eliminated the theatre reserve.

Schwarzkopf's aim was to effect what in military terminology is called a double envelopment, using XVIII Airborne Corps to the left and the JFC and MARCENT forces to the right as pincers, with the Euphrates valley and the sea providing natural barriers to the north and east. He also planned an envelopment within the envelopment, using VII Corps to place the Iraqi theatre reserve in a vice, with the British division providing the anvil against which the rest of VII Corps would hammer the trapped formations. The plan was intended not to push the Iraqi Army out of Kuwait, but to envelop and smash it in a gigantic battle of encirclement and annihilation. It was intended, in short, to emasculate Saddam's army, so preventing any repeat of the invasion of Kuwait a year before.

The western redeployment

In the event, the progress of the air campaign, which began on 16/17 January 1991, appeared to be so effective that several outside commentators — and even a number of Coalition commanders in private — began to wonder after a few weeks if a general ground offensive would actually be either necessary or desirable. The intense professional debate as to whether the air component on its own could have won the war will doubtless continue for some time.[12] What can be stated with certainty is that the air offensive created optimum conditions for the subsequent ground offensive. Coalition air forces achieved air supremacy very quickly, with the result that Schwarzkopf could choose to launch his ground offensive in the confidence that he controlled the skies above the battlefield. The Coalition's efforts to interdict its adversary's lines of communication with airpower also met with considerable success, significantly impairing the combat effectiveness of the Iraqi Army in the KTO. Finally, the use of airpower for what Pentagon spokesmen called 'battlefield preparation' greatly accelerated the process of eliminating or otherwise neutralising a large proportion of the Iraqi Army. The effect may not have been so much in direct loss of supplies or equipment as in a breakdown of leadership and morale, as the air campaign seriously degraded Iraq's military communications, with the result that the highly centralised Iraqi command and control system became badly disrupted before the ground war began.

Although, in Schwarzkopf's vivid image, the air campaign 'blinded' Saddam by driving his aircraft from the skies, CENTCOM took added precautions to ensure that the concurrent redeployment of ARCENT did not draw attention. One means used by Schwarzkopf to achieve this was the creation of 'ghost' formations in the areas vacated by the departing forces. Knowing that the Iraqis might still be able to hear, rather than see, what was happening on 'the other side of the hill', commanders made particular use of radio signals' traffic to simulate a continued presence. The British 1st Armoured Division left behind a formation known as 'Rhino Force', which broadcast radio recordings of divisional field exercises, while both XVIII Airborne Corps and VII Corps also left behind small units on the eastern seaboard to provide radio chatter for the Iraqis to detect.

Schwarzkopf's other principal means of drawing attention away from his redeployment was a ruse designed to reinforce Iraqi preconceptions that a Coalition offensive would emanate from the south, accompanied perhaps by flanking movements from the sea and from the area immediately to the west of the Kuwaiti-Saudi border. In the weeks before the ground offensive most fighting was, in any case, taking place on this southern border, and Schwarzkopf had the CENTCOM theatre reserve, the US 1st Armored Cavalry Division (a famous and extremely recognisable formation), mount demonstrations in the area of the Wadi al-Batin. Naval forces also continued their activities for an apparent landing, with minesweepers clearing approaches to the coast, battleships shelling coastal defences and amphibious forces conducting training exercises. Schwarzkopf himself joined in with this part of the deception operation when he told a press briefing on 30 January: 'I would be remiss if I didn't mention the readiness of our amphibious forces', knowing that this would be seen by Saddam Hussein on Cable News Network (CNN).[13] It was against this background of the air campaign and the deception operation that the Coalition began what has been described as 'the key maneuver of Desert Storm',[14] the movement of ARCENT's forces west towards Rafha.

The progress of this move was one of two crucial determinants that Schwarzkopf had to take into account in deciding exactly when to launch his ground offensive. The other was the progress of the air war, and more particularly the perceived effects of interdiction and battlefield preparation on Iraqi forces in the KTO, Schwarzkopf's clear intention being to attack only when the Iraqis had been sufficiently 'attrited'. The first of these considerations, that Schwarzkopf could not attack until all his forces were in place, was not one that was known to the public at the time, and it was the second which became a focus for discussion, with Coalition commanders being repeatedly quizzed about bomb damage assessment (BDA) and similar issues. As it happened, both considerations induced Schwarzkopf to delay his ground offensive for longer than he had intended. In the plan as it existed at the start of 'Desert Storm', the ARCENT deployment would have been completed by D+14 or thereabouts. But by the agreed date some elements of VII Corps were still arriving from Germany,[15] while even after the success of the Coalition forces in the ground clashes at Khafji and along the southern Kuwaiti border between 29 and 31 January, Schwarzkopf was still not convinced that air attrition of the Iraqi forces in the KTO had continued for long enough.

At this point, a third determinant began to have a countervailing effect — the pressure from Washington to launch a ground offensive before fissile tendencies appeared in the Coalition. The result of these conflicting pressures was that, when General Powell and Secretary for Defense Richard ('Dick') Cheney reached Riyadh to confer with Schwarzkopf on 8 February, the CENTCOM commander recommended that G-Day should be set at 21/22 February, or D+35/36. It appears that he may have asked subsequently for a further two-day extension to 24 February, although his exact reason for doing so is not obvious.

If Schwarzkopf did indeed ask for such an extension, then he had stalled the countdown to G-Day concurrently with a last-minute Soviet attempt to broker peace talks. In the event, Saddam's response to this initiative failed to find favour with the Coalition.[16] On 22 February President Bush offered Saddam, as he was later to put it, one last chance to do what he should have done more than six months earlier — withdraw from Kuwait.[17] Bush's deadline expired at noon, Saturday 23 February (EST), this being 8 pm Gulf time (all subsequent timings are Gulf time). American Forces FM Network radio in the Gulf, rather appropriately, played Elton John's *Saturday Night's All Right (For Fighting)* that night.[18]

In a sense, the fighting had begun some time before, with Coalition exercises giving way to preparatory actions such as the bulldozing of sand berms, the clearing of minefields, and the sabotaging of oil ducts leading to the Iraqi trenches. On 16 February the Coalition forces began 'shoot and scoot' artillery fire raids on the forward Iraqi positions from behind their own front lines. Helicopters also began to make raids across the border, and on 20 February an entire Iraqi dug-in battalion position surrendered to two American AH-64 Apache and two OH-58 Kiowa scout helicopters, with over 400 prisoners being lifted by transport helicopters back to American lines. On 22 February a 200-strong force of US Marines crossed the Saudi-Kuwaiti front line during a rainstorm at night to start work on reducing the Iraqi defences, particularly on clearing minefields. They apparently picked up some Iraqi deserters who later led them safely through the mines. Special Forces, meanwhile, had also been active deep behind Iraqi lines. Following the expiry of Bush's ultimatum, this fighting began to merge into a fully fledged ground offensive, which began formally at 4 am on Sunday, 24 February. The weather was not on the Coalition's side, being wet and overcast, but despite poor visibility caused by cloud cover, storms and the smoke from burning Kuwaiti oil wells set on fire by the Iraqis on 22 February, air and naval assets provided almost continuous support to the ground forces as they began their advance. This support was to continue almost unabated over the next 100 hours.

G-Day: Sunday, 24 February 1991

The Coalition offensive began as planned with a direct attack towards Kuwait City on the right and an outflanking movement on the extreme left. The drive towards Kuwait City was made by the JFCE forces moving up the coastal highway on the extreme right, and further inland by the land-based elements of MARCENT, comprising the US 1st and 2nd Marine Divisions supported by the 1st ('Tiger') Brigade from the US Army's 2nd Armored Division ('Hell on Wheels'). The outflanking move 480 km (300 miles) to the west, beyond the notice of Iraqi observers, was carried out by two divisions of XVIII Airborne Corps, the French light armoured *Division Daguet* with a motorised brigade of the 82nd Airborne Division attached, and the 101st Airborne Division (Air Assault), the famous 'Screaming Eagles'. The American air assault troops, positioned to the right of the *Division Daguet*, set off at 7.30 am rather than 4 am because of a delay caused by bad weather.

The attack on the Coalition right gave the JFCE and MARCENT groupings the unenviable task of having to penetrate one of the strongest parts of the much-vaunted Saddam Line. In the event, both groupings breached the barrier defences with ease, and then pushed on north and north-east respectively towards their intended objectives. In the process, the JFCE drove through the Iraqi 18th Infantry Division, while MARCENT shattered the 7th, 16th and 29th Infantry Divisions. Marines were reported to have crossed Iraqi minefields by stepping from one anti-tank mine to another, confident that the weight of a man would not trigger them, in order to avoid anti-personnel mines. By the end of the day the 1st Marine Division had secured Al-Jaber airfield.

The plan for the advance on the Coalition left had given the *Division Daguet* and the Screaming Eagles the different but nevertheless challenging task of sweeping around the Saddam Line to isolate the KTO and secure the left flank. The French troops, with their attached American brigade, soon secured their first objective, Objective Rochambeau, some 40 km (25 miles) inside Iraq, subduing *en route* a force of Iraqi tanks and infantry which they identified as the 45th Infantry Division. Simultaneously, the 101st Airborne Division mounted what has been described as 'the largest airmobile operation in history',[19] using some 300 helicopters to establish a Forward Operating Base — designated FOB Cobra — some 32 km (20 miles) in diameter about 112 km (70 miles) inside Iraqi territory. With the defending forces putting up little resistance, these first Coalition attacks on both left and right made rapid progress at minuscule cost in life. The first reports to Schwarzkopf were that MARCENT was through the Saddam Line without loss, and that XVIII Airborne Corps had one man wounded.[20]

Iraqi resistance was indeed so minimal that by mid-morning Schwarzkopf concluded that the enemy forces were in disarray, and therefore likely to be completely disorientated by a further massive blow. In the light of this assessment, and of reports that the weather was deteriorating rapidly (and also out of fear for the safety of civilians in Kuwait City, from which reports of arrests and atrocities were emerging), Schwarzkopf decided to move to the second phase of his offensive ahead of schedule, on the afternoon and evening of G-Day rather than the morning of G+1. Accordingly, he directed the remainder of XVIII Airborne Corps, consisting of the US 24th Infantry Division (Mechanised) and the US 3rd Armored Cavalry Regiment, together with the troops of VII Corps and the JFCN, to start their movement as soon as possible. This turned out to be within 12 hours in the case of most of the formations, but after as much as 15 hours for parts of VII Corps.

The JFCN forces began their advance later that day with an assault on the Saddam Line, moving much more slowly than the Marines to their right, who began to worry about their increasingly open left flank. The JFCN, like their fellow Arabs of the JFCE on the far right, found their task somewhat easier than Schwarzkopf had expected, although the Coalition's preparatory actions in this sector, encouraging the Iraqis to expect an attack, left the JFCN with a difficult breaching operation. The Egyptians effected the breach in four and a half hours, despite facing trenches of burning oil which briefly stalled their advance.

Out on the Coalition left, the 24th Infantry Division, with the 3rd Armored Cavalry acting in a screening role, moved forward at midday across initially undefended Iraqi territory. In between, some 140,000 troops and 1,300 tanks of VII Corps — the largest and strongest armoured corps in the history of battle — crossed into Iraq to breach defences that were more formidable than the virtually open ground facing XVIII Airborne Corps, but less so than those confronting the JFCN, or even MARCENT or the JFCE.

The VII Corps' breaching operation was led by the US 1st Infantry Division (Mechanised), the 'Big Red One', which started to make its breach at midday, pushing aside in the process Iraq's 26th Infantry Division and the unsuspecting 48th Infantry Division to its right. Just over an hour later, through the gap established by the Big Red One, followed the US 2nd Armored Cavalry Regiment, which went ahead to screen. The British 1st Armoured Division was to be next through the breach, on the morning of G+1, with the mission of protecting the right flank of VII Corps and blocking any move southwards by the Iraqi theatre reserve, as the 'anvil' on to which the rest of VII Corps would drive the Republican Guard if it tried to attack forward. The two other constituent divisions of VII Corps, the US 1st ('Old Ironsides') and 3rd ('Spearhead') Armored Divisions, which would provide the main driving force, also rolled into Iraq through breaches further to the west in the early afternoon. In CENTCOM's dramatic terminology, the Coalition offensive was named 'Desert Sword', with VII Corps' turning movement as 'Desert Saber' (the British insisting on their own spelling of 'Desert Sabre'), and the 3rd Armored Division's straight drive towards the enemy as (less officially) 'Desert Spear'.

All this was accompanied by continuing Coalition deception measures. The theatre reserve, the 1st Armored Cavalry Division, continued to demonstrate in the Wadi al-Batin, while naval forces also made demonstrations along the Kuwaiti coastline, as well as providing highly effective fire support to ground forces advancing up the coastal routes. These deception efforts, together with disinformation put out by radio broadcasts to the effect that the Coalition had landed paratroops in Kuwait City, and, apparently, the dropping of dummy parachutists in the Euphrates valley, all helped to increase Iraqi confusion. Schwarzkopf's press conference in Riyadh that afternoon, held in compensation for the Pentagon having imposed its news blackout at the start of the ground offensive, did nothing to elucidate the situation, merely referring to rapid progress, light resistance and very low Coalition casualties. When asked whether resistance was light because the Iraqis were retreating, not engaging Coalition forces or surrendering, the general replied: 'All of the above.' When pressed as to whether the Coalition was going through the Iraqis or around them, he responded that his troops were 'going to go around, over, through, on top, underneath, and any other way' to drive the Iraqis from Kuwait.[21]

G+1: Monday, 25 February 1991

The benefits of Schwarzkopf's decision to accelerate his schedules became increasingly apparent on the second day of the ground offensive, Monday 25 February, or G+1. The Iraqi command in the KTO appeared to be not only confused but disorientated by the sheer speed of the Coalition offensive, which gave them little chance to organise and respond adequately. They were to find that even the deteriorating weather conditions, notably sandstorms which in some areas reduced visibility to less than 27 metres (30 yards), offered them no help. They could not compete with the foul-weather and night-fighting capability of most Coalition vehicles, whose armoured commanders more often than not knew where they were, and where they were going, because of their global positioning satellite (GPS) systems. Coalition vehicles equipped with GPS receivers were able to identify their positions exactly even in featureless desert or at night.

The Iraqis did not even put up a good showing in those sectors against which they had expected major attacks to be mounted. The JFCE forces were delayed somewhat in their advance, but this appears to have been caused as much by poor visibility, traffic snarl-ups, and hoards of prisoners as by Iraqi resistance. The JFCN forces too made steady progress, the Egyptian 3rd Mechanised and 4th Armoured Divisions having at last secured a bridgehead across the barrier defences by mid-day on G+1 and reached their first objectives inside Kuwait by mid-afternoon.

Between the two Arab groupings, MARCENT came up against some Iraqi armoured resistance near Al-Jaber, where a counterattack was mounted against the 2nd Marine Division, but this turned out to be among the Iraqis' most costly ventures, being badly defeated. The Iraqi armour which met the 1st Marine Division near Al-Burgan oilfield also failed badly, becoming the victim of a divisional-sized 'time on target' artillery bombardment, in which every gun in the division — three or four artillery battalions in this case — hits the same target at exactly the same time. The remnants, as they tried to disengage, were destroyed by fire from Marine armour, artillery and AH-1 Cobra attack helicopters. Similarly, Iraqi armour from either the 3rd Armoured Division or the 5th Mechanised Division, standing in the way of the 2nd Marine Division and the Tiger Brigade as they pushed further north to Kuwait International Airport, fell prey to Coalition firepower. The day ended with MARCENT's forces only 16 km (10 miles) short of Kuwait City.

If the Iraqis were having little success in holding the Coalition attacks from the south, they still seemed to be unaware, or at best unable to do anything about, the Coalition forces moving from the west, which were rapidly gaining momentum. The *Division Daguet* continued to advance on the extreme left of the Coalition line, consolidating its first objective and proceeding to its second at As-Salman airfield, some 112 km (70 miles) inside Iraq, by nightfall, where it was ordered to pause. The 101st Airborne Division to its right had air-assaulted overnight to cut the Baghdad-Basra highway (Highway 8) between An-Nasiriya and As-Samara, establishing Area of Operations (AO) Eagle in the Euphrates valley between the two. During the afternoon the Screaming Eagles consolidated their blocking position within AO Eagle. To the east of the air-assault troops, the 24th Infantry Division, (the 'Victory Division'), was also approaching Talil airfield just south of Nasiriya and the Euphrates valley, having advanced 96 km (60 miles) into enemy territory without meeting a single Iraqi soldier.

To the right of the Victory Division's advance, VII Corps' formations were also making good progress. The movement through the breaches had continued overnight and into Monday morning, with the 1st Infantry Division consolidating its bridgehead, while the 1st and 3rd Armored Divisions advanced towards their first objectives with the 2nd Armored Cavalry screening. The British 1st Armoured Division, having passed through the 1st Infantry Division's bridgehead, now advanced. During the late afternoon and night of G+1, the British engaged and smashed the Iraqi 12th Armoured Division, still dug into its defensive positions behind the Iraqi 26th Infantry Division as a corps reserve. Meanwhile, the 1st Armored

Cavalry Division was withdrawn from the Wadi al-Batin and sent westwards towards VII Corps, an indication that the deception penetration of which it had been a part had now served its purpose.

By the end of G+1, therefore, the Coalition's ground offensive was going better than anyone had dared hope. Coalition forces in all sectors were achieving their objectives ahead of schedule, and had destroyed or routed seven Iraqi divisions while themselves suffering hardly any losses. They had also captured over 25,000 prisoners, and the number of Iraqis wanting to surrender was placing a greater brake on Coalition progress than those remaining Iraqis still trying to fight.

G+2: Tuesday, 26 February 1991

Confirmation that the Coalition forces were meeting with success, if any was needed, came early on the following day, Tuesday 26 February (G+2), when Baghdad Radio announced that Iraq was willing to withdraw its forces to those positions held before 2 August 1990. The Coalition, however, was in no mood to let Saddam off the hook and risk further aggression in the future. On the contrary, with XVIII Airborne Corps across Highway 8 and VII Corps prepared to wheel eastwards to take the Republican Guard in the flank, the Coalition's forces were well placed to smash the cornerstone of Saddam's regime. They proceeded to squeeze the Iraqis from the south and west into a rapidly shrinking pocket.

The Coalition's three groupings in the south continued throughout G+2 to push the remaining Iraqis back upon Kuwait City. The JFCE forces drove north along the coastal highway almost unopposed, and by the end of the day were poised to enter the city itself. To the left, one of the MARCENT task forces — apparently from the 1st Marine Division, which was fighting to secure Kuwait International Airport — ran into another sizeable Iraqi armoured formation on the outskirts of the city. This appears to have been part of Iraq's 3rd Armoured Division, or perhaps the 1st Mechanised Division which was positioned near the airport. The Coalition forces themselves freely admitted that, with the Iraqi Army disintegrating before them, identification of enemy units was virtually impossible, and often Iraqi prisoners had themslves only the haziest idea of their own location or division. The second MARCENT task force, from the 2nd Marine Division with the Tiger Brigade, started to bypass the city to the west to block any escape in that direction. JFCN forces continued their advance north-east on MARCENT's left, through the wreckage of the Iraqi 16th, 21st and 36th Infantry Divisions. By the evening they were approaching Kuwait City from the south-west, with a mixed Saudi-Kuwaiti formation designated 'Task Force Khalid' in the lead.

The only land route not cut by the evening of G+2 was to the north, along the main highway to Basra. This was perhaps a deliberate decision on Schwarzkopf's part, designed to avoid extremely costly and destructive house-to-house fighting by allowing the Iraqis an avenue of retreat, and then hitting them on the move. During the afternoon and early evening Iraqi troops in Kuwait City, panicking at the Coalition approach, began to flee northwards, providing Coalition air forces over the next 24 hours with the proverbial 'target-rich environment' of military jargon. Some Iraqis used light craft or rowing boats to escape northwards across the bay of Kuwait City harbour to the north, but many stole civilian cars or military trucks which they packed with personal loot, often simple essentials like boots and clothing. The road between Kuwait City and the Mutla Gap to the north, dubbed 'the Highway to Hell' by the media, became a deathtrap. By the early hours of the following morning Kuwait City was virtually devoid of Iraqi troops, and the Coalition forces were closing on an open city.

On the Coalition left, elements of XVIII Airborne Corps and VII Corps were about to start what has been claimed as the biggest tank battle in history, greater for sheer numbers involved even than the epic battle of Kursk, fought on the Eastern Front in July 1943. However, given that by this time over half the Iraqi tank force had been destroyed by Coalition air attacks or had fled northwards, historians may question whether the scale of actual fighting even exceeded the Arab-Israeli clashes in Sinai of 5–8 June 1967 or 14 October 1973, or on the Golan Heights of 6–9 October 1973. By no means all the Iraqis, however, were prepared to surrender at once, and some fierce actions took place in the next 24 hours.

The XVIII Airborne Corps strengthened its hold on the Euphrates valley, with the helicopters of the 101st Airborne Division resuming air assaults once the winds had died down. The 24th Infantry Division reached Highway 8 halfway between Talil and Jalibah airfields by early evening, and then turned eastwards, surging down the highway towards Basra with its attack helicopter regiment leading the way. In a phrase later used by Schwarzkopf, 'the door was closed'. As a brigade of Iraqi T-72s attempted to flee north-west it ran into the path of the Victory Division and was smashed, all 57 of its tanks being destroyed.

Meanwhile, VII Corps was closing on its prey — the Iraqi theatre reserve and in particular the Republican Guard. Despite high winds and poor visibility in the desert, the 2nd Armored Cavalry, screening as before in front of the 1st and 3rd Armored Divisions, managed late in the day to make contact with Republican Guard forces. The British 1st Armoured Division had completed its destruction of the luckless Iraqi 12th Armoured Division, and brushed aside elements of the 17th and 52nd Armoured Divisions lying near the Wadi al-Batin, accounting for an estimated 300 enemy armoured vehicles in the process. By midnight most of the British division had reached its main objective, codenamed Waterloo, at the southern end of Phase Line Smash, with the 1st Infantry Division prolonging the line northwards. The 1st Armored Cavalry Division, released to VII Corps' command on G+2, had also passed through the breach and was advancing north-westwards to support the final battle.

By the end of G+2 the Coalition forces were ideally placed to secure the kind of denouement of which even the Israeli Defence Forces would have been proud. The JFC and MARCENT forces were set to enter Kuwait City from the south and south-west, putting the last of the remaining Iraqis to flight in the process, while the city itself was already in the hands of Kuwaiti resistance fighters. At the same time, as far to the west the *Division Daguet* held secure against any Iraqi reinforcements, and helicopter forces

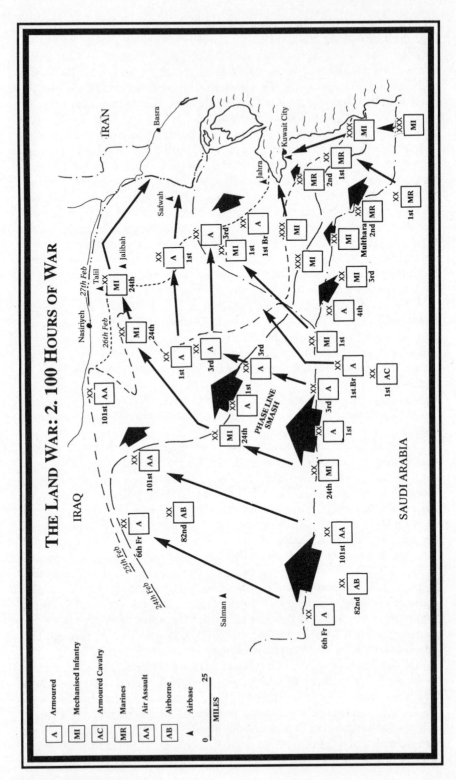

THE LAND WAR: 2. 100 HOURS OF WAR

closed the door to any organised escape, the flanking armour was deployed to fix and destroy the Iraqi theatre reserve along the Kuwaiti-Iraqi border.

G+3 and G+4: Wednesday, 27 February and Thursday, 28 February 1991
By the time that the final battle began, much of the Iraqi Army was already in rout. Its final disintegration and destruction took the remainder of Wednesday 27 February (G+3) and the first eight hours of Thursday 28 February (G+4). Coalition forces moving from the south reached their final objectives in the course of G+3. By the end of the day, while the 1st Marine Division finally defeated the last of a stubborn rearguard action at Kuwait International Airport, the 2nd Marine Division reached its blocking position at Al-Jahra, west of Kuwait City on the coastal highway. The Marines had opened their lines to give the honour of liberating Kuwait City to the Kuwaiti 35th Mechanised Brigade (the 'Al-Shahid' or Martyrs' Brigade), which entered the city at 9 am to considerable celebration and with minimal loss, followed by the Saudi 20th Mechanised Brigade, and later by American and JFCE forces from the south-west.

To the north and west of the Kuwaiti capital XVIII Airborne Corps and VII Corps were making a mockery of any remaining pretensions of the Republican Guard to military elitism. At dusk on G+2 the US 1st and 3rd Armored Divisions, together with the 24th Infantry Division and support from the 101st Airborne Division, had begun to take on the Guard in an armoured battle which continued throughout G+3 and into the morning of G+4. Although the exact details remain obscure, VII Corps' forces appear to have encountered all three of the Guard's best equipped divisions, the Tawakalna, Medina and Hammurabi Divisions, although the last may have been struck instead by the 24th Infantry Division advancing from Jalibah on the evening of G+4. (The Al-Faw, Nebuchadnezzar and Adnan Divisions may also have been engaged, although a dispute exists as to how many of these divisions were even in the KTO at this stage.) Advancing Coalition armour denied the Iraqi 'elite' formations of the Guard the chance to consolidate in what CENTCOM was now calling the Basra Pocket. Using classic 'hammer and anvil' tactics of fixing and destroying the enemy, the American armour, supported by airpower, moved forward to destroy the Tawakalna Division and the Medina Division, and to begin the destruction of the Hammurabi Division. Some of the Iraqi units put up a brave fight, but they were hopelessly overwhelmed by superior forces arriving from unexpected directions. American superiority was such that for some of its night engagements the 3rd Armored Division waved off its air support, judging the risk of loss from friendly fire greater than the Iraqi threat.

At this point the opportunity existed for General Schwarzkopf to complete the destruction and annihilation of the Iraqi forces, in the perfect 'Cannae' double encirclement which is judged as the pinnacle of manoeuvre warfare, and for which Schwarzkopf himself had aimed. He was denied his wish, although not through any defiant last stand of the Republican Guard. Rather, President Bush as American Commander-in-Chief, advised by Defense Secretary Cheney and General Powell, decided in Washington on the afternoon of Wednesday, 27 February (EST), to declare an end to the fighting. Apparently influenced by first reports of the carnage on the 'Highway to Hell', Bush was anxious, as one journalist put it, 'not to turn the public mood from one of relief and rejoicing into one of revulsion'.[22] No doubt Bush was influenced also by a concern to preserve the unity of the Coalition. The disintegration, as opposed to the humiliation, of Iraq was something that the Arab Coalition members had no wish to see. At 9 pm (EST) Bush announced in a television address that the Coalition would unilaterally suspend operations three hours later at midnight (8 am on 28 February in the Gulf). By this time Iraqi resistance in the vicinity of Kuwait City had virtually ceased, and there was a sudden scramble on the part of some Coalition units to reach acceptable stopping positions. The British 1st Armoured Division reached the Basra highway north of Kuwait City just as the ceasefire took effect. Taking up residence in an old Kuwaiti Army camp, the British cavalrymen were delighted to find a few horses to look after.

Coming when it did, the ceasefire meant that about 700 Iraqi tanks and 1,400 APCs escaped the Coalition net, including hundreds of T-72s belonging to the Republican Guard. Coalition forces were to reduce this number in some of the intermittent clashes which took place after the ceasefire, the biggest of which came on Saturday, 2 March, when units of the 24th Infantry Division smashed a Republican Guard column of the Hammurabi Division which had fired upon them while attempting to escape northwards along Highway 8. But elements of the scattered divisions of the Republican Guard (including part of the Hammurabi Division) did manage to limp back towards Baghdad. Although the Coalition had liberated Kuwait, it had not *wholly* accomplished its other mission, that of destroying the Republican Guard. There was no denying, however, that the Coalition had inflicted on the Iraqi Army the most comprehensive rout imaginable. Within only 100 hours, the Coalition had put to the sword or to flight the entire Iraqi Army in the KTO, humiliating Saddam Hussein and his supposed 'Prussians of the Middle East', while suffering only minuscule casualties. Altogether, the Coalition lost some 150 killed during the ground war, just over half of them Americans (of which 28 were victims of a Scud attack on Dhahran). Of these casualties, many were victims of 'friendly fire' incidents rather than of the Iraqis, including nine of the 16 British soldiers killed.

The reasons for victory
The events of Operation 'Desert Sword' seemed a far cry from any predictions made either by CENTCOM or outside observers before the ground war started. Shortly before G-Day, Baghdad Radio had promised that their enemy's cohorts would 'tumble into the great crater of death', and that the ground war would become a 'hellfire' for them.[23] With hindsight, these and similar outbursts made Saddam Hussein appear ridiculous even by the standards of Middle Eastern dictators, but he was not alone in the aftermath of the battle. Many Western 'experts' had offered equally dire predictions even after 38 days of Coalition bombing, forecasting a drawn-out land battle with heavy Coalition casualties — estimates ranged from

30,000 to 100,000.[24] Even the Coalition commanders, although apparently confident of victory, were apprehensive about the price to be paid.[25] At the final meeting between Schwarzkopf, Cheney and Powell on 8 February, approving the attack plan, the consensus was that the ground war would last for at least ten days and possibly as long as 30 days, while CENTCOM had fuel and ammunition stockpiled for a 60-day battle. At the same time, estimates of probable Coalition losses in the battle ranged from 10,000 to 50,000 casualties.

That nearly all these predictions proved excessively pessimistic was due in part to the fact that the Coalition was working from a 'database' on the Iraqi armed forces that took Saddam Hussein's absurd posturing at face value. The consensus was that the Iraqi Army was actually as huge as Saddam claimed, as well as being well equipped, well deployed and highly motivated. In this, although CENTCOM was itself in error, its estimates were treated throughout as over-optimistic by Washington and the Pentagon. In defiance of the normal situation in war, the further away they were from the front line, the more likely were Coalition leaders to view the enemy as a threat. The difference between what the Coalition imagined the Iraqi Army to be at the start of 'Desert Sword', and what it actually was, provides an instructive contrast, and goes far towards explaining the outcome of the ground war.

When the Coalition forces began to move into their pre-attack positions at the outset of the air campaign, US Intelligence credited Saddam Hussein with having over half a million men in the KTO, with several thousand tanks, APCs and artillery pieces of respectable quality, arrayed in the sort of defensive layout which had served him well against Iranian offensives, with a formidable barrier forming the outer layer. Furthermore, the Iraqi troops were regarded as tough and seasoned fighters. While there were doubts about the quality of the conscripts manning the outer layer of the Iraqi defences, there were none about the forces behind them, most notably the Republican Guard, which was considered an 'elite' or 'crack' body of troops, compared by some to Hitler's Waffen-SS.

It was clear to some observers at the time, particularly those who had made a close study of Arab armed forces in conflict with the Israelis, that these assessments both inflated the number of Iraqi troops in the KTO and flattered them in terms of capabilities. At the time that the Coalition forces began their deployment, according to estimates made after the war by the Pentagon, the Iraqis probably had no more than about 300,000 troops in the KTO, and perhaps even fewer. This was some 200,000 fewer than the original Coalition estimate, and also 200,000 fewer troops than the Coalition itself. If the more recent Pentagon figures are themselves correct, then far from having a 3:2 advantage over the Coalition, the Iraqis were actually at a disadvantage of 1:2 or more.

Saddam's armour inventory, also, was not much bigger than that of the Coalition (if at all), nor anywhere near as technologically advanced. It is true that Iraq's T-72 tank was slightly more modern than the US Marine Corps' M-60, but most of Iraq's tanks were not T-72s, they were older types such as the T-54/55 and the T-62. Moreover, most of the American tanks were not the M-60, but the M1A1 Abrams, a 'state-of-the-art' tank equipped with much better foul-weather and night-fighting capabilities, and at least a generation ahead of the T-72. Furthermore, the Iraqis were qualitatively inferior in every other weapons system having a bearing on the ground war, except possibly for artillery. Notably, they were greatly inferior in aircraft, and were bereft altogether of some systems readily available to the Coalition, such as satellites.

Iraqi defensive preparations, also, were never as redoubtable as Coalition commanders believed at the time. Oil-filled trenches turned out to be only a couple of metres (six feet) wide, and dugouts were often hardly strong enough to withstand a mortar round. Even before the air offensive began, Iraqi morale was also nowhere near as buoyant as the Coalition commanders feared. Many of Saddam's troops were disenchanted from the start, especially those conscript reservists who had already served in the long war against Iran, only to find that Saddam had returned their hard-won territorial gains as a bargaining ploy. As for the 'crack' Republican Guard, comparisons with the Waffen-SS were accurate only in so far as they had each begun life as a palace guard. Whatever its shortcomings, the Waffen-SS did at least fight ferociously against enemy armoured divisions, whereas the Republican Guard earned its reputation for tenacity against poorly armed Kurdish rebels or Iranian human-wave assaults. As one historian has commented, the Iraqis were perhaps not so much battle-hardened as battle-weary.[26]

It is clear that the Coalition grossly overestimated the strength and fighting abilities of the Iraqi Army. A cynical view is that this was done deliberately, in order to legitimise what was always going to be a massacre by creating a phantom ogre.[27] More probably, both CENTCOM and Washington were over-compensating for the malaise of Vietnam, and were desperate not to underestimate their enemy. Indeed, as Schwarzkopf is reputed to have told his staff and commanders repeatedly: 'never assume away the capabilities of the enemy',[28] citing the American operations in Vietnam and Grenada. As he observed in the celebrated 'Mother of All Briefings', his victory press conference on 27 February in Riyadh: 'When you're facing an enemy that is over 500,000 strong, with a reputation for being combat hardened veterans, you can't assume an easy fight.'[29] Schwarzkopf's insistence that Coalition forces should not 'assume away' enemy resistance was, in the light of the decades before the war, perfectly understandable. It was only in this particular case that it proved to be so pessimistic. The Americans had committed the elementary Intelligence error of treating every enemy division as if it were at full strength and the product of an advanced military culture, rather than looking at the past performance of the war machine and society which supported it. Fortunately, American Intelligence errors on this occasion meant that expectations were not pitched too high, and that casualties were much lower than expected, rather than higher.

If the comparison and correlation of forces meant that the Coalition was always likely to win the ground war, it did not necessarily mean that it was *bound* to win, at least so easily and quickly. Simple number-counting, beloved of some military analysts, tends to assume that all other things are equal, and in war they very seldom are. In particular, the Coalition might have dissipated its superiority on an unsuitable strategy or inappropriate operational method. The fact of superior numbers and superior technology — 'bean counting', as the Americans call it — offers only part of the explanation as to why the Coalition won the ground war so convincingly. The superior skill with which the forces were employed provides the rest.

Schwarzkopf and his CENTCOM staff may have erred on the side of pessimism when assessing the strength and fighting spirit of the defenders, but they were correct in their assessment of Iraqi fighting methods and the countermeasures required to overcome them. Saddam and his generals hoped to fight their own last war, pushing the Coalition into a *slugfest* that would play to Iraq's own presumed strengths. Schwarzkopf showed considerable skill in avoiding such a confrontation and fighting a battle which played instead to the strengths of his own forces, a mobile, all-arms and multi-dimensional battle. The result was a mismatch in which one side was fighting in the style of the First World War (or at best the Second World War without air cover), and the other was using methods devised for the next century. As one of Schwarzkopf's staff observed: 'The Iraqis were not capable of figuring out what was going on and telling someone. We fight fast and in three dimensions, and they were stalled at fighting World War I again.'[30] Or, as a captured Iraqi brigadier-general (no doubt boosting his enemy's reputation to mitigate his own defeat) concurred: 'You attacked us with the same NATO force that was designated to attack [*sic*] the entire Warsaw Pact, and the entire earth shook.'[31]

The earth had been shaking, of course, for 38 days before the ground attack actually began, and it has been asserted that Coalition airpower by itself defeated the Iraqi Army. These assertions overstate the case. In an incident typical of the ground war, one Iraqi artillery commander captured by the British revealed that, of his 100 artillery pieces, 80 had survived the air attacks while only seven remained after the artillery bombardment put down by the Coalition ground forces.[32] It was the ground forces and their tactical air support that actually destroyed the Iraqi Army, although there is no denying that the preceding air campaign had created highly favourable conditions for the ground forces to accomplish their mission, in particular by reducing Iraqi forces in the KTO to a number certainly well below 500,000.[33] Battlefield preparation by airpower weakened the Iraqi defences by burning off oil-filled trenches with napalm and smashing sand berms, and it had done much to shatter the already precarious morale of those Iraqi troops who were not already dead or deserting when the ground war began. How many of the missing Iraqi forces were casualties in the air and ground campaigns, and how many had simply deserted, is impossible to assess. American estimates have fluctuated from an initial claim of over 300,000 Iraqi military dead in the KTO to as few as 25,000. But, as one US Marine observed, once through the Saddam Line he and his fellows were more nervous of being hit by friendly fire than by the enemy,[34] a fear justified by the fact that a significant proportion of all Coalition casualties were incurred in friendly-fire incidents.

The air campaign had also smashed the Iraqis' communications system and capability to co-ordinate their forces. As one journalist put it:

> Saddam's generals were forced to rely on slow, circuitous means to send and receive messages from their field units; those units could not readily communicate among themselves. Lacking the aerial observation that could locate and track their enemy, unable to anticipate his movements or co-ordinate their own maneuvers with each other, the Iraqi armored forces would be fighting blind. In the end, every tank commander could be fighting for himself.[35]

Perhaps most beneficially of all, Coalition airpower had also isolated the KTO and deprived Iraqi forces there of their own air cover. To paraphrase General Powell, the Coalition had gone a very long way towards cutting off and killing the Iraqi Army in the KTO before the ground offensive had begun.

The decisive manoeuvre of the ground war to defeat Iraq actually took place concurrently with the air war, this being the concealed deployment of ARCENT to the far left of the Coalition line, rather than the subsequent drive forward on G-Day. Schwarzkopf, in his celebrated 'Mother of All Briefings' on 27 February, compared this with an American football play:

> As you know, very early on we took out the Iraqi Air Force. We knew that he had limited reconnaissance means. Therefore, when we took out his air force, for all intents and purposes we took out his ability to see what we were doing down here in Saudi Arabia. Once we had taken out his eyes, we did what could best be described as the 'Hail Mary' play in football. I think you recall when the quarterback is desperate for a touchdown at the very end, what he does is send every receiver way out to one flank, and they all run down the field as fast as they possibly can into the end zone, and he lobs the ball. In essence, that's what we did.[36]

The analogy once again shows Schwarzkopf erring on the side of pessimism — the desperate American quarterback looking to lob and pray — but it will no doubt become an historic one, much cited by those who wish to stress the continuing value of surprise in war. In fact, in football terms 'Desert Sword' was a much more conservative medium yardage play, a simple end-run with the British blocking. Whatever the value of the analogy, the 'Hail Mary' play was the key to the Coalition success. By maintaining his drive from the west, Schwarzkopf was able not only to avoid the heavy casualties that he feared would result from direct attack, but also to trap and destroy the Iraqi forces, rather than simply push them out of Kuwait as a drive from the south would have done, leaving the Republican Guard comparatively unscathed to fight another day. Even if they had detected the manoeuvre (and the Iraqi commanders' sand table captured in Kuwait City suggests that they had not), the Hail Mary play left the Iraqis in an untenable position. Once they were outflanked, the Iraqis could only withdraw at the risk of being pummelled from the air. As Schwarzkopf himself put it: 'So that's when I knew — we gotcha!.'[37]

That the ground war went so easily was therefore due not just to a favourable correlation of forces, but also to the operational method adopted by the Coalition. CENTCOM devised a plan in which each

Coalition member's role played to its particular strength: in particular the French with their fast, light armour screen, the Egyptians conducting a set-piece breakthrough, and the British placed where a dependable, high quality force might be most needed, all integrated into the American plan of manoeuvre at the operational level. It was an excellent example of coalition warfare, and of operational superiority. Schwarzkopf himself is reputed to be a student of military history, who drew inspiration for the battle from Cannae in 216 BC and, in terms of deception techniques, from the Second Battle of El Alamein in 1942. As one pair of reporters put it:

> If Schwarzkopf was looking for a place in military history, he had found it. Just as he studied Hannibal's and Montgomery's triumphs, future generations at military academies will pore over the plans of Schwarzkopf's 100-Hour War and marvel at how simple it all looked.[38]

Similarly, a biographer of Schwarzkopf has written that the ground war is 'destined to be taught and studied as one of the classic campaigns in military history'.[39] Both observations seem accurate. Having achieved a crushing mismatch, which compared with victories such as Agincourt in 1415, Plassey in 1757 or Omdurman in 1898, Schwarzkopf had certainly found his place in military history. And his 100 Hours War will no doubt be taught and studied for years to come.

Notes

1. Richard Pyle, *Schwarzkopf: The Man, The Mission, The Triumph* (Mandarin, London, 1991), p 143.
2. Lieutenant-Colonel Robert D Parrish and Colonel N A Andreacchio, *Schwarzkopf: An Insider's View of the Commander and His Victory* (Bantam, New York, 1991), p 72.
3. Pyle, op cit, p 119.
4. This paper is summarised in Roger Cohen and Claudio Gatti, *In the Eye of the Storm: The Life of General H Norman Schwarzkopf* (Bloomsbury, London, 1991), pp 234–235. For the Iraqi Army see above, Chapter 1.
5. Televised press conference by General H Norman Schwarzkopf, Riyadh, 27 February 1991. The ABC News version of this is available as a video cassette, 'Schwarzkopf: How the War Was Won' (Castle Vision, London, 1991). Transcripts are given in Pyle, op cit, pp 239–264 and Captain M E Morris, *H Norman Schwarzkopf: Road to Triumph* (Pan, London, 1991), pp. 239–277.
6. Norman Friedman, *Desert Victory: The War for Kuwait* (US Naval Institute Press, Annapolis, 1991), pp 119 and 217.
7. Schwarzkopf's televised press conference, Riyadh, 27 February 1991.
8. See above, Chapter 6.
9. See Cohen and Gatti, op cit, pp 235–243 for an account of this meeting.
10. See above, Chapter 3, for an explanation of AirLand Battle doctrine.
11. Cohen and Gatti, op cit, p 255.
12. See above, Chapter 5.
13. Quotation from Pyle, op cit, p 214.
14. Cohen and Gatti, op cit, p 264.
15. See above, Chapter 4, on the logistics of the deployment.
16. See below, Chapter 8, on the international consequences of the Gulf crisis.
17. Televised broadcast, cited in Jack Anderson and Dale van Atta, *Stormin' Norman: An American Hero* (Zebra, New York, 1991), p 176.
18. Ibid, pp 175–176.
19. Peter Tsouras and Elmo C Wright Jr, 'The Ground War', in Bruce Watson (ed), *Military Lessons of the Gulf War* (Greenhill, London, 1991), p 100.
20. Ben Brown and David Shukman, *All Necessary Means: Inside the Gulf War* (BBC Books, London, 1991), p 139.
21. Televised briefing by General H Norman Schwarzkopf, Riyadh, 24 February 1991. See Pyle, op cit, pp 235–238 for the transcript of this briefing, quotations at p 238.
22. John Simpson, *From the House of War* (Arrow, London, 1991), p 350.
23. Quoted in Anderson and van Atta, op cit, p 172.
24. Figures cited by Terry Manners, *The Gulf War* (Express Newspapers, London, 1991), p 33.

25. See, for example, Cohen and Gatti, op cit, pp 278-279.
26. Friedman, op cit, pp 111–112.
27. Such a view is expressed, for example, by Edward Pearce, 'War-Guilt, Zinoviev and the Boring Canadian: the Press and the War', in Victoria Brittain (ed), *The Gulf Between Us: the Gulf War and Beyond* (Virago Press, London, 1991), p 98.
28. Anderson and van Atta, op cit, p 135.
29. Morris, op cit, pp 260–261.
30. Cohen and Gatti, op cit, p 286.
31. Ibid, p 300.
32. John Witherow and Aidan Sullivan, *The Sunday Times War in the Gulf: a Pictorial History* (Sidgwick and Jackson, London, 1991) p 154.
33. Simpson, op cit, p 333, suggests that Iraqi strength fell from 260,000 on D-Day to less than 200,000 by G-Day.
34. Witherow and Sullivan, op cit, p 150.
35. Pyle, op cit, pp 139–140.
36. Schwarzkopf's televised press conference, Riyadh, 27 February 1991. Cited by Pyle, op cit, pp 241-262.
37. Pyle, op cit, p 141.
38. Witherow and Sullivan, op cit, p 174.
39. Morris, op cit, p 11.

Further Reading

Ben Brown and David Shukman, *All Necessary Means: Inside the Gulf War* (BBC Books, London, 1991).

Roger Cohen and Claudio Gatti, *In the Eye of the Storm: The Life of General H Norman Schwarzkopf* (Bloomsbury, London, 1991).

Norman Friedman, *Desert Victory: The War for Kuwait* (US Naval Institute Press, Annapolis, 1991)

Dilip Hiro, *Desert Shield to Desert Storm. The Second Gulf War* (Paladin, London, 1992).

CHAPTER 8
The Failure of the Iraqi Forces

Sean McKnight

'The Iraqi people are capable of fighting to the victorious end which God wants . . . the blood of our martyrs will burn you.'

Saddam Hussein, August 1990.

The Iraqi military myth

The months following Iraq's invasion of Kuwait saw saturation speculation on the war to come, as nightly the television pundits introduced the public to the 'realities' of modern war. The impressive size of the Iraqi armed forces, their recent experience of war and reports of sinister 'terror' weapons, made it easy to believe that forcing Iraq out of Kuwait would be a bloody affair for both sides. Saddam Hussein threatened the Coalition forces with 'the mother of battles', and the Iraqi armed forces were depicted as the fourth most powerful in the world, capable of confronting even the USA. Instead, the war failed to live up to its billing, as in just 100 hours the Coalition ground offensive shattered the Iraqi Army, at astonishingly little human cost to the allied side.

It is understandable that Western governments, public opinion and the media had all expected a more two-sided conflict. War is not an option to be undertaken lightly, and history is full of examples of nations losing through underestimating their enemies. On paper the Iraqi Army seemed a formidable force, and it was difficult to believe that it could be so incompetent at using its military resources. The long months of the Coalition build-up encouraged the media to concentrate on Iraqi hardware and weaponry, rather than on the more intangible question of their ability to use it. Some Iraqi weapons, in particular poison gas, Scud missiles and other 'terror' devices, caught the public imagination, further boosting the general expectation that war with Iraq would cost the Coalition thousands of lives.

This impression of Iraqi strength was not corrected by a more informed contribution from 'expert' pundits. One prominent British academic authority on warfare concluded on 12 February 1991 'that the Coalition is achieving the impossible: digging itself into quicksand. Having been confident of early victory, it is instead faced with very difficult choices against a formidable opponent,' and that, 'we will be lucky if the war is over within six months.'[1] Other views were less pessimistic, but there was a general uncertainty about the capability of the Iraqi armed forces. The more informed predictions, some of which were very accurate, tended to be lost in the mass.

It could be argued that in August 1990 the USA had little reliable intelligence on Iraq, leaving the media to fill the gap.[2] But the Iraqi armed forces had only recently finished fighting an eight-year war, and should not have been such an unknown quantity. The military conduct of the Iran-Iraq War received scant attention in the West, an omission which to a large extent explains the wild overestimation of Iraq's capabilities.

The performance of Iraq's armed forces in the Gulf War of 1991 was indeed so poor as to make an analysis of their strengths and weaknesses extremely hard, and their comprehensive defeat by the Coalition has caused the pendulum to swing the other way. The impression given before the war that Iraq was armed to the teeth with up-to-date weaponry obviously needs to be corrected, but it would be foolish to go to the opposite extreme. Iraq did have some weapons that needed to be taken very seriously, including some of surprising sophistication, even if they were not 'state-of-the-art' miracles of technology. However, in terms of its military equipment alone, Iraq was at a considerable disadvantage; and in some crucial areas, such as airpower, the disadvantage was such that Iraq's forces were of negligible military value. Rather than being dismissed as a rabble, the Iraqi armed forces should be assessed in the light of what they learned from their war with Iran. There had been clear improvement in that war, but there remained many obvious Iraqi weaknesses for the Coalition forces to exploit. Indeed, Saddam was aware of his armed forces' shortcomings, and his main hope was to avoid the necessity of waging a serious war against the Coalition.

Saddam's 'terror' weapons

In the months before the ground war, Saddam made Iraq's possession of weapons of 'mass destruction' very public. Convinced that the USA was afraid of the casualties which a war might inflict upon it, he attempted to intimidate the Coalition by painting a dire picture of the consequences of resorting to force. It seemed possible that Iraq had acquired fuel-air explosives, and there was even some uncertainty as to whether it could produce nuclear weapons. Saddam openly threatened to set fire to the oil wells in occupied Kuwait, which he claimed would produce conditions similar to a 'nuclear winter'. But the Iraqi weapons which caused most concern to the West were those which Iraq had already used against Iran: the modified Scud missile variants used in 1988, and chemical weapons, sometimes called 'the poor man's atomic bomb'.[3]

Iraq used various types of chemical weapons against Iran from 1982 until the end of the Iran-Iraq War in 1988, and it has been assumed that heavy casualties resulted from their use. At first, Iraq employed only mustard gas, a persistent agent used in the First World War, but later in the war with Iran it added nerve gases and hydrogen cyanide, with production rising to 70 tons of mustard and 12 tons of nerve gas a month by 1988.[4] Using aircraft, helicopters and artillery shells, Iraq could deliver a considerable volume of gas accurately against the relatively untrained Iranian troops. However, as late as April 1988 Iran claimed that, although it had suffered 25,600 casualties from gas in the course of the war, only 260 were fatal.[5] This low death rate is in keeping with the experience of chemical weapons in the First World War. In contrast, during the 1987 'Karbala 5' offensive, at least 20,000 Iranians lost their lives to conventional weapons. Even if their losses to chemical weapons were considerably understated, it appears certain that the vast bulk of Iranian casualties were caused by more conventional means. Only against unprepared civilians, such as the Kurds of Halabja who were gassed in March 1988, were mass casualties inflicted on the scale of which Saddam boasted.

Conditions for employing chemical weapons were very much less favourable to Iraq when facing the Coalition than they had been against Iran. The Iraqis were unable to deliver significant quantities of gas from the air, and their artillery was deprived of targeting information. Any chemical attack that the Iraqis had succeeded in launching would have been of modest proportions and, against troops better prepared for chemical warfare than the Iranians, it is unlikely that gas could have significantly influenced the course of the battle. An explanation of Iraq's failure to use chemical weapons does not need to include the dire but veiled threats of massive retaliation issued by the USA. For Iraq, it was far better to avoid the use of gas altogether than to use it ineffectively.

In 1987 Iraq claimed to have developed the new *Al-Hussein* missile with a range of 650 km, placing Tehran within its range. The *Al-Hussein* was in fact a variant of the Soviet Scud-B missile, given a longer range by several modifications, including reductions in the weight of its payload from 900 kg to under 250 kg, and by burning its fuel much earlier to reduce its in-flight weight. The Iraqis made similar but more drastic changes to the basic Scud missile in developing the *Al-Abbas*, with a maximum range of about 850 km.[6] During 1988 Iraq fired a total of 203 missiles at Iranian population centres. At least one million citizens of Tehran fled into the countryside for safety, not so much because of heavy casualties, but through fear that Iraq could use these missiles to launch gas attacks, fuelled by Iranian television pictures of the Kurds at Halabja.

The missiles used by Iraq had an important psychological impact on Iran, but in material terms they were not particularly effective weapons. The increased range had been gained by reductions not only in the payload of the standard Scud, but also in accuracy and reliability in flight. Even the unaltered Scud, which was originally built to carry a nuclear warhead, was not required to be particularly accurate, and Iraqi variants were so inaccurate that not even cities could be reliably targeted.[7] The Iraqi modificiations to the Scud also made it more likely to fall apart in flight. Both of these problems occurred when Iraqi missiles were launched in ideal circumstances. If launch procedures were rushed, inaccuracy and structural instability in flight would both increase.

Despite all these drawbacks, Saddam hoped to reap advantages from a missile campaign against the Coalition. Attacking Israel not only validated Saddam's claim to be fighting the 'Zionist enemy', which he denounced as responsible for the war, but an Israeli military response would make it difficult for Arab states to remain loyal to the Coalition. More specifically, military targets in Saudi Arabia included the areas of the Dhahran airbase, King Khalid military city and the port of Al Jubail, all of which were packed with Coalition troops and their equipment. It seemed possible that missile attacks could force the Coalition into a premature offensive.

Throughout the war, the Coalition remained uncertain whether Iraq's missiles could carry a chemical payload. The Soviet Union advised that Scuds were not capable of conversion to chemical warheads, but Israel believed that in a few cases the conversion had taken place.[8] Such warheads have been discovered in Iraq since the war's end by United Nations' inspectors. The high impact velocity of an incoming Scud would require the warhead to air-burst before impact for it to be effective, and, given the primitive state of much of Iraq's missile technology, it seemed reasonable to assume that the missiles could not be used to deliver chemicals effectively. However, in the absence of firm information, this assumption required a calculated risk which the American leaders of the Coalition were very reluctant to take.

Iraq succeeded in firing 86 Scud missiles and variants between 18 January and 26 February 1991. Despite the inordinate attention paid to it, this campaign achieved very little (see table below). The major Israeli urban centres of Jerusalem, Tel Aviv and Haifa are all within 400 km of western Iraq, but the Iraqis were unable to hit these targets with any degree of consistency, and the campaign did not damage Israel sufficiently to make a military response a domestic political necessity. The effect of the missile campaign was further reduced by the success of the American Patriot air-defence missile. The Coalition build-up was unaffected, and the Scud campaign appears to have had no influence on the decision to launch the ground offensive.

Iraqi Scud Attacks Jan/Feb 1991

	Hits	Misses*	Inter-cepted	Un-known	Total	Dead	Injured
Missiles fired against Israel	10	16	13	1	40	4	185
Missiles fired against Saudi Arabia	3	12	24	7	46	28	—
Totals	13	28	37	8	86	32	185

* A miss is defined as a missile doing neither injury nor damage

Source: An adaptation of a US briefing graphic, from Bruce Watson (ed), *Military Lessons of the Gulf War* (Greenhill Books, London, 1991), pp 224-5.

The missile war was not entirely a waste of time for Saddam. The Coalition was taken by surprise by Iraq's ability to continue firing Scud missiles from mobile launchers after the first few days of the air war, although the haste with which missiles were prepared and fired further reduced their accuracy. Alarmed by Iraq's unexpected ability to continue making Scud attacks, the Coalition tied up a considerable proportion of its airpower in the 'great

Scud hunt' between mid-January and early February. At the very least, the missile campaign gave Saddam the right to claim that Iraq was valiantly carrying the fight to the enemy, and attacking the hated Zionists on behalf of all Arabs. If the ground war had not been fought, the Scud campaign would have helped to create a myth of Iraqi victory.

Iraq's 'battle-hardened' forces

Having overestimated his own ability to intimidate the Coalition and underestimated American resolve, Saddam was unable to avoid the ground war. He may still have hoped that his ground forces would perform well enough either to persuade the Coalition to accept a compromise peace, or to lose valiantly against overwhelming odds. That the Iraqi Army failed to achieve either of these objectives is a comment on its many flaws as a fighting force.

The Iraqi Army was a numerically formidable force, and upon mobilisation it boasted over a million and a half men. It was organised into 60 divisions and 20-plus independent brigades (see table). This represented a considerable proportion of Iraq's population of approximately 20 million people. However, many Iraqi units were substantially under-manned, and few of the reserve formations were adequately trained.

Iraqi Armoured Fighting Vehicles

T-54/55, M-77 (Romanian version of the T-55)	1,500
T-59/T-69 (Chinese version of the T-55/T-62)	1,500
T-62	1,000
Chieftain Mks 3/5, M-60, M-47	30
T-72	500 to 1,000
Infantry Fighting Vehicles (BMP-1/-2)	1,500

Note: Many of Iraq's 6,000-odd AFVs had weapons added on, such as the Soviet wire-guided AT-3 Sagger anti-tank missile.

Iraqi Army Numbers and Organisation

955,000 men in the Regular Army (including a possible 480,000 recalled reserves)
850,000 men in the Popular Army (some mobilised)

Consisting of seven corps and the Republican Guard

6 regular, one reserve Armoured Divisions
3 Mechanised Infantry Divisions
10 Motorised Infantry Divisions
17 regular, 14 reserve Infantry Divisions
1 Naval Infantry Division[1]
1 Special Forces Division[2]
1 Air Assault Brigade
20+ separate Infantry Brigades

2 Armoured Republican Guard Divisions
2 Mechanised Infantry Divisions[3]
3 Motorised Infantry Divisions

Notes: 1. The Naval Infantry Division is an 'elite' unit able to select the 'cream' from regular units.
2. This was similar to the Naval Infantry Division in its elite status. Some descriptions of the Iraqi Army have included this as an eighth Republican Guard Division.

3. One of which consists of 4 rather than 3 Brigades and is permanently based in Baghdad.
Source: International Institute for Strategic Studies, *Military Balance* 1990/91.

The Iraqi forces were frequently described in the months before the ground war as 'battle-hardened'. The implications of this label were that, through the experience of the Iran-Iraq War, Iraqi troops had become competent or efficient soldiers. A closer examination of their performance in that war reveals serious shortcomings, which made them incapable of extracting the best from some of their weapons. One outstanding weakness was the Iraqi inability, both in the air and on the ground, to fight effectively at night. Despite its acquisition of sophisticated infra-red equipment, the Iraqi Army was frequently surprised by Iranian night attacks during the Iran-Iraq War.

The rapid expansion of Iraq's armed forces after 1980 had left them very short of technically skilled soldiers. This shortage largely accounts for the Iraqi Air Force's problems of maintenance on its more sophisticated aircraft, and it is clear that it had great trouble in keeping its modest force of MiG-29s at operational readiness. In the Iraqi Army a chronic shortage of mechanics led to a wasteful policy of replacing rather than repairing, compounded by the manner in which skilled drivers and technicians were frequently transferred to politically reliable 'elite' units.

Iraq's ability to import substantial quantities of weapons from the outside world seems to have resulted in a very profligate use of firepower in the Iran-Iraq War. With wire-guided anti-tank missiles such as the French-made Milan, the Iraqis fired six to eight missiles for every vehicle hit, and with the Soviet-made AT-3 Sagger the strike rate was as low as one hit for every 20 to 30 missiles.[9] Tank gunnery was similarly unimpressive, with targets engaged at less than 1,000 m frequently being missed. It appears that, even if sophisticated range-finding or detection equipment was fitted, Iraqi troops could not make it function or failed to use it properly.

During their war with Iran, the Iraqis had made efforts to improve the performance of their air force by importing new technology and sending some of their pilots overseas for training. More modern air-to-air missiles such as the French R-550 Matra had enabled the Iraqis to take on Iranian fighters on more even terms, and the Thomson CSF laser-designator pod allowed the firing of laser-guided missiles at ranges up to 10 km. However, the virtual disappearance of the Iranian Air Force from the sky in the second half of the war removed much of the impetus for the Iraqis to develop their aerial combat capabilities. Even in 1988, the manner in which they exploited their aerial dominance was very pedestrian, and despite possessing weapons guided by both laser and television they were unable to attack targets with the accuracy which such weapons could achieve. Their inability to do more than halt Iranian oil exports temporarily is testimony to their limitations. Iraqi pilots did finally learn to force home their attacks against ground forces at low level, but there was little point in attempting bolder tactics, especially since the loss of an aircraft was frequently a punishable offence. Only the most trusted pilots were sent abroad for retraining, because it was seen as a political risk to expose these vital military personnel to foreign influence. The limitations on Iraqi military training showed when Iraq's very first losses in the air, two MiG-29 pilots who were presumably the very cream of the Iraqi Air Force, accidentally shot each other down.[10]

Saddam Hussein's Republican Guard was frequently labelled an 'elite' force in the Western media. Throughout the Iran-Iraq War the Ba'athist regime saw the Guard as more politically reliable than other forces, trusting it to perform in a mobile attacking or counterattacking role. Iraqi Army units were required to pass their best men to the Guard (and to other 'elite' forces such as the Naval Infantry); it received the best of Iraq's weapons such as the T-72 tank; and it was trained to fight in a combined-arms mode. Reflecting the government's concern for its loyalty, pay and conditions in the Guard were better than in the rest of Iraq's armed forces. Unlike other formations in the Iraqi Army, the Guard was also allowed and expected to take tactical initiatives on the battlefield, although operational matters were still decided centrally. Since 1986 the Guard had expanded rapidly, and in 1991 it stood at two armoured divisions, three mechanised infantry divisions and three motorised infantry divisions, amounting to about 105,000 men.[11]

It is, however, questionable to describe the Republican Guard as a military elite. The primary function of the Guard was to protect the regime, which meant that officers were selected for political loyalty rather than military competence. The Guard had a high percentage of officers who were Ba'ath Party activists from Saddam's home district of Tikrit. The political role of the Guard ensured that it could not be used boldly or risk heavy casualties in battle; and its 'praetorian' role was not necessarily compatible with military excellence.

At the start of the Gulf War, four of the Republican Guard divisions had been in existence for barely a month. These new divisions were neither as well-armed nor as well-trained as the older Guard units, and amounted to little more than Iraqi Army motorised infantry under a new name. But even before the end of the Iran-Iraq War, a new 'praetorian guard' had been formed to protect the Ba'athist regime. Named the *Amn al-Khas* ('special security'),[12] it possessed a military arm equivalent to an armoured division. This 'guard within the Guard' would have received the lion's share of those Republican Guard officers with the unusual combination of competence and political reliability. Far too important to Saddam to risk against the Coalition, it remained in Baghdad throughout the Gulf War, and was crucial in preserving his power-base at the war's end. Overall, while there was some qualitative difference between the Republican Guard troops fought by the Coalition and the rest of the Iraqi armed forces, this difference was insufficient to justify the respect in which many commentators held the Guard before the war.

Even before the invasion of Kuwait, the Iraqis had suffered from problems of logistics and supply. Apart from the shortage of skilled personnel to maintain their equipment, their approach to logistics was very wasteful, substituting profligate use of resources for efficiency. Spare parts were regularly flown in by commercial courier services,[13] a costly exercise which reflected a lack of proper forward planning and suggested a limited stock of spare parts available inside Iraq. The United Nations' embargo, following the invasion of Kuwait, deprived Iraq of this external logistic support, greatly multiplying its supply problems.

The state of Iraqi forces immediately following their invasion of Kuwait also points to serious logistic problems. The initial deployment of the Republican Guard in a forward position on the Saudi-Kuwaiti border immediately after the invasion of Kuwait lends credence to the suggestion that Saddam Hussein may have intended to follow up his occupation by moving into Saudi Arabia. If so, logistic constraints may well have forced him to abandon the plan. The invasion of Kuwait required a far longer advance than Iraqi forces had ever previously conducted, and this seems to have led to a major breakdown in logistics. There are even reports that Iraqi soldiers were reduced to eating the animals in Kuwait's well-stocked zoo.[14] The invasion strained Iraq's limited capacity to maintain its vehicles, and it seems probable that the highly publicised 'withdrawal' of some Iraqi forces from Kuwait after a few days was forced on them by the need to transport vehicles back to Iraq for repair.

Weapons and equipment

The sheer size of Iraq's army and air force, and the number of weapons they possessed, were daunting on paper, but closer examination makes it clear just how misleading simply counting numbers can be in assessing military strength. An apparently strong Iraqi Air Force, for example, turned out to be of no value whatsoever against the Coalition. The single type of military aircraft which the Iraqis had in greatest numbers was the Soviet-made MiG-21 and its Chinese imitation, the Xian F-7M. The MiG-21 first entered Soviet service in 1958, and the Iraqi variant was an updated version produced in 1970. Armed with the obsolete AA-2 'Atoll' air-to-air missile, it had proved incapable of matching even what was left of the Iranian Air Force in 1980. The MiG-21s were unlikely to cause the Coalition any trouble, particularly as many had been sent to Yugoslavia for modernisation just before Iraq's invasion of Kuwait, and had not been returned. Much of Iraq's other equipment was obsolete or close to obsolete compared with that of the Coalition. Several aircraft types were only slightly younger than the MiG-21, and the Chinese-made Shenyang J-6 was a copy of the even older MiG-19.

Like many Soviet export models, the aircraft supplied to Iraq came without their most advanced equipment, and were not to be compared with those in Soviet service. Most of Iraq's MiG-23s had limited on-board radar and could carry only the AA-2 missile, rather than later versions. The most advanced Soviet aircraft supplied to Iraq was the MiG-29, comparable with the latest Coalition fighters, but at least ten of these lacked the crucial 'look-down/shoot-down' radar which made the MiG-29 so formidable.[15] The most numerous of Iraq's relatively modern combat aircraft was the multi-role Mirage F1 imported from France, which was respectable but elderly when compared with Coalition fighters. It is significant that Iraqi pilots apparently regarded their Mirage F1s as far superior to any Soviet-made aircraft in Iraqi service.[16]

It could be pointed out that the Coalition air forces also had many older aeroplanes. While this is true, an old-fashioned aircraft such as a MiG-21 is an asset only once the enemy air force has disappeared from the sky, as the Iraqis demonstrated in their war with Iran. In the Gulf War, the best they had with which to oppose the latest American air-superiority fighters were their Mirage F1s and a handful of MiG-29s. Simply in terms of aeroplanes and equipment, the Iraqi Air Force was inadequate to mount any serious challenge to the Coalition.

To defend themselves against air attack, the Iraqis had built an extensive ground-based air-defence system, chiefly consisting of surface-to-air missiles (SAMs) supplied by the Soviets. The main elements of this network depended on the SA-2, SA-3 and SA-6 missiles, all very well known to the Coalition from their use in earlier wars. The *Chel Ha'avir* (Israeli Air Force) had demonstrated in fighting against the Egyptians in the later stages of the October 1973 War, and against the Syrians in Lebanon in June 1982,[17] that it was possible for aircraft to overcome such a defence. The Iraqis had only a limited number of modern, more sophisticated SAMs, used by the trusted Republican Guard to defend key targets. The main SAM belt was supplemented by a lower-altitude layer of hand-held SAMs, such as the Soviet SA-7 'Strela', and conventional anti-aircraft artillery (AAA or 'triple-A'). Some of the guns, in particular the Soviet-manufactured ZSU-23-4, could make it dangerous for an aircraft to attack at low level, but again the Israelis had repeatedly demonstrated how such weapons could be defeated from the air. More importantly, this 'layered defence' depended on good radar and communications, and efficient co-operation between all its elements, none of which might be expected from the Iraqi levels of training and expertise. Indeed, despite the extensive air defences of Iraq, Iranian aircraft were able even in 1988 to penetrate unscathed deep into Iraqi airspace. Iraq had put a considerable effort into an air-defence network that was, in the light of Coalition capabilities and past experience, more than a little dated.

As with the air force, an uncritical numbers-count of weapons made the Iraqi Army appear much stronger than it was in reality. A total of between 5,000 and 6,000 tanks sounds very formidable, but approximately 90 per cent of these were models designed well over a quarter of a century ago. The most modern Iraqi tank was the Soviet-built T-72, vulnerable in Syrian hands to the Israeli Merkava in 1982, and by no means a match for either the American M1A1 Abrams or the British Challenger. It was reported before the war that many of Iraq's older T-55 tanks had been either up-gunned by the fitting of the T-72's powerful 125 mm main gun and automatic loader, or rebuilt with added composite armour.[18] All the accounts of the ground war so far, however, mention only Iraqi use of the older, very obsolete, versions of the T-55. It seems safe to assume that this modernisation programme was exaggerated for Iraqi propaganda purposes. Iraq's access to the international arms market did enable it to acquire sophisticated pieces of equipment, and there was some concern that French laser range-finders had been fitted to Iraqi tanks. But few examples of such technological 'implants' were discovered during the liberation of Kuwait, suggesting that the Iraqis had improved only a small number of their tanks in this way. Similarly, Iraq acquired some sophisticated infra-red jammers with which to defeat Coalition night-vision equipment, but these appear never to have been used.

The best of Iraq's mechanised infantry were equipped mainly with Soviet armoured vehicles, of which the most numerous model was the BMP-1. This is a rather elderly armoured fighting vehicle, and compares unfavourably with both the American Bradley and the British Warrior infantry fighting vehicles. Other Iraqi mechanised infantry had older Soviet or Chinese carriers. Most of the infantry divisions had only soft-top vehicles, and were extremely vulnerable while on the move.

Unlike its armoured vehicles, some of Iraq's artillery was at least as good as the equivalent Coalition weapons, if not better. However, it is important to remember that most Iraqi guns were older Soviet-manu-factured models of which only a few were self-propelled, unlike the standard American 155 mm field piece, the self-propelled M-109. Among the best Iraqi guns were the South African-built G5/6 and the Austrian GH-N45, both of 155 mm calibre and based on designs by the late Dr Gerald Bull, which outranged the American M-109.[19] The Iraqi home-produced *Al-Faw*, a six-wheeled gun of 210 mm calibre and a 57 km range, was proudly displayed at the Baghdad arms exposition in 1989. Saddam was an enthusiast for big guns, and it is clear that Iraq was working on several versions of a 'Supergun' based on Bull's designs when the invasion of Kuwait took place. The Iraqis also possessed some formidable multi-barrelled rocket launchers, such as the Soviet BM-21, and claimed to have developed a computer-controlled system called the *Ababil*, firing 12 or 16 missiles of 262 mm calibre, each containing 200 bomblets. Even if it had reached operational status, the *Ababil*, like many of Iraq's more vaunted weapons, does not appear to have been manufactured in large numbers, and there is no reliable information as to its effectiveness. More import-antly, the use of artillery is as much a matter of fire-control and target detection as the number or calibre of guns, and there was little to suggest that the Iraqi Army's ability to switch fire from one target to another was anything other than poor.

Iraq did possess a large helicopter force, most of which was operated by an army air corps. It included some impressive helicopters such as the Soviet Mi-24 Hind and the French Aerospatiale Gazelle. However, with 16 different types under its command, the Iraqi Army Air Corps did suffer from maintenance and operating problems. Iraqi helicopters had been used cautiously in the war with Iran, and operated only over the fringes of Iran's defensive positions.

Iraqi defensive doctrine

Iraq survived the war with Iran partly because it was able to develop an effective defensive system. Iraqi Army engineers certainly constructed some spectacular defensive barriers. In particular they proved very skilful at manipulating the marshes and waterways of southern Iraq. The impression of a powerful, well-organised defence of Kuwait was reinforced by comparing Iraqi defences with those of the First World War — suggesting strongly manned fixed defences built in great depth, and by likening its doctrines to the Soviet 'sword and shield' defence — which would aim to destroy an attacker rather than just repel him. Together these give a rather exaggerated picture of the quality of Iraqi defences, and it is important to realise that they possessed a number of basic weaknesses.

In its modern version, the 'sword and shield' concept as understood by the Soviets was a very aggressive form of defence. In particular, Soviet doctrine called for counter-penetration to be driven home to the enemy's depth, and successful use of the armoured 'sword' force to lead invariably to a counter-offensive before the enemy might recover. This was much more ambitious than Iraqi conduct in defence. The Iraqis relied on the defensive 'shield' far more than the 'sword', rarely drove home their counterattacks, and could not move from the defensive to the offensive as part of the same operational process. An Iraqi counterattack was a response to the failure of their 'shield', rather than the decisive stroke against an attacker who was already faltering.

The Iraqis' approach did not reflect just their tactical timidity — a consequence of their anxiety to minimise casualties — for although Iraqi resources appeared abundant, they were in reality thinly stretched, given the length of their front with Iran. The better-trained and armed formations, notably the Republican Guard, were a modest proportion of the Iraqi forces. Not only was it militarily unwise to risk these better-quality units, it was also politically dangerous for the Ba'athist regime to lose any of its more politically reliable troops. The mobile striking power of these select few was a last resort for the Iraqis. While their defensive layout may have resembled that of a textbook 'sword and shield', the Iraqi version was a weak and crude one.

Comparisons with the Western Front of the First World War have also given a very misleading impression of the Iraqi defences against Iran. Despite the competence of Iraqi Army engineers, many parts of the front lacked defences in depth, and even the deep defensive system covering Basra was only constructed over several years. In fact, the formidable defences of the Basra region make it clear just how thinly stretched Iraqi resources were. Just before the 'Karbala 5' offensive in 1987, there were only 50,000 Iraqi troops holding a defensive system which covered an area greater than the entire Verdun battlefield of 1916. It is worth remembering that, in the Battle of Verdun, over a million casualties were inflicted on both sides together. Iraqi defences by Western Front standards were in the main shallow, and even the more formidable defences were inadequately manned.

Central to the Iraqi defensive doctrine was an ability to use massed firepower against an attacking force. Once it had learned to fire accurately, Iraq's artillery inflicted very heavy casualties on the Iranians. The simplest way of achieving the necessary accuracy was to channel attackers into pre-surveyed killing zones, and Iraq used fortifications, obstacles and mine-fields to force attackers into areas already targeted by its artillery. Iraqi dominance of the air was sufficient to provide the additional and crucial information on precise enemy locations. Iraqi helicopters became practised at working with the artillery as spotters, and it was this that enabled Iraqi guns to fire accurately on targets of opportunity. During 'Karbala 5' the Iraqi Air Force also lost 50 aircraft forcing home low-level attacks against the Iranians, and these attacks by fixed-wing aircraft and helicopters supplemented Iraqi artillery fire.

The Iraqi concept of defence tied up the bulk of the army in static positions, sacrificed the mobility of tanks by digging them into defensive emplacements, and relied upon heavy artillery and aerial firepower against an attacking force. If the enemy penetrated too far, a limited mobile attack might be mounted to drive them back to their own lines. This defensive system was vulnerable even to the Iranians. Their attacks, normally launched at night, were often initially successful, and the static nature of Iraqi defences usually resulted in the capture of large numbers of Iraqi prisoners.

The defence of Kuwait
One Iraqi problem which received little attention before the war was the sheer length of front which had to be defended in Kuwait. Indeed, the general impression given was that Kuwait was quite a small country. Taken together, the Kuwaiti coast and common frontier with Saudi Arabia amounts to about 380 km (235 miles), a greater distance than the British sector of the Western Front in 1918. The common frontier between Saudi Arabia and Iraq, stretching to the Jordanian border, is almost 1,000 km (620 miles) long. When compared with the potential length of the front, the Iraqi Army suddenly looked very small indeed. Even if there had been 540,000 Iraqi troops in the Kuwaiti theatre of operations, as estimated by the Coalition, they would have been thinly stretched.

With the exception of a few coastal salt marshes and areas of soft sand, there were few natural features to aid the Iraqi defence, and commanders had neither the time nor the resources to build a comprehensive defensive system. Until very late in the day, the Iraqis seemed to have assumed that the Coalition would confine any ground fighting to Kuwait, and that an attack would come either by sea or would avoid the oilfields and drive down the only two highways to Kuwait City. The sand-table briefing model at Iraqi Army headquarters in Kuwait City, captured by US Marines at the end of the war, shows the construction of defences to have been directed primarily against these threats. But even these expected avenues of approach were not comprehensively defended, and eyewitnesses comment on the way that powerful defences alternated with relatively poorly fortified sections of the coast. A few kilometres to the west of the intersection of the Saudi, Kuwaiti and Iraqi borders the fortifications became negligible. These weaknesses in the defence of Kuwait reflect the magnitude of the problem facing Iraq, rather than incompetence.

Even in places where the Iraqis did construct defences, they were not always of a very high standard. In many cases fortifications offered no protection from air attack, the trenches were too shallow, and bunkers became very wet owing to the lack of drainage. Some bunkers, found in better condition, complete with carpets and televisions, seem to have been built in the rear for senior officers. Although tanks were integrated into the defensive system, their 'scrapes' were poorly constructed and sand channels often collapsed, making it difficult to move the vehicles. That the Iraqis expected these tanks to fight in a purely static role is shown by the addition to most of them of a fixed machine gun operated from the driver's seat.

The most impressive Iraqi fortifications were constructed along the coast, and to block the gaps between the oilfields through which the two highways ran. The old dhow harbour of Kuwait City was heavily fortified with belts of underwater mines, making a landing extremely hazardous. The two expected land-assault routes were blocked by three separate belts of fortifications, including overlapping anti-tank ditches about a kilometre (1,090 yards) long, up to four metres (13 ft) wide, and capable of being rapidly filled with oil. Something between half a million and a million mines were laid by the Iraqis in Kuwait, mostly in these areas. If, as General Norman Schwarzkopf feared, the Coalition forces had become 'hung up' in these defences, Iraq's artillery would have been able to fire into its predetermined killing zones, causing heavy Coalition casualties.

Ultimately, the purpose of the Iraqi defences in Kuwait may not have been to halt a Coalition advance. As with his 'terror' weapons, Saddam had hopes that fortifying Kuwait would frighten the Coalition into backing down. His frequent references to the 'mother of battles' reflected his belief that the Americans particularly were a cowardly people who would shy away from such a conflict. As Saddam told Ambassador April Glaspie in Baghdad shortly before the invasion of Kuwait: 'Yours is a society which cannot accept 10,000 dead in one battle.' Even if the ground offensive were launched, if Saddam's forces could inflict even moderate casualties on the Coalition he could claim a 'heroic defeat' amounting to a political victory. Both sides were well aware of the historical precedent of President Gamal Abdul Nasser's 'heroic defeat' in the 1956 Suez crisis.

Iraqi readiness for war
Since the end of the war, many commentators have suggested that the Coalition plan for its ground offensive was so obvious that Iraq's failure to predict the direction of the main thrust was a sign of incompetence. With the benefit of hindsight it is easy to point to the obvious nature of the Coalition's strategy, and it seems curious how quickly commentators in the West forget their many less accurate predictions.[20] Recollecting these inaccurate predictions is important, as it shows that predicting the direction of the Coalition attack was no easy matter. However, there were grave weaknesses in Iraq's gathering of intelligence. All three of Iraq's intelligence and security services were primarily focused inwards, against internal threats to the regime. Throughout the Iran-Iraq War the Iraqis gathered little intelligence about the enemy using their own resources. For detailed intelligence on Iranian troop deployments they relied on information from spy satellites passed to them by the USA. When Washington failed to warn Baghdad of an imminent Iranian offensive, as happened in 1986 when the Iranians attacked the Faw peninsula, the Iraqis were caught by surprise.

Throughout the war Iraq's own information-gathering was generally limited to whatever could be seen in the Iranian front lines, and despite their air superiority, the Iraqis knew little about Iranian troop dispositions and movements.

Given these weaknesses, it seems unlikely that Iraqi intelligence could have reliably predicted the direction of the Coalition attack. The Iraqis could have attempted to gather information from agents on the ground; indeed, it would be puzzling if they had not, since there were people in Saudi Arabia who might have been willing to help Iraq. One possible way of gathering such information was through the nomadic tribesmen who frequently cross international borders between Iraq, Kuwait and Saudi Arabia without formal checks. Shortly before the Coalition ground offensive, fear was expressed that such nomads might be reporting to Saddam from the region of Hafar al-Batin, and disclosing Coalition positions. The Iraqis may also have tried to exploit the large numbers of expatriate Arab workers in Saudi Arabia, many of whom had no love either for their Saudi 'hosts' or for the USA. Whatever the Iraqis may have attempted, sifting the truth from a mass of contradictory facts is a difficult process. Iraqi intelligence failed against the Iranians under far more favourable circumstances, and it seems unrealistic to suggest that it should have done any better against the Coalition.

Iraq's inability to gather intelligence had much wider implications. Lacking most of the means to locate Coalition forces except the good old-fashioned eyeball, the Iraqi Army could not direct its firepower accurately. Iraq's only hope of using its artillery to any effect was for the Coalition forces to dawdle within the Iraqi defences. When the Coalition proved unwilling to oblige, the military resources Iraq had locked up in its Kuwaiti defences became liabilities rather than assets.

The weaknesses in Iraq's defensive doctrine were exacerbated by the highly centralised Iraqi approach to command. Despite minor improvements during the war with Iran, officers in the Iraqi Army rarely made decisions on their own initiative, a flaw which may explain the unusually large numbers of field telephones possessed by Iraqi forces in Kuwait. The equipment available to the Iraqis to co-ordinate their forces was also inadequate. In the unlikely event of Iraq being allowed to operate its two Ilyushin Il-76 aircraft, they were still only capable of controlling up to four fighters each, and were in no way comparable with the American AWACS.[21] Iraq's ground-based air defences also lacked the technology to function as an integrated system. Finally, although the Iraqi Army had excellent telephone communications, it lacked the computer facilities to analyse data at high speed. A rapidly moving enemy was virtually certain to get inside the Iraqi 'decision loop'.

These limitations in the Iraqi approach to command were largely a consequence of the political requirements of the Ba'athist regime. Fear of a military coup continued to dominate the relationship between Saddam's regime and the Iraqi armed forces.[22] This was amply demonstrated by the different ways in which important facilities were protected in Iraq. Saddam's own headquarters, and the command structure of the Republican

Guard, were in deep, well constructed bunkers. In contrast, other important command centres such as the air force headquarters were well hardened but above ground.[23] The air force was particularly feared by Saddam, because of the well-known potential of such a force to decapitate a regime. Hence there were bunkers deep enough to protect the government and its guarantors, while the air force was located in buildings vulnerable to the Republican Guard. Even the hardened hangars which protected Iraqi aircraft were built in a way to make it hard for aeroplanes to be rapidly scrambled. That these precautions were necessary to enable the regime to survive had been demonstrated since the end of the Iran-Iraq War. There had been three serious attempts to overthrow Saddam by elements of the military, one of them involving officers of the Republican Guard.[24]

To the debilitating relationship between the Iraqi regime and its armed forces should be added the basic problems which the Iraqi state experienced in motivating loyalty in its citizens. It is important to remember the impact which this had on the fighting spirit of the Iraqi Army. It seems that, even before the ground war started, the fragile morale of Iraqi troops was already collapsing. Many Iraqi units were reduced to an active strength well below their official complement, partly from the normal Iraqi practice of fielding under-strength formations, but also through a high rate of desertion. Iraqi troops who did not desert before the ground war often placed themselves in a position of safety by abandoning their fighting posts. This happened particularly with the crews of armoured fighting vehicles, who, appreciating the accuracy of 'smart' weaponry, abandoned their tanks or carriers for the security of improvised dug-outs, a position of relative safety from which many never returned to their vehicles. Many of the tanks the Coalition 'engaged' in the ground war were probably empty. This is not to impute cowardice to the Iraqis, for to do so would be asinine racism. But, because they lacked devotion to the regime or a deep loyalty to the state, there was little to encourage them to draw from the well of courage common in most human beings.

Iraq endures the Coalition's aerial assault

The start of the Coalition air campaign on 16/17 January 1991 dramatically highlighted Iraq's inability to contest supremacy in the air. The power and accuracy of the Coalition's aerial assault was sufficient to knock out Iraq's extensive ground-based air defences in a matter of hours. The bulk of the 'Tall King', 'Squat Eye' and 'Bar Lock' radars were put out of action, and the command centres were destroyed. Deprived of their radars, many Iraqi SAM crews took to firing their missiles in unguided salvoes, but neither the missiles, nor the impressive volume of fire from the Iraqi anti-aircraft artillery, had much effect against the Coalition aircraft. After the war the commander of the Soviet Union's air defences stated that the 'layered defence' was discredited, and that an entirely new air-defence concept was required. Iraq's ground-based air defences never recovered from this first assault, and it seems that little or no attempt was made to repair the damage. Saddam expressed his displeasure at this performance by ordering the execution of the officers commanding both the air force and the air defence command. The air defences of specific targets, such as airfields, continued to be a threat to the attacking aircraft, but the Iraqi air-defence network had collapsed.

More might have been expected of the Iraqi Air Force, but without any guidance from the ground there was little that could be achieved. Iraqi aircraft had no effective Identification Friend or Foe (IFF) signalling system, and had not prepared to co-operate with the ground-based defences. During the weeks leading up to the outbreak of hostilities, Iraqi pilots had mounted 100 sorties a day. However, their encounters with Coalition fighters on combat air patrols near the common border served only to emphasise the qualitative edge, in aircraft and pilots, enjoyed by their opponents. In the first three days of the air war, the Iraqi sortie rate declined from approximately 50 combat sorties on the first day to 23 on the third, and after that only the occasional Iraqi aeroplane took off for a combat mission.[25] This should be compared with an Iraqi claim of 300 combat sorties flown on 13 June 1988 in support of just one of its offensives against Iran.

Whatever the reason, the challenge the Coalition expected from Iraq's air force simply never materialised. This may well have been a policy decision by Saddam to preserve some of Iraq's aircraft, and an unspecified number had already been sent to the safety of Yemen before the war started. When Iraqi aeroplanes did encounter Coalition aircraft, they very sensibly attempted to avoid combat. It has been suggested that many of Iraq's scarce foreign-trained pilots and aircrew were killed in the Coalition's first attack on Iraqi Air Force Headquarters. Iraq probably lost 35 aircraft in air-to-air combat, and the lowness of this figure points to its refusal to challenge the Coalition in the air.

The reluctance of the Iraqi Air Force to come up, fight, and be destroyed was frustrating for the Coalition. Until the end of the war Coalition commanders seem to have expected the Iraqis to attempt some desperate military gamble with their remaining aeroplanes, but as long as they remained protected by their well built concrete hangars (which the Iraqis possessed in greater numbers than aircraft), the Iraqi aircraft and aircrew remained relatively safe on the ground. The Iraqis proved very adept at repairing damaged runways and fooling Coalition reconnaissance by concealing the repairs with fake damage. Once the Coalition started systematically destroying the hangars from the air, Iraq's aeroplanes were moved to bases close to civilian population centres, mosques and major archaeological sites. Far from demonstrating incompetence, Iraq's refusal to allow its air force to be destroyed in 'gallant' aerial combat at least preserved it as a potential threat that the Coalition could not ignore.

Any fears that the Iraqi Air Force might come up and fight should have been laid to rest when, after a week of Coalition attacks, its aircraft started to fly for the safety of neutral Iran. The mass escape may have been part of a deliberate strategy on Saddam's part to preserve his air force, but Iran seems a peculiar sanctuary to select, and it must have been obvious even to Saddam that the Iranians would be unlikely to return his machines. It has been suggested that Iraqi pilots flew to Iran without orders, or at least without Saddam's personal sanction — a theory given some credence by the odd assortment of aircraft which made the flight, and the fact that several crashed on landing, which suggests that pilots were flying unfamiliar machines. The truth of this matter has yet to be established, but both interpretations — deliberate strategy or improvisation — recognise the central fact of Coalition dominance in the air. General Curtis LeMay of the USAF once remarked: 'Having a second-best airforce is like having a second-best poker hand — OK for a bluff, very poor for a call', a reality which the Coalition brought home to the Iraqis with devastating speed.

Having taken control of the air, the Coalition proceeded comprehensively to demolish Iraq's capacity to resist. Wherever it could, Iraq tried to minimise the impact of Coalition bombing, and it seems that the Coalition failed to prevent some supplies being moved south to Kuwait. The picture from Iraqi prisoners of war was a mixed one, with some apparently on the verge of starvation and others much better-off, sporting little luxuries like cigarettes. Attempts to target Iraqi troops and weaponry appear to have been very successful, although once again the Iraqis displayed skill in deception, and many of the targets attacked by the Coalition were dummies. In Kuwait, the Coalition bombing helped speed the collapse of Iraqi morale, which, given the insubstantial nature of much of the Iraqi defences, was hardly surprising.

The 'mother of battles'
It must have been clear to Saddam, as the Coalition aerial assault shattered much of the infrastructure of Iraq, that the Coalition intended to launch its ground offensive, and this helps to explain his decision to launch a ground attack of his own. The Iraqi seizure of the deserted Saudi town of Khafji on 29 January 1991 was bound to be a military failure. Launching an attack against a superior opponent, who is aware of your every move while you have only a hazy idea of his dispositions, is not a recipe for military success. However, in political terms this doomed attack made sense. The least result Saddam could expect was the appearance that Iraq had boldly wrested the initiative from the 'evil American imperialists'. The attack might also push the Coalition into an early attack against Kuwait while the city's defences were still relatively effective. It could even be that Saddam was aware of the speed at which the morale of his forces in Kuwait was collapsing, and hoped that precipitating the ground war would make politically embarrassing mass surrenders less likely.

The Iraqi 'Khafji offensive' was carried out by three brigades from the 5th Mechanised Infantry Division, and supported by a naval operation. The attempt to stage a seaborne assault was an expensive failure. The ground forces suffered an equally dire fate, with two of the three Iraqi columns failing to get anywhere near their objectives, and suffering heavy losses at the hands of US Marines. Operating at night, the Iraqi tanks found themselves outranged by the TOW anti-tank missiles from the Marines' Pirana light armoured vehicles (LAVs). The Iraqi column nearest the coast did get into Khafji, despite losing most of its supporting tanks to a Qatari unit equipped with French-made AMX-30 light tanks. Having got to Khafji the Iraqis did little, and once Qatari and Saudi troops, together with the Marines, launched a serious counterattack on the town, the Iraqis surrendered. Khafji underlined the limitations of the Iraqi Army. In particular, it demonstrated that it was not going to fight to anything like the last man.

Iraqi dispositions to defend Kuwait seem to have fitted their defensive doctrine. In the forward positions were the infantry, supported by dug-in tanks and artillery. Behind the infantry divisions were the better-equipped mechanised and armoured forces. Finally, furthest back, were the Republican Guard — most of which had been deployed in the Kuwaiti theatre of operations. A cynic might observe that the Republican Guard was as well positioned to retreat as to counterattack. The infantry divisions in the front line were among the least experienced troops in the Iraqi Army, and there were reports that, before the Coalition ground offensive, most of their officers had disappeared and up to 80 per cent of their soldiers had deserted. Iraqi morale was clearly very low, and many surrendering troops subsequently told their captors that it was only fear of their own security forces that had kept them from surrendering earlier.

The Coalition's ground offensive opened on 23/24 February 1991, precipitating an almost immediate collapse of the Iraqi Army in Kuwait and southern Iraq. The main Coalition thrust, by the US VII Corps to the west of the Wadi al-Batin, made rapid progress and, clearly, the Iraqis were incapable of responding to an attack from this unexpected direction. But even where the Coalition attacked in directions which the Iraqis had anticipated, the results were equally dismal for the Iraqi defenders. Indeed, it seems that if the Coalition had selected only the most obvious axis of advance, it would nonetheless have succeeded in liberating Kuwait rapidly and at little cost to itself.

The main Coalition thrust bypassed the stronger Iraqi fortifications, and only a counterattack delivered by a mobile Iraqi force could have hindered the advance. The Republican Guard was well placed to deliver a powerful counterattack, but the Iraqis proved incapable of organising such a response. The largest counterattack which VII Corps faced involved no more than 60 Iraqi tanks, hardly a sufficient force to disrupt the advance of a corps boasting over 1,300 tanks in its ranks. More typical of the Iraqi response was an action on the night of 24/25 February, involving the British 1st Armoured Division's medium reconnaissance regiment, the 16th/5th Queen's Royal Lancers. The Lancers were about 50 km (30 miles) beyond the main British force when they encountered Iraqi tanks moving into the regiment from several sides. This could have been a disastrous encounter for the British, as even the obsolete T-55 is more than a match for the thin armour of the Scimitar light tank, and the regiment's Swingfire anti-tank missiles were ineffective at the short range of the encounter. However, the Iraqi move was more an accidental blunder than a purposeful attack on enemy forces, and its main priority seemed to be to escape from the enemy. Most of the US VII Corps' clashes with the enemy, once the corps had broken through, were either accidental encounters like the British experience, or actions initiated by the Coalition forces. The Iraqi counterattacking 'sword' was never really used against the main Coalition thrust, and it seems clear that the Iraqis had no real grasp of what was being done to their forces west of the Wadi al-Batin.

Further east, the Coalition forces did encounter several more organised Iraqi counterattacks, and the US 1st Marine Division fought about 100 tanks of the Iraqi 3rd Armoured Division at Kuwait International Airport. These encounters demonstrated that, even when the Iraqis deliberately used their defensive 'sword', they were unable to inflict serious casualties on the Coalition. Iraqi tank gunnery was very inaccurate, and at the ranges at which Coalition tanks could engage them even their most accurate fire was ineffective. In contrast, Iraqi tanks were highly vulnerable to Coalition weapons.

The Iraqi defensive 'shield' proved to be no more effective than the counterattacking 'sword'. For example, the two US Marine Divisions rapidly broke through the more elaborate defences that the Iraqis had constructed behind the Kuwaiti-Saudi border, only to discover that many defensive positions had been abandoned. Even when an Egyptian force was delayed within the Iraqi defences (the most favourable scenario from the Iraqi point of view), Iraq's artillery failed to inflict more than minimal casualties. It seems that the Coalition air and artillery bombardment had either destroyed most of the guns or intimidated the Iraqi gunners to such an extent that few remained to operate their weapons. Any thoughts that the Iraqis may have had of an heroic last-ditch stand in Kuwait City — and some of their north-facing defences suggested that this option was considered — were abandoned as the retreat became an abject rout. Heroic defeat in the ruins of Kuwait City may have suited Saddam, but the Iraqi garrison was understandably less enamoured of the prospect.

Iraqi forces were incapable of responding at any level to the Coalition ground offensive. Many front-line Iraqi soldiers recognised this before the offensive began, and the advance of the Coalition was a welcome opportunity for them to surrender. Indeed, the single most important thing that the Iraqis did to slow the Coalition advance was to overburden its forces with prisoners of war.

The Iraqi armed forces had been given a task beyond their capacity in Kuwait. Their many weaknesses should have been apparent before the crisis erupted with Saddam's invasion and occupation of the emirate in August 1990. Explanations of the inevitable military defeat may be found in the nature of the Iraqi regime and state, the weapons possessed by the Iraqi armed forces, and Iraqi military skills, information on all of which was openly and widely available to the Coalition before the Gulf War began. Iraq withstood, albeit briefly, a military coalition of 30 nations and most of the world's great powers. Perhaps, rather than marvelling at the Coalition victory, it would be better to ponder the mighty effort required by the Coalition to overcome just one Third World state.

Notes

1. Dr Paul Rogers, quoted in *The Sunday Times* (London), 3 March 1991.
2. Norman Friedman suggests that the absence of any American human intelligence sources in Iraq left an information vacuum that was filled by the media, *Desert Victory: The War for Kuwait* (US Naval Institute Press, Annapolis, 1991), Introduction.
3. Anthony H Cordesman and Abraham R Wagner, *The Lessons of Modern War*, Vol II, 'The Iran-Iraq War' (Westview Press, Boulder, Colorado, 1990), p 513, quoting Ali Akbar Hashemi Rafsanjani, who was then Speaker of the Iranian *Majlis* (parliament).
4. Ibid, pp 506–12.
5. There are several different claims for Iranian casualties from Iraqi chemical attacks, but even the highest figures do not contradict the suggestion that such casualties were a relatively modest proportion of Iran's total casualties. This particular Iranian claim is quoted, ibid, p 516.
6. Ibid, pp 504–5.
7. The unaltered version of the Scud-B, which is more accurate, was reckoned to have a Circular Error Probable (CEP) of 1,500 m when used by the Soviets under operational conditions. The CEP is the radius within which 50 per cent of the missiles fired are expected to fall.
8. Friedman, op cit, p 339.
9. Cordesman and Wagner, op cit, p 443.
10. See above, Chapter 5.
11. Aaron Davis, 'A Military Analysis of Iraqi Army Operations', *Armor*, November/December 1990, p 13.
12. Andrew Rathwell, 'Iraqi Intelligence and Security Services', *International Defence Review*, May 1991, p 394.
13. Friedman, op cit, p 67.
14. Ibid, p 39.
15. Mike Gaines, 'Paper Tigers', *Flight International*, 9–15 January 1991, p 20.
16. Cordesman and Wagner, op cit, p 473.
17. In 1982 the Israeli Air Force destroyed Syrian SAM batteries in the Beqa'a Valley in Lebanon. They 'excited' the ground-based radars by flying Remotely Piloted Vehicles (RPVs) over the valley and, having collected the electronic 'signatures' of the radars, they jammed them. The radars were then destroyed by radiation homing missiles, which guided themselves down the radars' own beams. The missile batteries were destroyed by a mixture of laser-guided and free-fall bombs. The Israelis claim to have lost no aircraft in this operation.
18. Captain James M Warnford, 'The Tanks of Babylon', *Armor*, November/December 1990, p 23.
19. Major John F Antal, 'The Sword of Saddam', *Armor*, November/December 1990, p 12.
20. The War Studies Department at RMA Sandhurst was no exception to this, and our predictions ranged from an offensive near the Jordanian-Iraqi border to landings on the Faw peninsula.
21. Friedman, op cit, p 154.
22. Several of Iraq's more successful generals of the Iran-Iraq War disappeared from public view once the war ended. One of these was Maher Abd al-Rashid, the successful commander of the Iraqi offensive in 1988 which retook Faw. Even his relationship to Saddam by marriage did not prevent his disappearance, and there were rumours that he had been imprisoned or executed.
23. Friedman, op cit, p 25.
24. Efraim Karsh and Inauri Rautsi, *Saddam Hussein: A Political Biography* (Brassey's, London, 1991), p 207.
25. Bruce Watson (ed), *Military Lessons of the Gulf War* (Greenhill Books, London, 1991), p 69.

Further Reading

Anthony H Cordesman and Abraham R Wagner, *The Lessons of Modern War*, Vol II, 'The Iran-Iraq War' (Westview Press, Boulder, Colorado, 1990).

Norman Friedman, *Desert Victory: The War for Kuwait* (US Naval Institute Press, Annapolis, 1991).

Dilip Hiro, *Desert Shield to Desert Storm. The Second Gulf War* (Paladin, London, 1992).

Bruce Watson (ed), *Military Lessons of the Gulf War* (Greenhill Books, London, 1991).

CHAPTER 9
The International Ramifications

John Pimlott

'The military operation must go on until the decisions of the UN are enforced. Then we can start searching again, and searching hard, for lasting solutions to the problems of the area.'

British Prime Minister John Major, 17 January 1991

War and diplomacy

The beginning of Operation 'Desert Storm' on the night of 16/17 January 1991 seemed to mark the end of diplomatic efforts to resolve the crisis over Kuwait. Indeed, on 17 January the Secretary-General of the United Nations (UN), Javier Pérez de Cuéllar, went on record as saying: 'I do not think it is time for diplomacy at the very moment', adding, 'there is not much I can do.'[1] A restoration of stability would clearly have to wait until the battle was over.

This did not stop interested parties from involving themselves in political manoeuvrings, designed to give them advantage in the post-war world. Israel, under Scud missile attack from 12.05 am on 18 January (local time), showed great restraint in not retaliating against Iraq, fully realising that this was an opportunity to impress the Western members of the anti-Saddam Coalition and to store up favours for the future. Despite assurances from David Levy, the Israeli Foreign Minister, that Israel reserved the right to retaliate as it saw fit, it rapidly became apparent that political and financial considerations outweighed the satisfaction of hitting back. By 25 January Israel was being rewarded: the European Community (EC) had resumed full economic ties with the Jewish state, while US-Israeli relations had markedly improved.

Other Middle East countries were not so circumspect. On 6 February King Hussein of Jordan made what turned out to be an ill-considered speech, in which he described the war in the Gulf as one being conducted 'against all Arabs and Muslims and not against Iraq alone', with the intention of asserting 'foreign hegemony' in the region.[2] This went down badly in Washington, further souring relations with Amman and placing future US economic aid in jeopardy. King Hussein would have to work hard to reassert his position of influence once the war was over, although in fairness it should be added that he was under mounting pressure from the Palestinian population of Jordan, members of which were out in the streets cheering the Iraqi Scud attacks on Israel. He also made genuine efforts to mobilise Islamic and non-aligned countries in pursuit of a UN Security Council resolution imposing a ceasefire in the Gulf, although this never stood much chance of success when resolutions from the same body acted as justification for the use of force.

On a more realistic level, it was the Soviet Union that came closest to achieving a political settlement before the Coalition ground troops were committed to the liberation of Kuwait. As early as 11 February, President Mikhail Gorbachev sent his special envoy, Yevgeni Primakov, to Baghdad to explore the possibilities, believing that the imminent ground offensive went beyond the limits laid down in UN Resolution 678. There was undoubtedly more to it than that — Gorbachev was under enormous political and economic pressure at home, and may have been hoping to divert public attention elsewhere, while a diplomatic coup would ensure Soviet influence in the post-war Middle East — but some success was achieved. At first this was difficult to appreciate, for on 15 February, when Iraq announced its intention to withdraw from Kuwait (an announcement that led to widespread optimism among the Coalition powers), it soon became apparent that the conditions attached by Saddam Hussein were totally unrealistic. They included an immediate abrogation of all 12 UN resolutions passed against Iraq since 2 August 1990; a Security Council guarantee of Iraq's historic rights on land and sea (including, presumably, the claim to Kuwaiti islands); the overthrow of the Kuwaiti ruling family; an Israeli withdrawal from the Occupied Territories, the Golan Heights and southern Lebanon; and even a cancellation of Iraq's foreign debts. Denounced by President George Bush as 'a cruel hoax', the withdrawal offer was rejected immediately, even though it was later claimed that hasty translation of the offer into English had made the conditions appear more harsh than intended.[3]

Despite this disappointment, Primakov continued to work towards a peaceful settlement, holding talks with Iraqi Foreign Minister Tariq Aziz in Moscow between 18 and 21 February. By the end of these talks some progress seemed to have been made. The Soviets were insisting on an unconditional Iraqi withdrawal, but were offering guarantees of Iraqi safety and territorial integrity, while promising to urge the international community to deal effectively with the Arab-Israeli issue. But it was too late. With no firm Iraqi pledge to adhere to all outstanding UN resolutions, and with a feeling growing among the Coalition powers that Saddam was trying to avoid a land battle by initiating long-drawn-out negotiations (a feeling reinforced by a radio speech by Saddam later on 21 February, which contained nothing new), Bush had no hesitation in rejecting the Soviet plan. On 22 February, in his dramatic 'Rose Garden' speech, the President gave the Iraqis until 'noon Saturday' (Eastern Standard Time, 23 February) to give authoritative and public assurances that the withdrawal was taking place. Within hours, Primakov came forward with yet another proposal, based on a withdrawal to be completed within 21 days, upon which all UN resolutions would be lifted. By then the ground war had been ordered.

In retrospect, the basis for a compromise would appear to have existed. Iraq was accepting that a withdrawal would have to take place, but was not prepared to carry this out as quickly as Bush was demanding. The reason was obvious. After seven months of military preparations in Kuwait, much of the dug-in Iraqi weaponry could not be moved by 'noon Saturday' and would have to be abandoned — but this was exactly the motive behind Bush's ultimatum. The Americans were by now determined to defeat Saddam in as humiliating a fashion as possible, with no chance of him returning to cause future trouble. Similarly, Bush was insistent on Iraq's acceptance of all UN resolutions, partly to ensure that Saddam was punished for his original aggression and partly to undermine his position within Iraq. It seemed to work: on 25 February, as Coalition ground forces advanced against minimal opposition, Baghdad Radio announced that Iraqi forces were in the process of withdrawing from Kuwait, and by the 27th, when Bush decided to announce a unilateral ceasefire to avoid further one-sided slaughter, Aziz had indicated that Iraq would accept all 12 UN resolutions. Primakov remained convinced that a deal to avoid the land war had been possible, but Bush had maintained his resolve. His rewards were an unequivocal military victory and the liberation of Kuwait, although, with the return to diplomacy, his problems were immense.

The ceasefire

The first Coalition priority was to ensure that the ceasefire became permanent and binding. On 3 March General Norman Schwarzkopf met Iraqi military representatives at the captured airbase at Safwan, in occupied southern Iraq, to discuss a formal end to the war. By then, the UN Security Council had passed Resolution 686, calling for the immediate release of all prisoners of war and authorising the Coalition to resume hostilities if Saddam refused to accept ceasefire arrangements. In addition, Iraq was to rescind the annexation of Kuwait and agree to return all looted property. Although by no means unanimous — Cuba voted against the resolution, while China, Yemen and India abstained[4] — it was enough to persuade the Iraqis that the allies were still determined to impose terms. Late on 2 March Aziz indicated acceptance, and 24 hours later the Iraqi delegation at Safwan agreed to local ceasefire terms.

This was hardly surprising, for not only had Iraq suffered a comprehensive military defeat at the hands of the Coalition, but unrest was beginning to spread inside the country. By 5 March the southern city of Basra was reported to be in Shi'a rebel hands, while in the north the Iraqi Kurds were taking the opportunity to seize vast tracts of territory. The allies found themselves in a dilemma. On the one hand, the domestic attacks on Saddam and the Ba'ath Party seemed to satisfy Bush's call for a coup; on the other, if the fighting between Saddam's forces and the rebels escalated, the Coalition might well be drawn in. Bush was determined to avoid an open-ended commitment — parallels with Vietnam were already being drawn by US commentators — yet he needed to ensure that military victory was translated into a political settlement designed to avoid a recurrence of trouble in the Gulf and to enhance US influence in the Middle East.

Bush's plan for achieving this was outlined to Congress on 6 March. Based on reports from the US State Department and other government

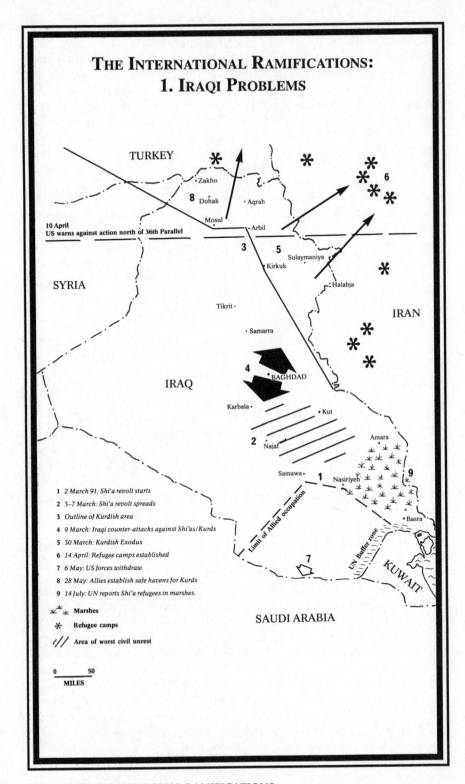

THE INTERNATIONAL RAMIFICATIONS:
1. IRAQI PROBLEMS

TURKEY

· Zakho

8 Dohak · Aqrah

Mosul

10 April
US warns against action north of 36th Parallel

· Arbil

3   **5**

Sulaymaniya

Kirkuk

· Halabja

SYRIA

Tikrit ·

· Samarra

IRAN

IRAQ

4 · BAGHDAD

Karbala ·

· Kut

2 Najaf

Amara

Samawa · **1** Nasiriyeh

9

· Basra

1 *2 March 91: Shi'a revolt starts*

2 *3–7 March: Shi'a revolt spreads*

3 *Outline of Kurdish area*

4 *9 March: Iraqi counter-attacks against Shi'as/Kurds*

5 *30 March: Kurdish Exodus*

6 *14 April: Refugee camps established*

7 *6 May: US forces withdraw*

8 *28 May: Allies establish safe havens for Kurds*

9 *14 July: UN reports Shi'a refugees in marshes.*

 Marshes

✳ **Refugee camps**

/// **Area of worst civil unrest**

Limit of Allied occupation

UN Buffer zone

KUWAIT

7

SAUDI ARABIA

0   50
MILES

agencies, put together while the war was going on, the plan contained four main strands which represented Bush's post-war aspirations as well as his justification for committing US and Coalition forces to battle. The first of these concerned the future security of the Gulf, which Bush was adamant should rest primarily with local states. Although US naval forces would remain in the region, no ground units were to be permanently stationed there. Indeed, plans were already advanced for the withdrawal of the 'Desert Storm' contingents, with a deadline of mid-June for completion. Coincidentally, as Bush was addressing Congress, the states of the Gulf Co-operation Council (GCC) — Saudi Arabia, Kuwait, Qatar, Bahrain, the United Arab Emirates and Oman — were meeting in Damascus with representatives of Egypt and Syria to discuss this very issue. The so-called Damascus Declaration, dated 6 March, seemed to accept Bush's proposal, containing plans that would enable Egyptian and Syrian troops to remain in Saudi Arabia as part of a Gulf security force, designed to deter future aggression from states such as Iraq.[5]

The other strands of Bush's policy seemed less likely to succeed. His second proposal was for the control of weapons of mass destruction (nuclear, chemical and biological devices, plus the long-range missiles needed to deliver them) in the Middle East. Not only did this imply outside interference, particularly if it was extended to more conventional weapons, but it also posed a threat to Israeli security, as that country's undoubted nuclear stockpile would have to be included. Bush's credibility was further undermined on 8 March, when he made a formal request to Congress to approve a $1.6 billion arms sale to Egypt, as well as an $18 billion package to rearm the Arab members of the Coalition. Admittedly, Bush later stalled on the issue, intending to use it as a means of pressurising the Arab powers into accepting more general arms control, but the damage had been done. A similar fate befell the third strand of Bush's policy, the creation of a regional development bank for the Middle East, funded by the rich oil-producing states and Western oil-users such as Germany and Japan for the benefit of poorer countries in the area. The Gulf states soon made it clear that they were unprepared to fund radical regimes which could be potential enemies. That left the final strand: an end to the Arab-Israeli conflict through negotiations based on UN Security Council Resolutions 242 and 338, implying adherence to the principle of Israel trading territory for peace, but this was so long-term and so fraught with diplomatic problems that any hopes of success were slim. To many commentators, Bush was being idealistically optimistic, linking these proposals to a vision of a 'new world order' that was already looking frayed.[6]

US Secretary of State James Baker left for a tour of the Middle East on 7 March, hoping to exploit what he described as a 'window of opportunity' in the relationship between Israel and her Arab neighbours, a window created by a war in which the Arabs and Israel had stood together against a common enemy. No-one expected an early breakthrough. More pressing matters took priority, forcing Bush to concentrate on events in Iraq. By 10 March he felt obliged to threaten renewed airstrikes if Saddam's forces used chemical weapons against the Shi'a rebels in the south or if fixed-wing aircraft were deployed in violation of the local ceasefire negotiated at Safwan. Ten days later, an Iraqi Sukhoi Su-22 attack aircraft was shot down by American fighters near Tikrit, increasing the pressure for a permanent, UN-backed ceasefire to be imposed. Until that happened, US combat units would have to remain in southern Iraq in case the war broke out again.

The result was UN Security Council Resolution 687, passed on 3 April.[7] Opposed by Cuba, with Ecuador and Yemen abstaining, it was one of the most complex resolutions ever voted, incorporating a whole series of measures to ensure that Iraq was denied the means to pose a future threat. The economic sanctions imposed in August 1990 were not lifted, although it was laid down that, as soon as Saddam accepted the terms of the resolution and a permanent ceasefire came into force, restrictions on the import of emergency civilian goods would be eased. This would also enable the UN Secretary-General to begin consultations with Iraq and Kuwait over demarcation of their common border, based on an agreement (never accepted by Iraq) of 1963, and to prepare plans for a lightly armed observer force to be deployed to monitor a buffer zone extending 9 km (5½ miles) into Iraq and 4 km (2½ miles) into Kuwait. Coalition forces would then be free to begin their complete withdrawal from southern Iraq.

But there was more to it than this. Within 15 days of acceptance, Iraq was to submit to the Secretary-General a list of the locations, amounts and types of its chemical and biological weapons, together with all ballistic missiles with a range in excess of 150 km (93 miles), and to inform the International Atomic Energy Agency (IAEA) in Vienna of all nuclear materials being held. This would allow the Secretary-General to prepare plans to inspect and ultimately destroy all such 'weapons of mass destruction'. Simultaneously, the Security Council would authorise the establishment of a special fund, taken from Iraqi oil revenues raised by UN-controlled sales, to pay compensation for war damages. Only then would arrangements be made for the lifting of economic sanctions and the unfreezing of Iraqi financial assets, although periodic meetings of the Security Council would still take place every 60 days to monitor events and, if necessary, re-impose appropriate penalties. Despite an angry Iraqi denunciation of the resolution, saying that it showed 'America's intention of robbing Iraq of its sovereignty and mortgaging its oil wealth', Saddam had little choice but to accept all the terms on 6 April. The ceasefire came into effect immediately.

Enforcing the ceasefire

From subsequent events, it appears that Saddam viewed these arrangements as so complex that they were unlikely to succeed. Certainly by early April, little over a month after the 'Desert Storm' victory, the Americans were clearly having second thoughts about the overthrow of the Iraqi leader.[8] Despite Bush's periodic calls for a coup, the situation inside Iraq posed a number of potential threats to regional security. If, for example, the Iraqi Kurds succeeded in creating an independent state in northern Iraq, neighbouring countries with their own Kurdish minorities, notably Turkey and Iran, would view it as a dangerous precedent; while a successful Shi'a revolt in the south, backed by Iraqi dissidents from within Iran, could cause a spread of Islamic fundamentalism to areas close to Saudi Arabia and the northern Gulf states. In such circumstances, it was not in US interests to intervene to support either of the Iraqi revolts, a policy which inevitably allowed Saddam to consolidate his power and survive the crisis. It also enabled the Americans to go ahead with their declared intention of withdrawing from occupied southern Iraq as quickly as possible. As early as 4 April Chairman of the Joint Chiefs of Staff General Colin Powell announced that the withdrawal would be completed by mid-June if Saddam accepted Resolution 687 and, when this occurred two days later, US units began to pull out.

This could only be achieved safely if a UN observer force replaced Coalition troops along the Iraq-Kuwait border. On 9 April the Security Council formally approved the despatch of 1,400 UN troops, to be commanded by Major-General Gunther Greindl from Austria. Twenty-four hours later it was announced that the observers would be backed by 600 infantry soldiers drawn from Canada, Ireland, Finland, Denmark and New Zealand. Greindl arrived in Kuwait on 13 April, and although it was to take a further two weeks for the rest of his command to be deployed, the pace of US troop withdrawal increased. On 14 April forward units, occupying positions in the Euphrates valley, were pulled back. Three days later Secretary of Defense 'Dick' Cheney announced that all US forces had left southern Iraq apart from some in a narrow buffer zone close to the border with Saudi Arabia. Iraqi refugees who had fled to the occupied zone, a total of about 50,000 people, were later flown by the US Air Force to a special camp at Rafha, under Saudi protection.

By then, Saddam's forces had effectively put down the Shi'a revolt around Basra, using tanks, artillery and helicopter gunships, but not deploying either fixed-wing aircraft or chemical weapons. Although the gunships were a violation of the local ceasefire negotiated on 3 March, none of the Coalition powers was prepared to back calls for military intervention in support of the Shi'as, leaving them to be ruthlessly suppressed. Bush reiterated his resolve not to keep US ground forces in the region, and on 9 May the last contingents left the buffer zone on the Saudi border. The US 3rd Armored Division was to remain in Saudi Arabia, together with the equivalent of a brigade (the 11th Armored Cavalry) in Kuwait, but only temporarily. Indeed, Cheney was already touring the Gulf area in an effort to negotiate a more lasting security arrangement, based on the assumption that the USA would provide no more than naval forces in support of ground units provided by the GCC, Egypt and Syria. On 9 May he appeared to succeed, with an agreement which included, in return for promises of naval support, local arrangements for joint US-GCC military exercises and pre-positioning logistic rights in Saudi Arabia and Kuwait.

This looked satisfactory, meeting one of the requirements for a post-war settlement outlined by Bush on 6 March, but negotiations between Egypt, Syria and the GCC were not going well. As the Egyptians threatened to withdraw all their troops from the region and the Syrians clearly lost interest, regional security began to fall apart. The situation was not helped by a Kuwaiti preference for continued Western protection (with their recent experiences, it was hardly surprising that they should distrust their neighbours), and by an Iranian insistence that they should be included in any security pact, a policy backed by Oman from within the GCC. Negotiations were still being conducted as late as 20 June, based on the creation of a 26,000-strong Arab force (including 6,000 from Egypt and Syria), but no formal agreement was signed.[9] One result was that neither US nor British contingents could be withdrawn from Kuwait until early September, finally leaving despite appeals from the Emir for them to remain.

Nevertheless, Bush had reason to be satisfied with this aspect of the ceasefire arrangements. United States troops had not been drawn in to the internal problems of southern Iraq, a UN-policed border between Iraq and Kuwait had been established, and the principle of Coalition withdrawal from the 'Desert Storm' war zone had been satisfied. The regional security pact proposed on 6 March in both Washington and Damascus may not have materialised, and Saddam had clearly not been overthrown, but one of the dangers for the USA of fighting a war in the Gulf, the need to secure the peace with permanent military garrisons, had been avoided. Unfortunately for the Americans, however, the post-war settlement was far more complex than this, requiring Bush to amend his policies and to use the threat of renewed attacks on Iraq in support of Resolution 687.

The Kurdish problem

The first of the problems began to emerge as early as March, before the ceasefire resolution had even been finalised. Saddam's forces, having contained the Shi'a revolt in the south, turned their attention to the Kurds in the north, mounting a sustained counterattack against the oil-producing city of Kirkuk on 28 March. The Kurdish rebels, equipped for guerrilla rather than conventional warfare, stood little chance against tanks, artillery and fixed-wing aircraft. By 1 April Saddam's Republican Guard had surrounded Kirkuk and swung north to cut the road to Arbil, forcing the Kurds to abandon most of their recent gains. As reports filtered through to the West of 'hundreds of thousands' of Kurdish refugees fleeing north to escape the wrath of Saddam, pressure mounted on Bush to intervene. At first he remained adamant that no US forces would be committed to any part of Iraq, restricting his response to a promise of humanitarian aid to Turkey, which suddenly faced the nightmare of an estimated one million refugees trekking towards its border across the snow-covered Zagros mountains. At the same time, a further 1.5 million were moving towards Iran. According to a spokesman for the Kurdish Democratic Party: 'A whole population is being annihilated, thousands have been killed and displaced. People are dying from cold and hunger, Iraqi helicopters are chasing fleeing citizens with their bombs and the world is watching in silence.'[10]

This was not strictly true, for if Bush was not prepared to get involved, other Western powers did not share his reluctance, and it was their actions which finally forced the Americans to change their policy. As early as 2

April France and Turkey raised the issue in the UN, and three days later the Security Council adopted Resolution 688, condemning Iraqi actions and demanding that Saddam allow international aid organisations to work among the refugees.[11] It was an unusual resolution, apparently ignoring the UN tradition of not interfering in the internal affairs of member states, which helps to explain why three members of the Security Council voted against it and two, China and India, abstained. But it did open the way for a closer involvement by the Western powers. By 7 April US aircraft were already dropping supplies to the refugees in the Zagros mountains.

Bush still seemed reluctant to go further, raising the need for more positive action from elsewhere. In the event, it was British Prime Minister John Major who took the initiative, presenting a plan for the establishment of 'safe havens' for the Kurds to an EC summit in Luxembourg on 8 April. Basing his ideas on proposals already put forward by Turkish Prime Minister Turgut Ozal, Major envisaged a two-phase operation. The first priority was to persuade the refugees to come down from the mountains into protected camps, free from Iraqi interference, and then to return them to their homes. Bush was initially opposed, realising that, for the plan to succeed, Western troops would have to be deployed to build and protect the camps, with military threats being made to keep the Iraqis away. By this time, however, US public pressure for action was growing, with opinions being expressed that Bush was deliberately ignoring the consequences of his decision to go to war in January. Presented with the *fait accompli* of Major's proposal, backed by the EC, he had little choice but to comply. After a 20-minute telephone conversation with Major on 10 April, the President announced his support. An exclusion zone was to be created in Iraq north of the 36th Parallel, covering significant parts of Iraqi Kurdistan, and Saddam was warned not to interfere with the construction of camps or the movement of refugees.

Bush hoped that the UN would quickly take over responsibility for policing the safe havens under the terms of Resolution 688, but this needed time to organise and the Kurds could not wait. On 11 April reports were received that Saddam's forces were still operating inside the exclusion zone, making the construction of camps and the issue of supplies potentially dangerous. If the safe havens were to be established, they would have to be protected by air and ground units, the first of which were deployed to southern Turkey on 13 April under the codename Operation 'Provide Comfort'. Two days later US Marines began to build a tented refugee camp at Silopi, inside Turkey, as part of a crash programme designed to provide shelter and protection to over 350,000 Kurds, many of them inside Iraq. French, Dutch and British troops — the last from 3rd Commando Brigade[12] — joined the Americans over the next few days.

The Western forces began to cross the border into Iraq on 20 April, moving towards the town of Zakho, chosen as a centre for the processing of refugees. But the operation was by no means straightforward. Zakho itself was garrisoned by an estimated 300 Iraqi paramilitary police, who initially refused to withdraw, and Bush had to make threats of renewed military action against Iraq to force them to comply. At the same time, efforts to persuade the UN to become involved were not going well. The Secretary-General was not enthusiastic about committing UN troops to Iraq without first gaining Saddam's support, and the Iraqis were protesting at the apparent violation of their sovereignty. This left the Americans convinced that 'Provide Comfort' represented the start of a commitment that they had been determined to avoid. To cap it all, Kurdish leaders announced that they were prepared to meet Saddam to discuss his recent renewal of an offer to grant autonomy to Iraqi Kurdistan, a decision that seemed to make the safe haven proposal redundant.

Nor was this the end of the difficulties, for despite an agreement by the Iraqis to pull out of Zakho on 25 April, leaving just 50 policemen behind, it soon became apparent that the refugees were reluctant to leave the mountains for fear of Iraqi reprisals. In an effort to improve the security of the safe havens, British Royal Marine Commandos extended their area of operations, advancing nearly 80 km (50 miles) to the east of Zakho by 2 May. By then a *de facto* Iraqi Kurdistan had been created, under Western protection. It was something that Bush had neither envisaged nor sought.

A combination of Western military posturing and diplomatic activity was now needed to avoid the potential quagmire. On 28 April British Foreign Secretary Douglas Hurd gained EC backing for demands that the UN should send a lightly armed police force to replace Western troops around the refugee camps. Although the Secretary-General was still not convinced, his special envoy in Iraq, Prince Sadruddin Aga Khan, opened negotiations with Saddam. While these were being conducted, in early May, US forces moved towards the Kurdish city of Dahuk, putting pressure on the Iraqi garrison to withdraw and allow the refugees to return. When the Iraqis stood firm, the possibility of renewed fighting suddenly increased. Saddam, realising that he was in no position to win, stepped down, agreeing on 18 May to allow the first UN guards to be deployed into Dahuk. In the event, the UN had problems finding the necessary manpower and money to carry out this new duty, and the agreement with Saddam did not prevent clashes between Iraqi police and angry Kurds, but at least the West could begin to pull back. By mid-June the last US troops had left the area around Dahuk, and Western force levels in Iraq had declined from a maximum of 13,000 to just over 7,000, with more withdrawing every day.

However, the West could not just abandon the Kurds. With only 400 UN guards available, their duties would clearly be restricted to supervising the distribution of aid, leaving Saddam free to attack again unless some sort of plausible deterrent threat was made. By mid-June the Western powers were discussing the creation of a rapid-reaction force of about 5,000 soldiers, backed by airpower, to be stationed in southern Turkey in case Saddam made threatening moves. Again, this was not something that Bush favoured, as it implied a long-term commitment, but he was by now enmeshed in an irreversible policy. On 13 July an announcement was made simultaneously in Washington, London, Paris and Rome that Western ground forces would withdraw completely from the safe havens two days later, leaving a reaction force at Silopi under the code-name Operation

'Poised Hammer', which would be used if Saddam moved troops or aircraft into a 'security zone' north of the 36th Parallel.

The last of the 'Provide Comfort' units moved out of northern Iraq on schedule, having achieved the humanitarian aim of helping the refugees. But the units had not solved the problems of the Kurds. Although Saddam remained quiet, maintaining negotiations over autonomy with the Kurdish leaders, it soon became apparent that the reaction force installed in Turkey was not a permanent arrangement. The Turks, concerned about the spread of Kurdish rebellion into their own territory, were never enthusiastic about playing host to Western forces, and by mid-September the ground elements of Operation 'Poised Hammer' were being withdrawn. Ozal allowed aircraft to remain at Incirlik, but this threat was not sufficient to prevent renewed Iraqi pressure on the Kurds. By early October Saddam's forces were reported to be closing in on Sulaymaniyah, outside the security zone, and a month later all remaining areas of Iraqi Kurdistan were being subjected to an economic blockade. Refugees began to appear again, but the West made no move to intervene. Bush, forced to react in April by a combination of public pressure and outside initiatives, had other things on his mind, and was no doubt pleased to have avoided a long-term involvement in Iraqi affairs, even if it meant that Saddam remained in power.

Disarming Iraq

Meanwhile, other aspects of Resolution 687 were being pursued with vigour. If there was no alternative but to accept that, short of full-scale military intervention, the Iraqi leader would survive at least the immediate post-war period, then it could be ensured that he was denied the power to threaten neighbouring states. Resolution 687 contained various clauses designed to rid Iraq of weapons of mass destruction, and Bush led the way in forcing Saddam to carry these out to the letter. It was not an easy process, involving political, economic and military threats, including two very public preparations for renewed airstrikes against Iraqi nuclear targets. By the beginning of 1992 there was still no guarantee that these had succeeded, but efforts continued to exploit the Iraqi weakness created by 'Desert Storm'.

At first Saddam appeared to comply with the UN demand for details of his weapons stockpile. By 18 April 1991 he had provided the IAEA in Vienna with a list of his nuclear materials, and the UN had received an account of his chemical and ballistic-missile capability. But the Americans refused to accept that these were complete, particularly as no reference was made to biological weapons, which US Intelligence was convinced existed. Under pressure from the UN, Saddam sent another letter to the IAEA on 29 April, virtually admitting that more nuclear material was being held, but insisting on guarantees that the Americans would not mount air attacks as soon as the locations were revealed. The Secretary-General rejected this as a violation of the ceasefire, which called for unconditional Iraqi compliance, and began to make arrangements for UN and IAEA inspection teams to visit Iraq. Their job would be to seek out all nuclear sites and material, preparatory to supervised destruction, after which the economic sanctions against Iraq would be reviewed.

In an effort to place this in the context of wider post-war policies, Bush revitalised his call for arms control in the Middle East. Evidence suggested that this was essential, for, almost as soon as 'Desert Storm' had ended, a number of countries in the region had begun to rearm. Some, notably in the Gulf itself, had done so with full US backing, but they had been restricted to conventional weapons only. Of far more concern to future security was an arms-spending spree by Syria, financed by money given to the country by Gulf states grateful for President Hafez Assad's commitment to the war against Iraq. An estimated $4 billion was involved, a significant proportion of which seems to have been devoted to purchasing ballistic missiles from China and North Korea, each with the range to threaten targets in Israel.[13] This, in turn, led to Israeli efforts to counter such missiles, turning to Washington for help. On 30 May Cheney announced US pledges of 'hundreds of millions of dollars' to Israel to research the Arrow anti-missile missile system, in addition to the normal US commitment of $1.8 billion of military aid per annum.[14]

It was an ill-timed move, coming less than 24 hours after Bush had outlined his proposals for regional arms control. Although the Arrow could be justified as a defensive reaction to Syrian rearming, it seemed to suggest that Israel would be excluded from any new arrangements. In his speech on 29 May, Bush called for a freeze on the supply of ballistic missiles to the Middle East, the introduction of controls on conventional arms exports to the region, a ban on the production of nuclear-weapons material by Middle East states, and restrictions on the transfer of chemical and biological capability. In addition, he advocated the creation of a UN register of all arms transfers — an idea originally mooted by Major in late April — and suggested that the five permanent members of the Security Council (the United States, the Soviet Union, Britain, France and China) should take a lead by curbing weapons sales.[15] The proposal lacked credibility in the light of the recent agreement with Israel, and was not enhanced by a further announcement on 4 June that the Americans would sell AH-64 Apache helicopters to both the UAE and Bahrain. In Bush's eyes such deals were not outside the parameters laid down in his speech, but to many observers they suggested a rather hypocritical approach.

On 26 June the Americans accused Iraq of pursuing a secret nuclear programme and of hiding evidence from UN inspectors, a team of which had been turned away from a site north of Baghdad by armed Iraqi soldiers, only to witness 'frenzied activity' as material was hastily removed. Twenty-four hours later, Bush advocated tightening the economic sanctions on Iraq as a punishment for non-compliance, and would not rule out the use of military action. By 29 June US forces in the Gulf region had been put on a war footing in response to Saddam's continued refusal to allow the inspectors unfettered access to nuclear sites, eight of which had been identified by US Intelligence from information provided by an Iraqi scientist who had defected in Kurdistan. On 1 July the inspectors delivered an ultimatum to the Iraqis, ordering them to open the sites to inspection or 'face the consequences', and speculation was rife that the Americans, backed by the British, were about to carry out selective airstrikes. In early

July the five permanent members of the Security Council agreed that the states of the Middle East should accept controls on their nuclear activities and eliminate ballistic missiles. The fact that this was not a formal UN resolution undermined its impact, although it did help to justify the continued pressure on Iraq to disarm.

Other instruments of pressure were applied, including an Anglo-American veto on attempts by Saddam to gain permission from the UN Sanctions Committee to sell $1.5 billion of oil to buy 'humanitarian goods'. On 12 July the five permanent members of the Security Council summoned Iraq's UN ambassador and ordered him to provide a full list of nuclear facilities within 14 days, and although they refused to support Bush's call for a formal UN ultimatum to Iraq to comply by 25 July or face military action, it was obvious that the international community was taking the crisis seriously. Despite an Iraqi denunciation of US policy — 'Bush is acting on behalf of Israel to fulfil the needs of international Zionism'[16] — Saddam had few options open to him. By 17 July the inspectors in Iraq were reporting that information was 'pouring out', enabling them to get on with their appointed task.

The Americans were still not convinced that Saddam was telling the whole truth about his nuclear capability, and issued warnings on 28 July and 2 August that military action had not yet been ruled out. There were even moves to press for a new UN resolution designed to enforce Iraq's compliance with international efforts to destroy its stockpile, although it was apparent that this would be opposed by permanent members of the Security Council concerned about US sabre-rattling. Indeed, throughout the rest of August and most of September, Saddam seemed to be obeying the rules. UN inspectors, for example, were allowed into a huge chemical-weapons complex at Salman Pak, 30 km (20 miles) south-east of Baghdad, and the Iraqis were being quite open about their 'Superguns'. This cleared the way for permission from the Sanctions Committee on 16 August for the supervised sale of $1.6 billion of Iraqi oil.[17]

It turned out to be a lull before the storm, diverting attention from the real issue of the nuclear stockpile. A new crisis emerged in mid-September, when Saddam refused to allow inspectors to use helicopters to fly over areas of Iraq suspected of containing secret nuclear sites. By 18 September Bush had ordered US aircraft back to bases in Saudi Arabia, saying that if the Iraqis did not comply with the inspectors' demands the helicopters would be escorted by fighters under orders to retaliate if fired upon. Five days later, as the Security Council agreed to discuss the issue, a further problem arose when the nuclear inspection team in Baghdad discovered what was described as a 'blueprint' for Iraq's nuclear programme during a dawn raid on an undeclared establishment. When the inspectors tried to remove the evidence, they were held at gunpoint by Iraqi soldiers and forced to hand back the documents. Less than 24 hours later an incident involving the same team, this time after it had seized lists of foreign companies which had reportedly aided Iraq in its nuclear development, led to a four-day siege in a Baghdad car-park as the inspectors barricaded themselves in their vehicles and refused to hand anything over to Saddam's men. The crisis was eventually resolved, but only after the Americans had deployed 100 Patriot missiles, with 1,300 military personnel, to Saudi Arabia, in preparation for possible Iraqi reaction to the planned airstrikes. Almost unnoticed, as Saddam stepped down, was his agreement to allow the UN helicopters to operate freely.

When the documents seized by the embattled UN inspectors were analysed, further evidence of the true state of the Iraqi nuclear programme emerged. According to reports by David Kay, the head of the inspection team, Saddam had a secret programme codenamed 'Petrochemical Three' to produce a nuclear device as well as a ballistic missile to deliver it to its target.[18] Sustained efforts had been made to keep this information from the UN. At Tuwaitha, troops had blown up evidence of a nuclear power plant, while at Tarmiyah they had paved over a floor to hide traces of uranium enrichment. When it was later revealed that Iraq was in the process of producing lithium-6, an element used in the manufacture of thermonuclear devices, international fears were revitalised. On 11 October the Security Council unanimously passed Resolution 715, prohibiting Iraq from any nuclear activity (including electricity generation) and from importing materials that might be used in the production of weapons of mass destruction.[19] By January 1992, with speculation rife that Saddam had already moved his stockpile of natural uranium to Algeria (a country then in the throes of a political crisis that seemed set to produce either a fundamentalist Muslim government or a civil war), it was obvious that the Iraqi leader was intent on retaining as much as possible of his weapons capability.

It would be wrong to conclude from this, however, that nothing had been achieved. The recognition of Iraq's capability alone was sufficient justification for American and UN actions, while the concurrent inspection and destruction of Iraqi non-nuclear weapons had undoubtedly weakened Saddam. By the beginning of 1992 UN teams had visited chemical and biological research installations, inspected Scud launching sites and supervised the destruction of missiles and 'Superguns', the latter comprising one complete weapon at Jabal Hamrayn, north of Baghdad, and one in bits elsewhere. In addition, UN economic sanctions had not been lifted, increasing the pressure on Saddam, while the Security Council had shown its willingness, through Resolution 715, to tighten the screw on Iraq if necessary, backing the various military threats and deployments put forward by the Americans.

If such international pressure could be sustained, there was little reason to doubt that the Iraqis would eventually be forced to comply with all the ceasefire terms laid down in Resolution 687, although the process would never be easy. It depended on US and UN resolve, on continued support of the inspection teams, and on public perceptions of anti-Iraq policies. By early 1992 it was already being suggested that Saddam was deliberately fuelling crises so that economic sanctions would not be lifted, leaving Bush and Major, both about to go to the polls, to cope with the impact on their electorates of starving and disease-ridden Iraqi children.[20] Many of these problems would have been solved if Saddam had been overthrown, but, faced with the reality of his survival, the international community seemed to be maintaining its resolve to ensure that he no longer posed a major regional threat.

The Arab-Israeli peace process

All the actions designed to disarm Iraq and to help the Kurds coincided with US-led efforts to resolve the long-running conflict between Israel and its Arab neighbours. Put forward as one of the four strands of post-war policy towards the Middle East in Bush's speech to Congress on 6 March 1991, recognition of the need for Arab-Israeli peace was an integral part of America's response to both the Gulf crisis and its aftermath. Promises that initiatives would be put forward had helped to create and maintain the anti-Saddam Coalition, undermining Saddam's own claims to be fighting to force such a settlement, and Bush's credibility at home and abroad depended to a significant extent on some form of breakthrough in this notoriously difficult area.

According to analysts in the US State Department, the 'Desert Storm' victory created a unique opportunity for negotiations to begin.[21] By early March 1991 the Americans were walking tall on the world stage, with a new-found reputation for getting things done, principally through a UN Security Council suddenly freed from the shackles of the Cold War. The unprecedented co-operation between Washington and Moscow meant that attempts to pursue peace in the Middle East were no longer stalled by Superpower confrontation. Moreover, there were optimistic signs from within the disputed region. The Israelis, aware that the USA might no longer view their country as an essential strategic outpost now that Soviet interest in the Middle East had declined, were susceptible to pressure to negotiate in return for continued economic support from Washington. The Syrians, aware that they had lost their Superpower backer now that Moscow had effectively withdrawn, were looking for better relations with the West. Lebanon, virtually under Syrian control, would follow Assad's lead. King Hussein of Jordan, desperate to improve his image and to rehabilitate himself with both the West and the more moderate Arab powers, would welcome a peace process in which he would hold centre stage, while the Palestine Liberation Organisation (PLO), having lost considerable credibility during the Gulf crisis and war by seeming to back Saddam, would be unable to put up strong opposition to any peace proposal.

Against this background, Secretary of State James Baker visited the Middle East in early March for the first of what would turn out to be eight exhausting trips. Almost immediately it was apparent that, despite the logic of the State Department analysis, the issues involved in a peace initiative were so complex, and the positions of the interested parties so entrenched, that a settlement was not going to be easy. Baker's proposal at this stage was for an international conference to be convened, under UN auspices, at which the various Arab-Israeli disputes would be discussed and solutions explored. Top of the list would be the Palestinian problem, which seemed to be the key to all others. If some settlement could be made involving an

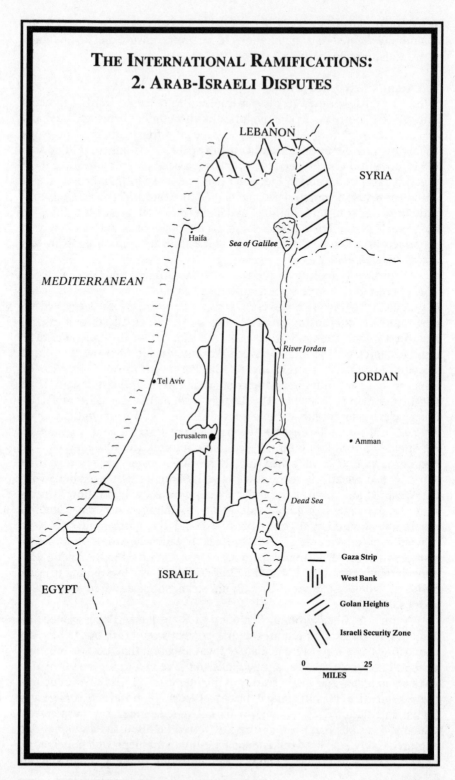

The International Ramifications:
2. Arab-Israeli Disputes

LEBANON

SYRIA

Haifa

Sea of Galilee

MEDITERRANEAN

River Jordan

JORDAN

Tel Aviv

Jerusalem

Amman

Dead Sea

ISRAEL

Gaza Strip

West Bank

Golan Heights

Israeli Security Zone

EGYPT

0   25
MILES

Israeli withdrawal from the Occupied Territories of the West Bank (including East Jerusalem) and the Gaza Strip as part of a process to create a Palestinian state, it was likely that other areas of contention — the future of the Golan Heights, the security of southern Lebanon, disputes over access to water resources, and arms control — would be relatively straightforward. During his first trip Baker received sympathetic backing from the Gulf states and Syria, the latter supporting the idea of a UN-sponsored conference, as this would imply international moves to impose a settlement based on UN Resolutions 242 and 338, which called for withdrawal from all occupied territories.

The Israelis opposed the plan. Prime Minister Yitzhak Shamir had already outlined his negotiating position. On 7 February, while the Gulf War was being waged, he had revitalised an Israeli initiative of May 1989, offering elections in the West Bank and Gaza Strip (but not in Arab East Jerusalem) leading to Palestinian autonomy over a five-year period.[22] He made no reference to the creation of a Palestinian state, fearing its potential strength so close to Israel, and insisted that any negotiations would have to be with Palestinian residents of the West Bank and Gaza Strip, not with the PLO. Shamir also made it clear that he was not prepared to trade land for peace, giving up territory which was considered vital to Israeli security in exchange for diplomatic recognition by Arab states he distrusted. In addition, he refused to accept any involvement by the UN, an organisation the Israelis disliked (not least because of Resolution 3379, passed by the General Assembly in November 1975, equating Zionism with racism), and insisted on a regional conference in which he could meet his Arab neighbours on equal terms, ree from the threat of international pressure.

When Baker returned to Washington on 12 March, therefore, the chances of success looked slim. However, it was apparent that common ground existed. Both sides seemed prepared to talk about the future of the Palestinians, and the idea of a conference of some sort had not been ruled out. What Baker had to do was bridge the gap between the Israeli and Arab positions, searching for compromises and, if necessary, exerting pressure to ensure that meetings took place. While in Israel, he met Palestinian leaders from the Occupied Territories in an effort to find delegates acceptable to Shamir, and then concentrated on widening the scope of the negotiations to increase international expectations of a breakthrough. On 12 April, while returning from his second trip to the region, he met the Jordanian Foreign Minister in Geneva (an event greeted by King Hussein as a sign that Jordan was being welcomed back on to the world stage). Four days later Baker consulted with EC foreign ministers, gaining their backing for an international conference.

Thus, when Baker returned to the Middle East, meeting Shamir on 19 April, he was looking for concessions from the Israelis in an effort to build Arab confidence in the peace process. By now the Syrians and Jordanians were making it clear that they would attend a conference only if the Israelis accepted Palestinian delegates from East Jerusalem and halted the building of new Jewish settlements in the Occupied Territories, two things that Shamir refused to contemplate. As far as he was concerned, Jerusalem was not negotiable (it was, after all, the self-proclaimed capital of Israel), and settlement-building was essential if all the estimated one million Jews arrived from the Soviet Union as expected over the next few months. In addition, of course, Shamir was under substantial pressure from the right wing of his coalition government, which comprised small parties dedicated not just to preserving the *status quo* but also to extending the frontiers of Israel, and there were limits to the concessions he could make. By the end of April the US initiative seemed to have stalled, even though Baker had gained Shamir's reluctant acceptance of EC participation as observers, and of co-sponsorship by the Soviet Union, the latter in exchange for promises from Moscow that full diplomatic relations with Israel, severed in the aftermath of the Six-Day War of 1967, would be restored. This in itself represented a considerable shift in US policy, which hitherto had deliberately excluded the Soviets from Middle East diplomacy. But Soviet participation was felt to be an essential prerequisite of Arab involvement, as well as an indication that any settlement would not be imposed by Washington alone.

The result was co-ordinated Superpower pressure. In early May both Baker and his Soviet opposite number, Alexander Bessmertnykh, were touring Middle East capitals, and compromises began to emerge. On 1 June Bush sent personal letters to the leaders of Israel and the Arab powers, outlining a number of new proposals. To resolve the problem of UN involvement, he suggested that the conference should be co-sponsored by Washington and Moscow, with UN representatives present as observers only. To quieten Israeli fears that a settlement would be imposed on them by the international community, Bush also assured Shamir that binding decisions would come only from bilateral talks between the Israelis and individual Arab delegations, including one made up of Palestinians from the Occupied Territories. International involvement would continue by means of periodic reviews of progress (Bush suggested a reconvening of the co-sponsored conference every six months), and wider regional issues such as economic development, water resources and arms control would be addressed separately in a multinational conference, to meet once the bilateral talks were off the ground. Shamir still had grave doubts. There was nothing in Bush's proposal about the make-up of the Palestinian delegation, nor any assurances that East Jerusalem was not on the agenda. But his position was effectively undermined when, on 14 July, in a belated response to Bush's letter, Syria accepted the plan, describing it as 'positive and balanced'. It was the breakthrough Baker had wanted, particularly as it soon became clear that the Syrian acceptance had come only after lengthy talks with the Egyptians, Jordanians and Palestinians.

Arab consensus increased the pressure on Shamir, not least because Bush's enthusiastic response to Syria's acceptance threatened to drive a wedge between Israel and her Superpower backer. Shamir offered concessions, agreeing to UN involvement in the conference as observers and welcoming Syria's offer of talks (chiefly because it implied Assad's acceptance of Israel's right to exist), but the Americans did not relax. On 16 July the leaders of the seven most powerful industrialised states in the world (the group of Seven, or G7), including Bush, urged Israel to stop settlement-building in exchange for the Arabs lifting their economic boycott of the Jewish state. When Baker began his fifth tour of the Middle East, two days later, he managed to persuade the PLO to drop its insistence on attending the conference, and accept his proposal for delegates to 'represent Palestinian interests'. At the same time, General Brent Scowcroft, Bush's National Security Adviser, let it be known that Israel's request for $10 billion of loan guarantees, due to be laid before Congress in September and vital if the country was to have the money needed to absorb the Soviet Jews, would be dependent on Shamir's positive reply to Bush's letter of 1 June. By 24 July Shamir was expressing optimism about the peace process, although he was still insisting on Israel's right to veto any list of Palestinian delegates and refusing to halt settlement-building.

On 30 July Bush and Gorbachev met in Moscow to sign the Strategic Arms Reduction Treaty (START), and took the opportunity to declare that they would co-sponsor a Middle East peace conference in October. Having gained promises that the Soviets intended to renew full diplomatic relations, and aware of mounting pressure from the West, Shamir indicated his acceptance on 1 August, receiving Israeli Cabinet backing four days later. Syria, Egypt, Jordan and Lebanon followed suit, but the problems were by no means over. Attention now shifted to the PLO, which refused to make any decision until a meeting of the Palestine National Council (PNC) in September, and let it be known that it would not accept an Israeli veto of delegates nor a continuation of settlement-building. PLO Chairman Yasser Arafat also demanded guarantees that any negotiations should be on the basis of UN Resolutions 242 and 338, and that the issue of East Jerusalem should be addressed.

The coup attempt in Moscow on 19–21 August led to a suspension of the peace process, but once Gorbachev had been restored to power, albeit temporarily, Bush and Baker returned to the fray. They were searching for more meaningful concessions from Israel, in particular over the question of settlement-building, which seemed to be the main block to progress. On 12 September Bush announced that he would veto the Israeli request for loan guarantees unless Congress agreed to a 120-day postponement. Six days later he linked this to demands for a freeze on all settlement-building in the Occupied Territories. Although the official reaction from Jerusalem was predictably hard-line — indeed, one of the more radical members of Shamir's coalition government publicly described Bush as 'a lying anti-Semite'[23] — it was obvious that US pressure on Israel was growing in an attempt to ensure a favourable response from the Palestinians. When the PNC met in Tunis in late September, Arafat succeeded in gaining permission for a team of 14 representatives from the West Bank and Gaza Strip to attend the conference as part of a joint delegation with the Jordanians. They would be backed by a further seven advisers from East Jerusalem, who would act as an unofficial link with the PLO but enjoy no rights of negotiation.

Opposition to the peace process was by now apparent among both Palestinians and Israelis. On 30 September there were reports that the leaders of the Popular Front for the Liberation of Palestine-General Command (PFLP-GC) and Hezbollah had met to co-ordinate a Rejectionist Front,[24] and ten days later militant Jewish settlers expressed their feelings by seizing Arab houses in East Jerusalem. But enough had been achieved to persuade the Americans to go ahead with the final arrangements. Baker travelled to the region in mid-October on his eighth trip, expressing confidence that all was well. Some issues still needed to be settled, not least the Israeli refusal to stop settlement-building, but when Moscow renewed diplomatic relations with Israel on 18 October and the Palestinians put forward a list of delegates which was acceptable to Shamir, the way was clear at last. Baker and the new Soviet Foreign Minister, Boris Pankin, issued formal invitations to Israel, Syria, Egypt, Lebanon, Jordan and the Palestinians to attend a preliminary conference in Madrid, starting on 30 October, after which bilateral talks would begin. A multinational conference to discuss the wider problems of the Middle East would convene two weeks later. The Israeli Cabinet accepted the invitation on 20 October, to be quickly followed by the Arab powers.

This in itself was a major achievement, representing a triumph for US diplomacy. Bush could now claim that one of his stated post-war aims had been pursued and, as far as he was concerned, crowned with success. After all, no-one had managed to get the Israelis and Arabs around the table before, and any agreements that emerged were the responsibility of the delegates, not of the USA. Furthermore, the road to Madrid had shown just how powerful the Americans now were, for although many questions had still to be answered, few people could doubt the manipulative capabilities of the Washington administration. Baker's ceaseless trips to the Middle East had been characterised by a carrot-and-stick approach, offering and demanding concessions which gradually bridged the gap between the contending powers. Before the Gulf crisis this would have been unthinkable, partly because of the perception that America was closely allied to Israel and partly because of Soviet influence with the Arab states. By October 1991 neither factor applied; Bush had shown his willingness and ability to ignore a domestic Jewish lobby, particularly over the question of the loan guarantees,[25] and the Soviet Union, beset with internal problems that would soon lead to a break-up of the republics, was no longer influential. The various delegations which gathered in Madrid on 30 October may not have done so willingly, and were certainly not expecting instant solutions, but each of them had been persuaded that the conference and subsequent talks were to its advantage. Each had made a deliberate and conscious calculation and, presumably, concluded that the potential gains from negotiation outweighed the costs of continued confrontation. Without the driving force of a confident and powerful United States, backed on occasion by its allies, this would not have happened.

The talks
Although Bush could claim to have carried out his promise of 6 March, he could not guarantee the success of the talks. When he and Gorbachev addressed the delegates in Madrid on 30 October, both leaders took an

optimistic line, describing the conference as a 'unique opportunity' and appealing to their audience to pursue 'real peace', out of which a Middle East could emerge that was 'no longer victimised by fear and terror'. It soon became apparent, however, that mutual suspicion and deep distrust prevailed. On 31 October Shamir (who had insisted on leading the Israeli team in preference to his Foreign Minister, David Levy)[26] made a speech in which it was clear that he had no intention of trading land for peace, only to be followed by representatives of Syria, Lebanon, Jordan and the Palestinians, all demanding an immediate Israeli withdrawal from the Occupied Territories. No-one walked out, but the mood was decribed as 'sharply confrontational'. It was made worse on 1 November when, in response to an Israeli description of Syria as 'one of the most oppressive states in the world', the Syrian Foreign Minister brandished a poster showing the young Shamir as a 'terrorist' in the war against the British in the 1940s. In his closing address, Baker openly rebuked the delegates: 'If you do not seize this historic opportunity, no one else can, no one else will and no one will blame anyone outside your region', but the prospects looked bleak. As one commentator put it: 'By Day Two [of the conference], everyone was talking but nobody was listening. Hope had become boredom; the fine phrases revealed the same old rhetoric.'[27]

The bilateral talks began in Madrid on 3 November, assuming a pattern that was soon to become familiar. Palestinian and Israeli delegates came face to face for the first time, conducting preliminary negotiations that were described as 'sombre and optimistic', but both the Syrians and Lebanese engaged in diplomatic brinkmanship, deliberately arriving late so that little could be achieved. Events in the Middle East also did nothing to lighten the atmosphere. On 3 November Hezbollah guerrillas attacked Israeli targets in southern Lebanon, triggering retaliatory airstrikes that led the Lebanese to threaten to walk out of the talks, and 24 hours later Syria expressed anger at the establishment of a new Jewish settlement on the Golan Heights. It was probably with some relief that the delegates agreed to a break in the proceedings for '2–3 weeks'. As they returned home it was obvious that peace was still a long way off. None of the key issues had yet been broached, relations between the various delegations were strained and, crucially, no-one had decided where the next round of talks would take place. Israel demanded meetings in the Middle East, away from the glare of Western publicity, but the Arabs, aware that they had scored something of a public relations victory in Madrid,[28] suggested a European location.

On 22 November Bush issued invitations to all parties to resume their negotiations in Washington on 4 December, only to alienate Shamir, angry that he had not been consulted. The Israelis, arguing that they needed more time to prepare — they were, after all, conducting three sets of talks simultaneously — asked for a five-day extension, and when this was refused they deliberately delayed their arrival. Thus, when the talks resumed on 10 December, there was increased resentment between the Arab and Jewish delegations which quickly spilt over into the meetings in the US State Department. Israel was still insisting on a move to the Middle East; relations with Syria were soured by suspicion (not least because of reported links between Damascus and the militant Palestinian groups in the Occupied Territories); Lebanon was complaining about new levels of violence on its southern border; and the Palestinian-Jordanian delegation was locked in procedural disputes with its Israeli counterpart. This last problem led to an almost farcical situation in which the delegates refused even to enter the allotted conference room, conducting heated debates in the corridor. The Israelis insisted on meeting the Palestinians and Jordanians together, while the Arab negotiators demanded separate talks in separate rooms. By 18 December no progress had been made and the talks were suspended.

The Americans, reluctant to intervene but feeling that there was little choice if the peace process was not to collapse entirely, used what pressure they could. Bush sent a message to all parties on 17 December arguing strongly that it was 'time to lay aside political posturing and to move on to issues of substance', and two days later Baker announced that the multinational conference on the Middle East would go ahead regardless, in Moscow on 28–29 January 1992. But the momentum built up before Madrid had clearly gone. Israel, despite welcoming a UN General Assembly vote on 16 December rescinding the 'Zionism is racism' resolution,[29] was refusing to consider any compromise over territory and continuing with its settlement-building programme. Indeed, when the annual budget was debated in the Knesset on 2/3 January, substantial additional funds were diverted to this. At the same time, militant Palestinians were creating trouble in the Occupied Territories in an effort to undermine the negotiations, and when the Israeli authorities responded by threatening to deport 12 of them, contrary to international convention,[30] the Palestinian delegation refused to return to Washington for a resumption of the bilateral talks.

Once again the Americans stepped in, voting in favour of a UN Security Council condemnation of Israeli actions, to reassure the Arabs, and reminding Shamir that the $10 billion loan guarantees were still to be debated. It was enough to get the parties back to the negotiating table and for the Israelis to agree to meet a Palestinian delegation (containing two Jordanians) separately from a Jordanian delegation (containing two Palestinians), but when news of this compromise reached Jerusalem, right-wing members of Shamir's Cabinet resigned, forcing a general election. As Israel prepared to go to the polls, the peace process ground to a halt.

An assessment

It was now a year since the opening of 'Desert Storm', and on the evidence of the peace process little had been achieved. Israel had made no major concessions in terms of the future of the Occupied Territories or the question of settlement-building; the Syrians and Lebanese had failed to come to any agreement with Israel over their border disputes; and the bilateral talks as a whole had bogged down in procedural debate, not least over where they were to take place in the future. Public expectations in the West of a breakthrough had declined significantly, leaving Bush with the difficult task of exerting sufficient pressure to maintain the momentum for peace while not alienating American domestic opinion in an election year.

Indeed, some commentators were arguing that, despite the military success of 'Desert Storm', the President had failed to exploit his new advantages on the world stage. A year after the war Saddam was still in power, having been allowed to slaughter those of his people who responded to Bush's calls for action against the dictator; the Western powers had been forced to intervene to save the Kurds, only to leave them to their fate after four months of military protection; and the Arab-Israeli conflict had not been resolved. In addition, Gulf security still seemed to be dependent on Western involvement, there having been no effective regional pact created; attempts at arms control had not stopped a number of local powers from increasing their stockpiles of weapons; and Bush's proposals for regional development had fallen on deaf ears. According to such analyses, the Middle East had not been changed by the war. If anything, attitudes had hardened and the endemic problems of the region — the gap between rich and poor, between moderate and radical Muslims, and between different ethnic or religious groups — had grown more acute.

But this is an unnecessarily pessimistic view. By January 1992 Bush and his erstwhile Coalition partners could look back to some positive gains over the preceding year. Saddam had been forced to relinquish Kuwait and accept humiliating ceasefire terms by means of a military campaign that was remarkable for its impact and brevity. Moreover, although Saddam had survived politically, his influence beyond Iraq had been seriously curtailed, removing an undoubted threat to the stability of the Middle East and allowing the West free access to vital oil supplies. Even within Iraq, the limits of Saddam's power had been defined by his enforced acceptance of military intervention in the north and of UN/IAEA inspectors throughout the country. The process of this enforcement may have been difficult, involving a mixture of threats usually associated with crisis management, but the fact that the Western powers, particularly the USA, were willing and able to respond was indicative of a new-found resolve which came directly from their success in the Gulf War.

Finally, although no-one could argue that the problems of the Middle East had been solved, significant progress had been made in key areas. The Madrid peace conference may have been followed by disappointing bilateral talks, but the fact that it had taken place at all was a major breakthrough. Nobody seriously believed that an Arab-Israeli peace initiative would lead to immediate success; it was always going to be a painfully slow process, based on a gradual build-up of confidence and compromise. The first signs of this may have been apparent with the Israeli agreement to treat the Palestinians and Jordanians as separate delegations. The fact that no-one had yet walked out of the bilateral talks was cause for some hope, as was the prospect of multinational talks in Moscow, despite both the Syrians and Lebanese announcing their refusal to attend.

Peace in the Middle East was, and will remain, a step-by-step process, dependent for success on the perceptions of those involved in negotiations. Israel needs US political and economic backing, and may be forced to compromise to ensure that it remains; Syria needs to regain the security of a Superpower ally or to mend fences with the West, and is susceptible to pressure for continued negotiations; Lebanon needs peace in order to recover from years of civil war; and both Jordan and the PLO need a restoration of international confidence to wipe out the memory of their policies during the Gulf crisis and war. As long as the USA, with its allies, continues to push for peace, the chance of success remains.

Notes

1. Quoted in *The Times* (London), Friday 18 January 1991.
2. Ibid, Friday 8 February 1991. King Hussein's anger was fuelled by the recent deaths of Jordanian truck drivers in Iraq, caught in Coalition air attacks.
3. Primakov's own account of his talks with Aziz appears in *Time International*, 4 March 1991, pp 32–3, and 11 March 1991, pp 64–5. The initial translation of Iraq's peace offer stated that withdrawal from Kuwait *'will* be linked' to the various conditions; only later was this amended to *'should* be linked', implying room for negotiation.
4. Since Resolution 678 in November 1990 (see Chapter 2, above), five non-veto members of the Security Council had been rotated: Austria, Belgium, Ecuador, India and Zimbabwe replaced Canada, Colombia, Finland, Malaysia and Ethiopia on 1 January 1991.
5. For details, see Rosemary Hollis, 'Security in the Gulf: No Panaceas', *Military Technology*, Vol XV, Issue 10, 1991, pp 52–62.
6. For an overview of the arguments for and against, see Lawrence Freedman, 'The Gulf war and the new world order', *Survival*, May/June 1991, pp 195–209.
7. The full text of Resolution 687 may be found in *Military Technology*, Vol XV, Issue 6, 1991, pp 140–44.
8. US Secretary of Defense Cheney admitted: 'I'm not sure whose side you'd want to be on', when first reports of the Shi'a revolt, led by fundamentalist mullahs, were received in Washington, *Time International*, 18 March 1991, p 26.
9. Hollis, op cit.
10. Quoted in *The Times*, Thursday 4 April 1991.
11. For the text, see *Military Technology*, 6/91, p 144.
12. 3rd Commando Brigade comprised Nos 40, 42 and 45 Commando, Royal Marines, with supporting arms. They worked under their own codename, Operation 'Safe Haven', although this was part of the overall US effort 'Provide Comfort'. Altogether in Turkey and Iraq, more than 23,000 troops from 13 nations were involved. A useful account of British experiences is in *The Sunday Times* (London), 4 August 1991, written by Major-General Robin Ross, Commander, HQ Commando Forces.
13. Details may be found in *Foreign Report* (The Economist Newspaper Ltd, London), 21 March and 7 November 1991. Assad regarded the acquisition of such missiles as a counter to the Israeli development of the Jericho II. For a wider view of ballistic-missile proliferation in the Middle East, see Frank Barnaby, 'Arms Control after the Gulf War', *Conflict Studies 240* (Research Institute for the Study of Conflict and Terrorism, London, April 1991).
14. According to *Foreign Report*, 25 July 1991, the Arrow is due to enter service in 1995; the Americans provided 80 per cent of the $180 million already spent and, on 30 May 1991, pledged 72 per cent of the $320 million second-stage, designed to make the missile smaller and more mobile.
15. *Sunday Times*, 2 June 1991.
16. Ibid, 16 July 1991.
17. In the event, Saddam refused to take advantage of this, seeing such supervision of oil-sales as a violation of Iraqi sovereignty. Of the $1.6 billion, $1 billion was to be used to purchase 'food and medicines', with the rest deposited in the UN 'war-compensation fund' set up under the terms of Resolution 687.
18. *The Times*, Saturday 5 October 1991.
19. Ibid, Saturday 12 October 1991.
20. According to a UN report in November 1991, 30 per cent of Iraqi children were malnourished and infant mortality had trebled since the Gulf War, *Sunday Times*, 1 December 1991.
21. *Newsweek*, 18 March 1991, pp 14–15.
22. Although put forward most recently in May 1989, the basics of the Israeli 'deal' dated back to the Camp David Accord of late 1978.
23. This was said by Rehavam Zeevi, head of the tiny Moledet Party and minister without portfolio in Shamir's Cabinet. *The Times*, Monday 16 September 1991. Shamir himself stated that 'Israel will never accept a choice between fidelity to its essential interests and money', but the

loan guarantees were desperately needed nonetheless.

24. A more formal Rejectionist Front, led by Iran, was created in Tehran in late October 1991, comprising Abu Mousa of the Fatah Uprising, Abbas Musawi of Hezbollah, Ahmed Jibril of the PFLP-GC, and Abu Nidal of the Fatah Revolutionary Council. The Front was dedicated to continuing the war against Israel whatever the outcome of the peace talks, ibid, Wednesday 23 October 1991.

25. The 'Jewish lobby' — or, more accurately, the American-Israel Public Affairs Committee (Aipac) — had tried to sway Congressional opinion in September, flying 1,000 prominent American Jews to Washington to lobby against a postponement of the loan-guarantee debate. The fact that this did not succeed was a blow to what had for long been regarded as an effective pressure group.

26. The 'official' reasons for snubbing Levy were given as his relatively poor command of English and his reputation in Likud Party circles as a man prepared to 'do a deal' with the Palestinians over territory. More cynical commentators observed that, as a Moroccan-born Sephardic (Middle Eastern) Jew, he never fitted easily into a Cabinet dominated by Ashkenazi (European) and Sabra (Israeli-born) Jews.

27. Coverage of the conference may be found in *The Times*, Thursday 31 October, Friday 1 November, and Saturday 2 November 1991, from where the quotations are drawn.

28. It was a general feeling among the press covering the conference that the Palestinian delegation, led by Haidar Abdel-Shafi (a respected doctor from the Gaza Strip) and spokeswoman Hanan Ashrawi (a professor of English at the Bir Zeit University on the West Bank), had appeared as erudite and reasonable. Indeed, one commentator observed that the main mistake made by the Israelis at Madrid was *not* to invite the PLO, ibid.

29. UN General Assembly Resolution 3379, originally passed on 10 November 1975, was rescinded by 111 votes to 25, ibid, Tuesday 17 December 1991. The fact that the Arab powers opposed the move alienated Israel, making the resumption of bilateral talks in January 1992 'frosty'.

30. Specifically, Article 49 of the Fourth Geneva Convention.

Further Reading

Tony Banks, 'After the Gulf War — The Prospects for Peace in the Islamic Crescent', *Jane's Intelligence Review*, pp 256–9.

Frank Barnaby, 'Arms Control after the Gulf War', *Conflict Studies 240* (Research Institute for the Study of Conflict and Terrorism, London, April 1991).

David Bradshaw, 'After the Gulf War: the Kurds', *The World Today*, pp 78–80.

Shahram Chubin, 'Post-war Gulf security', *Survival*, pp 140–57.

Lawrence Freedman, 'The Gulf war and the new world order', *Survival*, pp 195– 209.

Fred Halliday, 'The Gulf War and its aftermath: first reflections', *International Affairs*, pp 223–34.

Rosemary Hollis, 'Security in the Gulf: No Panaceas', *Military Technology*, Vol XV, Issue 10, 1991, pp 52–62.

CHAPTER 10
The Media War

Stephen Badsey

'Can one really distinguish between the mass media as
instruments of information and entertainment, and as
agents of manipulation and indoctrination?'
Herbert Marcuse, *One Dimensional Man* (1964)

The Military and the Media

From the Iraqi invasion of Kuwait in
August 1990, there was no aspect of
the Gulf War which was not directly
affected by the mass communications media. Although in previous
wars governments and armed forces
had grown increasingly sensitive to
the importance of war reporting, its problems and possibilities were
ultimately viewed as secondary to the war's prosecution. This time, the
world witnessed an unmistakable *media war*, ranking with the air war, the
ground war, the economic war and the political war in determining victory.
After the Gulf War, it will never again be possible to discuss the conduct of
war without reference to the media.

Nevertheless, the issue of military-media relations threatens to swamp
any investigation. Even without propaganda, psychological warfare and
commercial advertising, all of which had roles in the Gulf, the term 'media'
embraces all forms of print and broadcast journalism, from the supermarket
press to the international news agencies, and from local radio to global
satellite television. Generalisations about *the* military and *the* media in the
war hide a host of variations between disparate governments and armed
forces, and between state controlled, state sponsored, and commercial news
coverage. Military-media relations reached from the reporting teams with
the front-line combat troops through to the impact of global news networks
on the highest political and strategic direction of the war. Reported events
in Sydney, Moscow, Bangkok and Athens all became part of the global war
story. A Japanese news team secretly filmed Iraqi aircraft trapped in Iran for
world broadcast. As *Newsweek* argued, 'The globalization of news (a new
idea) ran smack into national allegiance in wartime (an old idea).'[1]
Uncensored television reports of the bombing of Baghdad were shown in
Saudi Arabia, Turkey, Israel and Iraq itself as it happened, while George
Bush and Saddam Hussein both watched CBS reporter Bob McKeown's
arrival in Kuwait City ahead of the Coalition ground forces at the end of the
war.

The relationship between all governments and their national media is
both complex and uneasy, and many nations — including all the Gulf states
— censor the media as a matter of course. Except for Egypt, the press

throughout the Arab world supported their respective governments without debate during the war, and the international press was censored accordingly, although access to uncensored overseas radio and even television was always possible, even in Iraq. In Western countries, while direct control of the media is rare, governments have for decades seen *news management*, or indirect influence, as quite legitimate. 'News generated by the action of the government as to content and timing,' as President Kennedy's Assistant Secretary of Defense for Public Affairs put it, 'is part of the arsenal of weaponry that a President has.'[2] The idea that different rules apply to media coverage in time of war is also widely accepted. One typical American opinion poll taken in the middle of the Gulf War found that 70 per cent of those questioned wanted *increased* government restrictions placed on the reporting of the war.

A fundamental belief which shaped military-media relations in the Gulf War was that the objectives of the armed forces would be in direct conflict with those of the media. In the famous British dictum, first heard in the Suez Crisis of 1956 and repeated during the Falklands conflict of 1982, 'the essence of successful warfare is secrecy; the essence of successful journalism is publicity', and there was a very real fear that open reporting would reveal the Coalition plans to the enemy. Some journalists believed that this attitude persisted even at the very highest levels. 'Mr Bush, Mr Schwarzkopf, did not want the war covered,' one argued, 'and all the rules of open society in America and in Western Europe simply were suspended.'[3] In fact this was not the case, as governments and their higher military advisers saw the co-operation of the media as vital in maintaining support for the prosecution of the war. According to *Newsweek* this gave the media more power than they realised, since 'the military needs TV to build and sustain support for the war even more than TV needs the military to build ratings',[4] and fewer restrictions on reporting should have been accepted.

The extent to which the Western media co-operated with the military in misleading both Iraq and their own people in the war is much disputed. Wittingly or not, the media played a crucial role in disguising the initial weakness of the American deployment to Saudi Arabia. As General Schwarzkopf confided at his victory press conference:

> I guess the one thing I would say to the Press that I was delighted with is, that in the very early stages of the operation when we were here building up, and we didn't have very much on the ground, y'all were giving us the credit for a whole lot more over here. And as a result that gave me a feeling of confidence that we might not be attacked quite as quickly as I thought we might be attacked.[5]

Schwarzkopf refused to be drawn on other aspects of the media's utility. It was acknowledged, however, that the Coalition deliberately used the international media as a weapon of psychological warfare, and that press conferences, interviews and media events were organised to convey information to the enemy. It has been claimed that the Coalition planners, by convincing Saddam Hussein through the media that their bombing targeters knew the location of every one of his communications centres, panicked him into using improvised, mobile communications.[6] There is no doubt that the Iraqis, also, attempted to use the media as a weapon, chiefly in allowing Western journalists to remain in Baghdad after the air war began, 'because they thought it would have a propaganda value — because they felt the West was squeamish about casualties, that public opinion would be undermined if they saw that happening'.[7] A significant number of journalists resisted these attempts by both sides to recruit them for the war effort, and resented the inevitable accusations of collaboration or bias in their reporting of the war.

At the operational level, a deep distrust of the media existed among military commanders preoccupied with winning the war and with the safety of their men. 'I suppose the press has its purpose,' one US Air Force commander told journalists, 'but one thing is certain: you can't do me any good, and you sure as hell can do me harm.'[8] This hostility was grounded in mutual ignorance, often reflecting the cultural separation between the armed forces and their societies in countries without compulsory military service. Military jargon, with its mixture of acronyms, euphemisms ('collateral damage equals genocide' as one opponent of the war put it), graveyard humour and frequent brutality was a rich source of misunderstanding. One journalist saw evidence of racism in an American pilot's account of Iraqi soldiers 'scattering like cockroaches when the light is turned on'. In fact this commonplace expression was applied by the military even to journalists themselves. Another pilot's description of air attacks at the Mutla Gap as 'the biggest Fourth of July show you ever saw' received similar criticism.

An almost universal counter-accusation against the media, particularly television, was that they covered the war like a sporting event or game show, without regard for the fact that people were being killed. Arab critics of American media coverage attributed this to simple racism:

> It was terrible, watching the violence. And also it was presented with a lot of euphoria and 'merry-go-round', that we are the clever guys, we are the producers of *Patriots*, we are the creators of all these high-tech weapons — some journalist said 'state-of-the-*art*'! — and we can destroy the natives, the invisible natives, easily.[9]

Perhaps more important was the media's own ignorance of the destructive nature of AirLand Battle and its associated technology, reflected in some curious statistics. One typical opinion poll in Britain at the start of 'Desert Storm' showed over 80 per cent popular support for military action, but only 60 per cent for liberating Kuwait at the cost of service lives. Even at the war's end the gap was 10 percentage points between support for the fighting and the realisation that to fight means to kill and to die.

Not every major newspaper or television station has a full-time defence correspondent, and very few of those reporting the war, particularly from their own capitals, were military specialists. In press conferences and studio interviews, newsmen lost credibility through ignorance. As in Vietnam, 'few knew the difference between, say, a mortar and a howitzer, battalions and divisions, logistics and tactics'.[10] The two British television news networks,

ITN and the BBC, between them identified USS *Missouri* as a battlecruiser with 18-inch guns, invented a British armoured regiment called the 15th/16th Lancers, and gave the FROG missile's country of origin as France. In defence terms this is broadly comparable with describing the Green Bay Packers as a cricket team.[11] The point is that these and many similar errors by British and American networks went unnoticed by the vast majority of the public, and were made by highly respected, experienced journalists at the very height of their profession.

While both the military and the media present to the outside world an image of omniscience, in a war such as the Gulf both were very limited in their knowledge. On several occasions during the war Coalition spokesmen claimed to have no information on an Iraqi action other than that given to them by the media. Some American analysts have even attempted to deflect on to the media the blame for their own intelligence failure:

> [Pre-war intelligence] relies largely on the sort of unclassified data that appear in standard military references and journals ... [Thus] whatever the local government manages to feed the media, particularly the specialist media, can have a disproportionate impact. Saddam Hussein seems to have understood this point particularly well ... [It] was, of course, our good fortune that Saddam was much less adept at warfare than at pre-war propaganda.[12]

In the war itself both the military and the media depended on inadequate information gathered with limited resources under impossible conditions. If the media misled the public and the military misled the media, this was often because they also misled themselves.

This similarity — almost a symbiosis — between the media and the military was most apparent at the front line, where it is not uncommon for newsmen to have seen more of war than the soldiers they accompany. Many common characteristics have been identified between the news-gathering team and the operational military unit, who often recognise kindred spirits in each other.[13] But both are also closed societies, deeply sensitive to outside criticism, claiming a high professional status seldom granted to them by the rest of the world. While the military have a rigid hierarchy, a formality of approach, and often a cult of good manners, the media tend towards egalitarianism, deliberate informality, and — at least in television — a cult of bad manners. Each sees in the other a distorted and rather distasteful image of itself, and often they will compare each other with children interfering in an adult world. As was seen in the Gulf, the best relationship they can hope for is one based on equality of dissatisfaction.

The evolution of media control

It has been suggested that the issue of military-media relations in the Gulf 'dates back to the Vietnam War'.[14] This is wrong by about a century. The first newspapers started life in Europe over 300 years ago as overtly political broadsheets or advertising circulars. Only with the development of the steamship and telegraph in the 1840s did it become practical to report news over long distances, and for newspapers to send their own reporters to war, gradually replacing the older tradition of soldiers writing their own newspaper dispatches as a sideline. The first major war to be reported by eyewitness newsmen was the Crimean War (1853–1856), of which a highly romanticised view, still current among modern journalists, sees the honest reporting of British military incompetence and the realities of war as responsible for the collapse of the government at home and the reform of the armed services. Since the Crimea, some war correspondents have seen their role as far more than simply that of reporters. Peter Arnett of CNN, who had also reported Vietnam, gave his reason for coming to Baghdad as 'because my contribution will be to somehow lessen the hostilities, if not this time, maybe next time'.[15]

Of far more importance to the development of war reporting was the first war fought by a literate democracy, the American Civil War (1861–1865). The issues of censorship and media responsibility raised by this war have remained unchanged to the present day. On one side, many like Major-General William T Sherman believed that the Federal Constitution should be suspended in war and reporters court-martialled as spies. The opposing view was that the Constitution, an essential part of the reason for going to war, should remain pristine — including its First Amendment stating that no law should be made restricting the freedom of the press. President Abraham Lincoln's government steered a middle course, calling on newspapers to co-operate by adopting voluntary self-censorship, with the government playing a passive role. 'You yourselves must decide what is proper to send,' Major-General Ulysses S Grant told newsmen with his command. 'I trust your discretion and honour to give no information of value to the enemy.'[16]

This compromise, in which newsmen voluntarily restrict their reporting in return for military facilities and access to the war zone, is against the deepest instincts of both sides. Nevertheless, forgotten and rediscovered in every war fought by democracies this century, it is the only system which works in practice, providing that the media accept the aims and objectives of the war itself. In the Gulf it was well understood by experienced journalists with the front-line media pools. As Kate Aidie of the BBC expressed it:

> I think that if you go into a war situation in which your own troops are involved; and you want to report in detail and as much as possible of what those troops are going to be involved in, you have to do a deal; and you must do it publicly.[17]

In the First and Second World Wars, in which national existence might be threatened, the co-operation of the national press could be virtually taken for granted. 'Gradually it became part of us all that the truth about anything was automatically secret', the novelist John Steinbeck wrote of his own experiences as a war correspondent, 'and that to trifle with it was to interfere with the War Effort.'[18] Indeed, it was at the request of the press itself that the USA introduced in the Second World War, and again in Korea, direct military censorship in the field to avoid the problems and uncertainties of self-censorship. The military disliked the responsibility, however, and despite further requests they refused to institute formal censorship in Vietnam. The field censorship units were downgraded to reserve status and in 1977 disbanded altogether. From Vietnam onwards the American government also insisted that accreditation of journalists should be made by the media themselves. 'As someone who works for the government,' argued Louis A ('Pete') Williams, Assistant Secretary of Defense for Public Affairs during the Gulf War, 'I can't decide who goes to cover the war and who doesn't.'[19] Central Command (CENTCOM) provided facilities for any journalist sent to Saudi Arabia, but would not take responsibility for them or their stories.

Because of its dominant position in world affairs, the United States' military experience is often taken as a model by other countries. However, in terms of media freedom it is an absolutely unique case. As Major-General Sherman found out, the only American legislation on the subject is the First Amendment, reinforced in 1966 by the Freedom of Information Act. There is no American legal authority for restriction, control or censorship of the press in peace or in war, in marked contrast to other countries. However, while the Constitution forbids censorship, it does not specifically guarantee to the media a right of access. In 1983 the American press decided against suing the government over its media handling in the invasion of Grenada, in case the ruling set a precedent for even tighter restrictions. Ultimately, as in the days of Sherman, the military can always control access to the battlefield. 'The soldiers have guns, the journalists have keyboards and cameras,' *The Economist* pointed out during the Gulf War. 'It is easy to see whose arguments will prevail.'[20]

Left to themselves, the military will tend to follow Sherman's line and exclude the press altogether from the war zone, as happened on all sides at the start of the First World War. It was not until the middle of that war that the lessons learned by Grant were again reapplied by the Allies, and they were never properly grasped by the Germans. But also after the First World War, British journalists boasted of a successful propaganda offensive against Germany which had destroyed the enemy's will to fight, particularly on the home front. This fitted perfectly with the beliefs of many Germans that their armies had been betrayed by a 'stab in the back' rather than defeated, leading to a wholly exaggerated view of the value of propaganda used against the enemy, and to the present meaning of 'propaganda' as distortion tantamount to lying. Adolf Hitler devoted several chapters of *Mein Kampf* to this use of propaganda, concluding: 'The enemy did only what was expected; and we ought to learn from the stand he took and the way he acted.'[21] The effectiveness of the lie became central to Nazi and other totalitarian views of media relations.

Ironically, there was hardly a word of truth to the British newsmen's boast. In military terms, although propaganda may work as a force multiplier, it has virtually no intrinsic offensive capability. That is to say, propaganda — or psychological warfare — works only in lowering the morale of an enemy already being defeated by other means. Even then, it requires detailed knowledge of the enemy to be effective. Coalition morale was considerably raised by the inept performance of the Iraqi propaganda radio station in the Gulf when the inevitable seductive voice — known with equal inevitability as 'Baghdad Betty' — told the troops that their wives had forgotten them and thought only of Hollywood stars, listing among others the cult cartoon figure Bart Simpson.

In the Gulf, as in previous wars, Anglo-American media policy also avoided aggressive propaganda aimed at their own armed forces, who were felt to need relief from boredom rather than repeated justifications of why they were fighting. Forces' overseas radio, sending out a mixture of light entertainment, music, news and current affairs taken mainly from national stations, was broadcasting to the Gulf almost from the start of 'Desert Shield', and by the end of 1990 both American Forces FM Network and British Forces Broadcasting Service 'Desert Radio' were established in Saudi Arabia. The programmes often reflected the bizarre, deadpan military humour which many journalists found so unsettling. Among the most frequent record requests from British troops were *Eve of Destruction* and *The Air That I Breathe*, which somehow escaped a BBC list of records (including *We Gotta Get Outta This Place* and *Walk Like An Egyptian*) not to be played.

Since the First World War this 'soft' style of information policy, aimed chiefly at the home front rather than at the armed forces of either side, has led to a largely unwritten doctrine of media-military relations based on a few commonsense principles. In the Gulf, press escort officers who had never heard of these principles nevertheless obeyed them, and most experienced journalists and officials understood them well. For convenience, they are reproduced here in tabular form. As with any 'principles of war', they are not absolute, but reflect a broad consensus. Both the military and the media, however, have poor institutional memories, being preoccupied with the immediate task in hand. The failure to codify these principles meant that they had to be rediscovered by yet another generation after the Second World War.

PRINCIPLES OF MEDIA-MILITARY RELATIONS

1. 'The propaganda of facts': an official statement should never contain a conscious lie. But there is no obligation to volunteer specific information unless asked, nor to correct errors of press interpretation.

2. 'Information must wait upon policy': information strategy is dictated by broader political and military strategy. It cannot rescue a political or military strategy which is itself misconceived.

3. 'PR is a command function': commanders must keep their media relations staff fully aware of what is happening, and must themselves be aware of the media implications of their actions.

4. 'Co-operate rather than censor': media relations work better by treating the media as allies rather than as enemies, and by trust rather than restriction.

5. 'Silence breeds speculation': cutting off information will not restrict the news flow. Telling the media nothing only forces them to guess, and they will often guess right.

6. 'Propaganda destroys credibility': the 'dirty tricks' of psychological warfare, such as black propaganda, should be kept entirely separate from any agency responsible for official contact with the media.

The impact of television

It is now a cliché — and almost a true one — that Vietnam was the first television war. Television news broadcasts began in the USA just after the Second World War, with the first live outside broadcasts following in the early 1950s. By the next decade there were about 100 million Western homes with televisions, and the majority of Americans saw television rather than newspapers as their most reliable source of news. By the height of the Vietnam War, in the late 1960s, all three major American television networks had full-time news staffs in Saigon, each producing up to three filmed reports daily, together with material provided by camera teams from the Department of Defense itself. By 1970 it was possible to transmit film, although not live pictures, across the Pacific by satellite, so that reports appeared on American television on the same day. All this was done without censorship or any attempt at media control. The US Army (unlike the Marines) did not even have press escort officers in the field. Instead, lacking a coherent media policy, the military improvised — disastrously. In contrast, the North Vietnamese maintained strict censorship inside their own country while mounting a sustained propaganda campaign abroad. Particularly after the 1968 Tet Offensive, when significant sectors of American public opinion turned firmly against the war, it was argued that uncontrolled television coverage, the images of death and destruction devoid of context or explanation, had undermined American government policy more than any other factor. The assessment by respected British television journalist Robin Day that 'the war was lost on the television screens of America' became a rallying cry for the American military.[22] If the war had been lost by such unconventional means, then the failure was not theirs. 'Next time I wouldn't tell the people anything until the war is over,' one suitably anonymous officer is reported as saying, 'and then I'd tell them who won.'[23]

Although widely believed by both the military and the media after Vietnam, this argument was little more than an updated version of the old 'stab in the back'. There is nothing in the statistical evidence to suggest that television coverage in itself produced popular discontent, or swung American public opinion against the war. At most, television may have amplified and reflected a popular disenchantment which existed well before 1968. Since Vietnam, armed forces have in fact discovered that there is almost no such thing as bad television publicity — American and British recruiting went up dramatically with television coverage during the Gulf War. It appears likely that the impact of television coverage of Vietnam was greatest not on the American people, but on the political elite in Washington, who had so lost control of the war that they depended on the nightly news bulletin, rather than their own command chain, to tell them who was winning.[24]

Nevertheless, it is undeniable that the replacement of newspapers by television as the dominant news medium has radically changed the way in which wars are reported. In a world of instant communications, newspapers produced once a day cannot hope to compete, and since the 1960s they have visibly reverted to their original function either as overt political broadsheets or as popular entertainment. As part of this change in the function of written reporting, Vietnam saw the first signs of 'advocacy journalism', in which, rather than reporting the facts, the journalist makes his own emotions and experience the story. Television or photo-journalists, in contrast, maintained the detachment implicit in their slogan not to take sides, only pictures. Both attitudes were heavily criticised by government and military, the first for bias and the second for lack of patriotism. But the change from print to pictures has in no way helped the reporting of events as complex as wars. Television is impressionistic and personal, poor at conveying an abstract concept or general trend. As a consensus medium it is also — particularly in the case of commercial networks — principally a form of mass entertainment rather than a source of information, in which minority interests and opinions tend to get squeezed out altogether. The decade before the Gulf War had already seen the development in America of 'Happy Talk News', the television version of the supermarket press. A large part of the military prejudice against television comes from the increasingly trivial nature of much of its output. The prize for the Gulf War went to a local American station which ran an item on the care of pets left behind when their owners left to fight in the Gulf.

The extent of the military reaction against the media over Vietnam became clear in 1982. Israel, although the most overtly democratic of the Middle East states, has since its foundation practised a form of 'censorship by co-operation', in which direct censorship exists but seldom needs to be applied, as if the country were permanently at war. However, for the invasion of Lebanon in June 1982 General Ariel Sharon as Minister of Defence decreed a policy of 'Battle Fog', in which all reporters were excluded from the front line. The press uproar produced the lifting of this ban within a week, leading one British general to observe: 'it is doubtful if any democracy could hold that line for much longer'.[25] Sharon's decision also left a legacy of international press ill-will from which Israel suffered for the next decade. At almost the same time, the British were themselves fighting in the Falklands conflict to similar press outrage, as only a handful of British journalists, and none from the international media, were allowed with the front-line troops. In this case the problem was not deliberate policy but the lack of one, as an entirely improvised war plan allowed the military to follow their first instincts. The result was arbitrary and inconsistent censorship, blatant news management, disinformation, and security failures through press speculation. After the war the British government set up major political, academic and service investigations into what had gone wrong.[26]

Meanwhile, the American military could hardly contain their admiration for how well the British had handled the press. For the 1983 invasion of Grenada military views were again allowed to dominate, and a policy of total exclusion was adopted. There was no public affairs officer on the planning staff, and even White House press officials were kept in the dark, with predictable results. 'The notion which evidently runs in the upper reaches of the White House,' one former press secretary commented, 'that a press officer who doesn't know can't get you into trouble, was discredited long ago.'[27] Television networks retaliated by showing film of Grenada provided by the government and captioned 'Cleared by Department of Defense Censors', when in fact there had been no formal censorship. Again, media pressure forced a reversal of the exclusion policy within a week, and subsequent press accounts of Grenada were overwhelmingly critical of American military performance. As a result a National Media Pool was established — civilian journalists with escort officers, to be part of the military planning on any future operation. This worked less than perfectly in Panama in 1989, when Secretary of Defense 'Dick' Cheney, acting on security grounds, delayed calling out the pool too long for the reporters to join the first assaults, bringing further accusations of bad faith from the media.[28]

Exclusion or direct censorship of the media by the military was not only legally doubtful and politically damaging, but investigations into media technology in the early 1980s showed that it was rapidly becoming physically impossible. At the time of Tet there were about 650 accredited reporters with the American forces in Vietnam, 100 more than with the Allied forces in Europe on D-Day in 1944. At the height of the Gulf War nearly 2,000 reporters were accredited to CENTCOM, over 1,000 of them from the United States alone. Cable television, direct satellite broadcasting, portable video cameras and electronic news gathering (ENG) equipment, the small broadcast-quality cameras operated by one man, all began to make a major impact in the USA during the late 1970s. By 1985 commercial television satellite coverage, either direct or linked to cable, was virtually global, and there were nearly 500 million homes with televisions worldwide. By the same date, laptop computers, portable fax (facsimile) machines and 'flyaway' satellite telephone dishes had become widely commercially available.[29]

These developments made an entirely new style of instant news possible, including satellite television news channels providing a continuous stream of updated reports and immediate reactions from anywhere in the world. Disparaged by critics as 'video cadet journalism' devoid of context and analysis, this highly entertaining format, backed by computer graphics and stylish packaging, has considerable popular and commercial appeal. Its greatest success story is Cable News Network, founded in Atlanta, Georgia, in 1979. Within four years CNN had reached 15 per cent of all American homes (not just those taking cable), and by 1990 claimed an American audience of 53 million and reception in a further 140 countries. During the Gulf War CNN occupied a unique place, being cited by heads of state and called upon as an authority in times of crisis. Even First Lady Barbara Bush, challenged on the American bombing of the Amiriyah shelter, replied: 'I believe what our Intelligence tells me and what CNN experts tell me, that it was a command post'. CNN has a policy of giving heads of state free access to its service, and was known to be a favourite with Saddam Hussein. According to the network itself, American planners judged that, after the first air-strikes of 'Desert Storm' destroyed Saddam's communications, 'CNN may have been the only accurate source of information that he had', and could be exploited accordingly. It is even claimed that Saddam's decision to attack Khafji stemmed from a routine ITN film report, relayed by CNN, showing the town unoccupied by Coalition troops.[30]

In the face of global, instant, television news both the Americans and British concluded by the end of the 1980s that any military control over the media in wartime would have to be institutional rather than physical, and based on co-operation rather than exclusion or coercion:

> Presumably listeners and viewers will continue to trust the sources of news they have learned to trust; and this will redound to the benefit of free societies practising open information policies, such as the United States . . . As long as this trust is not disturbed by censorship, one cannot see many people getting anything but a good laugh out of some Arab or Russian heavy [sic] churning out tales of disaster and prophesies of doom like the voice-over in an advertisement for a lavatory cleaner.[31]

The experience of the Falklands, Grenada and Panama was that, however the media themselves might grumble, most people would tolerate news blackouts and even disinformation in return for a quick victory:

> What does seem certain is that television coverage of armed conflict turns world opinion as a whole fairly rapidly against the war covered . . . Management of a body politic accustomed to being saturated with information does pose a problem in the political conduct of war just as difficult as the exercise of command on the military side. The only thing one can say with any certainty is that this problem puts a high premium on strategic surprise and swift decision.[32]

The impact of the media was central to the stress placed by the Reagan administration on the need for popular support and rapid success in limited war; and there was a genuine fear that sustained television reporting would undermine the war effort. Although the motives for much of Saddam Hussein's conduct from August 1990 onwards remain obscure, his actions become more explicable if it is assumed that he was aware — as he could hardly have been unaware — of this fear, and that the media war was intended as perhaps Iraq's principal line of defence. In this, as in all other aspects of the Gulf War, the Iraqis would be hopelessly outclassed.

The global home front
From the start of 'Desert Shield', opinion polls showed President George Bush's actions to have the support of about 80 per cent of the American people. This support declined to 60 per cent after September, climbed back with the additional troop deployment in November, and jumped to almost 90 per cent with the start of 'Desert Storm'. The British and French governments enjoyed similar levels of support for their war efforts, and in all three countries public support for the government went up during the fighting. As with Vietnam, the role of the media in influencing this support is subject to partisan debate. 'Belief in television's influence,' as was noted during the Vietnam War, 'is rather like the belief in life after death. Most of us would like to be able to prove it, but the evidence is inconclusive.'[33] Although in Britain the BBC was attacked from the left as 'the willing mouthpiece of the Ministry of Defence' and from the right as the 'Baghdad

Broadcasting Corporation', the overwhelming majority of viewers had no complaint. However, the television 'squeeze' effect on minorities led to objections from American war protestors that less coverage was being given to their views than to those of football players, and that only 1.5 per cent of nightly news broadcast content was being given to anti-war protests. Even so, opponents of the war continue to believe that, had the fighting lasted longer, the 'Vietnam Effect' would have defeated the Coalition. 'There was a correlation,' it is claimed, 'between knowledge — information — and opposition to the war.'[34]

The tendency for live studio television to confuse rather than to enlighten was increased by the over-use of live two-way links to the Gulf. Studio anchormen would demand instant reactions to an event in Washington or Moscow from a reporter in Dhahran with nothing to give but his own opinions. Networks would even read out the latest wire story to a front man in Saudi Arabia, to have it repeated back on camera as a personal report. Although the live link came into its own with the first Scud missile attacks on Saudi Arabia and Israel, producing some of the most dramatic scenes of the war, the reporter's personal response was still the only story. The handsome Arthur Kent of NBC earned the nickname of 'The Scud Stud' from the supermarket press; while Martha Teichner of CBS, who had quit a front-line pool as 'absolutely unworkable', also found herself a media celebrity. In military terms the Scud campaign against Saudi Arabia was ineffective and the danger was accurately assessed by Schwarzkopf as comparable with a Georgia thunderstorm. But the drama of the event, with the threat of a chemical or even nuclear warhead, made compulsive live television. The Saudi government actually had to explain to reporters that live coverage of incoming missiles could be used to correct the Iraqi aim. The publicity was so great that Iraq even complained of the Western media's error in calling the *Al-Hussein* missile the Scud and denying Iraq the credit for its development.

In its media handling of the Scud campaign the state of Israel showed once more its customary sophistication. Like Saudi Arabia, Israel blocked direct coverage of Scud attacks and accurate reporting of target locations after 23 January, but thereafter played brilliantly on the major media weakness by personalising the event. The world's press was allowed, within hours of a Scud attack, to interview survivors in the wreckage of their homes. Filming opportunities were offered, and accepted, of maternity wards full of gasmask-wearing mothers. On one celebrated occasion an Israeli minister's defence of his country's policies towards Arabs, given live on American television, was halted by an incoming Scud alert. The effect was to wash away the legacy of ill-ill which Israel had created in the West since 1982. At the cost of four dead, Israel used the media to secure a major military and political victory without firing a shot.

The view from Baghdad

The truth of the claim that Saddam Hussein expected to scare off the Coalition with media stories of Iraqi strength may never be established, although similar use of propaganda to disguise weakness was certainly part of Soviet doctrine, a major influence on Iraq. But from the invasion onwards Iraqi propaganda directed against the West was such a complete failure that, as with the air war, it is difficult to deduce exactly what was intended. Saddam's main successes came with those pan-Arabists already pre-disposed to support him against the USA, while Western support for Iraq — rather than opposition to the American government or to war in any form — remained negligible. An episode in late August 1990 which set the pattern was the Iraqi release of video tapes showing an avuncular Saddam chatting to some Western hostages, including one five-year-old British boy. The British Ambassador to Iraq assessed this as 'part of a very successful propaganda campaign which may be having an effect in some parts of the Arab world',[41] but to Western eyes the image, even down to the moustache, inevitably raised memories of Adolf Hitler. This comparison was at once taken up by the Coalition, with George Bush never failing to speak of 'Saddam Hussein the Dictator'. Soon networks were calling the Coalition forces *the Allies* as in the Second World War, and arguments over Western reporting from Baghdad were couched in similar terms. A popular emotional commitment for Total War was raised to support an entirely limited objective, and at the war's end a significant section of Western opinion fully expected to see Saddam tried for war crimes.

The need to maintain popular support brought sharply into focus the central role given to media management by the American Presidency, a process begun by Franklin D Roosevelt's appointment of the first permanent White House press secretary and culminating in the election of former actor Ronald Reagan as 'the great communicator' in 1980. There are few more striking images than George Bush's 'high noon' speech in the White House rose garden on Friday 22 February 1991, the President of the United States live on world television giving Saddam Hussein 24 hours to leave Kuwait. Indeed, as with CENTCOM's organisation of the military forces, much of the White House effort went into co-ordinating the American media war to stop the government fighting itself. Journalists often build stories by working on small differences between statements, trying to uncover a contradiction or disagreement. With reporters all over Washington demanding instant responses, the American government managed to ensure that it always spoke with the same voice. 'I've never seen it work better,' observed a former senior White House press official.[35] The only brief parting of this veil of unanimity came for a few hours on Thursday 21 February, when the State Department, taken by surprise by the Soviet-Iraqi peace plan, hinted that it might be acceptable before the White House could denounce it.

Also in parallel with CENTCOM's military organisation, the other leading Coalition nations followed the Americans in co-ordinating their media policies at the very highest level. The British in particular, despite their relatively small military commitment to the Gulf, played a surprisingly large part in the media war, chiefly through the wide overlap between American and British media. Reporters on both sides of the Atlantic again sought to build stories by exploiting the difference between American and British sources, while the British Ministry of Defence, criticised for being less open than the Americans, expressed the fear that too much was being given away. Against a more competent opponent than Iraq there might indeed have been a serious problem, since it was possible by using the open media to penetrate the Coalition military plans almost in their entirety. Just before the ground war started, CENTCOM actually published its Order of Battle, the list of its ground troops waiting to attack; while the left hook manoeuvre was 'nothing that anyone who had studied the campaigns of Civil War Major-General William T Sherman would not have predicted'.[36] Anthony Cordesman, ABC's resident military analyst, got it almost perfectly right.

In Washington, the Pentagon established from the start of 'Desert Storm' a daily hour-long televised press briefing at 3 pm EST. Usually the briefings were introduced by Assistant Secretary Williams and given by Lieutenant-General Thomas W Kelly and Rear-Admiral Michael Mc-Connell, the Joint Chiefs of Staff (JCS) Directors of Operations and Intelligence respectively. Secretary Cheney and General Colin Powell themselves gave the briefings for major events, Lieutenant-General Kelly and his staff worked for eight hours a day on each briefing and on trying to predict likely questions, which they did with considerable success:

> The first two rows were filled by the real pros — television and broadcast media in front; print media on the second row. They didn't ask many questions, but they asked the best questions, which always had probing followups. The middle rows were filled with neophytes and the back rows contained the amateurs, some of whom asked the dumb questions that eventually got parodied on *Saturday Night Live* — for example, 'What is your scheme of maneuver?'[37]

The Pentagon briefing was preceded at 10 am EST (6 pm in Saudi Arabia) by a half-hour live briefing from Riyadh, usually given by Brigadier-General Richard I ('Butch') Neal USMC, with officers from other services covering particular topics and General Schwarzkopf making occasional key appearances. The fact that Powell, Schwarzkopf and their staffs took so much time and trouble to appear before the press in the middle of a war underlines the media-consciousness of the modern military. Indeed, failure to understand the media could be fatal in career terms. The two highest ranking Coalition casualties of the war both fell victim to the media: USAF Chief of Staff General Michael Dugan in September 1990 and the Italian Navy commander in the Gulf, Vice-Admiral Mario Buracchio, in February 1991, both sacked for indiscreet press interviews.

The Coalition concern to present a united front to the media extended even to the pundits and interviewees for which live television developed an insatiable appetite during the war, CNN working its way through 2,500 interviews altogether and about 60 different 'experts' a day. On both sides of the Atlantic the military were anxious to avoid a repetition of the British experience in the Falklands, in which recently retired officers with close knowledge of serving commanders had speculated on their likely plans (although subsequent investigation dismissed claims of a real security threat). This time former officers were advised to talk in very general terms and to present a positive view of the war. 'The most important rule was that nobody should ever speculate about the operations which the Coalition might actually carry out.'[38] One result was that AirLand Battle was never properly explained. Lieutenant-General Kelly commented on CNN's two resident military pundits:

Major-General Perry Smith and former Major Jim Blackwell were the best, by a wide, wide margin. And the reason they were the best is that they explained to the American people what was going on at the time, rather than trying to predict the future . . . If I go on NBC News — I have a contract with them as a consultant — I will try to emulate Smith and Blackwell. They explained unclassified things about tactics and hardware to the American people, and they had a calming effect on their audience.[39]

Although there were honourable exceptions, civilian pundits, sometimes lacking inside knowledge, often did little better than their military counterparts. One British academic institution which deliberately maximised its services to the media to achieve publicity, giving over 200 interviews, confidently predicted a six-month war just over two weeks before it ended.[40]

A further contribution to the image of an evil enemy was the appearance, within days of the occupation of Kuwait, of Iraqi atrocity stories. Despite some prodding from Coalition governments, most of the Western media handled these stories with diffidence. The problem is not that these things happen — to the shame of mankind they do — but that people will repeat them in good faith whether they happen or not. One typical accusation, made by witnesses on American television and in an Amnesty International report in November 1990, was that Iraqi troops had removed incubators from Kuwait City Hospital, leaving the babies to die. On the liberation of Kuwait, reporters were told by nurses at the hospital that no such incident had taken place. A week later other reporters were shown a mass grave allegedly containing the bodies, but by that time television had lost interest in the story. The parallels with both the First and Second World Wars are striking, including the tendency of journalists to discount real atrocities through fear of invention, and the counter-accusation that 'Allied' bombing was the greatest atrocity of all.

The Iraqi government allowed Western journalists into Baghdad from mid-August 1990, housing them in the Al-Rashid Hotel. By the end of the year there were about 200 journalists in the Al-Rashid, representing some 50 media organisations, chiefly from British and American television networks and from France, Spain and Japan. Minister of Information Latif Nsayef Jassim regarded the American press as hopelessly prejudiced against Iraq, and most of the newspapermen were British or French. By negotiation and bribery, the journalists created facilities at the Al-Rashid for communicating with the outside world. CNN was particularly favoured, establishing by October a private 'four-wire' landline from Baghdad to Amman in Jordan, and from there by satellite line back to Atlanta. The networks also installed four Inmarsat flyaway telephone satellite dishes on the roof of the Al-Rashid, but until the start of the fighting all reporters except CNN used the Iraqi public telephone system. In theory this meant paying Iraq a hiring fee, forbidden under the United Nations embargo and United States law —

as CNN put it: 'we're running up a tab'. Despite initial denials, television tapes were censored before leaving the country, although negotiations had begun by January to add live satellite transmission equipment. According to CNN the Iraqis were in favour of live satellite pictures being broadcast, but CENTCOM warned the network that it would be jammed off the air if it tried.[42]

As the likelihood of fighting increased, most Western reporters left Iraq. When 'Desert Storm' began, on the night of 16/17 January 1991, pictures from the television landline were lost almost at once. Those journalists remaining in the Al-Rashid were able to describe from their windows the sight and sound of missiles and bombs falling on Baghdad, although this conveyed little but their personal impressions, and there was some criticism of CNN's 'Holy Cow!' style of reporting. Unusually, at the Pentagon press conference next afternoon Dick Cheney came to their defence: 'the best reporting that I've seen on what transpired in Baghdad was on CNN', he declared. Within hours, hits on the Baghdad telecommunications tower ended standard telephone services, leaving only CNN's private line functioning. Only after 17 hours did the Iraqi Ministry of Information forbid the continued transmission of uncensored news. Next day, 33 journalists elected to stay in the Al-Rashid, dependent on the Inmarsat terminals. The single largest national group was British, but the international nature of modern journalism showed in Alfonso Rojo of the Spanish El Mondo also reporting for the London Guardian, and in the NBC crew being Turkish and Jordanian with a New Zealand reporter. Other networks represented were RAI, NHK, BBC and ITN, and, of course, CNN, plus reporters and photo-journalists from several newspapers. Each team was given an Iraqi 'minder' who vetted stories before transmission, and the journalists showed great ingenuity in radioing back reports as personal messages or communications checks.

On 20 January further air strikes on the communications tower disrupted CNN's four-wire, and the Iraqi government, pleading lack of facilities, ordered everyone to leave for Amman. Peter Arnett of CNN was allowed to stay, and shortly afterwards announced himself as the only Western journalist left in Baghdad. Alfonso Rojo also remained, but had no access to Arnett's satellite telephone. Representatives of Arab, Soviet and other non-Western press stayed in Baghdad throughout the bombing. On 31 January, 16 Western journalists including an ITN crew received permission to return, and were later joined by others. Negotiations proved so difficult that when one freelance camera crew managed, at considerable risk, to film in the south of the country without a minder present, the networks refused to take the film for fear of antagonising Iraq.

Also on 20 January, Iraqi television showed interviews with captured American, British and Italian aircrew shot down in the first raids, who denounced their own side or called for peace. Except for ABC, all of the major Western networks took the pictures, backed by film, photographs and information from their own governments on the men and their normal appearance. The battered faces and remote, hesitant voices made it obvious that the airmen had been coerced, although most networks were scrupulous in adding that high-speed ejection from aircraft often causes facial bruising. The outraged Western reaction destroyed any Iraqi belief that the 'Vietnam Effect' might work for them, and on 24 January they announced that no further interviews would be shown. Four days later Coalition bombing took Iraqi television off the air for good, and the Ministry of Information directed its attention to the Arab supporters of Iraq, supplying wreckage of American aircraft for display to cheering crowds in Amman. At the same time, 'Voice of the People Radio' in Baghdad and 'Mother of Battles Radio' in Kuwait put out information, exultations and denunciations of Saddam's enemies in lurid terms.

Meanwhile, the Ministry of Information had prepared for the loss of live television by borrowing an idea from Hollywood. On 18 January it offered television stations a prepared videotape reel of scenes of Saddam Hussein, including his replies to apparent interview questions. Virtually all the film of Saddam shown on Western networks during the war came from this reel, while users in Arab countries edited the tape with studio scenes of their own reporters, creating the impression of personal interviews and reports from Baghdad. This reporting trick, at least 100 years old in its newspaper form and known as 'magic carpeting', enabled Saddam to appear in person throughout the Arab world. In fact he gave only one major television interview during the war, a taped conversation with Peter Arnett on 28 January, the day before the attack on Khafji. It was a remarkably cool performance, but, as *Time* noted, the Iraqi president's eyes were blinking at nearly 40 times a minute.

The weaknesses of the authoritarian Ba'athist state showed clearly in the Ministry of Information's inability to out-perform its enemies in a world of propaganda which demanded instantaneous responses. When, after the first Scud strikes, Baghdad Radio boasted that Tel Aviv was a crematorium, Israeli pictures and reports of the damage had already appeared. When, on 23 January, Peter Arnett and other reporters were taken to a 'baby milk plant' destroyed by bombing, the Coalition press briefing in Riyadh that afternoon provided plausible details of its military nature. In particular, Iraq could not produce evidence of the mass civilian casualities which it continued to claim that Coalition bombing was causing, and was handi-capped by its own censorship restrictions and strict control of Western newsmen in Baghdad. One ITN reporter admitted that, after a month of bombing, he personally had seen only one corpse. Iraqi film released on 28 January of injured children in a hospital ward denouncing 'the coward Bush who dares not face our glorious armies', was not an adequate substitute.

The greatest Iraqi propaganda strength actually came from their enemies. Saddam gained prestige simply by the length of time that he remained undefeated, and although Coalition leaders warned repeatedly of a long haul, the notorious American newspaper headline *Sixth Day — War Drags On* was an accurate reflection of the period from the end of January until the start of the ground war. When Saddam's troops moved into Khafji on 29 January the press, starved of actual news from the Coalition side, seized upon it as 'a major land battle', providing Iraq with a propaganda victory. Another media disaster for the Coalition was the Amiriyah bunker episode on 13 February. Although the Ministry of Information exploited the scenes of dead bodies to the full, allowing reports and film to pass uncensored (networks followed normal practice in editing themselves for taste), the Coalition response that the bunker was a military target into which the Iraqis themselves had put civilians, something for which they claimed to have evidence too secret to release, produced a massive credibility gap. The remark of the Iraqi Ambassador to Paris, 'They don't even have the decency to admit that they made a mistake, which of course they didn't, because they have a policy of killing civilians',[43] was particularly revealing. Whatever the truth of the matter, Iraq had its only case of mass casualties to show the world. The Western public response, however, was hardly the one predicted or feared before the war. Opinion polls taken after the Amiriyah episode showed a marked increase in the belief that television was being too critical of the Coalition and presenting too favourable a picture of the enemy. The Coalition military seems also to have learned its media lesson from Amiriyah. When on 16 February the Iraqis reported civilian casualties after a British attack on Fallouja, the RAF responded that one of their 'smart' bombs had malfunctioned and hit a market instead of its intended target.

After three weeks Saddam Hussein had his propaganda success in outlasting his enemies, and on 10 February he told the Iraqi people in a radio broadcast: 'We have already achieved victory in the eyes of God'. It was a temporary triumph, a media illusion which led Dick Cheney to complain to reporters: 'I don't buy the argument that he's winning by losing!'. But on 15 February Saddam may have tried to transform this into something more substantial, as Baghdad Radio broadcast a speech taken live by the American networks with simultaneous translation into English of its difficult and strangely-accented Arabic. From their Al-Rashid room, CNN's Iraqi minder obliged by translating for them to ensure accuracy. The speech was not addressed to the Coalition, with which Saddam had broken diplomatic ties five days earlier, and while mentioning the existence of Kuwait for the first time, it outlined peace terms so apparently outrageous as to provoke ridicule. Western linguistics specialists, working over the next two days, felt that the nuances of the speech probably contained a genuine offer to negotiate, but within two hours George Bush had himself gone on television to denounce the peace offer as 'a cruel hoax' and to call for Saddam's overthrow. The diplomacy of war and peace had been conducted through broadcast news, and the American government had responded not to the diplomatic gesture but to the media event.

The front line
With the decision to deploy American forces to the Gulf, Saudi Arabia agreed to accept the US National Media Pool, which arrived in Dharhan on 13 August 1990. The 17 journalists, representing AP, UPI, Reuters, CNN, *Time*, Scripps-Howard news service, *The Los Angeles Times* and *The Milwaukee Journal*, were typical of the tokenism inherent in pool selections. Wire service men intent on the latest hard news found

themselves joined with popular journalists whose story interests were rarely the same. As a further 300 journalists reached Saudi Arabia, the pool system ended on 26 August. The only press restrictions during most of 'Desert Shield' were the laws of Saudi Arabia itself together with accepted military peacetime practices — the US Marines expelled two women journalists from their camp for 'asking rude questions' — and by late 1990 the number of reporters accredited to CENTCOM had risen to over 800. A Joint Information Bureau (JIB) was established at Dhahran International Hotel, providing accommodation and facilities for the press and co-ordinating media policy, including the Free Kuwait Information Office. A second JIB was co-located with CENTCOM headquarters in the Hyatt Regency Hotel in Riyadh, with the fourth-floor ballroom turned into a press conference and briefing centre. For television, Forward Transmission Units (FTUs) were established at Dhahran and Riyadh, allowing either live relays or transmission of videotape, and at the start of 'Desert Storm' the US Air Force laid on a special aircraft to fly a further 126 media representatives to the Gulf.[44]

However, on 10 January 1991 a pool system was re-established by negotiation between Washington and the media organisations. Two 18-strong 'Media Response Teams' (MRTs) were formed, providing each division with four or five American broadcast or print journalists under escort officers. The British used a similar system with one MRT, made up of a television crew and four reporters, for each brigade. Each of the major warships was also given two or more reporters, and MRTs were established at the major airbases. The number of pool places allocated was fewer than 200 in total, leaving more than 1,000 frustrated journalists in Dhahran, many in no mood to do the Coalition any favours. Several American newspapers started legal proceedings in Washington against the government for violation of the First Amendment, while a separate suit was brought by a French news service demanding access to the American pool.

Journalists not given pool places remained almost entirely dependent on the JIB press briefings, and failed to impress many of their critics. Often their reporting ran behind information already available in Washington, while Brigadier-General Neal felt that their questions 'didn't lay a glove on him'.[45] The televised press briefings were found to be too restricting, and on 3 February Dhahran JIB began extra off-the-record briefings at the request of the journalists themselves, who were by then prepared to trade increased secrecy in return for increased information. This put CENTCOM in an enormously strong media position.

It was in this period, from the first bombing to the start of the ground offensive, that the major media failure in conveying the nature of the war occurred. From 18 January onwards CENTCOM released to the reporters waiting in Riyadh and Dhahran only a handful of video extracts showing 'smart' bombs and missiles striking Iraqi targets. The overwhelming media attention gained by this material was such that Rear-Admiral Brent Baker, the US Navy's Chief of Information, concluded:

Naval aviation was at a disadvantage, because our aircraft video mission recorder systems are old and do not meet broadcast standards. Copies of mission recordings were of poor quality after transferring to commercial tapes for news release. Modern aircraft video recorder systems are a must in a television war.[46]

CENTCOM refused to release video tapes of bombs that missed their targets, or any that included human casualties, and was able to exercise virtually total control over the public presentation of the air war. That the overwhelming weight of the air offensive consisted of conventional carpet bombing of Iraqi troops was never a secret. General Powell, for example, told a Pentagon press briefing on 19 January that troop concentrations in Kuwait were the main air target. But no emphasis was placed on this campaign by Iraq, which hoped to conceal its military losses and gain a propaganda victory from civilian deaths, by the Coalition, which wanted to show off its high-tech achievements and avoid comparisons with Vietnam, or by the media, with its fixation on spectacular visual images. As a result, the mass destruction of Iraqi forces in Kuwait came as a genuine surprise to many people after the war. The Gulf War became, as *The Economist* put it, 'history's most televised, least visible war'.[47]

Presentation of the war at sea was handicapped by resistance to publicity from the US Navy, which, like the Royal Navy in the Falklands conflict, showed a basic hostility towards the media (whose habit of identifying any aviator as an air force fighter pilot did not help). The navy also failed to make proper use of its own media resources. CENTCOM's Joint Combat Camera Team (JCCT) headquarters at Riyadh, with a staff of over 200 and 11 separate units, provided film, photographs and video to the open media throughout 'Desert Storm'. The French and British military ran smaller but similar units. The navy, however, allowed 40 per cent of its camera teams to be assigned to army and air force units, believing that eight cameramen were sufficient to cover all of its warships. Of bombing videos released through the JCCT to the media in Riyadh, 98 per cent came from the air force.[48]

Meanwhile, rather than wait in Dhahran, several reporters elected to cover the Coalition ground forces without their co-operation. Later termed 'unilateralists', they earned criticism from the military for irresponsibility and praise from their colleagues for providing the best news. Of the major networks only ABC rejected the pool system, guessing correctly that Saudi and Egyptian forces, despite close censorship of their own media, would welcome American attention. Forrest Sawyer's ABC camera crew obtained front-line material of the fighting at Khafji, and became the only crew allowed on a bombing mission. Unilateralists also provided the first film and reports of the Iraqi oil slick hitting Saudi beaches. But a unilateralist report of Coalition forces deploying west of Hafar al-Batin before the ground offensive also provided the worst security breach of the war, and a perfect Scud target for an enemy more alert than Iraq. Unilateralism was also a risky business in itself. A CBS crew with reporter Bob Simon, filming without an escort on the front line on 23 January, was captured by the Iraqis and not released until after the war.

The unilateralists who gathered in Hafar al-Batin as the ground war approached complained that pool journalists, afraid for their own positions, would betray them to the military authorities. CENTCOM could exclude any journalist from the front by physical force, but its only legal sanction was to request expulsion by the Saudi authorities. Usually the threat was enough, and only a handful of expulsions, two of them French journalists reporting on the Americans, took place, but this lack of legal authority did not stop unauthorised action against journalists. Former Ranger Captain John Koko, a Vietnam veteran turned press escort officer, earned a minor place in the war's history for a one-man crusade to clean the unilateralists out of Hafar al-Batin. 'We didn't want to catch them,' he explained later, 'We just wanted to make their life miserable'.[49] Most press escort officers had no special training (the British Army and Royal Navy had sent home most of their specially trained part-time escort officers, created in response to the Falklands, in December), and journalists complained that the co-operation they received varied immensely.

The problems of the Americans and British in media-military relations, however, were small compared with those of the French, who were without similar recent experience of a television war. On 18 February, after TF1 broadcast an unauthorised interview with French troops in Saudi Arabia critical of the war, the French Defence Ministry banned news crews from the front, offering to replace them with military cameramen. In retaliation all four French networks imposed a 24-hour ban on reporting their country's military activities in the Gulf. The Defence Ministry then proposed 'an immersion' of journalists with the front-line forces for brief periods only, and a 'French School of War Coverage', a pool of about 12 correspondents with permanent access to the troops, virtually excluding all others. The start of the ground war a few days later meant that neither suggestion was properly implemented. Although they were not very different from American practices, the sudden introduction of these restrictions in the middle of a war provoked massive press hostility.

In contrast, those American and British journalists who joined MRTs were deliberately made part of the military organisation, being looked after by their escort officers and drivers, which most took as no more than their due, and given survival training. It was later suggested that journalists might benefit from a peacetime course in 'military camping' and how to wear an NBC (Nuclear, Biological, Chemical) protection suit. They were also given very specific reporting rules and restrictions, with twelve main categories for the Americans and no fewer than 17 for the British. As Kate Aidie expressed it:

Apart from being practical and the arguments legally about being prisoners of war and other matters with regard to uniforms, the reason that we wore it was to say: 'We have changed our position slightly. I'm not just a reporter, reporting independently. I'm actually *with* the Army!' . . . And the journalists, on the whole, had to take a very careful line between not revealing the military tactics and not deceiving the people at home in their own country by telling lies or giving out disinformation.[50]

In late January the pool journalists were given detailed briefings on the war plans of their particular division. Having been placed in this position of trust, they were allowed to go anywhere within their assigned area and report anything, limited only by the presence of an escort officer. There was no formal censorship: military control was exercised by the initial agreement, by the threat of expulsion, and mainly by co-operation. American networks carried pool reports with the disclaimer 'Cleared by the US Military', and the British with their inimitable euphemism, 'certain operational facts have been omitted for reasons of national security'. Some journalists found the system unworkable and left; others found ways to bend the rules. When, despite numerous American stories on chaplains, the British insisted on their rule forbidding mention of religion, that Sunday's British pool broadcast began with a reference to 'a welfare meeting conducted by a welfare officer whose services are much in demand', over scenes of a church parade.

A notable result of the MRTs' existence was the effect that the arrival of a famous television reporter could have on soldiers. It was not the fact of being reported which boosted morale, so much as the presence of a celebrity. As Martha Teichner put it, she functioned as 'a talisman' for the troops. Otherwise, the Gulf War confirmed the belief that for combat troops the fact of support from home is the most important part of front-line reporting. One British officer told his men in front of the cameras:

> The country — in the UK — is living this war probably more than we are at this moment. They're glued to the television and the newspapers, and they're seeing Scuds and artillery raids and they're seeing much more than we are . . . And therefore they really feel very close to us.[51]

It was technically possible for live television broadcasts to come from the very front line. But television or satellite telephone signals posed a serious risk of Iraqi detection and hostile fire (in military terms, an electronic emission threat), and the FTUs were located either with divisional headquarters or, in some cases, even further back. Forward of this, the reporters depended on wheeled transport to get their tapes or copy back for transmission, and as this became apparent some journalists chose to remain at brigade or divisional headquarters to guarantee communications with the outside world when the ground war began.

The ground war

The week of intense diplomatic activity after Saddam's radio broadcast on 15 February was conducted in the full glare of the media, as the story moved between Riyadh, Baghdad, Moscow, and Washington, culminating in President Bush's ultimatum. While this was happening, media sources on the Coalition side began to dry up, and CENTCOM let it be known that a total news blackout would be imposed for the first 24 hours of the ground offensive. In response, on 19 February about 300 journalists in Dhahran, mainly European, threatened to turn unilateralist and storm the front unless given pool places by the Americans and British. In Baghdad the Ministry of Information was also suffering a growing credibility problem as Iraqi communications broke down under the bombing, claiming general panic in Israel, mass Coalition casualties from the air war, and announcing Scud strikes that had never taken place. On 22 February it reported that the ground war had already started with the repulse of an attack by a British armoured division. 'No-one here knows what the Iraqis are talking about,' was CENTCOM's comment, 'but then that's true most of the time'.

When the ground offensive began in earnest, on 24 February, the Coalition's carefully prepared plans for front-line media coverage broke down almost at once. The speed of the advance led to a greater gap than expected between forward units and divisional rear echelons, contact was lost for long periods between the reporters and the FTUs, and neither film nor copy could get through for transmission. In one extreme case, film of the US 1st Armored Division, taken during the first day's advance, did not reach its Riyadh FTU until two days after the end of the war, and was never shown. In addition to the practical difficulties of covering the front lines, the portability of ENG and other lightweight cameras was offset by the fact that much of the fighting took place at long range and at night, and that most cameramen were tied to reporters whose 'on-the-spot' description of events dominated the screen. Radio and print journalists also found that the technology hampered rather than enhanced their ability to report events:

> In the old days you could afford the luxury of fighting like hell through the desert to somewhere, taking at least 24 hours to find out what happened, finding a telephone and reporting it. That luxury is finished. As soon as you get there you can put up your telephone or you can put up your satellite and you can go 'live'. And about all you have to see is what's around you.[52]

Journalism at its best has been described as 'the first rough draft of history'. In those terms, the permanent value of both film and print reporting of ground combat in the Gulf was rather less than that of equivalent reporting in the Second World War, 50 years before.

The extent of the Coalition's success led General Schwarzkopf to break his own news blackout and give an eight-minute report to the press in Riyadh on the war's progress at 7 pm (local time) on 24 February. Within a few hours, the first pictures of the advance were appearing on Western television. Next morning, in the face of severe media pressure from Washington, CENTCOM re-established its daily Riyadh briefing; and at 9 pm on 27 February, with the war still going on, Schwarzkopf gave his celebrated hour-long briefing to the press at Riyadh JIB on how he had defeated the Iraqis. It was an unprecedented occasion, and a masterly media performance. Schwarzkopf was reporting total victory, and there was no-one in a position to contradict him.

With the start of the ground war many journalists had indeed driven towards the front, regardless of personal risks, and a few like Bob McKeown reached Kuwait City ahead of the Coalition forces. Most treated George Bush's announcement of a ceasefire on 28 February (local time) as if the final whistle had blown in a football game. As far as the journalists were concerned, reporting restrictions and obligations ceased at that moment. There was a mass exodus from Dhahran northwards, while pool journalists tried to order their escort drivers to break away from the advancing columns and drive at full speed for the Basra highway. A week later, over 40 journalists who had been captured in Basra were returned by Iraq to the Red Cross. 'We must drop the pretense,' Pete Williams concluded, 'that the safety of journalists isn't the government's concern.'[53]

Meanwhile, Iraq's media machine had disintegrated along with its armed forces. On 25 February the Ministry of Information in Baghdad dismissed reporters' stories of massed Iraqi prisoners as 'Western lies', only to be told by the reporters that television pictures of the prisoners had already appeared. Not only were the forces of AirLand Battle inside the Iraqi decision loop, but so were the Western media. That afternoon the Ministry of Information tried to refute claims that communications with the front had broken down by identifying the attacking forces as the US 2nd Armored and Egyptian 3rd Mechanised Divisions, an inadvertent proof that the Coalition deception plan had worked. Thereafter, Iraqi pronouncements took on an air of unreality. In the early hours of 26 February Baghdad Radio announced an organised, voluntary Iraqi withdrawal from Kuwait, and shortly before noon Saddam Hussein gave his own radio broadcast, proclaiming an Iraqi victory. 'I don't believe it,' one Arab supporter in Amman told the BBC. 'If Saddam is withdrawing, why aren't the Israelis withdrawing from Palestine?' Finally, the Iraqi government turned against the Western press. On 9 March the journalists were denounced for serving up 'a delicious plate of lies mixed with facts and poison mixed with reason', and expelled from Baghdad. Latif Nsayef Jassim was also sacked as Minister of Information. By that time, many of the leading journalists and camera teams were in northern Iraq, covering the fate of the Kurds under very different reporting conditions to those which had governed 'Desert Storm'.[54]

Conclusion

'Mutual mistrust is part of the shared heritage of soldiers and journalists in time of war', one American commentator wrote of the Gulf. 'So is mutual accommodation.'[55] Those on both sides who see media-military relations in terms of opposition agree that the military won this particular round at the expense of the media. Those, notably in the American government and military, who prefer to stress co-operation, argue that everybody won: the military did a good job and the press reported it accurately. Statistics indicate that over 80 per cent of American people thought better of the military than before the war, and about 60 per cent thought better of the media.

The experience of the Gulf War reaffirmed many old truths about war reporting and propaganda that governments, the military and the media themselves seem reluctant to learn. What makes the Gulf War perhaps unusual is that the military in most cases showed a better understanding of the strengths and weaknesses of the media than *vice versa*. The main military failing was their belief in the 'Vietnam Effect', which may now be put in its proper perspective. Those among the media who are critical of their own role express concern that their communications technology is out of control. In this they might learn from the military, who have faced similar problems for the last 20 years and made greater progress in overcoming them. The personalisation of news is also recognised as a problem. 'If the reporter becomes the story then it becomes strict theater,' as Peter Arnett put it. 'We'll lose our credibility and everyone will start reading newspapers again.'[56]

The basic issues of media-military relations remain as they have been in the past, although the specific problems will be different with each war. On the equality of dissatisfaction principle, the experience of both sides in the Gulf was about as good as they could reasonably expect. The disturbing possibility exists, and will continue to be investigated, that despite unprecedented openness and co-operation, the military and the media between them told their people nothing until the war was over, and then told them who won.

Notes

1. Jonathan Alter, 'Clippings From The Media War', *Newsweek*, 11 March 1991.
2. Arthur Sylvester, quoted in Derrik Mercer, Geoff Mungham and Kevin Williams, *The Fog of War. The Media on the Battlefield* (Heinemann, London, 1987), p 246. See also Philip M Taylor, *Munitions of the Mind* (Patrick Stephens, London, 1990), pp 220–232; Stuart Hood, *On Television* (2nd Edition, Pluto Press, London, 1980); Sarah Dickinson, *How To Take On The Media* (Weidenfeld and Nicholson, London, 1990).
3. British television interview with Richard Dowden of *The Independent*, from 'The Information War', TX Channel Four, 21 April 1991.
4. Alter, op cit.
5. Televised press conference by General H Norman Schwarzkopf, Riyadh, 27 February 1991. The ABC News version of this is available as a video cassette, 'Schwarzkopf: How The War Was Won' (Castle Vision, London, 1991).
6. Thomas B Allen, F Clifton Berry, Norman Polmar, *CNN — War in the Gulf* (Maxwell Macmillan International, London, 1991), pp 136–137, 160–162.
7. Interview with Richard Stourton, Diplomatic Editor of ITN, from 'The Information War'.
8. Unidentified US Air Force commander quoted in an article by Malcolm Brown, *The New York Times* and *The Sydney Morning Herald*, 13 March 1991.
9. Interview with Fadia Faqir, Jordanian writer, from 'The Information War'.
10. Peter Braestrupp, *Big Story* (Westview Press, Boulder, Colorado, 1977), p 14. See also Alan Hooper, *The Military and the Media* (Gower, London, 1982), pp 109–122.
11. To underscore the point: USS *Missouri* is a battleship with 16-inch guns; the British medium armoured reconnaissance regiment in the Gulf War was the 16th/5th Queen's Royal Lancers; FROG (Free Rocket Over Ground) is the NATO reporting name given to a missile of Soviet design used by the Iraqis in the Gulf War. The Green Bay Packers is not a cricket team.
12. Norman Friedman, *Desert Victory. The War for Kuwait* (Naval Institute Press, Annapolis, 1991), p 8.
13. See Hooper, op cit, pp 64–70.
14. Bruce W Watson, 'The Issue of Media Access to Information', in Bruce W Watson (ed), *Military Lessons of the Gul' War* (Greenhill, London, 1991), p 202.
15. Quoted in John Simpson, *From The House of War* (Arrow, London, 1991), p 321. For the popular journalist's view of the Crimean War, see in particular Phillip Knightley, *The First Casualty* (2nd Edition, Quartet, London, 1982), pp 3–18; and for its persistence in the Gulf War, see *The Education Guardian* supplement to *The Guardian*, 29 January 1991.
16. Quoted in John F Marszalek, *Sherman's Other War: The General and the Civil War Press* (Memphis State UP, Memphis, Tennessee, 1981), p 42. See also Knightley, op cit, pp 20–39.
17. British television interview with Kate Aidie, Senior Foreign Affairs Correspondent for the BBC, from 'Tales From The Gulf', TX BBC1, 19 July 1991.
18. John Steinbeck, *Once There Was A War* (Heinemann, London, 1959), Introduction, p xiii.
19. Pete Williams, 'The Press and the Persian Gulf War', *Parameters*, Autumn 1991, p 8.

20. 'The War on the Screen', *The Economist*, 19 January 1991. See also Mercer, Mungham and Williams, op cit, pp 4, 305.

21. Adolf Hitler, *Mein Kampf* (unexpurgated English language version translated by James Murphy, Hurst and Blackett, London, 1939), p 518; see also in particular ibid, pp 156–178 and Sir Campbell Stuart, *Secrets of Crewe House* (Hodder and Stoughton, London, 1920). For correctives see Nicholas Reeves, *Official British Film Propaganda in the First World War* (Croom Helm, London, 1986), pp 9–43; and M L Sanders and Philip M Taylor, *British Propaganda During the First World War* (Macmillan, London, 1982).

22. Steve Platt, 'Casualties of War', *New Statesman and Society*, 22 February 1991; Hooper, op cit, p 116.

23. Quoted in Robert Harris, *Gotcha! The Media, The Government and the Falklands Crisis* (Faber and Faber, London, 1983), p 65. See also Mercer, Mungham and Williams, op cit, pp 213–260; and William M Hammond, *Public Affairs: The Military and the Media 1962–1968* (United States Army in Vietnam Series, Center of Military History, United States Army, Washington DC, 1988).

24. Martin van Creveld, *Command in War* (Harvard UP, Cambridge, Mass., 1985), pp 256–257. See also Harris, op cit, pp 61–64.

25. General Sir Hugh Beach, 'News Management in a Conventional War', *British Army Review*, No 87, December 1987, p 4. See also Mercer, Mungham and Williams, op cit, pp 261–290.

26. Findings from the two main academic enquiries have been published as Mercer, Mungham and Williams, op cit, and as Valerie Adams, *The Media and the Falklands Campaign* (Macmillan, London, 1986). See also Hooper, op cit, pp 155–164; Harris, op cit; and The Glasgow University Media Group, *War and Peace News* (Open University Press, Milton Keynes, 1985).

27. Quoted in Mercer, Mungham and Williams, op cit, p 297.

28. Watson, op cit, pp 202–203; Major-General Winant Sidle, 'A Battle Behind the Scenes: The Gulf War Reheats the Military-Media Controversy', *Military Review*, Vol 71, No 9, September 1991, pp 52–63.

29. Beach, op cit, pp 4–7; Adams, op cit, pp 177–194; Mercer, Mungham and Williams, op cit, pp 2–15, 311–374; Hood, op cit, pp 98–121; Francis Wheen, *Television* (Century, London, 1985), pp 71–99, 243–252.

30. Allen, Berry and Polmar, op cit, p 236; Simpson, op cit, p 337.

31. Richard Simpkin, *Race To The Swift: Thoughts on Twenty-First Century Warfare* (Brassey's, London, 1985), p 173.

32. Ibid, p 174. See also Eugene J Carrol Jr and Gene R La Roque, 'Victory in the Desert: Superior Technology or Brute Force?' in Victoria Brittain (ed), *The Gulf Between Us. The Gulf War and Beyond* (Virago Press, London, 1991), pp 58–59.

33. Peter Black, *The Mirror in the Corner* (Hutchinson, London, 1972), p 226.

34. Grace Paley, 'Something about the Peace Movement: Something about the People's Right *Not* to Know', in Brittain, op cit, p 73.

35. British television news report, Channel Four News, TX 13 March 1991. See also Allen, Berry and Palmer, op cit, p 161.

36. John R Whiting, 'WAR — Live!', *United States Naval Institute Proceedings*, Vol 118, No 8, August 1991, p 65.

37. Interview with Lieutenant-General Thomas W Kelly USA (Rtd), *United States Naval Institute Proceedings*, Vol 118, No 9, September 1991, p 79.

38. Letter from Field Marshal Lord Stanier to *The Times*, 19 March 1991. See also Adams, op cit, pp 157–172.

39. Interview with Kelly, op cit, p 80.

40. 'How The Prophets of Doom Lost Face', *The Sunday Times*, 3 March 1991; 'Unhappy Media Pundits Find Some Profit Nevertheless', *The Times Higher Education Supplement*, 29 March 1991.

41. Quoted in Simpson, op cit, pp 154–155.

42. Steve Shaw, 'CNN Goes To War', *International Space Markets*, Vol 7, No 1, 1991, pp 3–6.

43. British radio interview with the Iraqi Ambassador to Paris, TX BBC Radio Three special Gulf coverage service, 1 pm (GMT) 14 February 1991.

44. Williams, op cit, pp 4–6; Watson, op cit, pp 203–204; Mike Sherman, 'Informing Through the JIB', *United States Naval Institute Proceedings*, Vol 118, No 8, August 1991, pp 59–61.

45. Quoted in Interview with Kelly, op cit, p 76.

46. Rear-Admiral Brent Baker, 'Last One in the Pool', *United States Naval Institute Proceedings*, Vol 118, No 8, August 1991, p 71.

47. 'Waging an Invisible War', *The Economist*, 16 February 1991. See also Daniel Hallin, 'TV's Clean Little War', *Bulletin of the Atomic Scientists*, Vol 47, No 4, May 1991, pp 17–19; and John Pilger, 'Liberal Triumphalism', *New Statesman and Society*, 15 March 1991.

48. Gary W Butterworth, 'Where Were the Navy Images?' *United States Naval Institute Proceedings*, Vol 118, No 8, August 1991, pp 73–76. See also Hans Halberstadt, 'The Navy Does Not Cooperate', pp 74–75; Brian Wolff, 'Tangled in Wires and Networks', pp 77–78 and Peter B Mersky, 'What Happened Out There?' pp 79–80, in the same issue of *Proceedings*.
49. Interview with Captain John Koko, from 'Tales From The Gulf'.
50. Interview with Kate Aidie, from 'The Information War'.
51. British television Gulf news pool report, TX BBC1 and Channel Four, 3 February 1991.
52. Interview with Deborah Amos, Foreign Correspondent US National Public Radio, from 'Tales From The Gulf'.
53. Williams, op cit, p 9.
54. Nik Gowing, 'The Media Dimension 1: TV and the Kurds', *World Today*, Vol 47, No 7, 1991, pp 111–112.
55. Arthur Lubow in *New Republic*, quoted by Williams, op cit, p 9.
56. Interview with Peter Arnett, Foreign Correspondent CNN, from 'Tales From The Gulf'.

Further Reading

Oliver Boyd-Barrett and Peter Braham, *Media, Knowledge and Power* (Routledge, London, 1987).

The Glasgow University Media Group, *Into The Media War* (Open University Press, Milton Keynes, 1992).

Derrik Mercer, Geoff Mungham, Kevin Williams, *The Fog of War. The Media on the Battlefield* (Heinemann, London, 1987).

David E. Morrison, *Television and the Gulf War* (John Libbey, London, 1992).

Philip M Taylor, *War and the Media: Propaganda and Persuasion in the Gulf* (Manchester UP, Manchester, 1992).

Francis Wheen, *Television* (Century, London, 1985).

CHAPTER 11
The Gulf War and the Environment

Ray Sibbald

'We won the air war, we won the land war, but we lost the ecological war.'

Dr Fatima Abdul, January 1992[1]

The threat

Saddam Hussein began to use the environmental 'wild card' as a potential weapon as soon as it became clear to him that the Coalition was serious in its threats to remove Iraqi troops from Kuwait by force. In September 1990, only a month after the invasion of Kuwait, the Iraqi leader warned the United States and its allies that any attempt to deprive him of his ill-gotten gains would be met with a deliberate destruction of Kuwaiti oil wells. Almost immediately, alarm bells were set off around the globe, warning of a possible ecological disaster.

Once the nature of the threat was apparent, the scientific world became the scene of a sharply divided debate. On one side there were those who spoke in almost apocalyptic terms about the possible results of Saddam's threatened actions. Ranged against them were those who belived that if the oil wells were set ablaze, the effects, although considerable, would be confined to the immediate region of the Gulf.

The debate was opened by King Hussein of Jordan at a World Climate Conference in Geneva in November 1990. Using data supplied by his chief adviser, Abdullah Toukan, he declared that igniting the oil wells would hasten the rate of global warming by increasing the amount of carbon dioxide in the atmosphere. King Hussein's perceived pro-Iraqi stance meant that his pronouncements were always likely to be viewed with scepticism in the West, but he was not the only person to prophesy dire results. American scientists such as Professor Carl Sagan thought that burning oil wells would produce an effect similar to that predicted after a nuclear war — 'nuclear winter'. In such a scenario, the smoke produced by the burning oil would undergo a process known as 'self-lofting'. The dark smoke emitted by the burning oil would absorb sunlight, heating the air around the smoke cloud. This would cause both the smoke and the heated air to rise, initiating storms which would project the clouds into the stratosphere, where they would remain for long periods, blocking out the sun's rays from significant parts of the planet.

These theories were vehemently attacked by other Western scientists, who accused both King Hussein and Sagan of allowing their judgement to be coloured by their anti-war attitudes. A scientist at the Lawrence Livermore National Laboratory in the United States, for example, declared that burning Kuwaiti oil-wells might produce pollution 'about as severe as that found on a bad day at Los Angeles airport'.[2] Weather experts at the British Meteorological Office believed that there would certainly be an increase in the levels of carbon dioxide in the atmosphere, but that this would be negligible when viewed on a global scale. However, they did express concern about the effects that smoke clouds from burning oil wells might have on the local environment of the Gulf region.

The basic problem with all these theories, both extreme and conservative, was that they were attempting to describe the results of something that the world had never seen. This led to a disparity of views split roughly along pro- or anti-war attitudes instead of being based on objective scientific evidence. Joel S Levine, a scientist working for the National Aeronautics and Space Administration (NASA) in the USA, summed up the reality of the situation, once Saddam had carried out his threat, when he described the Kuwaiti oilfields as 'the most intense burning source, probably in the history of the world'. Nothing more accurate was possible until the consequences had been experienced and studied.

During the early weeks of the crisis over Kuwait, politicians in the West were reluctant to discuss the problem of environmental warfare, dismissing it for the most part as being of little immediate consequence. In November 1990 John Major, newly installed as Britain's Prime Minister, declared that his government had no plans to call for international discussions on the possible environmental effects of conflict in the Gulf. A month later, Junior Foreign Office Minister Douglas Hogg stated that attempts to theorise about the effects of deliberate pollution were merely distracting attention from the real problem, that of evicting the Iraqis from Kuwait. This was all very well, but no-one really doubted Saddam's willingness to use the environmental weapon if he felt that it would help him to achieve his political objectives. The burning of Kuwaiti oil resources would be a dramatic and potentially far-reaching way of doing this, but it was not the only one available. As soon as Coalition air attacks on Iraq began, in January 1991, Saddam responded with actions which augured ill for the ecological future of the Gulf.

'... and numerous baby ducks'

On 2 February 1991 New Scientist made reference to a 'Doonesbury' cartoon of the 1970s.[3] A group of primary school children are watching a news report featuring endless lists of men killed in battle. The children watch this tale of carnage with equanimity until the announcer adds that numerous baby ducks have also died: the children are horrified. So, apparently, was the British government when Saddam made his first move in the 'environment war' in January 1991. Instead of the widely anticipated arson of Kuwaiti oil fields, Saddam began to release crude oil into the waters of the northern Gulf. Michael Heseltine, Britain's newly appointed

Secretary of State for the Environment, reacted with righteous indignation at the prospect of thousands of casualties among the marine population of the Gulf, particularly the rare Hawksbill Turtle and the Dugong.

The first oil slick was reported on 24 January 1991, but it probably resulted from actions taken at least four days earlier at the Mina al-Ahmadi oil refinery in southern Iraq. As soon as the problem became apparent, President George Bush publicly denounced Iraq, declaring on 25 January that Saddam had deliberately engineered the slick by ordering five oil tankers moored at Mina al-Ahmadi to empty their cargoes into the Gulf. The Iraqis responded by stating that the slick had occurred as a direct result of Coalition bombing.

Apportioning blame was not the key issue. Once the oil had been released, it was the results that were important. There were four main causes for concern: the immediate effect on wildlife in the Gulf region, the possibility that the oil would drift south and threaten Saudi Arabia's desalination plants (upon which the Coalition forces depended for their supplies of fresh water), the threat to the local fishing industry and the communities it supported, and the long-term damage to the ecology.

The Gulf is a unique and vulnerable ecosystem. Despite being close to the Equator, it is very different from other tropical seas. A crucial factor in determining the habitats and wildlife of the area is the fluctuation in temperature. In winter the air temperature can drop to freezing point, then in summer it can rise to more than 50° Celsius (122° Fahrenheit). The Gulf has a high salinity level caused by intense evaporation. In some areas the evaporation rate is 40 parts per thousand, while in shallow water this can rise to as much as 200 parts per thousand. There is a very weak anti-clockwise current, meaning that surface-water movement is dictated by wind rather than tide. The prevailing winds are northerly or northwesterly, pushing any oil-spill along the Saudi Arabian coastline towards Bahrain. Tidal range is low to moderate, ranging from one to four metres (three to 13 feet), and this, combined with the effect of the northerly winds in moving the fine-grained sand of the shoreline to form sandbanks, produces an enormous inter-tidal zone of mudflats and adjacent shallows. The largest mudflats are found at Dawhat, Abu Ali, Kuwait Bay and the Gulf of Salwah, and they, together with their neighbouring sub-tidal shallows, are extremely vulnerable to oil damage.

Two of the most important living components of the Gulf ecosystem are the species of seagrass that cover much of the sub-tidal zone and the algal mats that quite literally feed the sea. The algal mats are made up of groups of very basic organisms that are more like bacteria than algae. Between 20 and 30 different species of these creatures may be found growing in communities that also include colonies of green algae and quantities of anaerobic bacteria. A wide variety of invertebrates rely on the algal mats for sustenance, making the mats the base of the food chain which maintains virtually all the wildlife of the Gulf. As the mats rely heavily on photosynthesis for their growth, they can easily be damaged by oil, which cuts off the supply of direct sunlight. A major oil spill therefore has the potential to do enormous long-term ecological harm.

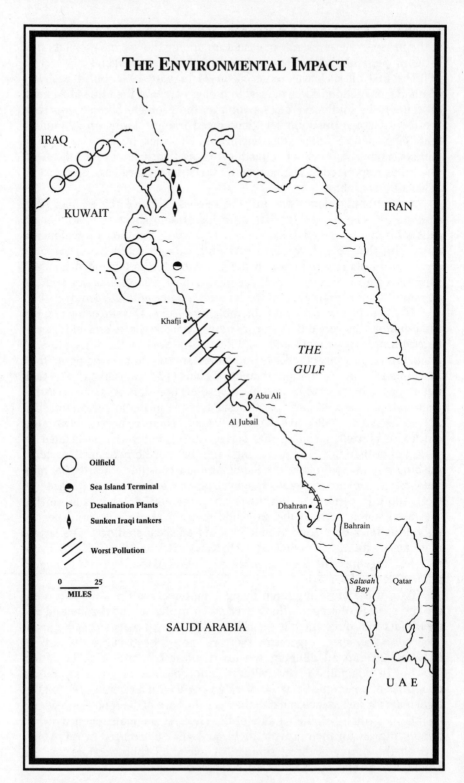

THE ENVIRONMENTAL IMPACT

IRAQ

KUWAIT

IRAN

Khafji

THE
GULF

Abu Ali

Al Jubail

○ Oilfield

● Sea Island Terminal

▷ Desalination Plants

◆ Sunken Iraqi tankers

/// Worst Pollution

0 ___ 25
MILES

Dhahran

Bahrain

Salwah
Bay

Qatar

SAUDI ARABIA

U A E

The clean-up

Once the Americans had announced the Mina al-Ahmadi incident, it quickly became apparent that this was not the first such oil spill. Reports emerged that Iraq had started to pump oil from Kuwait's Sea Island terminal as early as 19 January 1991, while oil from storage tanks damaged by Iraqi shelling of Khafji was also flowing into the waters of the Gulf. Initially it was virtually impossible to discover how much had been released. Estimates varied from the ridiculously low (50 million gallons) to the ludicrously high (500 million gallons), with an eventual consensus emerging of about 250 million gallons, a figure 20 times that spilt by the *Exxon Valdez* in Alaska in 1989.

Fortunately for the future of the Gulf, nature limited the immediate effects. As the current carried the slicks southwards along the coast of Saudi Arabia in March, a westerly wind altered their course, with the result that the bulk of the oil was confined by the Abu Ali island, jutting out into the Gulf, and kept away from the coasts of many of the more southerly states. Saddam's motives in releasing the oil seem to have been a mixture of revenge and military expediency. Befcre the conflict began, rumours were rife about a possible American amphibious landing on the coast of Kuwait, and the dumping of oil would appear to have been intended to counter this. Despite Coalition assurances that any such landing would not have been affected by the oil slick, several sources confirm that naval assault vessels would have experienced difficulty in crossing oil-covered water to reach the shore.

The top priority in any clean-up operation had to be the protection of the Saudi coastline and, in particular, its desalination plants. Almost as soon as the first slick was reported, a series of actions were taken that seemed to suggest a pre-planned operation. This was confirmed on 28 January 1991, when Dr Abdulbar Al-Gain, head of Saudi Arabia's Meteorology and Environmental Protection Administration (MEPA), stated: 'plans for the protection of important facilities were prepared well in advance of the spill. These facilities are either now protected or in the process of being protected.'[4] A variety of governmental and international bodies, spearheaded by conservation agencies from the USA, contributed to the relief effort. Britain's Oil Spill Service (owned in part by Saudi Arabia's Aramco) sent 90 workers immediately, and Norway despatched experts and equipment.

Together, they appeared to succeed in containing the worst of the disaster. A report in *Scientific American* in October 1991 stated: 'During the war, workers quickly deployed booms, nets and skimmers to protect water-intake pipes of Saudi desalination plants and refineries, which were crucial to the war effort.'[5] However, the author of the report, John Horgan, went on to quote a US Coast Guard officer in Saudi Arabia, who told Horgan in confidence: 'I'm not happy with any large scale operation that I've seen.'[6] What seems to have happened is that, once the top-priority task of ensuring the safety of water facilities had been carried out, the Saudis lost interest in dealing with any long-term and potentially far more damaging effects on the environment, such as the destruction of the algal mats or seagrass beds.

The only exception to this occurred when intense media attention on oil-affected wildlife forced the Saudis to act. A *New Scientist* report in February 1991 noted that 'a British television crew filmed thick surface oil and oil-soaked cormorants at Khafji, on the Saudi side of the border with Kuwait' in late January.[7] When the film was broadcast around the world, it caused an immediate outcry to which the Saudis had to respond. Bird-cleaning centres were set up at a number of locations in the kingdom, and the media was invited to report the work of the conservationists, which it duly did. The only problem was that, while such work provided excellent television footage, in a lot of cases it was largely ineffective. Of the 2,000 birds taken to the Al-Jubail conservation centre, for example, fewer than 400 survived the cleaning process. The United States National Oceanographic and Atmospheric Administration (NOAA) believed that the resources devoted to the cleaning centres could have been used far more effectively elsewhere, and that the whole affair represented an attempt to grab the headlines, rather than a serious conservation programme.[8]

Many conservationists thought the clean-up process should have targeted the algal mats, vital to the whole Gulf ecosystem, instead of diverting scarce resources into creating 'photo-opportunities' for the world press. Attempts were made to save the mats and the seagrass beds, but they were characterised by confusion and acrimony. The frustration of international conservationists centred on the apparent inability of the Saudis to control the contractors brought in to carry out the clean-up operation. Those responsible for one section of land, for example, would simply shift the oil from their allotted plot to another area of the shore, or dump the recovered oil so close to the waterline that environmentalists believed that it would soon seep back into the sea. In the event, the contractors were helped by the fact that the Gulf has been subject to man-made oil spills in the past, and that seepage from shallow oil deposits is a natural occurrence. Because of this, a community of bacteria has developed which lives by metabolizing oil; rather like antibodies that attack and destroy foreign bodies in humans, these 'oil-eating' bacteria attack and break up oil-spills in the Gulf. But this will take many years to effect. In the meantime, a large proportion of the areas vital to the ecosystem have either been destroyed or are in grave danger of destruction.

Poor organisation and disputes between MEPA and the various contractors caused problems in the clean-up process, and the situation was not helped by a shortage of funds. By June 1991 the $55 million donated by the Coalition and other international bodies had almost run out, leaving the Saudis to foot the rest of the bill. This posed a large question mark over the future of the operation. By early 1992 it was still too soon to assess the long-term damage inflicted on the Gulf ecosystem, but it should have been possible to draw lessons from the disaster through a monitoring programme set up in its aftermath. Unfortunately, this programme was hindered by a lack of co-operation. In June 1991, for example, at a United Nations meeting in Paris to discuss the creation of databases for the monitoring process, a dispute arose between the Saudis and Kuwaitis over where the monitoring apparatus should be sited and who should control the information derived from it. In this sort of situation only two things were certain: the ecosystem of the Gulf would suffer more damage, and any programme to monitor and combat the long-term effects of the wartime oil-slicks would be largely ineffective. Unless, of course, the world suddenly became more interested in boring scientific data than in photogenic wildlife.

Kuwait is burning

The conflagration of Kuwait's oil resources began at the end of January 1991, when Iraqi soldiers set fire to storage facilities at Al-Wafra and Shuaiba, producing a 'fat plume [of smoke] that is propelled high into the air'.[9] This immediately gave a boost to the sort of global catastrophe stories that had been prevalent since the start of the Gulf Crisis in August 1990. Newspapers and television stations around the world ran stories predicting mass starvation on the Indian subcontinent as smoke from the fires travelled vast distances in the upper atmosphere.

Evidence that the Iraqis had begun to burn Kuwaiti oil wells (as opposed to storage facilities) emerged on 21 February 1991, when an American satellite picked up images of smoke clouds emanating from the Mina al-Ahmadi refinery and the Burgan oilfield. Very quickly, the smoke from these fires grew and merged with other plumes as the Iraqis blew up more and more of Kuwait's oil resources. After a week, the smoke covered an area of 11,000 square kilometres (4,250 square miles) along the coast of Kuwait. Saddam's motives were probably the same as those displayed over the release of oil into the Gulf: a mixture of revenge and military expediency. Although Coalition commanders denied it, one of the first effects of the smoke plumes must have been to reduce visibility for pilots operating over Kuwait, at a time when the Coalition ground offensive was about to start. In addition, Coalition troops advancing into Kuwait would have to deal with the presence of sulphurous fumes from the burning oil, a situation not dissimilar to being under gas attack.

In the event, the smoke from the oil fires exhibited a totally different dispersion pattern to that from the refineries and storage facilities. Instead of racing upwards into the upper atmosphere, it stayed reasonably close to the ground, a phenomenon explained by Vipin Gupta, a scientist at Imperial College, London. He stated that refinery fires burnt large amounts of oil quickly, producing intense fires that sent plumes of smoke high into the air, whereas the flow of oil to well-fires was limited by the amount that could pass through the well-head.[10]

It soon became clear that the number of Kuwaiti oil wells set ablaze ran into hundreds (estimates tend to vary between 600 and 700), and that very few had escaped. Britain's Meteorological Office conducted an aerial survey, using a C-130 Hercules equipped as a research centre, to collect data from the smoke cloud and determine whether its effects would be confined to the Gulf region or would spread elsewhere. The findings confirmed Gupta's analysis: the smoke was staying close to the ground, affecting the local climate and environment but unlikely to have a global impact. Subsequent phenomena such as falls of black snow in the Himalayas may cast doubt over such an optimistic view, but the fact remains that it was the Kuwaitis who suffered the most from Saddam's actions. When the fighting stopped in late February 1991, they faced two immense and interconnected problems — the oil-fires themselves and the health hazards caused by the fall-out of soot.

Extinguishing the fires

Of these problems, the more pressing was how to stop the burning oil wells from turning Kuwait into an uninhabitable wasteland. The obvious solution was to put out the fires, but that was easier said than done. According to official Kuwaiti sources, six billion gallons of oil a day were going up in smoke. Three Texan oil-fighting teams, one led by Red Adair and the others from Boots and Coots and Wild Well Control, were hired by the Kuwaiti government in February 1991, and they were soon joined by a Canadian group known as Safety Boss. Together, they faced the greatest oil conflagration ever seen. Moreover, the inevitable dangers of their trade were made worse by the fact that they had to operate in a recently vacated battle area, full of unexploded munitions.

Procedures for extinguishing an oil blaze had been developed by the Texan Myron Kinley in the 1940s, based on the idea of using dynamite to blow out the fire. Positioning the explosives close to the well-head was achieved by deploying a bulldozer with a projecting boom attached, which could place the dynamite, contained in an oil drum, exactly where it was needed. The bulldozer driver was protected from the intense heat by a box of corrugated iron which surrounded his cab, while both the vehicle and well-head were drenched by a constant stream of water delivered by high-pressure hoses. This enabled the drum containing the dynamite to be placed to the side of the burning well and detonated. The resulting explosion sucked the air from the vicinity of the well-head, depriving the fire of oxygen and, in theory, extinguishing the blaze. In reality, most oil fires needed several bulldozer assaults before they went out.

Initially, it was estimated that it would take at least two years to extinguish all the fires in Kuwait. In the event it took only half that time, with the last of the blazes being subdued in December 1991. The remarkable speed of the operation was a tribute to the skill and dedication of the fire-fighting teams, although they were helped by the arrival of a newly invented machine in August. Known as 'Big Wind', this was a jet engine adapted to blow out the fires, and once deployed it increased the rate of extinction from two fires a day to six.

However, even this record of success could not prevent the spread of very high levels of pollution inside Kuwait. The burning oil produced clouds of smoke that contained various substances, such as hydrocarbons, sulphur dioxide and nitrous oxides, which were harmful to humans and wildlife. Even more dangerous were the fine particles of heavy metals such as lead and vanadium. In Kuwait, large numbers of people soon began to experience symptoms associated with respiratory illness — breathing difficulties, giddiness and nausea — although when these did not coincide with an increase in the death-rate, as predicted by a number of 'doom-watchers', health workers in Kuwait neglected to collect relevant data. Reports of respiratory illness went largely unrecorded, with the result that it was impossible to distinguish normal sickness from that caused by the oil fires. As the Director of Birmingham University's Institute of Occupational Health pointed out in October 1991: 'Data on the acute effects [of the smoke] are not so good . . . we don't really know what happened.'[11]

The only way forward was for scientists to set up long-term monitoring programmes to study the people of Kuwait, identifying their health problems and compiling information that would allow preventive action to be taken in the event of future oil disasters. One such programme has been established in the Al-Ahmadi area, in which 400 Kuwaiti families will be screened for the next 25 years, but if this is the norm it will be decades before the true effects of the oil smoke are known. It is perhaps typical of humanity that reasonable data exists on the number of seabirds injured by the oil slicks, but precious little information is available on the human casualties of the smoke cloud. In mitigation, it should be pointed out that scientists are working largely in the dark, and that no similar disaster can be studied to gain comparative data, but it is worrying that the full effects of Saddam's decision to burn the oil wells cannot be foreseen. Jassim Al-Hassan, Professor of Biochemistry at the University of Kuwait, summed up the problem in late 1991: 'No-one knows how to look at the effects of oxidised hydrocarbons. Everyone is looking at the classic pollutants like sulphur dioxide and nitrous oxides. Yet there are so many unknowns in the air and in our food.'[12]

When the last oil fire was extinguished, in Decembr 1991, it was an occasion for great celebration in Kuwait, and rightly so, but the removal of one menace merely served to highlight the existence of another. In many cases, despite the extinction of the fires, oil continued to flow out of the damaged well-heads, creating huge oil lakes, some of them up to six metres (20 feet) deep and several kilometres long. They posed a number of problems for conservationists. In the heat of the desert, the rapid evaporation of the shallow lakes added yet more pollutants to the already murky atmosphere of Kuwait, and although many of the lakes were quickly contained by specially constructed sand barriers, the oil could still seep out and find its way into the waters of the Gulf, increasing the contamination caused by the original oil spills. Equally worrying was the possibility that the oil would seep downwards to contaminate ground-water resources. The Kuwaitis seemed at a loss as to how to cope with all this, merely covering the oil with a thin layer of sand. By early 1992 the problem was still unsolved.

Kuwait inherited one other major hazard from the Gulf War. During the conflict the Coalition dropped thousands of tons of explosives on to Iraqi positions in the country, and about 30,000 tons of these failed to explode. In addition, the Iraqi retreat left enormous quantities of munitions strewn around Kuwait. It is not hyperbole to describe parts of the Emirate as being carpeted in high explosives. An international effort to deal with the complicated and dangerous task of clearing the munitions was mounted as soon as the war was over. The British Royal Ordnance Company, for example, had over 500 personnel working in Kuwait by May 1991. By February 1992, 84 explosives experts from around the world had been killed while clearing munitions in Kuwait, and over 1,400 Kuwaitis had died in incidents involving unexploded and abandoned explosives. The Kuwaiti government has estimated that it will cost $1 billion and take five more years to remove the bulk of the discarded munitions. Some areas will remain dangerous for generations.[13]

Thus, although Kuwait was liberated in February 1991 and must be regarded as a victor in the Gulf War, the effects of that victory on the environment inhabited by the Kuwaiti people have been disastrous. The air that Kuwaitis breathe poses a direct if unquantifiable threat to public health, the waters of the Gulf and its ecosystem have been badly damaged, the area's agriculture and fisheries have been virtually destroyed, and large parts of Kuwait are literally minefields impassable to all but explosives experts. Kuwaitis might be forgiven for asking, if this is victory, how much worse can defeat be? To answer their question, they need only look northwards into Iraq.

The destruction of the Iraqi environment

Since the Gulf War ended, most of the studies of its environmental impact have been confined to the natural world or to the consequences for humanity, principally in Kuwait. Yet there can be little doubt that Iraq suffered just as much, if not more, in environmental terms. Some of the first reports of damage caused by smoke from burning oil wells dealt with a fall-out of soot on to Iraqi farming regions, caused in part by Coalition bombing of oil facilities such as those at Basra. It proved very difficult to estimate such damage, chiefly because the USA refused to release satellite pictures showing the smoke clouds generated by Coalition attacks, but some experts speculated that it was as bad as that caused by Iraqi sabotage in Kuwait. Much more extensive damage was done by Coalition bombing of water installations and power stations, for these formed part of Iraq's irrigation system. One of the consequences was that the Iraqi grain harvest in 1991 was poor, with a shortfall of about three million tons. In normal times this would not have been a major problem. Iraq would merely have used its oil wealth to purchase extra grain on the world market. But with United Nations sanctions remaining in force, it was impossible for the Iraqis to feed themselves. Widespread malnutrition, especially of children, was unavoidable.

An even greater impact must have been felt in the urban areas of Iraq, where key strategic targets such as power stations and communications centres were located. Their destruction was an integral part of the Coalition bombing campaign, and although the number of civilians killed as a direct result of the attacks was remarkably small, it would be naive to imagine that the death toll came to an abrupt end when the fighting stopped in late February 1991. Among the Coalition targets were water and sewage plants, the destruction of which would be sure to have long-term effects on the health and well-being of Iraqi citizens. Indeed, almost as soon as the war ended, World Health Organisation (WHO) officials visiting Iraq commented on the problems caused by a lack of clean drinking water, estimating that the supply in some areas had been reduced to five per cent of its pre-war rate. According to Ali Kohogali of the WHO, the average Iraqi had to make do with little more than a litre of clean water a day, when the minimum required to ensure healthy living was reckoned to be about 40 litres. Observers noted that many Iraqis were drawing water directly from the Tigris River, known to be a major health hazard as it contains high levels of bacteria harmful to human life.[14] This was particularly worrying in Baghdad, where Dr Gordon Cook of the London School of Tropical Medicine predicted outbreaks of typhoid, cholera, amoebiasis and hepatitis unless urgent measures were taken to improve matters,[15] while throughout Iraq doctors were reporting significant increases in cases of diarrhoea, especially among children.

The situation did not improve as time passed. A survey group organised by Harvard University completed a report in October 1991 that described a steadily worsening state of affairs in Iraq. The group found that the death rate among children under the age of five had increased fourfold since the Gulf War. Moreover, two out of every three water samples collected from the rivers of Iraq had shown contamination from raw sewage. This had contributed to the spread of diarrhoea, which was now one of the main reasons for high infant mortality. In such circumstances a further increase in the child mortality rate was to be expected, particularly as nearly 900,000 children were estimated to be in a weakened condition because of malnutrition.[16]

Nor was Baghdad the worst affected, for the Shi'as in the south of Iraq had suffered far more. By late 1991 the infrastructure of the region had been devastated, first by the Coalition during the war and then by Saddam's troops as the Shi'a insurrection was brutally suppressed. Nearly all systems that people depended on for survival had been either destroyed or so badly damaged as to be rendered useless. Sewage plants, water-purification facilities and power stations had all ceased to function, leaving the population at grave risk from starvation and disease. Similar problems affected the Kurdish region of northern Iraq, leaving few areas free from the impact of the war and its aftermath, especially as UN sanctions continued to be applied. The tragic irony was that the man against whom the war had been fought and sanctions imposed, Saddam Hussein, remained in control of the country, suffering from neither hunger nor disease.

The future

What will happen to the environment in the coming years as a result of the Gulf War seems, at first glance, to be clear. The prophets of doom appear to have been wrong. Their picture of global catastrophe, painted in response to the oil spills and fires of January-February 1991, has been discredited by a scientific community apparently united behind a scenario of limited regional effects. Yet an unsettling number of reports of freak climatic conditions continue to disturb this cosy image. As early as April 1991 'black rain in Baluchistan' was noted in the world press,[17] followed by similar reports from areas that the doom-watchers had predicted would be affected by the burning oil.

The scientific establishment has continued to ignore evidence that contradicts its 'local effect' theory, even though examples may be drawn from history to suggest that natural disasters can affect vast areas of the globe. According to Benjamin Franklin, for instance, the eruption of the Laki volcano in Iceland in 1783 caused 'a constant fog over all Europe and a great part of North America',[18] while 100 years later the eruption of Krakatoa in the East Indies had such an effect on the world's atmosphere that sunlight levels in parts of Europe were reduced by up to 20 per cent for some time. It may be, of course, that circumstances were different during the Gulf War and that the scientists were right to play down the global implications of what happened, but nagging doubts remain. These are reinforced when it is realised that insufficient time has elapsed for a full evaluation of the available data to take place. As Jonathon Porritt, former Director of Greenpeace, has pointed out: 'Nobody really knew what was going to happen because nobody had ever simultaneously set fire to 600 oil wells before'.[19] At the same time there are disturbing hints that the United States government has tried to stifle scientific debate about the environmental impact of the war. In October 1991 *Scientific American* reported the existence of a memorandum from the US Department of Energy to the Lawrence Livermore National Laboratory, dated 25 January 1991, requesting researchers not to discuss war-related topics with the media.[20]

Lack of clarity about the possible global impact of the oil fires is matched by uncertainty over the full regional effects of the calamity. Because of a lack of reliable data and problems of co-operation concerning the gathering of information in the future, all that can be said with any accuracy is that the damage caused to the Gulf environment is extensive. It is clear, for example, that almost all of Kuwait's agriculture is in ruins. Millions of tons of smoke particles have been deposited on to Kuwait and its neighbours, turning vast areas into ash-covered wasteland and destroying plant life. This, in turn, has affected the animals which depend on the plants for food, not least the camel and cattle herds belonging to Bedouin nomads.

The future of the clean-up operation, on land as well as in the waters of the Gulf, is also unclear. Once the funds set aside by the Coalition had been exhausted, individual countries in the region seemed reluctant to spend much more. In Saudi Arabia, for example, one of the only projects to have been properly funded since June 1991 has been the cleaning of a hunting reserve used by Saudi princes. In addition, there is evidence of a lack of understanding about the true nature of the catastrophe. In April 1991 an article in *New Scientist* pointed out the dangers of putting out oil fires too quickly, before the wells were ready to be capped, but this is exactly what seems to have happened. Fire-fighters were given orders to extinguish as many blazes as possible in the shortest time, leaving uncapped wells to pour oil into the surrounding desert. This helped to create the oil lakes that are now such a problem to the Kuwaitis.

It may be overstating the case to suggest, as one American official did, that 'if CNN [Cable News Network] hadn't been broadcasting this spill, the Saudis wouldn't have done squat',[21] but a similar attitude of indifference can be discerned in Kuwait's response to oil pollution. An overriding impulse seems to have been a desire on the part of both Aramco and the Kuwaiti government to restore oil production as quickly as possible, regardless of the fact that this has led to other problems, not least the creation of oil lakes. Both the clean-up programme and the establishment of scientific databases from which to study the long-term effects on the environment seem to have been relegated in favour of financial gain. It would appear, for example, that the more powerful sectors of the Kuwaiti population do not spend much time in their own country, regarding it as little more than a convenient source of income. If so, this may help to explain the drive to restore oil production at the expense of the Kuwaiti environment.

The country most obviously affected by the Gulf War, Iraq, has largely been ignored. Initially, the tragic plight of the Kurds obscured events elsewhere, but as that ceased to be front-page news, a more accurate picture of the results of the 'video war' began to emerge. Far from being a war of precise surgical strikes, it is clear that it was the same old dirty war in which the weaker members of the enemy state suffer the consequences of attacks on sewage works and power stations, while their leaders remain in power. If the Gulf conflict is viewed just from the perspective of the ceasefire, it is easy to regard it as a 'clean' war, but the long-term realities are much less acceptable. It may be some time before the full extent of those realities is recognised.

Notes
1. 'The Audit of War', Channel 4 *Dispatches* documentary, TX Thursday, 16 January 1992.
2. Quoted in Thomas Kuhn, 'Up in Flames', *Scientific American*, May 1991, p 8.
3. *New Scientist*, 2 February 1991, p 23.
4. Quoted in Michael McKinnon and Peter Vine, *Tides of War: Eco-Disaster in the Gulf* (Boxtree, London, 1991), pp 115–6.
5. Quoted in John Horgan, 'The Muddled Cleanup in the Persian Gulf', *Scientific American*, October 1991, pp 86–8.
6. Ibid, p 87.
7. Fred Pearse, 'Wildlife choked by world's worst oil slick', *New Scientist*, 2 February 1991, p 24.
8. Horgan, op cit, p 86.
9. Fred Pearse, 'Kuwait's oil wells send smoke to Iraq', *New Scientist*, 2 March 1991, p 12.
10. Ibid.
11. Quoted in Stephanie Pain, 'Is Kuwait's foul air fit to breathe?', *New Scientist*, 26 October 1991, p 13.
12. Ibid.
13. Report on Channel 4 News, Thursday, 27 February 1992.
14. Phyllida Brown, 'Risk of epidemics threatens bombed Baghdad', *New Scientist*, 9 March 1991, p 13.
15. Kuhn, op cit, p 8.
16. Ibid.
17. Fred Pearse and Stephanie Pain, 'Oil from Kuwaiti wells still pouring into the desert', *New Scientist*, 9 November 1991, p 14.
18. McKinnon and Vine, op cit, p 159.
19. Fred Pearse, 'Desert fires cast a shadow over Asia', *New Scientist*, 16 February 1991, pp 30–1.
20. McKinnon and Vine, op cit, p 165.
21. Horgan, op cit, p 87.

Further reading
Michael McKinnon and Peter Vine, *Tides of War: Eco-Disaster in the Gulf* (Boxtree, London, 1991).
Fred Pearse, *Green Warriors* (The Bodley Head, London, 1991).

CHAPTER 12
Conclusion

'If we see the confrontation in traditional material and
technological terms, then the camp of the faithful was
defeated.'

Saddam Hussein, 17 January 1992

The anniversary

One year to the day from the start of
the Gulf War, President Saddam
Hussein addressed the Iraqi people
on television in Baghdad, acknow-
ledging for the first time the crushing defeat which had been inflicted
on himself and his country by the
forces of the Coalition. But Saddam went on to argue, as he had throughout
the conflict, that this defeat represented a moral victory for Iraq, as well as
for the Arab nation and the Islamic world. Just as after the Iran-Iraq War of
1980–88 Saddam conveniently marginalised his original reasons for
aggression, while laying claim to an 'heroic defeat' which would enhance
his own prestige. He portrayed the events of the war as a temporary setback
for his own ambitions and the aspirations of the Iraqi people, promising
that he would rebuild a prosperous economy and an influential military
capability for Iraq once again.

If Saddam were right, then the Gulf War was simply one more event in
a sadly familiar pattern. At the time of the Gulf War between 20 and 30
other violent conflicts were happening in the world, each of which deserved
by some definition to be called a war. Although the locations have varied,
this level of world disorder and violence has remained broadly constant
since the Second World War, something obscured in Western perceptions
by the fact that virtually none of these wars has taken place in North
America or Western Europe. In Western popular thinking, the Second
World War, now fading into history, still remains 'the last war', against
which existing political, social and military developments are measured. It
is not yet clear what effect the Gulf War and the events of 1991 will have on
this perspective. The defeat of Saddam may stand out as a turning point in
world history, or simply as a dramatic event without wider significance.

Research into public understanding of the Gulf War has confirmed
that, as in previous wars, most people were aware that the version of events
they received while the war was being fought was not complete, understood
the reasons for this, but expected that the truth would be revealed in due
course. The authors of this book began their own studies virtually from the
start of the Gulf Crisis, working without direct access to privileged
information of any kind. Although much detail on the conduct of the war
has emerged since its end, particularly from the technical press, new
evidence has confirmed rather than overturned our original assessments.

This suggests that our basic methodological position — that an understanding of history and context makes it practical to follow and predict the events of a major modern conflict with considerable accuracy — has been valid in this case. This, in turn, has significant implications for the role which military history might play in future crisis management and warfighting, and for the importance of treating military studies as central to mainstream international politics. In particular, closer study of the Iran-Iraq War, and of earlier Arab-Israeli wars, would have considerably eased the Coalition's task in assessing the Iraqi threat.

It is, however, a truism that there are no 'lessons' to history. While an understanding of military history in context made possible our predictions of how the two sides would perform in the war, specific events were obviously not predictable. We are also aware that our assessment at the moment is tentative, and that future revelations may overturn it. Also, thanks in large part to the Gulf War's ambiguous ending, certain major facts may never be accurately established. To take the most obvious example, in the course of the year estimates of Iraqi military dead in the Kuwait Theater of Operations (KTO) have fluctuated from 300,000 down to 25,000 or less. A major dispute has also developed over the effectiveness of air weapons technology in the Gulf. It has, for example, been claimed by critics that the MIM-104 Patriot missile system defending Israel and Saudi Arabia against Scud missile attacks failed to achieve a single direct intercept. The historically minded reader is directed to disputes concerning the number of casualties in the Third Battle of Ypres of 1917, or the effectiveness of the RAF 'Dambusters' raid of 1943, and to many other similar disputes which remain unresolved after years or even centuries.

The public bickering among the US armed forces over their relative contributions to victory, which began virtually with the end of the Gulf War and was aimed at securing larger slices of a diminishing defence budget, has also been a major obstacle to understanding the war. Further, many of the war's most interesting and significant aspects, both in political and military terms, will by their nature remain secret for many years. This is particularly true of clandestine or covert operations, intelligence gathering, and electronic warfare.

One of the most surprising, and most interesting, aspects of the Gulf War was the Western public response to its ending. In the USA and in Britain, although not in France or the Arab states, public interest in the war evaporated within a month of the ceasefire. The untidy political resolution to the war may have been a factor in this, as may the complexities which surrounded its conduct. The sudden drop in public interest may also have been due to media saturation during the war. This raises the moral and political point that, although they were largely aware that the truth was being withheld from them at the time, the majority of people may come through indifference to accept the partial version available at the time as history. Western post-war boredom and disappointment, following inflated expectations of the war, have in turn increased Saddam Hussein's credibility with his own people in claiming victory.

The Gulf War and the new world order

The problem of understanding and assessing the Gulf War was made more acute by the fact that it coincided with the collapse of the framework which had determined international political relations since the Second World War. The Gulf War was clearly part of that collapse, and of the emergence of a new world order, but the precise relationship cannot at the moment be established. In particular, any connection existing between the Gulf War and the failed coup against President Mikhail Gorbachev of the Soviet Union on 19 August 1991 remains barely explored.

From the start of the Gulf Crisis, Saddam and his supporters (and many others) argued that the problem was a regional one to be managed by the Gulf states, or by the wider Arab — or even Islamic — world, rather than by the international community or the Superpowers. American participation in the war stemmed from the opposing belief, firmly held by President George Bush (and by many Arab leaders), that the Iraqi invasion of Kuwait had far wider implications. Successful co-operation over the Gulf Crisis would, it was believed, cement confidence between the Superpowers in their new relationship. Whatever Saddam may have hoped or believed, neither the USA nor the Soviet Union saw the invasion of Kuwait at any time purely as a regional issue.

This version of a new world order barely survived the Gulf War itself. By the end of the year the Soviet Union had passed out of existence, with Gorbachev resigning on 25 December, to be replaced by the Commonwealth of Independent States (CIS) including all former Soviet states except Georgia and the three Baltic republics of Latvia, Lithuania and Estonia. The Soviet Union's permanent seat on the United Nations (UN) Security Council was inherited by the Russian Federation (later renamed simply Russia) under President Boris Yeltsin. But when considering these dramatic events in relation to the Gulf War, not too much hindsight should be allowed. The Soviet Union between August 1990 and February 1991 was still a world Superpower feeling its way in a new and unaccustomed role. The first major indications of the end of Soviet domination of eastern Europe came with the overthrow of President Nicolae Ceausecu of Romania in December 1989, reached a high point with the unification of Germany in October 1990, and concluded with the formal dissolution of the Warsaw Pact in Prague on 1 July 1991. The facade of the Soviet Union's power stayed intact for a short time after the substance had crumbled, and that time coincided with the Gulf Crisis and War. It may have been Saddam's error to misjudge the political situation outside his own region by even a few months, expecting that Soviet antagonism towards the USA would act as a restraint on any American military response as in the past.

The events of 1991 left the USA as the world's remaining Superpower, in a position of unique dominance for any country in the 20th century. However, the difficulties of capitalising on this victory to produce the Middle East peace conference, the problems accompanying the Soviet Union's collapse, and the forthcoming Presidential election campaign of 1992, all combined to limit US enthusiasm for overseas ventures. When, on 26 June 1991, Croatia and Slovenia announced their 'disfederation' from the state of Yugoslavia, precipitating a slow-motion war that ran through 14 ineffective ceasefires before the end of the year, overt US political and military involvement was conspicuous by its absence. Not until February 1992 was agreement reached on a 14,000-strong UN multinational peacekeeping force for Yugoslavia. How the USA will interpret its own new international role will depend, in the short term at least, on the results of the 1992 Presidential election. In turn, it is not yet clear what part American conduct in the Gulf War has played in that election's outcome.

The role of the UN in the Gulf War was perhaps the most clear indication of a fundamental change in the international system. The war represented only the second occasion on which countries had gone to war to carry out a UN Security Council resolution, the other being the Korean War of 1950-53. The two cases were not quite identical — in 1950 the UN Security Council authorised the use of force against North Korea and a unified UN command (resolutions considered invalid by the Soviet Union, which had boycotted the Security Council at the time), whereas in 1990 the Security Council authorised only 'all necessary means' to be used against Iraq, and there was no formal UN leadership of the Coalition. Nevertheless, the UN had acted against aggression in the Gulf with an effectiveness unknown for a generation. By February 1992, with 175 members (including all the former states of the Soviet Union except Georgia), the UN stood at its strongest and most prestigious for decades.

In the atmosphere of US success created by the Gulf War many long-standing international wars or disputes seemed ripe for resolution, of which the question of Israel's relations with its neighbours was only the largest. By February 1992 the long-standing civil wars in El Salvador and Colombia were being brought to an end, a multinational force was overseeing a similar settlement in Cambodia, negotiations had opened to resolve the Turkish occupation of northern Cyprus, and even the Republic of South Africa had made progress towards liberalisation (the claim from white right-wingers that they were facing black 'communist' extremists sounding particularly hollow in the existing international climate). These events all helped foster the impression that a new world order was coming into being, towards which the Soviet Union and the USA had been moving before the Gulf War.

With the withdrawal of Soviet support and pressure from many client states, allies and left-wing movements worldwide it remains to be seen whether this trend will continue, or whether the world will simply exchange one set of troubles for another. The intermittent violence in eastern Europe, central Asia, and the Indian subcontinent in 1991 were indications that the latter might be the case, and underlined the continued ineffectiveness of the UN without US Superpower support. In the long term, US global intervention will almost certainly continue to be in support of its own interests, rather than in pursuit of peace or stability in the abstract. In this respect, very little may have really changed.

The Gulf War and the Middle East

The Iraqi invasion of Kuwait was not predicted with any accuracy much in advance; and the confident predictions of stability in the Middle East following the Iran-Iraq War of 1980-88 produced sufficient embarrassment in August 1990 to make further predictions less assured. Although Saddam Hussein appeared confident both in his own continued future and that of his country in January 1992, as these words are being written there is no way of knowing how long he will remain in power in Iraq. The extent of long-term damage to the infrastructure and ecology of Iraq caused by Coalition bombing during the Gulf War, plus the continued pressure of UN sanctions and the refusal of other states to normalise relations with Iraq as long as Saddam remains in power, all present the Iraqi leader with a severe challenge, and make even the continuation of Iraq as a political entity appear problematical in the near future. On the other hand, the ability of Saddam and his country to survive after a year of disastrous war, insurrection, famine, sanctions and lost oil revenue suggests strongly that he miscalculated in believing in August 1990 that the wealth of Kuwait was necessary for Iraq's continued existence, and point to the remarkable resilience of the Iraqi Ba'athist regime.

If the War of Attrition of 1969-70 and the *Intifada* uprising are not counted, the Gulf War was the sixth war involving the state of Israel since its foundation, in a slightly irregular pattern of one every decade. In the process, by the skilled use of diplomacy and military force, Israel has gradually transformed its position, from being surrounded by hostile enemies and threatened with extinction, to the possession of secure frontiers and progress towards *de facto* recognition from nearly all of its neighbours. During the Gulf War the most likely Israeli ground involvement, threatened by Israeli 'hawks' at the time, was an offensive to occupy part of the neighbouring country of Jordan, rather than being at risk of ground attack itself, while its airpower and (officially non-existent) nuclear weapons provided a constant threat to Iraq. Whether Israeli restraint in the Gulf War will pay off in the long term is no easy judgement, but despite a perceived continued threat from Iraq and some confrontational posturing at the Middle East peace talks, the acceptance of Israel into the framework of the Middle East by its neighbours appears greater following the Gulf War than at any time in the past.

In contrast, the decision of the Palestine Liberation Organisation (PLO) to offer support to Iraq in its occupation of Kuwait has resulted in a considerable loss of status and credibility in the Arab world, not least among Palestinians formerly resident in Kuwait. Indirect PLO participation in the Middle East peace talks has gone only part of the way to redress this, and a Palestinian political entity independent of PLO control appears increasingly possible. Another marked loser from the war has been the newly unified state of Yemen. In 1990, as a rotating member of the UN Security Council, Yemen was the only Arab state to abstain or to vote consistently against resolutions in support of Kuwait, and also acted as a sanctuary for Iraqi aircraft. As a result, Yemen has had crucial economic support withdrawn by the USA and Saudi Arabia, and has also lost the patronage of the Soviet Union. The stability of the country, not markedly strong after unification, appears to be seriously threatened. King Hussein of Jordan performed no small feat in maintaining the overt neutrality and integrity of his own country throughout the Gulf War, but he also faces great problems in assimilating Palestinians expelled from Iraq and Kuwait during and after the war.

The position of Syria under the ageing President Hafez Assad now appears much stronger than before the Gulf War. Effectively replacing Soviet patronage and economic support with American, Syria has largely re-equipped its armed forces with weaponry obtained from former Warsaw Pact countries and also from North Korea and the People's Republic of China, including Scud missiles, and has secured its position in Lebanon. Improved Syrian relations with the West following the Gulf War also appear to have had an indirect bearing on the release of Western hostages held in Lebanon since 1985, starting with the British journalist John McCarthy on 8 August 1991. At present, if Syrian relations with Israel cannot be described as cordial, there seems less immediate prospect of a war than in the past. Continued tension between Syria and its fellow Ba'athist state of Iraq makes some form of confrontation on their common frontier appear more likely than war with Israel. Egypt also has emerged as one of the winners from the war, both in terms of support from the West and enhanced prestige within the Arab world. Part of this prestige has been the participation of its armed forces in a genuine military victory for the first time in living memory. A further consequence of Syrian and Egyptian participation in the Gulf War is that the USA now has direct influence, for the first time, on both sides in the Middle East peace process.

Turkey has emerged from the Gulf War as a potential player of new significance in the complex game of Middle East politics. A member of NATO, secular in outlook and possessing little affinity with its Arab neighbours, Turkey's political and military orientation before the Gulf War was largely northwards and westwards, and it was seen by the USA as a potential counterweight to Syria in the defence of Israel. The events of 1991 have changed this position considerably. In the Gulf War, in allowing US air raids to take place from its territory, Turkey earned Iraqi and some wider Arab enmity without doing enough to secure American gratitude. Stalled in its attempts to join the European Community (EC), with hostilities and instability on its common frontiers with Iraq and Armenia, evidence is growing that Turkey may be drawn more closely into involvement in central Asia and the Arabian peninsula. Its role in the Middle East, and in the wider world, will be of considerable future importance.

The political weakness displayed by the Arab states in failing to provide a regional solution to the Gulf Crisis has left a legacy which will endure for some time, together with the environmental damage to Kuwait and Saudi Arabia caused by the war and the accompanying oil pollution. Not the least of the problems are the massive arms and ordnance dumps that still litter the former KTO, as easy and accessible sources of supply for guerrilla groups. Although the rest of the world refused to treat the Gulf Crisis as a regional issue, the ensuing war has certainly had a permanent and significant effect on the region. Perhaps these wider considerations should not obscure the obvious point that a major achievement of the Gulf War was the restoration of the previous government of Kuwait, driven from its country by the Iraqi invasion, and the protection of Saudi Arabia and the smaller Gulf states from further aggression. But as long as 'the hungry and the angry' remain unsatisfied, it would be brave indeed to predict any other future for the Middle East than further instability, outside intervention, and probable war.

The Gulf conflict and the future of war

Even the present cursory assessment of the Gulf Crisis and War reveals that the confrontation between the USA and Iraq was, by any standards, not a fair fight. From the first hours of the Gulf Crisis the US government displayed almost total superiority over its opponent, manipulating the levers of political, economic and military force to create an environment in which Iraq was virtually helpless. Each Iraqi attempt to recover the initiative was either pre-empted or met with a devastating response. Purely quantitative measures of conventional military power counted for very little in judging the relative strengths of the two sides. Iraq was a wealthy Third World country, while the size and strength of its armed forces made it (by some estimates) the fourth or fifth military power in the world. But the difference between this and the USA as the world's Superpower turned out to be not one of degree, but of an absolute nature.

This has led to an argument based on a crude but persuasive historical analogy. During the 18th and early 19th centuries European colonial powers enjoyed only relative military superiority over Asian or African forces. Small but cumulative improvements in military technology and methods in the second half of the 19th century transformed this into an absolute European military dominance, typified by one-sided massacres such as the battle of Omdurman in 1898, which in turn fostered an era of colonial stability. In the mid-20th century the pendulum appeared to swing the other way, as forms of war were developed which produced defeat for the colonial powers on the battlefield. Arguably, the Gulf War demonstrated a level of US superiority over its enemies similar to that enjoyed by the late 19th century and early 20th century colonial powers, marking an era of world stability based on a *pax Americana*.

Against that, for many people the central fact of the Gulf War was that Saddam Hussein remained in power after his defeat. As President Bush began his re-election campaign in February 1992, opinion polls showed his popularity to be half that of a year before, and the possibility emerged that Saddam might actually outlast Bush in power. Although the USA fought the Gulf War very largely in accordance with the changes to its Limited War doctrine made after Vietnam, and with its formally declared war aims, this doctrine still presents political problems for the US government. In particular, the perceived need to maintain domestic support for the war, by a media campaign portraying Saddam and his regime as evil, obscured or distorted the US war aims for many Americans. The official US objective in fighting the war was the expulsion of Iraqi forces from Kuwait and 'the restoration of peace and stability to the region', and it was emphasised that the death or overthrow of Saddam was not part of this objective. At the same time, President Bush called repeatedly for Saddam's overthrow by others, and in the war's aftermath the official American position has remained that no normal relations with Iraq are possible as long as Saddam remains in power. The expectation that the war would end with Saddam's fall remained very high, and like his predecessors who fought Limited Wars, George Bush paid a political penalty for failing to deliver the outright victory that his people expected. This effect has been compounded by the US claim to have won such a victory on the battlefield.

The risks of war-making have increased in the 20th century to the point at which it is now well established that a government which loses a war cannot expect to remain in power. However, the single large exception to this global rule has been the Arab governments of the Middle East, which have frequently been able to survive the popular discontent following a lost war. A plausible explanation is found in the lack of strong loyalties to the state which characterises many Arab countries, together with the degree of political control exercised by their leaders. Simply, there is less popular trust to betray, and Arab governments have usually been able to deflect popular discontent away from themselves towards some traditional internal or external enemy. The survival of Saddam Hussein after the Gulf War is perhaps an extreme example of this phenomenon, arising particularly from his post-war position of being able to blame his country's ills on UN sanctions and US hostility. The reduced personal political risk for Middle East leaders of going to war may also help explain the comparatively high frequency of major wars in the region. This is not, of course, to follow Saddam in suggesting that Iraq won the Gulf War.

In the Gulf Crisis, of the traditional instruments of power it was military force that — as often in the past — proved to be the most blunt. The greatest achievement of the US government in the Gulf Crisis was the maintenance and even increase of support at home and abroad for nearly six months while its cumbersome military forces were made ready for combat. The US military was presented with a political framework within which defeat was virtually impossible. The methods by which this was done will repay much future study, but the price paid by the US government for this support was a high one. In forming military strategy for the war, US planners were limited in particular by the need to keep the political support of the Arab members of the Coalition, and by their own fears of a 'quagmire' or prolonged conflict. It was also a severe limitation that, from nearly 500,000 American service personnel deployed in the Gulf, a casualty level in excess of 10,000, or 2 per cent, was deemed domestically unacceptable.

Four major US strategic decisions, stemming from these overriding limitations, are likely to remain controversial. The first was the doubling of ground forces in November 1990 by the addition of heavy armour. It has been suggested that this was unnecessary, and that had the American logistic deployment worked properly, the war could have been fought successfully with the Coalition airpower, seapower and light forces present in the Gulf in autumn 1990. The second was the decision not to drive on

Baghdad, taken in order to preserve Arab support for the Coalition and out of fear of either a protracted war or heavy American casualties. The third, which has received much less attention, was the decision to stop short of Basra and complete the destruction of the Iraqi forces. The extent of American military opposition to this decision is only just emerging. The final controversial decision was the speed with which American troops were withdrawn from the region. Logistic considerations, rather than politics or military strategy, were more important to all four decisions than has been realised. In particular, logistic issues made the dispatch of heavy armour to the Gulf in November 1990 the single most important decision of the war, on which all else subsequently turned. This decision also coincided with, and represented, the fundamental shift in US policy from crisis management to crisis resolution.

Immediately after the Second World War there was some speculation that conventional war had become impossible, and that guerrilla or low-intensity war would be the only form practical in the future, short of a nuclear exchange. Since then, many conventional high-intensity wars of considerable size have taken place worldwide. However, the argument is once more gaining ground that the use of military force on a large scale (recognisable to Western domestic public opinion as a 'war') as an instrument of policy is ceasing to be a realistic option for modern states, even for the USA with its Superpower status. In the new international environment it has become much harder to reap dramatic gains from military victories, while, as Saddam found out, conquest has become increasingly politically unacceptable within the international system. Even in simple terms of cost and gain (including financial cost), large-scale war appears less attractive than the use of force without war for symbolic or deterrent purposes, such as the US Air Force and US Navy air raid on Tripoli in 1986.

Instead of large-scale conventional war, the late 20th century has seen increasing examples of a highly politicised and diffuse type of slow-motion war, for which a name does not yet exist, such as that fought by the Republic of South Africa against the 'front-line' southern African states in the 1980s. Even such comparatively orthodox military operations as the Falklands conflict in 1982 or Panama in 1989 were accompanied by considerable political interaction. This may well represent the future of warfare, or more precisely the final breakdown of the 19th century European distinctions between war and peace as separate conditions and of the state as absolute controller of military force. Like all apparently new phenomena, this form of gradual or slow-motion war has a history, and origins which may be profitably studied.

Despite its size and conventional nature, the Gulf War appears to fit this pattern closely. As was pointed out at the time, the event which became known as the 'Gulf War' started with the original Iraqi invasion of Kuwait in August 1990, and was fought by political, economic and propaganda weapons throughout its course. Coalition military forces (particularly naval and air forces) also formed a major part of the war effort from August 1990 onwards; their final use in January and February 1991 was only the culmination of the process. With hindsight, the Gulf War may appear as a halfway house between the large conventional wars of a bygone age and new ways of projecting force as a more precise political instrument. We have either seen the end of an era, or the first war of the 21st century.

The conduct of the Gulf War

After August 1990 Saddam Hussein threatened a form of war which, if not completely new, was far removed from conventional Western military thinking. Saddam's strategy was global and based on deterrence, threatening drastic retaliation if his control of Kuwait were challenged. The USA and other Western members of the Coalition were promised a sustained terrorist campaign on their own territory, including the use of biological or chemical weapons to attack their civilian populations. Defence against Western retaliation would come from the use of hostages, and from a sustained campaign of media manipulation and political initiatives. Coalition forces and civilians in Saudi Arabia would also be subject to terrorist attacks, and to missile strikes using either conventional warheads, or escalating to the use of biological, chemical or nuclear weapons, again accompanied by political and media campaigns and attempts to secure external political intervention. Saddam was sufficiently politically sophisticated to include an ecological threat aimed chiefly at Western sensibilities.

Had this form of war been carried out in the autumn of 1990, while the American military machine was being assembled in the Gulf, it might have been enough to break the Coalition or dissuade it from attack. Instead, the world saw a highly conventional and rather traditional form of war imposed by the US government, in which the strengths and weaknesses which have featured in American war-fighting since the First World War were once more displayed. The US war machine was strong on technology, on firepower, and, after a false start, on logistics. But although it was strong on information gathering, it was very weak on intelligence and information assessment, and unprepared to take risks. Also as in the past, its approach to alliance warfare was to dominate the alliance, and impose an American way of war.

Why some of Saddam's threats came to nothing is likely to remain one of the most obscure parts of the Gulf War story. But others could be reasonably dismissed as fantasy, propaganda, or a gross overestimation by Saddam of his abilities to confront modern states and control modern technology. In wider terms, the kind of war threatened by Saddam, if successfully carried out by a more sophisticated state, might easily render irrelevant the conventional measures of military force which determined success in the Gulf War. Although there are exceptions, most Western military thought has scarcely begun to consider this new form of war, managing only to brand it and its weapons as 'unconventional' and therefore outside mainstream considerations. It is sufficient here to note that within living memory unconventional weapons have included the aircraft, the tank and the submarine.

Being relatively cheap and extremely difficult to defend against, unconventional war and its weapons have proved attractive to Third World countries. Even before the Gulf War, the spread of nuclear and missile technologies in the Third World, together with international terrorism, was already a principal Western concern, although the experience of the Gulf confirmed that unconventional war is harder to use effectively than many believed. Despite the agreement in 1991 of both France and the People's Republic of China to sign the Nuclear Non-Proliferation Treaty, the limited political success of Iraq's Scud campaign in the midst of what was otherwise a catastrophic defeat, together with the escape of nuclear and missile technology from the disintegrating Soviet Union, has made future nuclear proliferation much more likely. Further, if Iraq had the capability during the Gulf War to use nuclear warheads, then the world may have also seen an unusually clear case of nuclear deterrence, with the veiled threat of retaliation from the USA and Israel acting as a restraint.

The basis of Limited War since the Korean War has been that the first use of nuclear weapons would mark a major threshold in the conduct of war. However, the Gulf War has demonstrated in practice something which had become increasingly apparent in the previous decade. The level of destructiveness of modern conventional bombs, such as fuel-air explosives (FAE) or the BLU-28 'Daisy Cutter', together with the massive power of modern air forces, has virtually eroded the distinction between conventional and small-scale nuclear weapons. If the reported figures are correct, the tonnage of bombs dropped by Coalition air forces in the KTO which *failed to explode* was still greater than the total tonnage dropped on Berlin in the Second World War, and twice as great as the Hiroshima bomb (estimated at 12–16 kilotons). As the memory of the Second World War recedes, all these trends have increased the likelihood of nuclear weapons being used, somewhere in the world, in the near future.

The Gulf War also provided the first major demonstration of the weapons technology which had been under development since the Vietnam era. American conservatism in planning and fighting the war is partly explained by anxieties over how well this largely untried technology would work. It was also a consideration that this was the first US attempt to fight large-scale conventional manoeuvre war since the Korean War. As a rough guide of which all military men are painfully aware, 20th century weapons technology takes about a human generation of 30 years to perform on the battlefield the roles claimed for it by its manufacturers, and slightly longer to become accepted and understood by those who use it in war. The Gulf War was fought with technology and concepts first developed in the late 1960s and early 1970s, barely enough time for them to reach maturity. It was historically predictable that after 20 years the weapons systems would perform adequately but not perfectly, and would still rest largely on the doctrinal framework of a previous generation, in the same way as submarines or aircraft used by Western armed forces before 1914, or tanks before 1939.

In broad terms, this appears to have happened to AirLand Battle and its associated technology in the Gulf War. The war also confirmed a trend that dates back to the Second World War, but became clearly visible in the Arab-Israeli War of October 1973, that in modern warfare electronic superiority over the enemy has become the most important single factor in determining victory. Control of the electronic spectrum governs the ability to communicate, to gather intelligence, to strike and defend, and to prevent the enemy from doing the same. Even more than air superiority, the massive electronic superiority of the Coalition over the Iraqis from the start of the Gulf War established the framework for the apparently easy win.

The claim by the US Air Force that airpower alone defeated the Iraqi Army, made in the first flush of victory, has not withstood even brief examination. Institutional arguments continue over whether the Coalition air forces fought a separate 'air campaign', or only 'air operations' in a wider context, and over whether Coalition strategy followed the doctrine of AirLand Battle or represented a refined form of independent strategic bombing, plus a largely unnecessary ground war. In the present climate of dispute the only assessment possible is both trite and obvious: AirLand Battle was an untried global war-fighting doctrine which the US armed forces expected to use for the defence of Western Europe against the Warsaw Pact. Its application to offensive operations in the Gulf War marked the difference between doctrine and reality. Once again the Gulf War may be seen as a halfway position between the expectations of the future and US war-fighting methods of the past. As a result of the Gulf War, the US Army and US Air Force issued in September 1991 a preliminary pamphlet defining more carefully the role of each in the extended battlefield, and changing the name of the doctrine to 'AirLand Operations'.

American conservatism regarding the use of helicopter forces and airmobility in the ground war has made any assessment of their future importance very difficult. Before the Gulf War it was assumed that any NATO or Warsaw Pact 'out-of-area' ground deployments would consist of light forces only. The decision that heavy armour, which for practical purposes cannot be airlifted and takes weeks or months to be prepared for battle, was needed in the Gulf has major implications. If only heavy armoured formations can overcome armour and fixed defences, then the timescales and difficulties in deploying armour globally mean that future land wars of intervention have become virtually impossible, except against countries or alliances with very small armed forces, or those who commit Saddam's error of allowing enemies the time to deploy.

It is, however, probable that the Gulf War represents in this respect a special case. The logistic burden imposed on US armed forces planning to fight a 38-day air war and a 60-day ground war, the failures of a seaborne deployment system which never expected to have to function in reality, the nature of the enemy, terrain and mission, and the refusal to take even calculated risks all combined to establish the unusually large size and timescale of the US deployment. With the removal of the major monolithic threat from the Soviet Union, US and European NATO thinking has turned increasingly to power projection and improvised overseas deployments, preferably in company with allies, for which the Gulf War will serve as a major learning experience and precedent. This should give naval forces an enhanced importance and role. The quiet success of the US Navy and its Coalition partners in the Gulf War, although obscured through their failure to manage the media with the same sophistication as rival services, is one of lasting importance.

The overwhelming impression of the Gulf War has been as a television war, and immediate reactions have confirmed the enhanced importance of the media in Western military and political thought. It is significant that *Time* magazine named Ted Turner, the owner of CNN (Cable News Network), rather than General Norman Schwarzkopf, its 'Man of the Year' in 1991. Indeed, media war played an even greater part in the Gulf Crisis than was first apparent. It has emerged that, after the Iraqi occupation of August 1990, the Kuwaiti government-in-exile hired a leading US advertising firm to front a major media campaign at a cost of some $10 million, selling the importance of liberating Kuwait to the American public. The sole eyewitness who testified, at Senate hearings in November 1990, to the atrocity story of babies being taken from incubators by Iraqi troops in Kuwait City, was in fact the daughter of the Kuwaiti ambassador to Washington. The Kuwaitis cannot be faulted for this. Their country had been taken from them, and only the USA had the political and military power to recover it. They used their only available weapon — money — to mount a media campaign aimed at the American government and people, which ultimately proved successful.

In assessing the conduct of the Gulf War, the overwhelming impression which remains is that the war was neither clean nor brief. It arose from complex political considerations, was conducted with extreme violence, and produced a legacy of intractable problems, both for the region and the world. It was, for everyone involved, a learning process and a test of institutions and ideas, both old and new. Further assessment must await a more distant perspective.

Further Reading

Christy Campbell, *AirLand Battle 2000* (Hamlyn, London, 1986).

Martin van Creveld, *On Future War* (Brasseys, London, 1991). US title: *The Tranformations of War*.

Hirsh Goodman and W Seth Carus, *The Future Battlefield and the Arab-Israeli Conflict* (Transactions, London, 1990).

Paddy Griffith, *The Ultimate Weaponry* (Sidgwick and Jackson, London, 1991).

Joseph Hanlon, *Apartheid's Second Front* (Penguin, London, 1986).

Chronology of the Gulf Crisis and War

1990

2 August: At 2 am (local time), Iraqi forces invade Kuwait; the UN Security Council passes Resolution 660, condemning Iraq and urging a ceasefire; the USA, Britain and France freeze Iraqi assets

3 August: Arab League foreign ministers, meeting in Cairo, condemn the Iraqi invasion of Kuwait; 2,000 Egyptian troops airlifted to Saudi Arabia

6 August: The UN Security Council passes Resolution 661, imposing mandatory sanctions and an embargo on Iraq and occupied Kuwait; US Secretary of Defense Richard 'Dick' Cheney meets King Fahd, who invites US forces to Saudi Arabia to reinforce its defence; President George Bush orders US fighter aircraft and troops to move to Saudi Arabia

8 August: Iraq announces that Kuwait is now the '19th province' of Iraq

9 August: The UN Security Council passes Resolution 662, declaring the Iraqi absorption of Kuwait 'null and void'

10 August: The Arab League summit in Cairo condemns the Iraqi invasion and absorption of Kuwait, and agrees to send troops to Saudi Arabia

11 August: Saddam Hussein offers a peace initiative, linking an Iraqi withdrawal from Kuwait to an Israeli withdrawal from the Occu-pied Territories and a Syrian withdrawal from Lebanon; Bush rejects the proposal

14 August: Saddam Hussein makes peace with Iran

17 August: Iraq's National Assembly agrees to detain nationals of those countries which have decided to participate in the embargo against Iraq

18 August: The UN Security Council passes Resolution 664, demanding the 'immediate departure from Kuwait and Iraq' of all foreign nationals

21 August: Syria sends 1,200 troops to Saudi Arabia

25 August: The UN Security Council passes Resolution 665, authorising 'such measures ... as may be necessary' to halt ships trading with Iraq, in accordance with Resolution 661

5 September: Saddam Hussein calls on 'faithful Arabs and Muslims everywhere' to wage a holy war against Saudi rulers and their supporters

9 September: At the end of the Helsinki Summit, Presidents Bush and Gorbachev call on Iraq to withdraw unconditionally from Kuwait

16 September: The UN Security Council passes Resolution 667, condemning Iraqi acts of violence against diplomatic missions in Kuwait

17 September: General Michael Dugan, USAF Chief of Staff, is sacked for suggesting that, in any war with Iraq, Saddam Hussein will be a target

25 September: The UN Security Council passes Resolution 670, extending sanctions against Iraq to cover all means of transport, including aircraft

1 October: President Bush addresses the UN General Assembly, stating that once Iraq has evacuated Kuwait there will be opportunities to settle wider issues of the Middle East

8 October: Israeli police shoot dead 18 Palestinians at the Temple Mount in Jerusalem

12 October: The UN Security Council passes Resolution 672, expressing alarm at Israeli actions at the Temple Mount

13 October: In Lebanon, Syrian troops defeat the forces of General Michel Aoun

21 October: Former British Prime Minister Edward Heath meets Saddam Hussein in Baghdad and secures the release of 38 sick and elderly British hostages

31 October: Bush decides secretly to double the number of US troops in the Gulf to 430,000 and to mount an air assault on Iraq in mid-January 1991

8 November: Two days after the mid-term elections in the USA, Bush makes public his decision to double the number of troops in the Gulf

9 November: Former West German Chancellor Willi Brandt secures the release of 206 Western hostages from Iraq after talks with Saddam Hussein

18 November: Saddam Hussein agrees to release all 'foreign guests' from Iraq between 25 December and 25 March

28 November: John Major takes over from Margaret Thatcher as British Prime Minister

29 November: Britain decides to renew diplomatic relations with Syria; the UN Security Council passes Resolution 678, authorising 'all necessary means' to ensure that Iraq withdraws from Kuwait unless Iraq agrees to abide by all relevant UN Resolutions passed since 2 August

30 November: Bush invites Tariq Aziz, Iraq's Foreign Minister, to talks in Washington before 15 December, and offers to send James Baker, US Secretary of State, to Baghdad for talks with Saddam Hussein between 15 December and 15 January

6 December: Saddam Hussein recommends to the Iraqi National Assembly that all foreign nationals should be released

13 December: The last of the US hostages leave Iraq

1991

3 January: Bush offers to send Baker to Geneva for talks with Aziz

4 January: Iraq agrees to the Geneva talks, to take place on 9 January

9 January: After six and a half hours of talks, Baker and Aziz fail to reach agreement

11 January: Javier Pérez de Cuéllar, the UN Secretary-General, flies to Baghdad for last-minute talks with Saddam Hussein

12 January: The US Congress authorises Bush to use force in pursuit of UN Security Council Resolution 678

13 January: Talks between Pérez de Cuéllar and Saddam Hussein fail

15 January: The UN deadline passes with no sign of an Iraqi withdrawal from Kuwait

16/17 January: Operation 'Desert Storm' begins, with Coalition air attacks on targets in Iraq

18 January: Twelve Iraqi Scud missiles land in Israel

20 January: Iraq displays captured Coalition pilots on television; eight Iraqi Scuds are fired at Saudi Arabia

26 January: The first Iraqi aircraft seek refuge in Iran

27 January: The first oil slick in the Gulf to be caused by war action threatens ecological damage

29 January: Iraqi forces capture the Saudi border town of Khafji; Coalition forces counterattack to liberate it

1 February: Coalition troops recapture Khafji

13 February: A Coalition airstrike hits an air-raid shelter in Amiriya, killing many civilians; the Americans insist that it was a command and control bunker

15 February: An Iraqi 'peace offer', including a withdrawal from Kuwait, is put forward, but it includes too many impossible conditions. Bush dismisses it as a 'cruel hoax'

18 February: After meeting Aziz, Gorbachev forwards to Bush a new peace proposal; Bush lays down the conditions acceptable to the Coalition

21 February: Iraq responds positively to Gorbachev's peace plan, but still insists on conditions unacceptable to Bush

22 February: Bush rejects the Gorbachev peace plan and gives Saddam Hussein until noon EST on 23 February to accept publicly the Coalition conditions; Gorbachev puts forward a revised proposal, accepted by Iraq

23 February: Aziz announces that Iraq will withdraw from Kuwait in line with the latest Gorbachev proposal; Bush rejects the arrangement and orders General Norman Schwarzkopf, CENTCOM commander, to eject the Iraqis from Kuwait by force

24 February: Operation 'Desert Saber' begins as Coalition ground forces enter Kuwait and southern Iraq

25 February: The Soviet Union proposes a new peace plan, accepted by Saddam Hussein, who orders his troops to withdraw from Kuwait

26 February: Bush rejects the latest Soviet peace plan; Iraqi troops leave Kuwait City but are caught in Coalition air attacks to the north, on the Mutla Ridge

27 February: Coalition troops control Kuwait City; Aziz writes to the UN Secretary-General accepting Resolutions 660, 662 and 664, but rejecting those concerned with the embargo on Iraq. The five permanent members of the Security Council insist on a full Iraqi acceptance of all Resolutions. Bush orders a unilateral ceasefire from midnight EST, 27/28 February; it is accepted by Iraq

2 March: The UN Security Council passes Resolution 686, setting out ceasefire terms; a Shi'a revolt begins in southern Iraq

6 March: In Damascus, the foreign ministers of Egypt, Syria and the Gulf Co-operation Council agree to the setting up of a peacekeeping force for the Gulf. In Washington, Bush outlines his post-war goals, including Arab-Israeli negotiations

9 March: Iraqi forces loyal to Saddam Hussein counterattack the Shi'a strongholds in southern Iraq

14 March: Kurdish forces in northern Iraq take territory

30 March: In the face of Iraqi counterattacks, Kurdish civilians begin to flee towards the Iranian and Turkish borders

3 April: The UN Security Council passes Resolution 687, setting out the details of the ceasefire with Iraq and war reparations

5 April: The UN Security Council passes Resolution 688, condemning Iraq for the suppression of its people

11 April: Ceasefire now in permanent effect in the Gulf

16 April: In line with Resolution 688, the USA and UK prepare to send troops to protect Kurdish refugees in northern Iraq (Operation 'Provide Comfort/Safe Haven')

17 April: Iraq begins to provide information to the UN about its chemical, nuclear and missile programmes, in accordance with Resolution 687

6 May: US forces withdraw from southern Iraq

15 May: Kurdish refugees begin to return home, protected by Western troops

16 June: Kurdish leaders announce an agreement with Saddam Hussein about the future of Kurdistan

14 July: Bush threatens renewed airstrikes against Iraq if Saddam Hussein continues to persecute Shias and Kurds

15 July: Western troops leave northern Iraq at the end of Operation 'Provide Comfort/Safe Haven'

1 August: Israel agrees to participate in a Middle East peace conference

18 September: Bush threatens military action unless Saddam Hussein agrees to abide by the terms of Resolution 687

20 September: Kuwait signs a ten-year defence co-operation agreement with the USA

24 September: UN inspectors are held at gunpoint in Baghdad

27 September: The UN inspectors are released

18 October: Baker and the new Soviet Foreign Minister, Boris Pankin, issue invitations to Israel, Syria, Egypt, Lebanon, Jordan and the Palestinians to attend a conference on the Middle East, to be held in Madrid on 30 October

30 October to 1 November: Madrid Conference on the Middle East

3 November: Bilateral talks between Israel and delegations from Syria, Lebanon, Jordan and the Palestinians begin in Madrid

10–18 December: The second round of bilateral talks in Washington fails to produce any agreements

16 December: The UN General Assembly rescinds Resolution 3379, equating Zionism with racism

1992

28–29 January: Multilateral talks on the Middle East in Moscow fail to reach any agreement

Index

Washington Bilateral Talks, 213–14
Military Assistance Command Vietnam
  (MACV), 64–5
Military Doctrines:
  Britain, 63, 67, 72–5, 76
  France, 67, 72
  Iraq, 30–1, 76, 182–4
  Israel, 62
  Soviet Union, 57, 63, 68, 76, 231
  United States, 57–71 *passim*, 272
Military Vehicles, 85–6, 92, 95, 100
Mines, naval, 127, 134, 139–41
Mine Countermeasures (MCM), 127, 129,
  133, 141
Mine Countermeasures Vessels (MCMVs),
  127, 130, 134, 140–1, 144; *see also* Warships,
  RN
Mitterand, François, 72
Mixson, Rear Admiral Riley D, 125, 136
Morocco, 46
Moscow, 41, 47–8, 50, 194, 207, 211–12, 219,
  230, 240; *see also* Middle East Peace Process
Moscow coup attempt (August 1991), 211
MSR Dodge (Tapline Road), 99, 101–2
MSR Sultan, 99, 100
Mubarak, Hosni, 36, 40, 42–3, 45–6, 77
Multinational Interception Force (MNIF),
  131
Mutla Ridge, 121, 221

N
Nasser, Gamal Abdul, 17, 25, 185
National Aeronautics and Space
  Administration (NASA), 248
National Assembly (Iraq), 27–8
National Broadcasting Corporation (BBC);
  see Television Networks
National Defence Council (Iraq), 30
National Media Pool (US), 228, 236–7
National Oceanographic and Atmospheric
  Administration (US), 252
National Security Council (US), 41–3
Nayif, Abd al Razzaq al, 20
Neal, Richard I ('Butch'), 232, 237
Netherlands, 134
'New Look' (US), 60, 73
'New Naval Policy' (US), 144
New Scientist, 248, 252, 258
Newsweek, 219–20
'New World Order', 35, 197
North Atlantic Treaty Organisation (NATO),
  58–9, 61, 68, 72–5, 132–4, 266, 272
North Korea, 127, 204, 264, 266
Norway, 139
Nuclear Weapons, 60–1, 66, 68, 230, 265,
  270–1

O
Occupied Territories, 46–7, 49, 51, 194,
  209–14 *passim*
Oilfields (Kuwait), 247–8
Oil Lakes, 255
Oil Revenues (Iraq), 21
Oil Wells, burning, 253–4

Oman, 46, 197, 200; *see also* Armed Forces,
  Oman
Ordnance Depots (British), 93, 97
Organisation of Petroleum Exporting
  Countries (OPEC), 36–7
Otis, General Glen K, 66
Ottoman Empire, 13, 16
Ozal, Turgut, 201, 203

P
Paton, James A, 89–90
Palestine/Palestinians, 51, 193, 210, 212–15
  passim
Palestine Liberation Organisation (PLO), 43,
  45–6, 207, 209, 211, 216, 265
Pan-Arab Nationalism, 15–16
Panama, US Invasion of (1989), 67, 69, 228,
  229, 269
Pankin, Boris, 212
Pentagon, 41, 109, 129, 141
Pérez de Cuéllar, Javier, 54, 193
Planning, Air War, 109–13
'Poised Hammer', Operation, 202–3
Pollution, Oil, 249
Poos, Jacques, 54
Popular Front for the Liberation of Palestine –
  General Command (PFLP-GC), 212, 217n
Porritt, Jonathan, 258
Powell, General Colin, 43, 82, 96, 116, 117,
  199, 232, 238
Prepositioned War Reserve Materiel Stores
  (PWRMS), 98
Primakov, Yevgeni, 50, 194–5, 216n
Propaganda, 269–70, 273
'Provide Comfort', Operation, 201–3, 216n

Q
Qaruh Island, 137
Qassem, Abd al-Karim, 17, 18
Qatar, 46, 197

R
Radio, 224–5, 235–6, 240–2
Rafha, 98–100
Rafsanjani, Ali Akbar Hashemi, 47
Railway Systems, 87, 92, 97
Rapid Deployment Joint Task Force (RDJTF),
  40
Rashid Ali, al-Kaylani, 17, 19
Reagan, Ronald, 58–9, 66–7, 128, 229, 231
Red Adair, 254
Red Sea, 130–4, 136
Regional Development Bank (Middle East),
  197, 215
Rejectionist Front, 212, 217n
Republican Guard; *see* Armed Forces, Iraq
Revolutionary Command Council (RCC)
  (Iraq), 20, 27, 30
Riyadh, 42, 44, 82, 96, 110, 119, 132, 232, 235,
  237–8, 240–1
Rodgers, General Bernard, 74
'Rose Garden' Speech, 194
Rumailla Oilfield, 37
Russian Federation, 263